The Drive for Self

RELATED BOOKS BY EDWARD HOFFMAN

Wilhelm Reich: The Man Who Dreamed of Tomorrow
The Right to Be Human: A Biography of Abraham Maslow
Visions of Innocence: Spiritual and Inspirational Experiences
of Childhood
Future Visions: The Unpublished Papers of Abraham Maslow

The Drive for Self

*Alfred Adler and the
Founding of
Individual Psychology*

EDWARD HOFFMAN

Foreword by

KURT A. ADLER, M.D., Ph.D.

ADDISON-WESLEY PUBLISHING COMPANY, INC.
*Reading, Massachusetts • Menlo Park, California • New York • Don Mills, Ontario
Harlow, England • Amsterdam • Bonn • Sydney • Singapore
Tokyo • Madrid • San Juan • Paris • Seoul • Milan • Mexico City • Taipei*

Many of the designations used by manufacturers and sellers to distinguish their products are claimed as trademarks. Where those designations appear in this book and Addison-Wesley was aware of a trademark claim, the designations have been printed in initial capital letters.

Grateful acknowledgment is made to the following for permission to reprint previously published material:

Sigmund Freud Copyrights, Wivenhoe, England: Personal correspondence between Sigmund Freud and Alfred Adler.

The Houghton Library, Harvard University: Personal correspondence between Raissa Adler and Leon Trotsky; and between Raissa Adler and the Austrian Communist Party.

The Albert Einstein Archives, the Hebrew University of Jerusalem, Israel: Personal correspondence between Albert Einstein and Alfred Adler.

Library of Congress Cataloging-in-Publication Data

Hoffman, Edward
    The drive for self : Alfred Adler and the founding of individual psychology / Edward Hoffman.
        p. cm.
    Includes bibliographical references and index.
    ISBN 0-201-63280-2
    ISBN 0-201-44194-2 (pbk.)
    1. Adler, Alfred, 1870–1937. 2. Psychoanalysts—Austria—Biography. 3. Adlerian psychology. I. Title.
BF109.A4H65 1994
150.19′53′092—dc20
[B]   94-5160
                                       CIP

Cover design by Suzanne Heiser
Text design by Janis Owens
Set in 10-point Baskerville by G & S Typesetters, Inc., Austin, Texas

1 2 3 4 5 6 7 8 9-MA-0099989796
First printing, June 1994
First paperback printing, September 1996

We can never know what actions will characterize a man if we know only whence he comes. But if we know whither he is going we can prophesy his steps and his movements toward his objective.

ALFRED ADLER

To the memory of Jack Lipitz

Contents

PART ONE

Contents

Contents

Foreword

As I reflect upon my father's life, I am impressed by his ability to affect so many people—not only as a social theorist and the creator of individual psychology—but also as a parent, healer, teacher, lecturer and friend. Never seeking to isolate his work from the wider social and political events of his time, my father was the complete antithesis of the armchair intellectual. He considered himself a man of the people and not of the intellectual elite. Despite the many philosophical, psychological, and sociological formulations and constructs he expounded, he always tried to use simple language, so that his ideas could be understood by all.

At the end of the first World War, during which he served as a military physician, his belief in democratic socialism became even stronger than it had been in his student years. It was at that time that he developed the key concept of *social interest* (*Gemeinschaftsgefühl*), by which he meant the need to be and to feel at one with all humankind. He considered social interest the only salvation for humanity, and the only valid test of an individual's mental health. Modern psychologists acknowledge that Alfred Adler, with ideas like social interest, returned dignity to human beings—a dignity that the instinct theories had stolen from them. My father placed psychology back in the hands of us all by declaring that the self-created goals of each individual are the determining influences that create the human character.

Previous books about Alfred Adler have been fragmentary. However noteworthy, they have examined only bits and pieces of his career, such as his initial involvement and subsequent decisive break with Sigmund Freud. Other volumes have tended to focus on particular features of my father's theories and therapeutic methods concerning children, adults, and families.

This work is the first full-length biography to paint a vivid picture of both the man and his times. It is the story of his life, as well as his development and emergence as the great psychologist who influenced not only the thousands of people he dealt with directly, but also the whole realm of modern psychology.

Having personally experienced many of the tumultuous historical events described by *The Drive for Self,* I often found myself deeply moved in reading it. Men and women who were important in my father's life are given here their rightful due. His family members, friends and co-workers, critics and opponents are discussed objectively. Long-ago scenes and conversations are brought to life.

Especially valuable in *The Drive for Self* is the fascinating account of Alfred Adler's career in the United States. Having emigrated from fascist Austria as a young man with my family in the 1930s, I can well remember how much he liked his new homeland and its opportunities for individual freedom and accomplishment. During those final years in his late fifties and sixties, he was highly active, publicly visible, and extremely productive, and Edward Hoffman's book dramatically makes this clear for perhaps the first time.

Late in my father's career, he became convinced for several reasons that a comprehensive biography about his life was necessary. Undoubtedly, he wished to "set the record straight" about many aspects of his work, for controversy had never ceased to dog him. It was not only the matter of his break with Freud and the unrelenting hostility he bore from Freudian loyalists for challenging their master's dogmatism; because of Alfred Adler's impassioned ideals as a democratic socialist, he was often the target of politically-motivated ideological attacks that maligned his psychological approach. Unfortunately, my father never had the chance to detail such issues, for he died suddenly while on lecture tour in Scotland. Thus, besides lucidly presenting his notions, *The Drive for Self* is unique in placing Alfred Adler's life in a meaningful historical context. No doubt, this major biography will succeed in helping a new generation discover the timely relevance of his teachings. For as my father always believed, our world can only benefit from the power of psychological knowledge and insight.

Kurt A. Adler, M.D., Ph.D.

Acknowledgments

D uring the past four years, the challenging task of constructing Alfred Adler's biography would scarcely have been possible without the help of many people. Alfred Adler's two surviving children, Dr. Alexandra Adler and Dr. Kurt Adler, have been generous with their time and assistance beyond any biographer's expectations. Both psychiatrists, they have been able to offer special insights about their father's influential career in historical context. As members of Alfred Adler's extended family, Margot and Tanya Adler have likewise been most helpful.

Of the many academicians who provided assistance on this project from its initial conception, Dr. Heinz L. Ansbacher, professor emeritus of the University of Vermont, receives my foremost gratitude. We first became acquainted through my earlier biography of his colleague and friend Abraham Maslow. Dr. Ansbacher has not only been a gracious host and energetic correspondent, but he has also shared invaluable recollections and materials pertaining to Adler's life and times. I am deeply appreciative for his critical reading of this manuscript also meticulously provided by Dr. Kurt Adler and Dr. Henry Stein.

For their conceptual or research contributions to my efforts, I am indebted to Dr. Daniel Benveninte, Vanessa Brown, Dr. H. Cammaer, Stephen Citron, Dr. Adele K. Davidson, Dr. Don Dinkmeyer Jr., Dr. Gerald Epstein, Dr. Lawrence Epstein, Eric Freedman, Dorothy Greenberg, Dr. Helmut Gruber, Alan Hovhaness, Dr. Joseph Heller, Aaron Hostyk, Dr. Guy Manaster, Dr. W. Edward Mann, Dr. Rollo May, Thomas O'Brien, Mrs. Sydney Roth, Dr. Paul Stepansky, Jenka Sperber, Dr. Henry Stein, Dr. Irma Sutton, and Dr. Jack Zipes.

For their extensive archival assistance, I wish to thank Jack E. Termine, archivist of the State University of New York Health Science Center at Brooklyn; Victoria Jones, manuscripts curator of the University of Oregon; and James H. Hutson, chief of the Manuscripts Division of the United States Library of Congress.

The following individuals also provided archival assistance: Karen Drescher of The Adler School in Chicago; Friederike Zeitlhofer of the Austrian Cultural Institute in New York City; Dr. Diane R. Spielmann of the Leo Baeck Institute; Diane Davenport, reference library supervisor of the Berkeley Public Library; Patty Graziano of the *Cleveland Plain-Dealer* Library; Bernard R. Crystal, Hollee Haswell, Rhea E. Pliakas, and Dr. Corinne H. Rieder of Columbia University; Fred Winston of the Commack, New York, Public Library; Kay Aler-Maida of the Community Church of New York; Barbara L. Krieger, archive assistant of the Darmouth College Library; Jennie Rathbun of Harvard University's Houghton Library, where the Trotsky Collection is housed; Deborah Rand, medical library director of the Long Island Jewish Medical Center; Barbara M. Niss, archivist of the Mount Sinai Medical Center; Dr. Virginia Torgenev, archivist of the Museum of the Diaspora in Israel; Eda Regan, research librarian of Mills College; Robert A. Gates, vice provost of the New School for Social Research; Ella Dabney, librarian of the New York State Medical Society; Gloria A. Roberts, head librarian of Planned Parenthood Federation of America; Beth S. Curran, reference librarian, Providence Public Library; Gary Ink, research librarian of *Publisher's Weekly;* Nikki Bengal of the *San Francisco Chronicle;* Dr. Esther Katz of New York University, editor/director of The Margaret Sanger Papers; Colin A. McLaren, head of Special Collections, University of Aberdeen; Adrian Allan, assistant archivist of the University of Liverpool; Dr. Donald E. Riggs and his staff at the University of Michigan; Mary M. Huth, assistant head of the University of Rochester Department of Rare Books and Special Collections; Nancy S. MacKenchie, curator of Rare Books and Manuscripts of the Vassar College Libraries; Patricia Bartkowski and Leslie S. Hough of the Walter P. Reuther Library of Wayne State University; William Prescott Jr., headmaster of the Wheeler School; President William A. Kinnison of Wittenberg University.

To portray the colorful life of Adler's chief American benefactor, Charles Henry Davis, has been a task requiring extensive historical research. I am grateful to his grandchildren Thor Brandt-Erichsen, Charles Matteson, and Jean Nandi for offering personal recollections and materials. In providing additional information about Mr. Davis, the following individuals were likewise helpful: Dr. Joseph P. Barratta; Bainbridge Crist; Dr. James Good; Dr. James Gould; Remsen M. Kinne III; James Light; Nancy Stewart, librarian for the South Yarmouth Library Association; Charles A. Ruch of the Westinghouse Corporation; Dr. Herbert N. Foerstel of the Engineering & Physical Science Library of the University of Maryland; and Dr. Wesley T. Wooley.

Acknowledgments

For their fine translation work pertaining to source material, I wish to thank Anna Bernstein, Jonathan Skolnick, and Martina Sonntag-Butsch. Research assistance was ably provided by Susan Brook, Maria Gillen, Harvey Gitlin, and Elizabeth McLaughlin. The enthusiasm of my literary agent, Alice Fried Martell, has been an important motivating force from the outset. Gratitude is likewise extended to my editors Amy Gash and Sharon Broll for their editorial judgment and sustained commitment to publishing a full account of Adler's life and career. My parents and brother, as well as Gertrude Brainin, and Alyce and Robert Tresenfeld, have been a constant font of encouragement during my research and writing.

Above all, I would like to thank three individuals for their boundless patience and encouragement. My children, Aaron and Jeremy, often insisting that I take a break to play with them, helped me stay balanced and cheerful. My wife, Laurel, more than any other person, gave me the intellectual and emotional support to complete this project and fulfill my own goals for it.

Some readers of this book's first edition have been puzzled by its title. Therefore, I wish to explain that my choice of wording—*The Drive for Self*—was intended to describe Adler's own, intense ambition for accomplishment in the world. Specifically, he sought to apply psychological knowledge for widespread social improvement. In an unceasing way, Adler placed his energy, intelligence, and creativity in the service of this goal.

PROLOGUE

═══

With a lively, inquisitive expression, the peasant family of six gazes at its observer. The young mother and father, sitting next to each other over a small table draped by a simple cloth, are wearing rough and heavy clothes. Their heads are also covered, and so perhaps it is a winter's day. Behind the mother, two young children can be seen: A pensive bonneted girl hovers close; her barefoot brother sits contentedly on the floor. At his feet, a gray-and-white kitten peers out from beneath cooking pottery, a big ladle, and a wicker basket lying awry.

Next to his bearded father stands an older barefoot youngster, a wooden flute held to his carefully pursed lips. Absorbed in the musical activity, he has turned toward his seated grandmother, as though awaiting her reaction. Obviously older than the others but erect and clear-eyed, she holds a glass of wine poised in midair. On her lap rests a large pitcher. In the corner, a small dog gazes alertly toward the little boy relaxing on the floor.

The family can hardly be called high-spirited. But neither does it seem sad or downtrodden. Not one of its members appears angry, frightened, or lonely. Rather, their group portrait exudes an atmosphere of serenity and dignity. Whatever their lives are about in seventeenth-century rural France, they are, for the moment, experiencing them together.

Family of Country People was painted around 1640 by artist Louis Le Nain, and has long been displayed in the Louvre. It was Alfred Adler's favorite painting, and for a man whose public persona of genial psychological brilliance was rarely penetrated, it offers a valuable window into his own personality.

Alongside Sigmund Freud and Carl Jung, Adler has for more than six decades been acclaimed a cofounder of modern personality theory and psychotherapy. Not only did he exert a tremendous influence on the growth of such allied fields as child guidance and social work, but his ideas have also had considerable impact on wider Western culture. Spending most of his life in his native Austria before eagerly emigrating to the United States, Adler was driven by an almost unshakable desire to create and promulgate his own psychological system for the world.

It was a system borne of his conviction that, like the six figures in Le Nain's vivid group portrait, we all have an inborn capacity for "social feeling"—companionship, camaraderie, friendship, community, and love—and that we are most fulfilled when this quality is vibrant within us. For Adler, who broke decisively with Freud after nine years, it is not our sexual drive that is paramount, but our early sense of helplessness and inferiority. What determines our life's course is not primarily how we handle our sexual feelings, but rather how we express our innate striving for mastery, competence, and power. Through biological makeup and social aspects like birth order, each of the three adults and three children in the French painting manifests this drive differently.

It is likely that *Family of Country People* also appealed to Adler because of his lifelong predilection for the simple pleasures of food, drink, and good company. From his earliest years, he enjoyed being with friends, and as a young man spent countless hours in Vienna's cafés debating psychology and social ideas. Soon after leaving Freud's circle, Adler began to develop an optimistic psychological approach aimed especially at parents, teachers, and others involved with children, a task that would occupy him for the next thirty-six years. In many ways he became the complete antithesis of the aloof and scholarly Freud. Acquiring a celebrated international reputation by middle age, Adler avidly wrote articles about child rearing for mass magazines, and became a ubiquitous lecturer throughout Europe and the United States. Indeed, he was one of the two figures along with behaviorist John B. Watson to help create modern popular psychology in his new homeland.

Until literally his last day of life at the age of sixty-seven, Adler zealously promoted his ideas to professional and lay audiences. With a materially modest life-style, his chief motive for such tireless proselytizing seemed to be the fervent belief that individual psychology (as he called his viewpoint) could succeed in creating a better world when all other philosophical systems, as well as organized religion, seemed to have failed.

Reflecting the bubbling optimism of its founder, Adler's system contains little of the dark ruminations found in the Freudian or Jungian labyrinths. When personal tragedy involving his oldest adult child struck him late in life, there was an element of irony involved, for Adler had never devoted much attention to the capacity for violence and destructiveness. At the time of his death, shortly before Hitler launched World War II, there was arguably more need than ever to uncover this shadowy aspect of the human soul.

Today, we live in a culture dominated by psychological and therapeutic ideas. It has therefore become increasingly important to understand how our major theories of human nature, articulated by such figures as Freud, Jung, Maslow, Skinner, and others, ultimately reflect the impulses and struggles of their respective founders. After the long absence of a truly definitive biography of Alfred Adler, the time is right for a probing look at the life of the creator of individual psychology.

Part One

===

For a long time now, I have been convinced
that all the questions of life can be
subordinated to the three major problems—
the problems of communal life, of work, and
of love . . . These . . . confront us continually,
compelling and challenging us.

ALFRED ADLER

CHAPTER ONE

A Viennese Boyhood

*Struggling within the incalculable
compass of his potentialities, the child
by means of trial and error receives
training and follows a . . . path
towards a goal . . . that appears
to offer him fulfillment.*

ALFRED ADLER

For centuries, Vienna stood as a natural gateway in Europe between East and West. Since medieval times, the city's strategic location on the Danube River and below the Austrian Alps made it a key trading center. Ruled by the Hapsburgs for more than half a millenium, it was under the benevolent reign of Maria Theresa and Joseph II in the late eighteenth century that Vienna also acquired an international reputation as a world capital of music. There, Haydn, Mozart, Beethoven, and Schubert dazzled all with their brilliance. But despite such glitter, many ethnic and religious minorities like the Jews found little to celebrate within the Austro-Hungarian Empire. Prince Klemens von Metternich, Emperor Franz Joseph's foreign minister and state chancellor since 1809, kept political conditions extremely repressive in a time of rapid industrial change.

Then came the revolution of 1848. Throughout the empire, popular movements arose to defy Metternich's brutal rule. Although it was quickly extinguished, the revolution brought in its wake many ideals and principles that subsequently made their way into law, among them Jewish emancipation from the ghetto. In 1849, Emperor Franz Joseph promulgated a new constitution that mandated that "civil and political rights are not dependent on religion." Soon after, specific restrictions and levies on the Jewish community were lifted. Previously, the only learned profession open to Jews had been medicine; now a wide range of career options beckoned. Jews could also own real estate, keep Christian domestics, and live anywhere in the empire. Before long, some Jews were even elected to the Vienna City Council, and finally, in 1867, a new constitution was adopted for Austro-Hungary. While it affirmed the Dual Monarchy as a Christian country, it proclaimed freedom of religion and civil rights for all the empire's citizens.

To be sure, anti-Semitism still flourished. Yet most Western nations had already begun ending formal discrimination against Jews, and Franz Joseph was determined to create a multinational empire on the basis of civil and political equality. As a result of his liberal outlook, Vienna's Jewish population soared from around 6,000 in 1860 to nearly 150,000 in 1900. Both in absolute numbers and as a percentage of its total population, fin de siècle Vienna comprised the largest Jewish community of any city in Western Europe; on the entire Continent, only Budapest and Warsaw had more Jewish residents.

The first wave of Jewish immigrants to Vienna consisted mainly of Hungarians, followed by an influx of Czechoslovakian Jews from Bohemia and Moravia. Among the former group was Alfred Adler's paternal grandfather, Simon Adler. A master furrier from Kittsee in the Burgenland, he was married to Katharina Lampl. Throughout the centuries, the Burgenland had been a buffer zone between Hungary and Austria, and at the time of Simon Adler's departure, the region actually belonged to Hungary, although the Hungarian nobility who owned it were friendly with Austria. It was a picturesque countryside, with lakes surrounded by reeds, fields and groves, hilltop castles and vineyards, and small villages, and it boasted such native-born composers as Haydn and Lizst. In the mid-nineteenth century, the Burgenland numbered about 300,000 people, the majority of whom were German speaking. Residing there, too, were Hungarians, Croatian immigrants, Gypsies, and prosperous Jewish families.

Most Burgenland Jews enjoyed a political climate far more tolerant than the rest of their coreligionists in the far-flung Austro-Hungarian Empire. Many worked as well-traveled traders, and as such, they served as intermediary agents between the ghetto Jews of Pressburg and Vienna's commercial centers. Relatively affluent and unhindered, Burgenland's Jewish inhabitants rarely felt like members of a persecuted minority. By the 1850s, most spoke German or Hungarian rather than Yiddish and closely emulated their gentile neighbors in accent and attire.

Almost nothing has been recorded about Simon and Katharina Adler, other than they had at least two children who lived to maturity. David, born in 1831, was married in Vienna in 1862 and worked as a tailor. His younger brother, Leopold (Alfred's father), was born in 1835. Both were probably born in the Burgenland and came to the Vienna area in the 1850s or 1860s. When he wedded Pauline Beer (Alfred's mother) in 1866 at the age of thirty-one, Leopold's marriage certificate identified his address as identical to that of his in-laws. Most likely, Leopold was already living in their house and working for their thriving family business.

Alfred's maternal grandparents were Hermann and Elisabeth Beer, Czechoslovakian Jews who hailed from the town of Trebitsch in Moravia, the same region that produced Sigmund Freud. It is not known how long the Beers had lived in Moravia, but when they migrated to Penzing on Vienna's outskirts around 1859, they already had at least five children: Ignaz (born before 1839), Moritz (born in 1843), Pauline (1845), Salomon (1849), and Albert (1858). Two other children were born in Penzing: Ludwig (1859) and Julius (1861).

Hermann Beer had founded the small firm Hermann Beer and Sons, dealers in bran, oats, and wheat. At the time it was a prosperous enterprise, but with the advent of railway transportation which greatly increased competition, such businesses were eventually doomed. Later, Salomon took over the firm from his father. In 1861, two years after settling in Penzing, the Beers bought a house, and lived there for many years.

Leopold and Pauline Adler spent their early married years in the neighboring villages of Penzing and Rudolfsheim. He was a grain merchant with little formal education or intellectual drive. Several grandchildren recalled him as a generous and elegantly dressed old man with virtually no Jewish religiosity. Pauline was described as more high-strung and frail than her husband. By all accounts, she was a hard-working mother and homemaker who simultaneously helped Leopold run the family grain business.

The Adlers' first child, Sigmund, was born in 1868. Two years later, in the village of Rudolfsheim near Vienna, Alfred was born on February 7, 1870. The apartment house comprised fifteen small units and faced an open marketplace. Nearby was a great expanse of open land, where neighborhood children always played. In later life, Adler regularly attributed his psychological approach to his earliest years: "As far as I can look back, I was always surrounded by friends and comrades, and for the most part, I was a well-loved playmate. This development began early and has never ceased. It is probably this feeling of solidarity with others that my understanding of the need for cooperation arose, a motive which has become the key to Individual Psychology."

Indeed, throughout his adult life, Adler displayed a gregarious personality and the ability to make friends easily. Even well into middle age as a busy figure of international acclaim, he clearly liked being around other people, almost never preferring solitude. Possessed of an easy-going, genial manner, he enjoyed forming new acquaintances and deepening them through shared activity. In that young Alfred was not especially close to either parent, it seems likely that peer relationships were important in helping him to gain an early sense of self-confidence and personal optimism.

Alfred's convivial temperament was undoubtedly strengthened by his large family of siblings. Following his birth were those of five more children: Hermine (1871), Rudolf (1873), Irma (1874), Max (1877), and Richard (1884). He enjoyed his siblings' company while growing up, but did not remain close with them in adult life. None would ever achieve fame or wide influence.

Only a few steps from the large Adler household lay the spacious grounds of Austria's imperial palace of Schönbrunn. Its beautiful gardens were renowned throughout the empire and later immortalized in a painting by Gustav Klimt. As a preschooler, Alfred was attracted to the public park's impressive grounds, and delighted in plucking the magnificent blossoms found there. But, as he humorously recalled, "My criminal career was short-lived. One day, entrance to the gardens was forbidden to me by order of the castle guard."

For the young Alfred, however, his older brother, Sigmund, was a far more formidable figure than Schönbrunn's sentries. Bright and domineering, he habitually made Alfred feel embattled in an intense struggle for his parents' attention. As the first-born male child, Sigmund also occupied a traditionally favored status in the Adler's Jewish household. Perhaps even more frustrating for Alfred was the fact that his older brother enjoyed much better physical health. In Adler's own psychological theory, our earliest memories offer an important clue to key inner themes of later adult life. It is therefore striking to see how many of his own early remembrances revolve around sickness and medical intervention.

In his few, scattered autobiographical accounts, Adler related how, as a toddler, whenever he became angry he suffered from a mild spasm of breathlessness caused by a contraction of the glottis. Decades later, when he was known for his pugnaciousness, he recalled rather jokingly that, "The situation was so agonizing that at the age of three, I decided to give up being angry altogether. From that day, I have never been angry."

More serious was Alfred's falling sick with rickets, a condition that was quite common for youngsters of the time, and one that seems to have accentuated his rivalry with Sigmund. "One of my earliest recollections is of sitting on a bench [and] bandaged up on account of rickets, with my healthy elder brother sitting opposite me. He could run, jump and move about quite effortlessly, while for me movement of any sort was a strain. . . . Everyone went to great pains to help me." To strengthen Alfred's stamina, Pauline and Leopold were glad to satisfy his desire for outdoor play, and since they lived in one of the last houses on Vienna's outskirts, such activity was easy to accomplish. In the wide meadows that stretched behind the house, Alfred joined his many friends in vigorous games, and his rickets eventually fully dissipated.

Although Leopold and Pauline were not intellectuals, their household was one that valued music. Alfred learned the piano, occasionally tried his hand at composing, and especially enjoyed singing Schubert and German folk songs in what would mature into a rich baritone voice. One day when he was about three, his parents had to attend a relative's wedding and left the children in the care of a governess. When they returned home in the evening, they were astounded to find Alfred standing atop the dining-room table and bellowing out a popular street ballad. The inane song told of a woman who prided herself on her gentleness; so intense was her feeling that she cried to see a chicken's neck wrung. The chorus went: "If the sorrows of a chicken are so difficult to bear, why pulverize poor Hubby with the kitchenware?"

Leopold smiled at little Alfred's tuneful mastery, until he realized that the governess must have taken the children to a local cabaret without asking permission. She was immediately fired, and Alfred gained more freedom for unsupervised activity in her absence.

Shortly after this comical episode, little Rudolf fell ill with diptheria. In those days, medical knowledge of the dread and often fatal illness was limited. Alfred and Rudolf were allowed to continue sleeping in the same room, and no precautions were taken to avoid contagion. Worried but helpless, the family physician advised the Adlers to keep a tub of hot water standing in the sickroom and, from time to time, to throw tall grasses and dried flowers into it. Not long after this doubtful remedy was implemented, four-year-old Alfred awoke one morning and found Rudolf lying dead in the bed beside him.

Traumatized by this experience, Alfred was taken on the day of Rudolf's funeral to his maternal grandparents' house, where relatives were gathered in mourning. He was not particularly close to Hermann and Elisabeth Beer, and the day seemed interminable. Riding back home by carriage, he noticed how his mother, "clothed all in black and wearing a black veil, went on crying and crying. My grandfather [Hermann] turned to comfort her and whispered a few words which brought a smile to her face. He must have spoken of the possible blessing of future children." But at the time Alfred felt instant shock and revulsion at the sight of his mother's fleeting smiling countenance. Crossing his mind was the clear thought: "How could a mother smile on her child's burial-day!" For years after, he bore her deep, unspoken resentment for this behavior.

Not long after, when he was about five, Alfred too faced a life-threatening illness. One winter's day, an older boy took him ice-skating. The lad soon skated out of sight, and Alfred, who remained standing on the ice, became increasingly cold. The youngster never returned. Anxious and plagued with spasms of shivering, Alfred managed to find his way home. Exhausted, he fell asleep instantly on the living-room couch. Busy with housework, Pauline noticed nothing unusual. But the moment Leopold entered the house, he looked at Alfred's sleeping form and shouted to her room in alarm.

As night fell, a doctor was summoned. Alfred dimly regained consciousness and saw the stranger hovering over him. After examining Alfred and feeling his weak pulse, the physician turned to Leopold and said, "Give yourself no more trouble. The boy is lost." Alfred understood the death sentence well, especially coming so soon on the heels of Rudolf's miserable demise. After losing consciousness again, Alfred next awoke to find another doctor standing nearby and his parents holding down their son's arms and legs. He felt severe prickings on his left thigh, and looked down in horror. Blood was pouring out in streams, and several leeches were lying on his body. Although frantic, Alfred was unable to remove them.

Miraculously, Alfred recovered from his bout with pneumonia, and then and there decided his future occupation. He vowed to become a doctor. A few years later, his parents recounted the physician's frightening warning: Another encounter with pneumonia might well prove fatal to their second-born son. Upon hearing it, Adler recalled during midlife, "My decision was confirmed. I *must* become a physician. To this decision, I always remained true."

━━━━━

Certainly, from an early age, Alfred was more interested in medicine and science than in religion. In Penzing and Rudolfsheim, his family lived predominantly amidst gentiles who tended to be tolerant of the Adlers' religious background. But like many Hungarian Jews of their generation, Leopold and Pauline Adler had minimal interest in Jewish observance. Aside from occasional synagogue attendance and a few rituals halfheartedly practiced on major holidays, they deemed Judaism irrelevant to their lives.

For them, it belonged to the ancient Israelite past, and not to the new age of the steam engine and the locomotive.

In adulthood, Adler could recall only a few early episodes related to his Jewish heritage and these were not uplifting. One day when he was about five, the family was attending synagogue. Bored by the seemingly interminable silent prayers, Alfred spied a piece of vestment sticking out of a cupboard drawer within his reach. Very slowly and cautiously, he began to tug at this mysterious and intriguing piece of cloth, which emerged like a snake from the old cabinet. Then, suddenly, the whole cupboard lurched forward and fell with a tremendous crash to the floor. Alfred leaped to his feet and dashed out of the synagogue, fully believing that he had brought down heavenly wrath upon the entire congregation.

On another occasion, the Adler family was celebrating Passover at home. Skeptical when told that an angel would be inspecting every Jewish household to make sure that it contained only unleavened bread, Alfred decided to hold a test. On Passover night, after the rest of his family had gone to bed, Alfred crept downstairs and substituted leavened bread for the matzos in the cupboard. He sat up for hours with the door ajar, seeking to discover the effect upon the heavenly visitor. "I was not altogether surprised," he humorously recalled, "when the angel did not turn up."

Despite such early skepticism, Alfred found the Bible to be a source of psychological wisdom. He particularly liked the stories of Genesis, such as those about Joseph and his jealous brothers, that chronicled all-too-human foibles in family relations. Throughout Adler's later career in lecturing and writing, he often cited biblical tales to illustrate such concepts of individual psychology as sibling rivalry, dream interpretation, or the inferiority complex. As a parent who rejected religious observance, he would nonetheless teach his children to value the Bible for its insights into human nature.

Although most Viennese Jews at the time resembled the Adlers in eagerly seeking to shed their ancestral ways, they nevertheless clustered in certain of the twenty-one different districts within the imperial city. They also preferred to socialize and do business with one another. As Sigmund Freud's son Martin later recalled, "Rich and poor . . . we moved in Jewish circles. Our friends were Jews, our doctor was Jewish, our lawyer was Jewish. If one was in business, one's partner was Jewish. One read a newspaper that was written and directed by Jews and went for holidays to places where Jews were in the majority."

The most ethnically Jewish district in Vienna was the Leopoldstadt, to which Alfred's family relocated from the villagelike Penzing-Rudolfsheim area when he was seven years old. Situated between the Danube Canal and the Danube River, it housed the largest concentration of Vienna's growing Jewish population and was derisively known as Matzo Island. Centuries before, during the Renaissance, Leopoldstadt had been mandated the Jewish ghetto for Vienna, where all Jews on pain of imprisonment or death were obliged to return every nightfall. Although such repressive restrictions had long since been abolished, by the late nineteenth century, so many working-class Jewish immigrants were settling in crowded Leopoldstadt that it was again becoming a de facto ghetto. Why Leopold and Pauline Adler relocated there is not clear, although economic reasons such as less expensive housing were probably important.

It is significant, though, that Adler's autobiographical accounts never mention his childhood years spent in this heavily Jewish district. Coupled with the fact that he would later convert to Protestantism, it seems likely that Adler felt no pride in his Jewish background. Indeed, quite unlike Freud in later years, he probably viewed it as an embarrassment. In this respect, Adler was far from unique. During his four boyhood years in the Leopoldstadt, most of its Jewish inhabitants were immersing themselves in German rather than Judaic culture. By 1880 in Vienna, after-school Hebrew education for Jewish boys, as well as synagogue attendance, had clearly begun to decline. The city's one rabbinic seminary, established by a Galician scholar, had virtually no contact with local Viennese Jews. As late as 1900, Vienna would still lack a rabbi who had been born in the city.

This assimilationist emphasis prevailed culturally as well as theologically in Vienna. Jewish newspapers were printed there, but unlike their counterparts in London and Paris, none was written in Yiddish; nor did any make a reference to Jews or Judaism in their titles. Two Yiddish theaters operated in the Leopoldstadt, but no significant Yiddish literature was being published in Vienna. It therefore seems hardly surprising that Adler, like many of his peers, grew to maturity with virtually no interest in Judaism.

In 1881, the Adler family moved out of the urban clutter of Leopoldstadt to Hernals, a largely rural section outside Vienna's borders at the time. Alfred was probably pleased, for Hernals resembled the sparsely populated Penzing-Rudolfsheim area that he had enjoyed several years before. The Adlers rented two adjoining houses that belonged to a dairy farm owned by Count Palffy, a Hungarian magnate from the Burgenland. Most likely, Leopold was employed as a middleman for the sale of the count's produce.

During the same year, Alfred's grandfather Hermann died; the following year, his grandmother Elisabeth was buried. With both their parents deceased, Pauline and her six living siblings divided the estate. She sold her share of the property to one of her brothers, and in July 1883, the Adlers purchased a home in Währing. This district also lay outside Vienna's immediate boundaries and still had a pastoral ambience of one-story houses and gardens. The home was a typical commercial dwelling for the time, and comprised business premises with a first-floor dwelling and stables below. It nearly fronted on the famous cemetery (now known as Schubert Park) that held the tombs of Beethoven and Schubert.

Alfred liked the country atmosphere of Währing. The family kept chickens, rabbits, and even cows, goats, and horses. But relentless competition with his older brother, Sigmund, made adolescence difficult. Alfred always felt eclipsed by his "model brother" and resented his favored status in the family. Years later, Adler, as a world-renowned psychological theorist, would poetically compare the emotional development of siblings close in age to struggling garden saplings, each competing for adequate light and space for growth. Even in middle age, he would feel moved to comment wearily that wealthy businessman Sigmund, "a good industrious fellow [who] was always ahead of me—is *still* ahead of me!"

Whether Alfred found or sought teenage love outside his family is not known historically. Especially for those of Jewish background, middle-class adolescents had little opportunity for actual romance. Proper young women were expected to be virgins upon marriage and to resist all efforts against womanly modesty. For well-bred young men, the sexual double standard was common: They were tacitly permitted and sometimes even encouraged by older male relatives to find sexual outlet in brothels. Short-lived and discreet affairs with lower-class women like servants or shopworkers were also deemed acceptable in the cultural milieu.

But in all probability, Alfred led a rather chaste adolescence. The only surviving photograph of his teenage years reveals a slender and pensive fifteen year old with wide, innocent eyes. As an adult, he never alluded to any romantic infatuations prior to meeting his future wife, Raissa, when both had been university students. In fatherhood, Adler would broach the topic of sex only once with his adult son; and that was to advise a surprised young Kurt, before his celebratory, post-graduation tour of Italy, that "the only sure prevention of venereal disease is love."

═══

Since early childhood, Alfred enjoyed playing outdoors and socializing with friends. Schooling was a very different matter, however. From the outset, young son. Ironically, they had little interest in intellectual pursuit for its own sake, and were not well-read in either Judaic texts like the Talmud or in wider European literature. But similar to the overwhelming majority of Jewish parents inhabiting the Austro-Hungarian Empire, the Adlers valued education pragmatically: as the means to provide a better future for their children. Although Leopold might devote his life to buying and selling grain to support his large family, his dream was that Alfred would excel academically, and then attain a coveted career in an elite profession like law or medicine.

Middle-class men and women like the Adlers regarded such professions as providing lifetime security against the inevitable ups and downs of business activity. Striving for acceptance into wider European society, these families also hoped that a university education might gain their sons more favorable acceptance among Vienna's sophisticated gentiles than mere financial success could bring.

Certainly, the Adlers were well acquainted with the educational path necessary for their second-born son to attain the lofty goal of attorney or physician. First, little Alfred, like all other Viennese children, would attend an elementary school (*Volksschule*) from the ages of six through ten. Then, assuming Alfred performed scholastically according to expectations, he would be enrolled in a prestigious secondary school (*Gymnasium*) for eight years of rigorous study. This stint would culminate in admission to the University of Vienna and, finally, to legal or medical certification and a prestigious practice.

As writer Stefan Zweig recalled in his memoirs of prewar Vienna, "Every well-to-do family took care to have its sons 'educated' if only for purely social reasons. . . . Only the so-called 'academic' education, which led to the University, carried full value in those days of enlightened liberalism, and that is why it was the ambition of every 'good' family to have some sort of doctor's title prefixed to the name of at least one of its sons."

Initially, Alfred probably made his parents happy in their cherished plan, for he encountered little difficulty in elementary school. This achievement was hardly suprising, however. During the late nineteenth century, Vienna's *Volksschules* provided only a rudimentary training for pupils in four basic areas: reading, writing, arithmetic, and religion. In the semirural areas of Penzing and Rudolfsheim, few families shared the Adlers' Jewish heritage emphasizing educational accomplishment, and Alfred probably experienced minimal competition from his classmates. Indeed, he gained special popularity for his academic ability by serving as a friendly tutor to many popularity for his academic ability by serving as a friendly tutor to many neighborhood youngsters. As Adler himself would later coin the phrase, he was clearly *compensating* for physical weakness by achieving success in a different realm of youthful development.

But when Alfred turned nine, his happy school days abruptly ended. Having successfully completed the elementary grades, he was now ready to enter *Gymnasium* and begin the long, formidable preparation leading to the venerated University of Vienna. Meanwhile, the bulk of his classmates were embarking on the very different, nonacademic track of vocational training, which terminated when they reached fourteen. For such children of laborers or peasants, the only options for attaining high-social status lay in the army and the priesthood. Likewise, virtually no gentile artisans or shop-keepers sent their youngsters to *Gymnasium*; nor, generally, did Vienna's non-Jewish businessmen seek higher education for their sons.

In the fall of 1879, Alfred's parents placed him in the well-regarded Communales Real-und Obergymnasium. Situated in the Sperlgasse section of Vienna, the school was better known as the Sperlgymnasium or Sperläum. Coincidentally, the young Sigmund Freud had attended school there fourteen years earlier. In the ensuing time, the institution's regulation had changed and was now mandating ten years as the minimum pupil age for admission. Perhaps through the deliberate deception of Alfred's parents, he was dutifully enrolled, for school records erroneously listed his birth year as 1869.

Socially as well as intellectually, Alfred found the Sperläum quite a different place from his semirural elementary school. For one thing, enrollment in Austria's prestigious *Gymnasien* was limited only to boys and would remain so for more than forty years. Nearly all educators believed that such superior schooling would be wasted on "mere girls," and they would certainly prove distracting to the boys for whom secondary education was considered a necessity.

Perhaps even more surprising for nine-year-old Alfred was the fact that so many of his new *Gymnasium* classmates shared his middle-class Jewish background. Yet, as Leopold and Pauline Adler undoubtedly knew, Jews had been attending Austria's *Gymnasien* for nearly a hundred years, since Emperor Joseph II had abolished restrictions against their presence in schools. The first European monarch to encourage Jews to pursue secular education as a means toward assimilation, Joseph II had also, in 1782, dissolved several specific levies on the Jewish community. Over the ensuing decades, a steady growth had occurred in the number of Jews seeking entry into wider European culture through secular education, the so-called *Haskalah* ("Enlightenment") movement. Such Jews fervently regarded the *Gymnasium* as a key avenue for social integration and acceptance.

Curiously though, *Gymnasium* schooling was not generally a path for upward social mobility in nineteenth-century Austria. The dominant, two-track system of education made it difficult for the sons of artisans, manual laborers, or shopkeepers to gain higher education. The issue, it seems, was not simply financial. Tuition fees were typically low and were often waived for needy pupils. Rather, the matter may have been partly psychological, for most working-class Viennese probably never even considered sending their offspring to prestigious secondary schools. Originally from peasant backgrounds, they were accustomed to servility toward their social superiors, not to sitting beside them in class. In contrast, most Jews like the Adlers lacked any such tradition of social obeisance.

For whatever reasons, Jews attended almost all Viennese *Gymnasien* in numbers greatly exceeding their actual percentage in the imperial capital's large population. It has been estimated that in fin de siècle Vienna, Jewish residents comprised about 8 percent of the city's populace. Yet among *Gymnasien* in such districts as the Inner City (I), Leopoldstadt (III), and the Alsergrund (IX), Jewish students numbered between 40 and 80 percent of the attendees. As early as 1875, four years before Alfred began *Gymnasium,* Jews comprised about 30 percent of all such pupils. Significantly though, they rarely attended the two most prestigious secondary schools in Vienna: the Gymnasium zu den Schotten and the Theresianische Akademie. These offered the most elite education in all Vienna, and were the preparatory academies for many of the capital's political leaders.

One year younger than most of his highly competitive classmates and under strong parental pressure to succeed, Alfred found the Sperläum a difficult adjustment. With mathematics proving especially troublesome, he actually failed his first year and was obliged to repeat it. Alfred's scholastic performance was so poor that Leopold angrily threatened to remove him from *Gymnasium* and instead obtain for him a shoemaker's apprenticeship.

Such parental threats were rather typical among middle-class Jewish parents like the Adlers, but they were farfetched. Only a miniscule number of Jewish boys in Vienna were involved with apprenticeships for manual trades like shoemaking or attended lower-class vocational programs. Even in schools for the needle trades leading to tailoring work, Jews comprised only 2 percent of the students. Indeed, Jewish youngsters shunned such institutions, in part because anti-Semitism was more common and overt than in the more cosmopolitan *Gymnasien*. Additionally, even those Jewish families who were struggling financially regarded trade and commerce careers as more promising for their sons than futures in shoemaking or tailoring.

Nevertheless, Adler later recalled that he had been truly frightened by his father's forceful threat to have him apprenticed. Perhaps he was thinking of his uncle David's difficult life as a tailor and feared following in his footsteps. Eventually, as a new physician, Adler would write his first publication on the health hazards of small-business tailoring work in Vienna. In any case, he immediately decided to work harder in *Gymnasium,* and soon his grades vastly improved.

As for his difficulty with mathematics, Adler recalled in later years—perhaps apocryphally—an occasion when his teacher was stumped by a seemingly insoluble problem. Adler was the only student who saw the answer and recollected that, "The success changed my whole attitude toward mathematics. Where previously I had withdrawn my interest from the whole subject, now I began to enjoy it and use every opportunity for increasing my ability. In consequence, I became one of the best mathematicians in my school. The experience helped me . . . to see the fallacy of theories of special talents or inborn capacities."

Yet, it would be quite inaccurate to say that Adler ever truly enjoyed *Gymnasium*. Throughout Central Europe, schools like the Sperläum saw their mission quite traditionally: to provide rigorous training in the Greek and Latin classics to youngsters being groomed for the university and high-status careers in the professions or civil service. These humanistic (rather than church-oriented) educational institutions had been founded in the late eighteenth century. The educators who designed the curriculum had felt strongly that the study of Latin and Greek grammar was vital to the development of logical thought patterns, that exposure to classical literature was essential for gaining aesthetic sensitivity, and that a grasp of ancient history and philosophy would stimulate noble sentiments. A decade before Adler began the Sperläum, the *Gymnasium* curriculum in Austro-Hungary was placed under governmental control and therefore standardized throughout the empire, with virtually no innovation or variation permitted.

By our own educational standards, the curriculum was extremely rigorous. The ten- to eighteen-year-old students learned Greek, Latin, German language and literature, history and geography, mathematics, physics, and religion. They also took electives in French and English. In German class, sixth-year pupils (sixteen year olds) like Alfred learned Middle High German, studied German literature from its inception to Martin Luther, and analyzed verses of the *Nibelungenlied*. The following year, pupils studied New High German, literature from Luther to Goethe, and the works of Goethe and Schiller in depth. In the final year, they analyzed German literature from the romantic period to the present.

In later life, Adler never showed much interest in German letters, and it is unlikely that he found such *Gymnasium* lessons particularly uplifting. Perhaps even less compelling was the core curriculum emphasizing Latin grammar and literature. Depending on grade level, students were required to take Latin for five to eight hours weekly in all eight years of *Gymnasium* attendance, and Greek for four to five hours weekly from the third to the final year. Students read the *Iliad* and the *Odyssey,* as well as Plato and Sophocles, all in the original. They were exposed to the works of Cicero, Horace, Livy, Ovid, Tacitus, Virgil, and Julius Caesar. In contrast, *Gymnasium* pupils spent only three hours each week in mathematics or science. Gymnastics, singing, drawing, and handwriting completed the curriculum.

In 1881, when the Adlers moved from the Leopoldstadt to Hernals for Leopold's business activity, Alfred transferred to the Heralser *Gymnasium* on the street bearing the same name. He continued to attend this second *Gymnasium* when the family moved once again, this time to the neighboring area of Währing, and remained there until he was eighteen years old and received his matriculation degree. Unfortunately, the school's archives were destroyed during World War II, making it impossible to document his performance.

Nevertheless, it seems clear that Adler's eight years at the Heralser *Gymnasium* and the Sperläum were rather unsatisfying. In the extensive writings of his later life, he never alluded to a single inspiring teacher or an exciting learning experience. Indeed, Adler would emerge as a major educational reformer in postwar Austria who, even early in his career, had allied himself with firebrand socialist critics like Carl Furtmüller. In their view, the entire system of schooling required radical overhaul. Although many Austrian *Gymnasium* graduates chose careers in fields other than psychology or education, they undoubtedly felt the same way. They regarded their professional accomplishments in the arts or sciences as having been in spite of, rather than due to, their youthful schooling.

"It was more than too much," caustically recalled writer Stefan Zweig, "and scarcely left any time for physical development and sports, to say nothing of recreation and gaiety. . . . The entire period of my [*Gymnasium* education] was nothing more than a constant and wearisome boredom. . . . I cannot recall ever having been either 'joyous' or 'blissful' during that monotonous, heartless, and lifeless schooling, which thoroughly spoiled the best and freest period of our existence."

For one thing, most *Gymnasium* environments were architecturally and physically dreary. Classrooms were often badly whitewashed and without adorning pictures or other decorations. Students sat in pairs for hours at a time on uncomfortable, low wooden benches; lavatory odors were sometimes pervasive. The curriculum itself was regimented and inflexible. "For eight years," observed writer Zweig, "no teacher ever asked us even once what we personally wished to learn, and that encouraging stimulus, for which every young person secretly longs, was totally lacking."

Indeed, the dominant teaching method was to emphasize the number of mistakes students had made in their preceding lesson. No interaction among them was permitted, whether in pairs or small groups. The teachers sat rigidly at their front desks and the pupils sat below them on wooden benches. They answered specific questions as the teachers deemed fit: Everything was subordinated to the standardized curriculum. "For a teacher to regard a pupil as an individual," Zweig reminisced," would have demanded particular attention to [his] special qualities . . . and at that time exceeded not only the teacher's authority but his capabilities as well."

Even worse than such indifference was that students were infantalized. In the process, their intellectual and creative energy inevitably suffered. Even eighteen year olds, in their final year of *Gymnasium* attendance, were treated like children. They were punished if caught with a cigarette and required to raise their hands obediently for permission to use the lavatory. Not once in his writings did Adler ever wax nostalgic or seek to romanticize Austria's fin de siècle schooling system. In words that well summed up Adler's own memories of *Gymnasium* life, Zweig remarked that, "For us school was compulsion, ennui, dreariness, a place where we had to assimilate the 'science of the not-worth knowing' in exactly measured portions. . . . It was a dull, pointless learning that the old pedagogy forced upon us. The only truly joyful moment of happiness for which I have to thank my school was the day that I was able to shut the door behind me forever."

For young Adler, that blessed day occurred in the spring of 1888, when he received his graduation certificate from the Hernals *Gymnasium*. At the age of eighteen, he was accepted into the University of Vienna, ready to embark on a premedical curriculum. Alfred's older brother, Sigmund, had already been forced to drop out of *Gymnasium* to join his hard-pressed father in the grain business. For struggling Leopold and Pauline, their dream of Alfred as a successful physician served as a beacon to illumine a better future for their children.

CHAPTER TWO

The Making of a Radical Physician

*To grow up means to have more
power, and it is better to strive
for progress than to look for
the paradise of the past.*

ALFRED ADLER

In the fall of 1888, Adler enrolled in medical school at the University of Vienna. He already had decided to become a practicing physician rather than a researcher; and perhaps mainly for this reason, his course work held little appeal. In later years, Adler could remember almost nothing inspiring or intellectually stimulating about his medical training. Certainly, his academic record was undistinguished. He completed medical studies in the average length of seven years, took only the obligatory courses necessary to pass his formal examinations, and passed his three *Rigorosa* (qualifying tests) with the grade *genugend* ("adequate"), the lowest possible.

In view of the medical faculty's orientation, it is difficult to imagine how matters for Adler could have been otherwise. His professors strongly emphasized experimentalism and diagnostic exactitude rather than patient care. By the mid-nineteenth century, their medical philosophy was derided by humanistic practitioners as "therapeutic nihilism" for having so little to say about compassionate treatment for suffering individuals. One Heidelberg-trained physician was so horrified by the Viennese faculty's callousness, that in mid-century he wrote a poem satirizing them for allowing a patient to die while they debated the man's diagnosis. But such criticism generally had little impact on medical practices there.

Undoubtedly, the school's most notorious case of therapeutic nihilism concerned Hungarian-born obstetrician Ignaz Semmelweiss. At the university's General Hospital in 1847, he discovered that dreaded childbed fever resulted when doctors coming directly from the dissecting room unwittingly introduced bacteria into a mother's womb. For daring to insist that his Viennese colleagues adopt adequate sanitary precautions, Semmelweiss was denounced and then ridiculed until his death in 1861.

When Adler began medical study at the university twenty-seven years later, not much had changed. The city's poor dreaded entering the General Hospital, fearing they would never leave alive. Incoming patients had to pay in advance, and all who died underwent autopsy to help advance the diagnostic process. One medical alumnus later recalled hearing about an episode during this era in which a group of students eagerly surrounded a woman dying of pleurisy or pneumonia in order to hear the crepitation in her lungs as her last moments approached. When confronted by a visiting colleague shocked by such callousness, a Viennese professor rebutted, "Treatment, treatment, that is nothing. It is the diagnosis that we want."

Such a cold-blooded approach was antithetical to Adler's entire motivation for becoming a physician as the best means to help humanity. But he was determined to reach his goal despite the unsatisfying curriculum, and had several outlets to keep him from becoming discouraged. By now, Adler had long since overcome—or compensated for—his early physical weaknesses, and had matured into a sturdy and active young man. Standing barely five feet seven inches tall, he was not physically imposing, but he enjoyed participating with friends in swimming, hiking, and occasionally mountain climbing. In later life, he would advise parental audiences to help foster self-confidence in their children by teaching them swimming or other pleasurable forms of demanding exercise.

Even more satisfying for Adler during his college years was to socialize with friends every evening at the nearby, inexpensive Café Griensteidl. He rarely felt drawn to solitude; even when intellectually excited, he never seems to have kept a diary or journal. Much more stimulating was to discuss ideas, whether philosophical or social, amidst friendly company in a relaxed public setting. In coming decades, as Adler became an increasingly well-known figure in Vienna and abroad, such activity would be his hallmark.

Since at that time psychiatry was not an obligatory course at university, Adler received no formal psychiatric training. Nor did he hear the lectures of *Privadozent* ("instructor") Sigmund Freud on hysteria. In his fifth semester, however, Adler took Richard von Krafft-Ebing's course on "the most important diseases of the nervous system." One of Vienna's most renowned psychiatrists, Krafft-Ebing was a German-born Catholic who helped discover how syphilis causes paralysis. He was probably best known for coining the term *masochism* and for his 1866 volume on sexual deviancy, an influential work for over fifty years.

Adler's university records reveal that his fifth, sixth, and seventh semesters were particularly strenuous. During these three semesters, he took, among others, ten-hour weekly courses in both surgery and medicine. The latter was taught by the internist Hermann Nothnagel, a staunch advocate of humanistic treatment. "It is true that our prospects and the possibilities of influencing the nature of pathological processes are very limited for the time being," he wrote. "However, this does not mean that medicine is condemned to the role of an idle spectator or to passive laissez-faire." Like Adler, Nothnagel had chosen a medical career in order to aid others, and his famous maxim was, "Only a good man can be a great physician." A productive and innovative researcher, he widely studied brain diseases and was also the first to perfect the measurement of blood pressure in diagnosis. Nothnagel's lectures included material on neurological disorders, and he was among the handful of professors whom Adler found stimulating.

When Adler's seventh semester ended, he passed his first qualifying examination on March 24, 1892. The following week, he began half of his one-year obligatory military service and was placed with the First and Fourth Tyroler-Kaiserjäger-Regiment until October 1.

Among Adler's courses in his ninth semester was the pathology of the nervous system with Salomon Stricker. A leading histologist, Stricker was known for research on vascular nerves and new techniques for studying dead tissue. For Adler's tenth and final semester, he enrolled only in a ten-hour weekly course of surgery. Adler passed his second *Rigorosum* on May 22, 1894, and then waited almost a year and a half before presenting himself for the final qualifying examination.

For medical students like Adler planning on clinical practice rather than academic research or specialization, two institutions were typically available: the forementioned General Hospital and the considerably smaller Viennese Poliklinik. Paid positions at the General Hospital were available to Austrian citizens only. Because Adler held Hungarian citizenship due to his parentage (he would not gain Austrian citizenship until 1911), volunteer medical work would have been Adler's sole option there.

The Poliklinik was founded in 1871 by the iconoclastic Moritz Benedikt to provide free medical care to working-class families at a time before social security legislation existed in Austria. As an associate professor at the Uni-

versity of Vienna, the German-born Benedikt had become interested in util-
izing hypnosis to treat hysteria (antedating young Freud's interest by several
years), but was warned by senior faculty to abandon this unconventional
and taboo field. Never accepted by his more conservative colleagues, it was
only after a lifetime of work that Benedikt would be awarded the title of full
professor in 1899. It seems likely that Adler was inspired by Benedikt's fierce
intellectual independence and indifference to medical orthodoxy. Such
qualities would soon dominate Adler's entire professional outlook.

Medical staff at the Poliklinik were not paid for their services, but they
received an excellent opportunity to gain direct clinical experience and
perhaps prospective patients as well. In 1895, Adler began working in the
opthamology department under Professor August von Reuss. On November 12 of that year, he passed his third and final qualifying exam. He was
awarded his medical degree ten days later on November 22.

Leopold and Pauline Adler must have been delighted with their second-
born son's accomplishment and his promising career prospects. He was the
first family member to achieve professional status. For the next few months,
Adler continued to perform opthamological work at the Poliklinik, but he
was called away to begin his remaining half year of obligatory military service on April 1. Assigned to a Hungarian unit where he was identified as
Aladar Adler, he was stationed at the Eighteenth Military Hospital of Pressburg. His tour of duty was completed on September 30, 1896.

———

Adler's medical treatment of poor patients at the Poliklinik reflected his
wider political outlook, for by the mid-1890s, he had become strongly
drawn to socialism. The writings of Marx and Engels excited him intellectually, and seemed to offer a real path for actualizing his idealistic ambition
to help humanity through medical intervention. He was much less drawn
to economic theory and analysis than to socialism's optimistic viewpoint
that peoples' lives could be immeasurably enhanced through specific societal action.

Each evening at the Café Dom near Vienna's famous Stephansdom, Adler
enjoyed sitting for hours over coffee and inexpensive food and fiercely debating philosophical ideas with friends. Although uninterested in joining
the rough-and-tumble world of political-party organizing, he soon began to
frequent socialist meetings. As Adler's longtime colleague Carl Furtmüller
later recalled, "There was an intense intellectual life among members of
this circle, and an enthusiasm to prepare the world for a better future, very

different from the superficiality with which the [German] nationalist group handled political and social problems. A high percentage of this circle . . . played important roles in public life."

Indeed, during Adler's university years, a nationalistically motivated form of anti-Semitism gradually began to emerge throughout Central Europe, including Austria and the celebrated University of Vienna. Such hostility toward Jews was hardly comparable with the organized brutality to occur decades later under European fascism's banner, but it did mark a definite change in the school's social atmosphere. "Grouped into so-called *Burschenschaften* [German students' association]," remembered Stefan Zweig, "[were] scar-faced, drunken, and brutal [youths who] dominated the University Hall . . . and were armed with hard, heavy sticks. Unceasingly aggressive, they attacked the Jewish, the Slavic, the Catholic, and the Italian students turn by turn, and drove them, defenseless, out of the University. On the occasion of every *Bummel* (as the Saturday student spree was called) blood flowed."

There is no evidence that Adler was ever victimized by these anti-Semitic gangs, but their presence helped to unify those students who were not German nationalists into sympathizing, albeit loosely, with the internationally oriented socialist cause. Although raised in a religiously nonobservant household, Adler as a Jew harbored little attraction for German nationalistic striving. Instead, the socialist movement offered many young Jewish intellectuals like him the alluring values of economic justice and concern for the disadvantaged with an emphasis on rationality and progress.

For such secular Viennese, Judaism, by comparison, appeared irrelevant and outmoded in the new industrial age. It seems no historical accident that most of Austria's socialist leaders came from this same secular-Jewish background, including the highly influential Viktor Adler (no relation to Alfred, a generation older).

Known as the father of Austrian socialism, Viktor Adler might well have served as a role model for Alfred Adler. Although the two men never became close, their lives had striking parallels. Born in 1852 to assimilated Jewish parents, Viktor Adler received medical training at the University of Vienna. He initially decided to become a psychiatrist and, like young Freud, went to Paris for postgraduate study. But soon he chose to become a general practitioner among the poor, and finally, in the mid-1880s, turned his full effort to organizing Austria's badly demoralized and split socialist movement. Using the Anarchist Law of 1886 as legal justification, Austro-Hungarian Prime Minister Eduard Graf von Taaffe had him arrested and jailed numerous times for sedition. But with unshakable perseverance, he succeeded in creating a united Social Democratic party in December 1888.

In the ensuing years, Viktor Adler became a vital figure in guiding Austrian socialism into democratic rather than violent modes of political expression. A staunch defender of the Hapsburg Empire, he declared in 1889 that, "Except for France and England, Austria has perhaps the most liberal laws in all Europe, so much so that it resembles a republic which has a monarch in place of a president at its head."

The following year, Viktor Adler revealed his talent as an organizer by inaugurating socialist May Day in Vienna and making it the occasion to demand a standard eight-hour day for workers. Another key item on the socialist agenda was the enacting of universal suffrage, for hundreds of thousands if not millions were disenfranchised by their inability to afford the five-gülden poll tax.

Carrying red flags and singing, tens of thousands of workers and their children marched four deep along the wide Praterstrasse, as imperial soldiers stood a watchful guard. As Zweig later recalled, "[The] main avenue [was] a lovely, broad, chestnut-lined boulevard [on which] usually only the carriages and equipages of the aristocracy and the wealthy middle classes appeared. Socialists! The word had a peculiar taste of blood and terror in the Germany and Austria of those days."

Vienna's 1890 May Day demonstration was the most successful conducted by any European socialist party of the time, and left a vivid impression on those who witnessed it. Although eminently peaceful, it worried moderates like the establishment's *Neue Freie Presse,* which reported that, "Food is being hoarded as though for an impending siege, everybody's mind is weighed down by grave worries. . . . This fear is humiliating and would never have arisen if the middle class had not sunk so low, if it had not lost all confidence."

Adler was an impressionable youth of twenty at the time, more worried about his father Leopold's increasing business problems than about safeguarding middle-class Vienna's esteem. Perhaps the experience of seeing the family sink into financial duress was radicalizing; in any event, the Adler residence in scenic Währing became heavily mortgaged, and the following year, they were forced to sell the property at a loss and return to the far more urban Leopoldstadt district. There the Adlers lived in considerable economic strain until Alfred's brother, Sigmund, became a successful businessman and managed to reestablish all his relatives in comfortable living conditions.

Alfred Adler never wrote about either his childhood or early adulthood in Vienna's crowded working-class Jewish district, and he may have felt resentment about those years. In this respect, his attitude toward Judaism was not wholly unlike that of socialist leader Viktor Adler, who, although raised in a Jewish family, felt only antipathy toward his ancestral religion and, joined by his father, converted to Protestantism at the age of twenty-six. It was Viktor Adler's fervent hope that socialism would speed assimilation so that Judaism and Jewish culture would both disappear from the world. Alfred Adler never publicly voiced such sentiments, but he would eventually convert to Protestantism as well, and divorce himself completely from Austria's Jewish community.

Most Jewish intellectuals who embraced Austrian socialism felt the same way. They saw nothing of value within their religious and cultural heritage worth preserving. Politically, they were delighted that Viktor Adler had brilliantly succeeded in unifying for the first time their country's socialist movement's moderate and radical factions. Indeed, with the successful incorporation of the country's active trade unions, the Social Democratic party grew rapidly, and in 1897, it experienced unprecedented parliamentary gains.

During the summer of 1897, Adler fell deeply in love for what was likely the first—and only—time in his life. The precise circumstances in which he met Raissa Timofeivna Epstein remain unknown. Characteristically reserved about personal matters, Adler never wrote or spoke publicly about the courtship. Nor could his adult children Alexandra and Kurt ever recall hearing him reminisce about romancing their mother or engaging in any other youthful love affairs.

According to the powerful social dictates that dominated middle-class Viennese life, the young professional Adler was expected to remain single until he achieved financial independence. He was also expected to enjoy solely platonic involvement with women of his own social class. As has been noted, sexual relations for middle-class bachelors were fully permitted, but only tacitly, and exclusively, with women of the lower classes. As Zweig later recalled, "[typical] were brief liaisons with lower-class women such as shop-girls and waitresses, the artistic women who worked as actresses, dancers, and artistes, and much more commonly, prostitution."

While no information exists on Adler's own behavior in this regard prior to marriage, in his early writings he would strongly condemn such mores as hypocritical and antifeminist. For "proper" middle-class women like his younger sisters, Hermine and Irma, social convention governing sexuality was even more restrictive: Complete sexual abstinence until marriage was the inviolate rule. "In order to protect young girls," Zweig observed, "they were not left alone for a single moment. They were given a governess whose duty it was to see that they did not step out of the house unaccompanied, that they were taken to school, to their dancing lessons, to their music lessons, and brought home in the same manner. . . . They were akin to the exotic delicacy of a hothouse plant cultivated under glass in an artificially over-warmed atmosphere."

In her own way, Raissa rebelled vigorously against a similar upbringing in Russia. Born in Moscow on November 9, 1873, she was the second child of Anna and Timofei Epstein. They were affluent, relatively assimilated Jews, and seemed to have valued education for women: Raissa was encouraged to develop her intellect and her older sister, Rosa, would later become a librarian. The sisters were fortunate that their father had extremely wealthy relatives, owners of vast tracts of wooded land that provided the extensive lumber necessary for building the railroad between Moscow and distant St. Petersburg.

With her mother, Anna, dying early in life, Raissa did not enjoy a happy childhood. It is not clear when Timofei remarried and produced a son, but Raissa and her stepmother got along poorly. In the climate of anti-Semitism that flourished in late nineteenth-century Russia, Raissa also felt insecure and inhibited as a bright Jewish girl growing to maturity. The University of Moscow barred her attendance as a female, and so at the age of twenty-two she went to Switzerland. There, she attended the University of Zurich for three semesters in 1895–96, and took courses in biology, microscopy, and zoology, apparently planning a major in the natural sciences.

Raissa's reasons for moving to Vienna the following year are unclear. By then, she was already quite interested in socialism, and it seems likely that Alfred first encountered the petite, fair-skinned female Russian student at a socialist function during March or April 1897. Having already received his medical degree, and now single in his late twenties, Adler was certainly at an age when marriage had become socially appropriate.

The courtship was swift and intense. Adler found Raissa physically attractive and felt immediately exhilarated by her intelligence, idealism, and like-minded commitment to world betterment through socialist activity. He also may have regarded Raissa's Russian background as intriguingly exotic, and yet at the same time her Jewish ethnicity made him feel secure. Although

Adler was not religious, he probably experienced some modest family pressure to marry within the faith.

The twenty-three-year-old Raissa seems to have been flattered by this young Viennese physician's polite and adoring manner. In a letter of July 11 addressed to "respectful Miss" and signed "with heartfelt greetings," Adler expressed his disappointment to Raissa at not finding her at home (probably a boardinghouse for female students) during the past weekend. Feeling forlorn by Raissa's unexpected absence during his appointed "calling hour" early Saturday evening, Adler had wandered aimlessly for hours through Vienna's winding streets. On Sunday, he likewise returned twice to her residence before writing to her.

During the next few weeks, Adler became increasingly infatuated. By August 13, he was still addressing Raissa as "respectful miss," but was beginning to bare his soul poetically in a manner never duplicated in later life:

> I have burned my bridges behind me, and a simple vessel carries me out to the rolling die of time. Since my gaze is no more directed upon sinking shores, it has become freerer and lighter. And with the fundamental knowledgeable air, I gather my strength, search behind the wonders for the world of the-thing-itself, behind the magic of beauty for its molecular unity. . . . When one extracts the root from his life . . . one becomes a seer: all-knowing, all-powerful, all-wise. Just so, he is a knower of good and evil. Our gazes become sharper; with X-ray vision we glance through the shell, until we spy the true core.

How often Raissa answered her ardent suitor's letters is unknown, as not one of her replies has survived. Although rapid, their course of love was not altogether smooth. Experiencing either a quarrel or blow of rejection later that summer, Adler penned a passionate response:

> Raissa! My soul yet heaves at the sound of your name, and mists dance before my eyes. And as the weakness summoned by this frightening word passes, terrible thoughts, on a wild flight, chase all over, all over this wreck which was once an audacious sailor. . . . Yes, your bold cry shrilled over ruins with the hardness of a conqueror when you uttered that word which makes me suffer so. Of difficulty, suffering and privation—you met the riddles of my life straight on and see, flowing from every vein large and small, my life's current, which goes out to you from my warmed heart. . . . Dear lady! I do not want to trick or disappoint you. What remains of me I would gladly give to the hounds to eat. I know that your noble character will try to save me. . . . I have nothing more to lose, and therefore nothing to fear. . . . I would fulfill an invitation with the greatest pleasure.

By early September, Raissa left Vienna and returned to Russia. Marriage plans were in the air, and she had begun making preparations for the wedding. On September 17, an elated Alfred wrote that he had received her letter:

> When there is news from you, when I inhale your holy words with my whole soul, when I try to stammer what your love gives me in words—Child, I veer thus between the highest disquiet and the highest joy—I would curse the misfortune which separates me from you, I would rejoice about the rapture of [our] soon belonging to each other completely.

In the same letter, Adler discussed how friends had advised him to postpone marrying Raissa until he was more established professionally. His hard-pressed parents would be unlikely to provide much help if financial difficulties arose for the newlyweds. Adler quoted a warning, " 'Just think, if you were to fall sick, unable to work, how would your wife and children live?' " But with characteristic self-confidence, he went on to reassure Raissa that, "So speak the newly wise, as if I did not know all this better. 'But must the devil come instantly to take me away the minute I start being happy?' I answer them, and [also that] 'I have never been sick.' "

As plans for a December wedding in far-off Russia began to materialize, Leopold and other family members expressed interest in making the journey. Although willing to allow his brother Sigmund and a few additional relatives to attend, Alfred dissuaded his sixty-two-year-old father from making the arduous winter voyage.

While busily getting his foreign travel papers in order, he was also seeking a suitable place in Vienna for them to rent. The process was time-consuming, and the local realtor whose services he was using could find nothing appealing. Finally entrusting the apartment-hunting effort to friends, he decided to leave immediately for Moscow and spend time with Raissa before the wedding. Daring not to inform her parents of this impetuous and unconventional action, on October 4 he wrote Raissa:

> Your father has not written to me yet. It is already too late for me. But if your father is good, he could write a few words to my father, perhaps to tell him that he has learned of my proposition and wishes to get to know me better. It is probably impudent of me with regards to your family to come like this, without invitation. But I must, that is simply the case.

And then, with almost euphoric excitement, Adler added:

I am already starting to pack my bag. My books and papers lie wildly all over my room. . . . After you get this letter, write me no more, for I am leaving on Friday. All my papers are in order, my passport is good for 6 months, now all I need is permission to marry in Russia, and that I shall pick up from the Russian consulate tomorrow. If I can't get it right away, I will have them send it to me. Hurrah, my child, yell loudly: Hurrah! Only a few days and I will have you in my arms!

CHAPTER THREE

On His Own

*For me there can be no doubt that
every individual conducts himself in
life as if he had a definite idea of
his power and his capacities.*

ALFRED ADLER

A lfred and Raissa were married in Smolensk, Russia, on December 23, 1897, in a festive Jewish wedding attended by family and friends. He was twenty-seven; his new bride had just turned twenty-four. The small, industrial city of forty-five thousand inhabitants, which lay several hours due west of Moscow by railroad, was where her wealthy relatives resided. They were among Smolensk's moderately sized Jewish community of forty-five hundred, many of whom were similarly involved in the timber business.

Growing up in a far more ethnically and religiously assimilated family than Raissa's, Alfred probably found the sacred Hebrew wedding prayers and rituals relatively strange. Available historical evidence indicates that this might well have been the last time Alfred Adler would ever participate in formal Jewish worship. Typical of Russian-Jewish weddings of the time, it is likely that the exchange of Hebrew vows was followed by a celebratory banquet enlivened by a boisterous *klezmer* (Yiddish folk-music) band.

Soon after the momentous day, the newlyweds returned to Vienna to set up their household. Alfred's friends had apparently failed to find them a suitable apartment to live in the months he had been away. So rather generously, Leopold and Pauline Adler temporarily vacated their quarters at Eisengasse 22 (today Wilhelm Exnerstrasse) until their son and new daughter-in-law could obtain something more permanent.

Situated in a row of high, old-fashioned houses with French architecture, the Adlers' first home was located in Vienna's Ninth District. It stood on a narrow and dark, sloping street, leading down into the heart of Vienna, and was not far from the hospitals Alfred visited frequently.

Initially, Adler felt euphoric about living with Raissa. He seemed more relaxed and self-confident to those who knew him. With a striking metaphor, he impulsively confided to one friend that, "If I had made her in a laboratory, I could not have found her more to my taste!" But without much organized activity to absorb Raissa's inquisitive mind, she soon began to miss her family members and acquaintances hundreds of miles away in Russia. To a certain extent, the loneliness was interrupted by a new, transformative event in her life: On August 5, 1898, the Adlers' first child, Valentine Dina, was born. Her birthdate was seven and a half months after the wedding; it is unclear whether she had been born premature. It is certain, however, that little Valentine gave Raissa something important with which to occupy the day while her physician-husband was away working.

For several years, Adler had been eagerly planning a medical career in clinical practice rather than in academic research. Soon after marrying Raissa, he was delighted to open a private office as an internist at Czeringasse 7 in the Leopoldstadt. Within the same pleasant building containing a courtyard and fountain, they occupied a comfortable adjacent apartment facing the Praterstrasse. It was the couple's first permanent residence. A photograph taken of him during this period shows a handsome, serious young man wearing a well-tailored vest-suit and necktie. His short hair is brushed straight back to reveal a prominent forehead, spectacles, and a handlebar mustache.

Scattered information about these years reveals Adler as an idealistic and hard-working physician. Not much interested in writing at this early point in his career, he devoted most of his professional time to building his private practice through diligent, attentive patient care. Possessing strong physical stamina, he required little sleep and almost never missed a day's work. Though Adler liked smoking cigarettes and cigars, he rarely indulged in liquor. Perhaps as a compensatory legacy from childhood, his health habits were good and he took them seriously.

Evening hours were spent with Raissa and friends in café camaraderie with fellow socialists, intellectuals, and artists. Relaxing over coffee and pastry (Adler would soon begin acquiring the paunch typical for successful men of his milieu), and perusing the latest newspapers and magazines, he was happiest in lively conversation about politics, philosophy, and, to a lesser extent, theater and the arts. Adler still enjoyed attending musical performances, and played the piano and sang occasionally; however, growing professional duties reduced the time available for all such leisure. He visited his parents only occasionally, and neither seems to have exerted much influence on Adler's professional or adult family life.

Situated in a predominantly lower-middle-class neighborhood with a heavy Jewish population, Adler's office lacked the prestigious address of Eisengasse, where many distinguished specialists maintained their private practices. But he had greater opportunities for establishing himself in the Prater area, home to Vienna's famous amusement park. First opened to the Austrian public by Emperor Franz Joseph II in 1766, the vast former imperial hunting reserve on the Danube's right bank eventually incorporated playing fields, a zoo, and a circus. Much beloved by the city's schoolchildren, its towering Ferris wheel was later immortalized in film director Carol Reed's famous murder mystery, *The Third Man,* set against the dark backdrop of post–World War II Vienna.

With a pleasant and discerning manner, Adler soon became a well-regarded physician in the growing Leopoldstadt community. He was particularly admired by both patients and colleagues for his intuitive, often uncanny ability to diagnose symptoms accurately. His first psychiatric case was reportedly that of a distant cousin who complained of suffering from an acute headache. "But no one," Adler gently responded, "has *only* a headache. Are you sure that your married life is a happy one?" Offended by his implication, the cousin angrily stormed out the office; but within a month she had applied for divorce.

Adler's patients were not wealthy, but this fact meant little to him. He wanted to make a real difference in the world with his medical career, not to amass personal wealth. His case histories reveal a varied clientele of merchants and students, accountants and attorneys, writers and civil-service officials, and even many cooks, assistant shopkeepers, governesses, and bookkeepers.

Perhaps his most colorful patients were those employed at the Prater's amusement park, including strongmen, trapeze artists, and acrobats. These men and women, who earned their living through their extraordinary bodily strength and skill, shared with young doctor Adler their life experiences, frustrations and desires, expectations and goals. To help his patients more fully, he decided to delve seriously into the hidden and seemingly mysterious bonds between body and mind.

During these years, Adler especially began to ponder the role of what he would later call *organ inferiority* in determining adult personality and habitual behavior. He found it intriguing that many of the amusement park's entertainers had suffered from a congenital weakness early in life and then strove successfully to overcome it through athletic prowess. Such cases undoubtedly evoked memories of his own childhood struggle for physical stamina. Within a few years, Adler's observations about this drive to surmount such difficulties would steadily coalesce into his theories of *compensation* and *overcompensation,* which have become bulwarks of modern psychology and have penetrated the popular English language.

During the years when Adler was establishing himself as a young, independent practitioner, Vienna was politically dominated by a local church-inspired, middle-class group, the Christian Social party. Its leader was the demagogic Karl Lueger. The son of a janitor at Vienna's Polytechnic College, he had earned a law degree and early entered politics, performing grass-roots organizing for the Liberal Party that had run Vienna for three decades. Sensing the growing discontent of the imperial city's artisans and shopkeepers who felt threatened by new economic realities, Lueger began to inveigh against capitalists and "the Jews." Drifting toward the moderate political left, he thus helped build a new political movement in the late 1880s.

Tall, elegant, and handsome, Lueger successfully led the Christian Socials into becoming Vienna's strongest political party. In 1895, the city council elected him mayor, but Emperor Franz Joseph refused to confirm the rabid anti-Semite for the post. The city council insisted on another vote, and the emperor again rejected Lueger's election. After the city council had voted in favor of Lueger a third and then a fourth time, Franz Joseph, in a one-hour audience, prevailed on the Christian Social leader to step aside "for the time being" and accept instead the position of deputy mayor. In April 1897, Lueger was elected mayor in a fifth council vote, and this time the emperor confirmed him.

Elected three times and holding office for thirteen years until his death in 1910, Lueger wielded considerable power in Vienna. His Christian Social party proclaimed itself the advocate of the "little people" who resented corruption in city hall, the power of bankers and industrialists, and widespread Jewish influence in the capital's business and cultural life. Effectively using anti-Semitic rhetoric to gain lower-middle-class support among shopkeepers and artisans fearing competition from the new department stores and mass-marketing practices, Lueger's speeches would later inspire the young Hitler, who in *Mein Kampf* would praise him as "the most formidable German mayor of all time."

Yet, Lueger was not a proto-Nazi seeking to destroy his opponents. He once jokingly defined anti-Semitism as "not hating Jews any more than necessary" and even had a few Jewish backers and friends in Vienna's elite circles. As the uncrowned King of Vienna, he also initiated a significant array of modernization and reform projects. Under his direction, the public sector was broadened in power by municipalizing the gas works and electric power plants. Lueger likewise authorized the development of Vienna's transportation network, instituted labor exchanges, and helped dot the city with more than a hundred new schools. He improved its water supply by the construction of a 150-mile aqueduct from the Alps in the south, and promoted afforestation in the Vienna Woods to save the capital's dwindling greenbelt. The city even bought up and ran two undertaking establishments, and created municipal agencies that created housing, employment, life insurance, and a savings bank that eventually attracted a hundred thousand depositors.

Lueger's civic-mindedness also included a variety of measures designed to improve the quality of urban hygiene and ambience. Besides increasing the amount of municipal land set aside for parks, gardens, and forest preserves, he helped to build a modern slaughterhouse, an orphanage, a tubercular sanatorium, a mental hospital, and a recreational beachfront. Lueger also established a system of sanitary ambulances and a network of public baths for the city's poor. His parks had playgrounds and tubs of flowers around each lamppost. The public schools were attractively designed and free lunches were served to poor students.

Meanwhile, the Social Democratic party, with whom Alfred Adler felt closely allied, continued to press for its own program of far-reaching political and economic reforms. Viewing capitalism as the enemy, its leaders like Viktor Adler saw themselves as part of an international movement linking workers throughout Europe and abroad to help achieve a new world order. They regarded local Vienna, with its 1,675,000 inhabitants divided among a few exceedingly wealthy capitalists, a smugly self-satisfied bourgeoisie, and a great mass of lower-class workers struggling to eke out a living, as a teeming microcosm of the capitalist system and its inherently inequitable distribution.

═══════

It is against this political-economic backdrop that Adler, at the age of twenty-eight, produced his first professional publication. Appearing in 1898, *Health*

Book for the Tailor Trade, a monograph of thirty-one pages, was the fifth in a series entitled "Guides to Occupational Hygiene: Advice for the Prevention of Occupational Diseases and Industrial Accidents," edited by Dr. E. Golebiewski of Berlin. Earlier monographs had dealt respectively with the baking, wooden-match, textile, and coal-mining industries. Ostensibly written for the workers themselves, the inexpensive booklets bore the encouraging motto, To know a danger is the first step toward its prevention!

At the time, the Austrian tailor trade was a dying home industry whose remaining practitioners were leading a dismal and unhealthy life. They were plagued by erratic, seasonal work and irregular wage practices conducted by the often exploitative entrepreneurs who hired them. Forced to labor in filthy homes up to eighteen hours a day, Vienna's tailors included Adler's paternal uncle David, whose hard life, as earlier noted, may have provided a personal impetus for the project.

Adler's goal for the monograph was "to describe the connection between the economic condition of a trade and its disease, and the dangers for public health of a lowered standard of living." According to its socialist author, disease among Central Europe's tailors was higher than in any other trade, and their average life expectancy was the lowest. In the booklet's first two sections he sketched a general socioeconomic picture of the tailoring trade in Austria and Germany during the preceding decades. Once, tailors like David Adler had proudly worked independently for individual customers and had been united and protected by their guilds. The advent of ready-made clothes had decisively changed that centuries-old arrangement, however.

Adler argued that large-factory conditions were now much better because of closer governmental regulation. Tailors employed by such companies also possessed greater ability to unify and fight for their rights as a group. In contrast, tailoring conditions in small enterprises were definitely more difficult for several reasons. There was less technological innovation, with tailors still using only conventional sewing machines. Serving small local markets also made these operations much more subject to economic fluctuations. This usually resulted in a hugely uneven distribution of work throughout the year. A tailor might spend five or six months working up to eighteen hours per day, assisted by his toiling wife and children. Then, in the remainder of the year, almost no work at all existed, and tailors were left unemployed or forced to work at vastly inferior wages.

The monograph also painted a dismal portrait of the specific working conditions of tailors. Because little governmental monitoring was involved in home-industry work, the typical tailor worked and lived in the same space, which was generally situated in the dingiest and unhealthiest section of a town. It was damp, dark, airless, and overcrowded—conditions that encouraged the rampant spread of contagious diseases. When epidemics did arise, the situation became dangerous for customers as well. Emotional stress also undermined the health of tailors.

The second part of *Health Book for the Tailor Trade* described the specific illnesses common to small-business tailors. Presenting two statistical tables of previously-published data, Adler showed that pulmonary diseases were dominant. This fact was not surprising, since tailors typically worked in a stooped, sitting position and spent many hours each day inhaling the dust from cloth. The dread disease of pulmonary tuberculosis was twice as frequent for tailors as for those employed in other trades. The chronically stooped sitting posture also brought on other medical problems, including circulatory disturbances like varicose veins and hemorrhoids, as well as frequent stomach and intestinal problems, ailments that afflicted more than 30 percent of the subjects. Likewise, the stooping increased the incidence of arthritis, rheumatism, and scoliosis. Two other reasons for tailors' poor health was their exposure to toxic dyes and to infectious diseases transmitted through old clothes brought by customers for mending.

In summarizing the causes for the high morbidity rate among tailors, Adler stressed the factors of chronic undernourishment, poor housing conditions, overwork, the lack of governmental protection, and the fact that many tailors chose this trade because they were physically unfit for other activities.

In the third and final section, Adler offered his recommendations for ending this unsatisfactory situation. Insisting on the immediate necessity for new labor legislation, he articulated an agenda that included some very modern ideas: rigorous enforcement of existing regulations, accident insurance for small businesses and not just those employing twenty or more workers, mandatory retirement and unemployment insurance, setting a maximum number of hours for the workweek, separating tailors' working and living quarters, and prohibiting piecework compensation. Finally, he urged that more adequate housing and dining facilities be built for tailors.

Adler's purpose in *Health Book for the Tailor Trade* was clearly not to provide a dispassionate, scholarly tome. Rather, in a pattern that was to become characteristic of Adler throughout his career, he explicitly linked his writing to the need for definite action. With a Marxist perspective, he also denounced unregulated capitalism by complaining that, "it is the unbridled competition of the world market that compels the small master to rely on the cheapest help he can get, to the most far-reaching exploitation of his assistants, and to recourse to seasonal work."

Also foreshadowing Adler's later outlook was the book's emphasis on the specific role of physician as social activist and reformer. With an obvious allusion to his recent alma mater and its notorious "therapeutic nihilism," Adler attacked mainstream "contemporary academic medicine, which ignores the very existence of social diseases . . . [whereas these] will be successfully controlled only by . . . a new social medicine of which present-day medicine is unaware."

He insisted that ultimately the elimination of widespread occupational diseases, such as those experienced by Europe's struggling tailors, depended on the medical profession's willingness to adopt a new social responsibility. Specifically, suggested Adler, this would involve the mandating of health inspectors to supervise basic hygienic requirements, including adequate air, space, and light. Physicians would also become eager to provide public education, so that, for instance, tailors would be well informed about the health risks of their chosen trade.

═══

Little information has survived concerning Adler's next three years. He saw his parents occasionally, but was not particularly close with either Leopold or Pauline. Neither one was well educated nor intellectually oriented, and he may have found himself gradually outgrowing their predictable conversation. According to several of Leopold's grandchildren, he probably read a daily newspaper but otherwise was mostly concerned during his elderly years with maintaining an elegant appearance of finely tailored clothes and well-polished boots. Adler's later writings were suprisingly harsh about grandparental tendencies to spoil their grandchildren, so he may also have experienced friction with Leopold and Pauline over child-rearing issues.

While friendly with his youngest teenage sibling, Richard, who was developing his talent as a pianist, Adler was not especially intimate with his two sisters and two other brothers. Hermine did not get along with Raissa, and soon had little contact with the newlyweds. Alfred's relations with the older Sigmund continued to be marked by tension and rivalry. To help support the family financially, Sigmund had gone into business with Leopold rather than attain a university education; perhaps for this reason, he bore a thinly concealed resentment toward his younger brother.

On September 24, 1901, the Adlers' second child, Alexandra, was born. Soon afterward, Alfred and Raissa's marital strains seem to have become exacerbated, producing a situation not unlike that experienced by many well-educated or dual-career couples today. With two young children at home, the twenty-eight-year-old Raissa now found herself even more bur-dened with time-consuming housekeeping and child-rearing chores. Keenly interested in political affairs and with an intellectually inquisitive mind, she experienced no pleasure in the everyday routines of household mainte-nance. Nor did she have available in Austria the emotional support of ei-ther family members or longtime acquaintances for this new stage of her adult life.

Undoubtedly influenced by the social mores of the time, Adler expected his wife to perform domestic tasks eagerly and happily. From his own per-spective, he was increasingly busy with the responsibilities of his practice and the support of their growing family. Because his clientele was princi-pally drawn from working-class Leopoldstadt, many of his patients paid little for his time and some nothing at all. Indeed, it would be characteristic of Adler throughout his medical career to charge relatively modest fees and to criticize colleagues who sought to become wealthy through clinical work.

Typically after putting in long hours at his office, Adler came home briefly, and then was off to meet with friends for hours at the Café Grien-steidl, a favorite haunt of Vienna's socialists. Raissa could not have been very happy about having no respite from child-care duties, especially since she enjoyed discussing political and social ideas, too.

Adler was not blind to Raissa's feelings. In a letter to his journalist friend Franz Blei, he remarked that, "Since the second child, my wife is tied far too much to the house. Luckily, the little one is already beginning to walk. Hopefully, it will be better then." But within three years, their third child, Kurt, would be born, and Raissa would feel even more constrained and burdened.

The truth seems to be that Adler, like most men of his nineteenth-century upbringing, was rarely involved in domestic duties even when physically present at home. He instead tended to be absorbed by work-related inter-ests. Sophie, the family cook and maid for more than twenty years, later reminisced that, "When I first came to the Adler family, Herr Doktor was never without a book or pen in his hand. When he came in from his rounds, he would sit up to all hours of the morning, writing and reading. It was not so later, for people came to the house all day long—and far into the night—but when he was a young man, he did not talk very much."

At times, Alfred and Raissa experienced significant personality clashes. How much of these reflected their differing cultural backgrounds is not altogether clear, but as a native Viennese he seems to have been disappointed by her nonconforming disinterest in dressing well and fashionably, as befitted her new social status as a doctor's wife. Adler tended to be outgoing, buoyant and tactful. When potential arguments arose between them, he strove to avoid confrontation and instead diplomatically sought to defuse tensions with genial humor. Raissa was typically far more blunt and even harsh in her manner.

With Adler mainly concerned with his professional work and Raissa feeling overburdened with domestic concerns, their child rearing was sometimes lax. Once while guests were visiting, one of the Adler youngsters quietly entered the kitchen and emerged brandishing a large carving knife. "Look at how they watch me!" the child proclaimed contemptuously to the astonished adults sitting in the dining room. But such incidents seem to have been rare. Both Alexandra and Kurt later recalled their father as an extremely warm and caring man who never once resorted to physical punishment. His approach was to employ reason rather than fiats or threats when making requests of them. In this regard, he practiced what he later preached to innumerable audiences of parents and professionals throughout the world.

———

After a hiatus of four years dominated by daily clinical responsibilities, Adler published two articles in 1902 in *Aertzliche Standeszeitung* ("Medical News Bulletin"). Newly founded by Heinrich Gruen, it was a bimonthly periodical aimed at advancing the professional interests of Austria's physicians. Adler had apparently been recruited in the planning stage to be a key contributor, for the premiere issue featured his manifestolike article, "The Penetration of Social Forces into Medicine."

Continuing to articulate the progressive ideas of *Health Book for the Tailor Trade,* Adler urged his colleagues to become more committed to social medicine, specifically to prophylaxis, or disease prevention, "the most valuable fruit that scientific medicine has offered the people." He deplored that governmental agencies as well as other professions had begun taking the lead away from his fellow doctors regarding the important issue of public health. Already, policy questions involving occupational hygiene and the treatment of mass diseases like tuberculosis were beginning to be evaluated by nonphysicians, for "in the little worries of daily life, in the always illusory expectations attached to elegant research projects, the medical profession [has] again lost the long-range vision."

Demanding that this situation be reversed, Adler declared that, "Only then will humanity move . . . from the time of hesitating, difficult, often hopeless therapy to the time of victory-assured prophylaxis, from the time of powerlessness or small medicine to the time of self-assured action."

In this piece, Adler praised Rudolf Virchow (1821–1902) as a key role model for socially concerned physicians. "There was a time . . . when young Virchow and like-minded men urged vehemently for a social solution of the disease problem," Adler commented. "It is not a mere coincidence that it was the courageous founder of cellular pathology who regarded the living body as a social organization of cells, who was also the first to have shouted the courageous call for a social therapy."

An eminent researcher who had originally espoused a mechanistic philosophy, Virchow became a staunch advocate for the poor and a founder of social medicine in Germany. In 1848, he established a liberal periodical, *Medical Reform,* and later served in the German parliament, where he fought for civic-minded causes. Eventually embracing medical humanism, he proclaimed that, "It is high time that we give up the scientific prudery of regarding living processes as nothing more than the mechanical resultant of molecular forces inherent in the constitutive particles." Later he said that, "Life cannot be simply reduced to physical and chemical forces." Virchow's long career of effective social activism and renowned medical work would inspire Adler throughout his own life.

Later that year, Adler published a second article, "An Academic Chair for Social Medicine," in *Aertzliche Standeszeitung.* He now specifically proposed that a university professorship and seminar be created for the purpose of improving public hygiene. The envisioned medical post would involve a collaboration with economists and sociologists, as well as those active in public education. In Adler's optimistic view, governmental and scientific backing for the new chair and its affiliated seminars would

> finally provide the undergirding for a system to replace the presently involved tangle of our hygiene. And the illumination that would be ignited there would also bring light not only to the heads and hearts of all listeners, but to the people themselves. Ten years of hygienic popular education, the freeing of hygiene from the fetters of politics and bungling exploitation—and then we will be able to discuss the mass epidemics!

In addition to evincing a continued concern for social medicine, this brief article crucially foreshadows Adler's later emphasis on education as a lynchpin for societal improvement. The coming decades would see Adler

emerge in Austria as a key figure in schooling reform, particularly in training teachers and clinicians to better understand children's emotional needs.
Indeed, more than twenty years after writing this essay, Adler would come
to advocate a university chair (in what we would now call special education)
to "curtail and eliminate" juvenile maladjustment and deliquency.

Although impassioned about the need for societal reform through preventive medicine, he was nevertheless obliged to continue with military
service. From mid-August through mid-September of 1902, Adler spent
thirty-five days with the Eighteenth Infantry Regiment of the Honved, the
Hungarian reserve army. Composed mainly of German-speaking soldiers,
the regiment was stationed in the Burgenland town of Oedenburg.

Soon after returning home to Vienna, Adler penned a chatty letter on
September 30 to his friend Blei. He apologized for not replying sooner due
to his military activity, and happily recounted a recent family trip enjoying
"the splendor of Hungary. That was a gypsy life!" Turning briefly to professional interests, Adler commented that, "I have begun to write to the editor
Muller. Up to now, I have no news of him. Did he move to the moon?" He
also asked if Blei had read a recent article by a local Viennese physician
named Sigmund Freud.

――――――――

How Adler and Freud first came to know each other has never been satisfactorily determined. Each of their respective psychological movements has
for more than a half century provided a differing account, and both of these
are false.

Perhaps it was Adler's novelist friend–biographer, Phyllis Bottome, who
initiated the Adlerian myth: One day between 1900 and 1902, an article
appeared in Vienna's influential *Neue Freie Presse* mocking Freud's new tome,
The Interpretation of Dreams. Finding the book worthwhile, Adler felt impelled to defend it by writing a review or public letter. In response, a grateful Freud invited his younger colleague to attend an informal seminar
devoted to psychoanalysis, a gathering that was to become known as the
Wednesday Psychological Society. Unfortunately, this account has no sub-
stantiation. No such article or letter written by Adler defending Freud has
ever been found, either in the *Neue Freie Presse* or any other Viennese
publication.

As for the spurious Freudian version, it originated with the psychoanalytic founder himself. In his 1914 monograph, *The History of the Psychoanalytic Movement,* he recounted that a group of early admirers had sought him

out to teach them psychoanalysis, and that among these was Alfred Adler. Freud paternally agreed to do so, and such was the origin of the Wednesday Psychological Society. Ever since this condescending account was published, Freudian adherents have described Adler as a mere "pupil" or even a "disciple" of their esteemed leader. Freud's version is likewise erroneous, more for its crucial omissions than for what it baldly presents.

This much is known for sure: The Viennese physician William Stekel underwent brief, successful treatment with Freud to alleviate symptoms of psychological impotence. Extremely impressed with Freud's insights about the human mind, Stekel urged him in 1902 to organize a weekly meeting for other colleagues who might likewise be interested in this innovative approach. Feeling professionally isolated at the time, Freud welcomed the suggestion. In the fall, he sent invitational postcards to Stekel and three other Viennese physicians, all considerably younger than himself, to attend an informal discussion group at his professional office at Berggasse 19. Two of these, Max Kahane and Rudolf Reitler, were acquainted with Freud through his psychoanalytic lectures on "The Psychology of the Neuroses" at the University of Vienna. Like Freud, Kahane had translated a volume of Jean Charcot's French psychiatric lectures into German; also, it was Kahane who had originally introduced Stekel to Freud's writings.

The fifth and youngest member comprising this tiny group was an independent physician of seven years post-graduate experience who almost certainly had neither been treated by Freud nor attended his university lectures: Alfred Adler. Dated November 2, this was Freud's message to him in its entirety:

> Very honored Sir Colleague:
> A small circle of colleagues and followers is going to give me the pleasure of meeting at my house once a week in the evening at half past eight in order to discuss the themes which interest us, psychology and neuropathology. I know of Reitler, Max Kahane, and Stekel. Will you have the goodness to join? We have agreed upon next Thursday, and I am expecting your kind answer whether you would like to come and whether this evening would suit you.
> With hearty greetings as your colleague,
> DR. FREUD

Decades after the two men would bitterly terminate their relationship, Adler would show the faded postcard to reporters as tangible proof that Freud, fourteen years his senior, had initially sought his intellectual companionship, and not the other way around.

How, then, did Freud come to request his socialist-minded colleague's presence in the weekly discussions? Some historians have recently suggested that Freud had heard about Adler through his growing reputation as a skillful practitioner devoted to progressive ideas in medicine—or possibly, Adler had treated one of Freud's own relatives or acquaintances.

What seems definite is that Adler could little have suspected how this single postcard would affect the entire course of his own life—and that of modern psychology.

CHAPTER FOUR

Early Years with Psychoanalysis

*I remember well when I was very
discontented with the state of
psychiatry as a young student
and medical man. I found Freud
was courageous enough
to go another way.*

ALFRED ADLER

In the fall of 1902, Freud, then forty-six, was emerging successfully from a long period of introspective isolation. He had finally been granted a much-coveted and prestigious, albeit unpaid, professorial position at the medical school at the University of Vienna. That same year, his second major book on the human mind, *The Psychopathology of Everyday Life*, had just been published. Although his earlier, seminal work of 1899, *The Interpretation of Dreams*, had attracted disappointingly little interest among Austria's medical colleagues or its educated public, Freud was becoming increasingly convinced of his ultimate historical fame and destiny.

It certainly had not been this way for several long years. From boyhood days, Freud had shown academic brilliance and had been the outstanding student of his *Gymnasium*. As a youngster, he knew full well that his intellectual talents were extraordinary. In medical school at Vienna, he had shown considerable research talent, combining a painstaking approach to detail with an original, creative flair. But wanting to marry and support his fiancée, Martha Bernays, in affluent style, and lacking independent wealth, Freud had felt obliged to abandon a promising career as a medical researcher. His interests in the mid-1880s had included the psychological effects of cocaine and, working with the venerated Jean Charcot in Paris, the use of hypnosis as a therapeutic tool. But soon after returning from his French sabbatical, Freud, then thirty-one, felt it was time to marry and pursue the more financially rewarding path of private medical practice.

Over the ensuing sixteen years, Freud struggled to support his large, growing family while simultaneously deepening his interest in the hidden workings of the human psyche. During the 1890s, he became convinced that hysteric symptoms (such as unexplainable paralysis) originated in unconscious sexual tensions, and in 1895, coauthored with Josef Breuer his first psychological work, *Studies in Hysteria,* dealing with this issue. Initially, Freud had been sure that virtually all hysteric disorders could be traced to childhood experiences of sexual abuse, and in 1896, courageously lectured on this viewpoint before Viennese medical colleagues. The response to his "seduction theory," which had been built on many quiet, persistent years of work, was so incredulous and skeptical (the influential Krafft-Ebing called it "a scientific fairy tale") that Freud plunged into a depression for nearly a year.

In the late 1890s, Freud felt impelled to initiate an intensive self-analysis involving free association and dreams, and at the same time rework his theory of hysteria. He became sure that the seduction experiences vividly recalled by hysteric patients had never actually happened, but instead represented long-suppressed sexual fantasies and wishes. It was proving evident to him that all individuals—not just neurotic or hysteric patients—have intense, unconscious sexual feelings that can exert a tremendous impact on their emotional and physical health. *The Interpretation of Dreams* had been meticulously prepared to buttress this emerging new theory, as had his latest work, *The Psychopathology of Everyday Life,* which examined "slips of the tongue" for their revelatory insights into personality. Most recently, he had finished writing the intriguing case of his teenage female patient, "Dora," which would be published several years later.

Although pleased to be so productive in his mid-forties, Freud nevertheless was still experiencing an acute sense of professional seclusion. *The Interpretation of Dreams* remained almost completely ignored or ridiculed by fellow physicians. Indeed, he had found it irritatingly necessary to prepare a time-consuming abridgment, *On Dreams,* in hopes of increasing public attention to his work. Also, Freud had always found it congenial to exchange psychological viewpoints with sympathetic thinkers, and had recently terminated such a relationship with the physician Wilhelm Fliess. Stekel's encouragement to organize a small discussion group devoted to psychoanalysis therefore seemed quite sensible.

On the preannounced date marked on their respective postcards, Adler, Kahane, Reitler, and Stekel arrived at Berggasse 19 in the fashionable Alsergrund neighborhood for their first evening meeting. For Adler and Stekel, who both lived in the more heavily Jewish Leopoldstadt district, it was a leisurely walk to Freud's apartment building, which housed his spacious apartment-office suite. Cordially seating themselves around Freud's waiting room, the five physicians eventually conversed on the psychological implications of smoking. The lively session was repeated and formalized as the Wednesday Psychological Society, with Freud as discussion leader. Initially, the early gatherings seemed to have been marked by a genial camaraderie. Although almost surely with effusive exaggeration, Stekel later reminisced that there had reigned "complete harmony among the five, no dissonances; we were like pioneers in a newly discovered land, and Freud was the leader. A spark seemed to jump from one mind to the other, and every evening was like a revelation."

Certainly, Adler found the meetings intellectually stimulating and attended quite regularly. There is no doubt that he found Freud to be erudite and brilliant and an excitingly original theorist. He was friendly with Stekel, but less so with Kahane and Reitler, who may have seemed to hold rather conventional psychological ideas. Probably from the outset as well, Freud regarded Adler as the most creative and articulate thinker of those joining the fledgling group. But despite such mutual respect, the two men never became friends, or even close socially. There is no evidence that they ever corresponded with each other while traveling; nor did their respective families share any social bonds.

Outwardly, Freud and Adler had a great deal in common. Both had grown up in largely assimilated Jewish families who had emigrated to Vienna in mid-century from outlying regions of the Austro-Hungarian Empire. Although Freud had received more exposure to Judaism and felt more ethnically tied to his heritage, neither man held the slightest interest in ritual observance and instead were proud secularists. Both their fathers had been unsuccessful and nonintellectual merchants who had failed to provide steady material security for their offspring. Both thinkers had spent boyhood years living in the ethnically Jewish Leopoldstadt, although Adler had also resided in more rural and gentile-dominated sections of outlying Vienna.

Both Freud and Adler had pursued the medical profession as their primary career choice. They had studied under many of the same professors at the University of Vienna and had even attended the same *Gymnasium*. Unlike the academically brilliant Freud, however, Adler had only been an average pupil. Soon after completing medical graduation, both men had fallen in love, married Jewish wives, and produced large families. They shared a strong interest in the human mind and were critical of many aspects of Viennese and larger Austrian society.

Given the many commonalities of background and interest, why did Adler never even briefly become emotionally close with Freud? Several important considerations exist. First, the age difference of fourteen years probably precluded the possibility of real friendship from arising. Freud, who was in early middle age, was also much too young to constitute a father figure for Adler. More plausible might have been his serving as a mentor-like older-brother figure, except for the fact that Adler had always gotten along poorly with his actual older brother, Sigmund. Indeed, the intense sibling rivalry and simmering resentment between the two Adlers may have unconsciously spilled over to Alfred's own unsettled relations with Freud.

Temperamentally, the two physicians were also quite different. Freud's major motive for entering medicine had been research, and he remained highly cerebral and bookish throughout his life. To family and associates alike, he made it clear that treating patients was for him a largely unpleasant financial necessity. Freud could be cordial when circumstances required, but few except his most ardent admirers would ever describe him as a warm or jovial person. In contrast, Adler had chosen medicine for a clinical career and had never been drawn to laboratory investigation. He enjoyed treating patients, as well as lecturing before a wide variety of nonprofessional audiences. Possessed of a genial and outgoing personality, Adler's favorite activity was to spend his evening hours conversing with friends in a bustling café.

Freud and Adler also differed politically. Over the decades, historians of varying viewpoints have provided strikingly diverse portraits of Freud's political outlook. It seems clear that in his early career he embraced a generally liberal viewpoint; but quite unlike Adler, he had aristocratic tastes and felt condescension toward the working-class masses. Likewise, Freud was never actively drawn toward socialism and stayed far removed from the Social Democratic party, even when it dominated Vienna after World War I. Nor did he ever emulate Adler's voiced contempt for the conservative-minded administration of their mutual alma mater.

Even more different in personality were their respective wives, who almost certainly could never have become friendly with each other. Their twelve-year age difference was probably the least important factor in this equation. By all accounts, German-Jewish Martha Freud was a devoted, somewhat subservient homemaker with little interest in intellectual or political affairs. According to historian Peter Gay, "she was the complete bourgeoise. Loving and efficient with her family, she was weighed down by an unremitting sense of her calling to domestic duty, and severe with lapses from middle-class morality." Raised in an observant Orthodox home, Martha was warmly attached to Judaism. Indeed, she once confided to a cousin that one of the more upsetting moments in her life had come on the first Friday night after marrying Freud, when he had vehemently forbidden her to light Sabbath candles in their new home.

In contrast, Russian-Jewish Raissa Adler was an irreligious political revolutionary, an active Trotskyite for most of her adult European life. She was an ardent feminist who disliked domesticity, and instead most enjoyed associating with other women who shared her intense socialist convictions. Intellectually active, Raissa did professional work as a translator after her children grew up. Throughout her marriage with Adler, she insisted upon her independence and was the complete antithesis of the subservient house-wife of bourgeois Vienna.

Over the ensuing months and years, membership in the Wednesday Psychological Society steadily grew. One member would introduce another, and relatively few dropped out. Recruitment was conducted through unanimous agreement, but that was probably a mere formality in the highly informal atmosphere that initially reigned. By 1906, the year Freud turned fifty, membership stood at seventeen, and a dozen attendees could almost always be expected to provide an animated discussion around the long dining table moved into his waiting-room. At the time, the group was quite homogeneous: Almost all were physicians younger and less established than Freud. Everyone was of Jewish background, and no women had yet been invited.

Freud especially prized the presence of nonphysicians like bookseller-publisher Hugo Heller and musicologist Max Graf; their participation suggested that psychoanalysis might eventually transcend its narrow medical base. As Graf later recalled, "The [society] gatherings followed a definite ritual. First, one of the members would present a paper. Then, black coffee and cakes were served; cigars and cigarettes were on the table and were consumed in great quantities. After a social quarter of an hour, the discussion would begin. The last and the decisive word was always by Freud himself." Though he still admired Freud's brilliance after he left, Graf would eventually become dismayed by "the atmosphere of the foundation of a religion" at Berggasse 19 and permanently quit the association.

═══

For the first four years of the Wednesday Psychological Society, no formal minutes were kept. It is therefore impossible to determine precisely how Adler was influenced in his clinical practice by these weekly meetings, which he actively attended. His first subsequent professional publications revealed no discernible exposure to psychoanalysis.

In 1903, Adler produced two articles for *Aertzliche Standeszeitung*, both continuing his focus on social medicine. The first, entitled "City and Country," was a three-part series challenging the prevalent assumption that country living in Austria was more healthful than its urban counterpart. Adler insisted that the opposite was actually true, pointing out that municipalities utilized more advanced hygienic methods and also received better public-health services due to their greater political clout.

In keeping with his earlier predilection for making specific policy recommendations, Adler urged that uniform sanitary protection laws be enacted to apply equally to Austria's urban and rural areas. He argued that existing regulations, which applied only to cities, ignored the increasing interaction between urban areas and the countryside. Adler also noted cogently that ultimately only national laws regulating water and food supplies could protect cities from epidemics originating in rural regions.

In "State Help or Self-Help?" Adler called for his medical colleagues to become more involved with societal welfare and improvement. His tone was definitely more caustic and his approach more Marxist than in previous articles. He called on his fellow physicians to stop deluding themselves with the expectation that Austria's public officials were truly interested in medicine, for "no government can affect anything in its work, beyond conducting the business of politically influential strata whose interests it perceives" and that "[as] the manager of the politically influential classes, [government] cared for medical help only as long as it had to. . . . What remains now of the medical profession no longer has unconditional importance."

Only by joining forces with the working-class struggle could physicians gain true, legitimate political power, Adler insisted. He argued that conservative authorities typically hampered medical progress due to "the hesitating social precautions of our time" and specifically noted the extent to which the University of Vienna medical faculty appointments were influenced by the meddling of politicians. Sarcastically, Adler remarked that his alma mater's academic decline constituted "a gain for our ruling classes of the first order." Simply put, by adopting an unthinking subservience to Austria's elite, capitalist class, his country's physicians were dooming themselves to political, and ultimately professional, impotence.

In 1904, Adler published the most important article of his career to date.

Again appearing in *Aertzliche Standeszeitung,* it was entitled "The Physician as Educator" and foreshadowed many important themes of his later influential work. At the outset, he acknowledged that, "We owe to Freud much enlightenment regarding the enormous part played by infantile impressions, experiences, and developments in normal and neurotic individuals." He then added that, "Possibly, the powerful accent was needed with which Freud considers the life of the child and the demonstration of the tragic conflicts which arise from anomalies of childhood experiences, to make us realize the high significance of a science of education."

Throughout the article, Adler emphasized the primary importance of prevention, asserting that, "Not to treat and cure sick children, but to protect healthy children from sickness is the logical and noble challenge of the science of medicine." He had articulated this notion in earlier papers appearing in the same journal; but now, for the first time, he suggested that physicians become educators by helping teachers and parents to prevent emotional problems from arising in their youngsters. His specific recommendations for raising healthy children included the following:

1 That such adults must win the child's love. "The most important aid in education is love. . . . The child's love . . . is the surest guaranty for educability."

2 That the best support for a child's progress is "confidence in [his or her] own strength." Also, that "the child's self-confidence, its personal courage, is its greatest fortune. Courageous children will later on meet their fate not as coming from the outside, but as coming from their own strength."

3 That "weak and sickly children" easily lose their self-confidence as do "pampered and overprotected children."

4 That "under no circumstances should the child be afraid of its educator" and "under no circumstances, even [in response to] sexual transgressions, may one scare a child, because this way one never achieves one's purpose, deprives the child of its self-confidence and greatly confuses the child."

5 That praise and reward are to be preferred over punishment, and that punishment, when implemented, should teach the child his or her mistake and focus attention on alternative behavior.

6 That instead of demanding blind obedience, adults should seek to "leave the child freedom of decision"—that is, offer specific choices.

In this article, Adler did not attempt to examine the social or economic forces that might be contributing to children's emotional difficulties. For instance, he never ventured any Marxist conjectures as to why parents might be finding it hard to raise their children without creating psychological disturbances. Nor did Adler ever suggest that perhaps some rebellious youngsters might be better off refusing to conform to society as it presently existed. Such an intriguing line of criticism would wait until the appearance of Wilhelm Reich's powerful effort to synthesize psychoanalysis and Marxism in the late 1920s.

Nevertheless, "The Physician as Educator" was Adler's first publication to focus on children and their psychological upbringing. In this respect, he may have been strongly influenced by a young educator destined to become a close friend and major collaborator, Carl Furtmüller. By his mid-twenties, Furtmüller had already gained a national and controversial reputation as an educational reformer allied closely with the Social Democratic party.

Born in 1880 and raised in Vienna, Furtmüller was the product of a religiously mixed marriage. His mother, Caroline Biermann, who was the daughter of a Jewish businessman, had converted to Catholicism and become a strict practitioner. After attending the renowned Schottengymnasium, Furtmüller entered the University of Vienna in 1898. There he majored in German language and literature and minored in philosophy and French. It was at the university that he first became politically active, especially with the Social Science Education Organization (SSEO). The organization had been founded in 1895 with the expressed aim of disseminating high German culture to the general public, and it regularly sponsored presentations by prominent scholars. In 1901, at the age of twenty-one, Furtmüller was voted secretary of the SSEO; at the time, the president and vice president were Michael Hainisch and Karl Renner respectively, two future presidents of the Austrian Republic. In the same year, Furtmüller was elected the youngest member on the founding board of the Volksheim, the country's first center for adult education. Some twenty years later, his close friend Adler would gain considerable prominence in offering public lectures there.

While attending the university, Furtmüller fell in love with Aline Klatschko, a Russian-Jewish student three years his junior. Her father, Samuel, was a key, beloved figure in Vienna's close-knit Russian-socialist emigré community. Warm and sociable, he quickly became friendly with young Furtmüller, who shared the same impassioned political and cultural ideals. After four years of academic study, Furtmüller received his doctorate in 1902 for a dissertation on "The Theory of Epic in the Schlegel Brothers, the Classics, and Wilhelm von Humboldt."

Since early adolescence, Furtmüller had helped support himself financially, and during university vacations he worked as a tutor for wealthy families. In 1901, he began teaching middle school as an uncertified teacher at Vienna's Sophiengymnasium. In 1903, he gained certification in German, with Latin and Greek as secondary subjects. Carl's mother died that same year, and soon after, he and his father converted to the Lutheran church; at the time, civil servants were required to have religious affiliation. In November 1904, Furtmüller and Aline Klatschko were married. Unfortunately, the only teaching offer he received was an apprenticeship in the German-Bohemian town of Kadan, and they were forced to relocate far from Vienna's glittering cultural life.

It is almost a certainty that Furtmüller and Adler first became acquainted through their Russian-born wives. Aline shared Raissa's feminist and socialist convictions, but tended to be even more politically active. Eventually, she would gain elective power as a Social Democrat, serving on Vienna's municipal council. Although a decade younger than Adler, Furtmüller exhibited an attractive blend of intellectuality and social idealism that matched his older acquaintance's personality well. Before long, they were spending many stimulating hours together, joined by like-minded friends, at the Café Griendsteidl and later the Café Central, sharing their plans and visions for reforming Austrian society. Adler introduced Furtmüller to new ideas about public health and medical treatment, including Freud's work in psychoanalysis. In turn, the young teacher emphasized the importance of educational innovation as an instrument of social transformation.

═══

It seems plausible that Furtmüller exerted not only an intellectual but an emotional influence as well, for Adler formally abandoned Judaism on October 17, 1904, just before his friend's marriage. Together with his young daughters, Valentine and Alexandra, but without Raissa, he underwent Protestant baptism in the Church of the Dorotheergasse. Among his younger siblings, Max would later become a Catholic and serve in the Vatican, and Richard would legally terminate his Jewish heritage by declaring himself *konfessionslos,* a citizen "without religious affiliation." Raissa was not at all religiously observant, but she had grown up in a Russian-Jewish milieu permeated by a vibrant Yiddish folk culture absent in her husband's assimilated Viennese upbringing. She probably therefore felt a stronger ethnic identity. Perhaps, too, she regarded Alfred's important decision as a misguided attempt to circumvent anti-Semitism. It is not known how his aged parents viewed the decision. Pauline was a frail sixty-five, and would live only another two years; Leopold was much heartier, and would survive her by fifteen years, but did not seem to be close with Alfred's growing family.

Why Adler chose conversion to Christianity has never been satisfactorily explained by his followers, but it was certainly not motivated by religious conviction. Decades later, when asked whether his father had ever attended church or taught Christianity to his children, Kurt burst out laughing. He confided that, aside from his own infant baptism, he had only once in his life ever set foot in a church and definitely considered himself an atheist. He fondly recalled, however, that a Christmas tree unfailingly adorned the Adler household every year. Since Freud and his wife, who ethnically identified themselves as Jewish, likewise observed this custom, it undoubtedly held minimal religious significance for most urbane Viennese citizens.

Adler's conversion to Christianity was far from unusual for those of his background. As historically unprecedented opportunities beckoned in nineteenth-century European society, Jews began converting in record numbers. The process had been initiated with Europe's wealthiest Jewish families as early as the years between 1780 and the end of the Napoleonic wars, and steadily continued through ensuing decades. In Austria, the trend started before the revolution of 1848, when both the Arnsteins and the Eskeles, the two most prominent Jewish families in Vienna, had their children (although not themselves) baptized. Especially in liberal countries like Germany, Jewish converts regarded their act as the appropriate way to gain acceptance and entree into fashionable society. In the famous, cynical aphorism of the German-Jewish poet and convert Heinrich Heine, the baptismal certificate served as the necessary "ticket of admission to Western culture."

For many European Jews of Adler's generation, such wider culture had far more appeal than their own ancestral religion. The journalist Arnold Hollriegel reminisced that, "I considered myself a German; my Judaism meant little to me." Recalling her own Viennese childhood, Toni Cassirer (wife of philosopher Ernst Cassirer) likewise observed that, "We were raised without religion. Father's family hadn't observed the rituals for three generations." The celebrated playright Arthur Schnitzler recollected that his grandmother fasted on the Day of Atonement and ate *matzos* on Passover, but "the generation which followed . . . tended to display indifference to the spirit of Jewish religion and opposition, sometimes even a sarcastic attitude to its formalities."

Another factor encouraging conversion was that European countries often barred Jews from participating in certain professions; to become a Christian therefore presented the only means for career advancement. Even with the widespread introduction of legal rights for Jews by the late nineteenth century, many individuals still found that conversion immediately opened doors of social and economic opportunity that "paper rights" never could.

Such motivation was especially common in Adler's hometown of Vienna, which exhibited the highest Jewish conversion rate by far of anywhere in Europe. Although Vienna was a predominantly Catholic city, only half of all Jewish converts accepted baptism in the Roman faith. On the average, about one quarter of all Jewish converts chose the Protestant church like Adler, and another quarter decided to become *konfessionslos*. The capital city's famous converts to Christianity included musicians Gustav Mahler and Arnold Schönberg, writers Karl Kraus and Otto Weininger, and political activists Viktor Adler and his son, Friedrich. Other well-known figures, like municipal politician Wilhelm Ellenbogen and psychoanalyst Otto Rank, left Judaism by officially declaring themselves *konfessionslos*.

One key reason for Vienna's high conversion rate was undoubtedly its repressive law prohibiting a Jew from marrying a non-Jew. For nearly a century, such discriminatory ordinances had been eliminated from public life in France and Germany. But for Austrian mixed couples to marry, one of the partners had either to convert to the other's religion or legally bear the category of *konfessionslos*. Indeed, it has been estimated that over 80 percent of all Jews who converted during the era of 1870–1910 were single, and many were presumably seeking to marry a non-Jewish spouse.

But, Adler was already married to a Jewish woman when he converted to Protestantism. He had also long completed schooling and established himself professionally as an independent physician. Certainly, Jews were not prohibited from medical practice; his coreligionists comprised a sizable minority of Austria's esteemed medical profession. Anti-Semitism probably hampered their successful career advancement, however; such was definitely Freud's lifelong conviction. But perhaps feeling more ethnic loyalty for his ancestral heritage, he adamantly refused to convert to Christianity, as Adler did, or to declare himself *konfessionslos*, as his young protégé Otto (née Rosenfeld) Rank did.

Freud never commented publicly on Adler's conversion but almost certainly knew and disapproved of it. A proud atheist who ridiculed all religious sentiment as a sign of emotional immaturity, Freud nevertheless valued his Jewish ethnicity. In a letter to colleague Karl Abraham in 1907, he wrote, "The fact that things will be difficult for you as a Jew will have the effect, as it has with all of us, of bringing out the best of which you are capable." Writing at the same time, Freud implored musicologist Max Graf not to baptize his son in an effort to avoid confrontation with anti-Semitism. "Develop in him all the energy he will need for that struggle. Do not deprive him of that advantage."

━━━━━

Such an attitude meant little to Adler, for on February 25, 1905, his third child, Kurt, was born and soon after, like his sisters, was baptized. Perhaps more obliged to help Raissa with the additional child-rearing responsibilities, Kurt's father published only two short articles that year. Appearing in a German periodical, "The Sex Problem in Education" echoed Freud's viewpoint that children possess sexual feelings that should be recognized by educators. As for the rather technical "Three Psychoanalyses of Ideas of Numbers and Obsessive Numbers," Adler sought to validate Freud's notion of unconscious motivation by demonstrating how a seemingly random number verbalized by a patient actually possessed hidden and specific psychological meaning.

In November 1906, Adler offered a major presentation before the Wednesday Psychological Society. Several weeks before, Freud had encouraged its members to professionalize their meetings, which were now attracting up to twenty members on a regular basis. They had agreed to hire a paid secretary to record attendance, keep track of dues, and take extensive notes on each meeting. That secretary was Otto Rank, who was twenty-one at the time and was a diminuitive and gifted young philosophy student at the University of Vienna.

Freud liked young Rank very much, who, while living in the Leopold-stadt, had been seeing Adler in the role of family physician in October 1904 for a lung ailment. The two men apparently began discussing psychology, for Rank subsequently borrowed Adler's personal copy of *The Interpretation of Dreams*. After reading Freud's other two books, Rank had excitedly begun analyzing his own dreams. Then, in April 1905, Adler lectured before the Teachers' Temperance Union and spotted Rank in the audience. The next month, Adler brought his former patient to a Wednesday Psychological Society meeting, and Rank became a dedicated attendee.

Rank's minutes for the November 6 meeting record Adler as the primary speaker, addressing the group in a talk entitled "On the Organic Bases of Neuroses." It was an effort to summarize his forthcoming first book, which, when it was published in Germany in 1907, was entitled *A Study of Organ*

Inferiority (in later English translation, the title would be enlarged with the phrase *and its Psychical Compensation;* there would also be a subtitle, *A Contribution to Clinical Medicine*). It is not known how many other chief presentations Adler had given, nor on what topics, since cofounding the society with Freud, Kahane, Reitler, and Stekel four years earlier. Rank's minutes for this November session do indicate, however, that Adler's talk represented a follow-up of his earlier reported research into the "Physiology and Pathology of the Erotogenic Zones."

Adler's crucial lecture highlighted the notions that would subsequently appear in *A Study of Organ Inferiority*. In essence, he argued three basic points before his colleagues: First, virtually all neurosis derives from congenital weakness—organ inferiority—such as visual or hearing impairment, or muscular debility. Second, the major cause of sexual precocity lies in such childhood defects, since presumably any bodily weakness will adversely affect sexual vitality as well. Third, people inevitably strive to overcome their congenital debility in a struggle for social adaptation. Adler called this latter process *compensation,* and stressed that often such striving actually leads to overcompensation; that is, the "supervalence," or triumphant dominance, of the initially inferior organ.

It is this latter concept, of course, that has become well accepted in modern psychology for nearly ninety years. Besides describing specific cases from his own medical practice, Adler depicted such well-known historical examples of overcompensation as composers Beethoven (who became deaf), Mozart (who was said to have misshapen ears), and Schumann (who suffered from a psychosis that began with auditory hallucinations). He likewise cited the presence of early speech defects in famous orators like Demosthenes and Moses.

Most of those attending the meeting were drawn to Adler's third and most intriguing point, especially Freud. "He attributed great importance to Adler's work; it has brought his own work a step further," dutifully recorded young Rank. "[Freud stated that] to judge from the immediate impression, much of what Adler said may be correct." To buttress Adler's insight about overcompensation, Freud suggested the case of the contemporary German painter Franz von Lenbach, who was blind in one eye. Following lively speculation about the differing types of organ inferiority and resulting occurences of overcompensation among various professions, including painters, musicians, and poets, Freud remarked that "good cooks are always severely abnormal" emotionally and mentioned that "his own cook invariably cooks particularly well when a period of illness is imminent."

Not all who attended the lecture were impressed with Adler. Some criticized his reliance upon anecdotal cases rather than hard statistical data; such an objection would later dog Adler throughout his wide-ranging career. Others felt that he was exaggerating the importance of congenital causes in affecting adult personality and also that he needed to be more specific in defining organ inferiority.

Published several months later, *A Study of Organ Inferiority* was a detailed and well-reasoned work for its time. The slender book was replete with case studies illustrating the nature of overcompensation as a verifiable phenomenon of human personality. Although offering little empirical data, Adler did incorporate the results of a medical study cited at the November society meeting, in which 70 percent of a sample of German art students were found to have visual anomalies.

Throughout the book, Adler revealed a clear and explicit intellectual debt to Freud. But he insisted that "the interesting psychic phenomena of repression, substitution, [and] conversion which Freud demonstrated in his psychoanalyses and which I have also found to be the most important constituents of the psychoneuroses, develop [as a result] of inferior organs." In other words, it was congenital weakness—and one's resulting sense of inferiority—that initiated the hidden emotional processes that Freud had discovered: If a person failed to *compensate* adequately, then neurosis happened.

Undoubtedly anticipating skepticism in the notion that auditory or visual impairments could produce sexual repression, Adler declared that a link indeed existed: "This seems to me to be a fundamental law of the theory of organ inferiority, namely, that every organ inferiority carries its heredity through, and makes itself felt by reason of an accompanying inferiority in the sexual function."

This idea, of course, has not stood the test of time. It lacked supporting evidence, and Adler himself abandoned it within just a few years. Far more crucial in the evolution of his growing psychological thinking was a rather implicit point in *A Study of Organ Inferiority:* If compensation and overcompensation are such basic human characteristics, then there must exist a natural, inborn drive for mastery and competence in the social world. Adler did not yet say so directly and probably had not even made the conceptual leap in his own mind, but he may have already sensed, however vaguely, that by alluding to the power of this drive rather than to that of sexuality, he was on the road toward a radical divergence from Freud.

Adler further developed his viewpoint throughout 1907. In a lecture before the University of Vienna's Philosophical Society, he emphasized that a true definition of organ inferiority always involved an interplay between the individual's unique biological makeup and the society's external demands. Presumably, for example, a woman with a congenital leg weakness might be much less likely to experience a drive toward compensation if she inhabited an urban society where few people need to hike long distances.

In a paper published that year entitled the "Developmental Defects of the Child," Adler blended his socialistic emphasis on preventive medicine with his new work on organ inferiority. He urged parents to become interested in education as a means to insure their offspring's healthy development:

> In our children rests the future of the people! All the creations of peoples, all urging forward, the destruction of old barriers and prejudices, usually happen for the sake of progeny and are meant first of all to help them. While today the struggle for mental freedom rages, while we are shaking the pillars of superstition and serfdom, tomorrow our children will sun themselves in the mild light of freedom and drink from the fountains of pure knowledge, unconcerned about the threats of a decaying manner of thought.

Adler identified such factors as inadequate housing, parental malnourishment, the overwork of pregnant women, and the abuses inherent in child employment as contributing to developmental abnormalities. He ended his article with an optimistic, almost evangelical fervor:

> Whereas today the old and rotten collapses, having lost its right of existence, some day the church of true humanity will arise more proud and daring than our thoughts can comprehend, before which any falsehood and deceit will be reduced to dust. For our children! They shall enjoy that to which we yearningly aspire: air, light, nourishment, which today are still kept from the people—our children shall fully partake of them! We are fighting for sanitary housing, adequate wages, for the dignity of labor, for solid knowledge, that these may some day be assured for our children. Our sweat is their peace; their health is our struggle.

With Raissa and friends like Furtmüller sharing his impassioned viewpoint, Adler felt certain that his path would lead decisively to social betterment. And although he continued an active association with the Vienna Psychoanalytic Society, he would increasingly find that an equally adamant Freud viewed all such matters quite differently.

CHAPTER FIVE

═══

Breaking with Freud

Don't worry too much about the
Freudian brood and its cackle. Since
the first significant steps of its creator, the
best that [the psychoanalysts] could
do was to cackle at what we said.

ALFRED ADLER

A dler was immensely gratified by the response to his first book.
A Study of Organ Inferiority was well received by his Viennese medical colleagues including fellow members of the Wednesday Psychological Society. Virtually everyone who attended the weekly meetings
at Freud's office suite deemed it an important work, a major contribution toward better understanding the biological forces affecting neurotic
development.

Within the society that year, major changes were underway. Its members
were expected to pay dues to cover expenses, the largest portion of which
went toward Rank's salary as secretary. The total membership climbed to
twenty-one, with newcomers more than replacing resignations, and perhaps
inevitably, the atmosphere of the growing association began changing as
well. Gone was the warm, unified spirit that Stekel had so fondly evoked in
his reminiscence of the society's early days. Members were increasingly
combative toward one another, and began resorting to ad hominem attack:
psychoanalytic character assassination. Since Freud frequently relied upon
this technique in later years, it seems plausible that members took the master's lead in this regard. Some of the exchanges were quite brutal, such as
Eduard Hitschmann's accusation that physician Fritz Wittels was interested
in the three topics of pregnancy, chaste female medical students, and syphilis because he was personally thwarted sexually by all three.

As a result of such lurid exchanges, the society formally adopted new rules in February 1908. Its members voted to devote several sessions each year to reviewing new books and journal articles. As official secretary, Rank was encharged with this responsibility; Hitschmann was to assist him. Each member would henceforth be expected to offer a major presentation annually. To control the group's unruliness, Freud agreed to intervene as chairperson if a speaker found himself (the society was still all male) inappropriately distracted by counter-conversations or directly interrupted. An irritated Freud remarked that he found it professionally embarrassing to have to reprimand anyone and threatened to end the society's meetings if they could not be conducted more civilly. He offered hope that "deeper psychological understanding would overcome the difficulties in personal contacts."

It is unlikely that Adler became embroiled in the society's increasingly contentious atmosphere, for his manner was typically conciliatory. Although clearly beginning to forge an independent psychological system, he sought to maintain good relations with other society members. Yet he never became emotionally close with its regulars, or with its key foreign supporters, such as the Hungarian Sandor Ferenczi, the Britisher Ernest Jones, or the Swiss psychiatrist Carl Jung. Perhaps such early international exponents of psychoanalysis sensed from the outset that Adler never quite shared their intense admiration for Freud; possibly, they also found him too independent-minded and too zealous an advocate for socialism to gain their friendship. In any case, Adler worked without medical collaborators during his final three years of society participation.

Perhaps his closest intellectual ally during this period was Carl Furtmüller, who in 1908 left Kadan, after four years, to take a teaching position at a Viennese secondary school. Life in Kadan had initially been intellectually confining for him and Aline, but they had quickly become politically active, participating in Social Democratic party meetings and founding a local chapter of the newly formed anticlerical organization, Free School. Its fiery leader was Otto Glöckel, who would later direct Vienna's school board for more than a dozen years during its socialist heyday after World War I.

During the Furtmüllers' strong effort to combat church influence over public schooling, they became targets of abuse. In November 1906, a Kadan-area newspaper ridiculed the "sir who should be [called] Professor *Durchwühler* [a molelike animal that rhymed with Furtmüller] and his "better or perhaps even worse half . . . the frightful shrew." That same year, he gained teaching certification in philosophy and, in 1908, in French as well.

By his mid-twenties, Furtmüller was already publishing critical essays concerning classical education. He had also become intrigued by Adler's conversations about psychoanalysis, and had eagerly attended Freud's 1906 lectures at the University of Vienna.

The year of Furtmüller's enthusiastic return to Vienna also marked his older friend's first clear divergence from Freud. In "The Aggression Drive in Life and in Neurosis," which appeared in a major medical journal, Adler argued that two key personality drives exist: sexuality and aggression. Both, claimed Adler, are aimed at satisfying physiological needs and garnering pleasure from the environment. Since Freud had already discussed libido extensively, Adler focused more prominently on aggression, arguing that:

> From early childhood . . . from the first day (first cry), [we find] a stand of the child toward the environment which cannot be called anything but *hostile*. On closer examination, one finds this attitude determined by the difficulty in gaining pleasure for the organ. This circumstance as well as the further relationships of the hostile, belligerent position of the individual toward the environment indicates a drive toward fighting for satisfaction which I shall call *aggression drive*.

In this seminal paper, Adler was clearly struggling to define precisely what he meant by the term *aggression*. He explicitly mentioned that it constituted an interplay, or *confluence,* of several, different instinctual drives, such as the impulse "to see, to hear, and to touch." Adler also remarked that this confluence induces not only destructive and criminal behavior, but also the beneficial actions committed by clergy, judges, police officers, physicians, teachers, and "revolutionary heroes."

From our perspective today, Adler as a psychological pioneer was groping in this article for a description of the human tendency toward assertiveness; his term *aggression drive* therefore was actually a misnomer, and before long, he would stop using it in this context. Ironically, after witnessing the mass horrors of World War I, Freud would emulate Adler's original formulation by positing the existence of an innate human urge for destruction. In this same 1908 article, however, Adler was already suggesting that our so-called aggression drive often transforms itself into socially useful channels:

> Charity, sympathy, altruism, and sensitive interest in misery represent new satisfactions on which the drive, which originally tended toward cruelty, feeds. . . . The greater the aggression drive, the stronger will become this cultural transformation. Thus the pessimist becomes the preventor of dangers, Cassandra becomes a warner and a prophet.

Adler's viewpoint on aggression intrigued Freud, who published a mildly favorable article the following year. Readily conceding the reality of human aggressive tendencies, Freud nevertheless denied his colleague's contention that such impulses exist independently of sexuality or libido:

> Alfred Adler, in a suggestive paper, has recently developed the view that anxiety arises from the suppression of what he calls the *aggressive instinct,* and by a very sweeping synthetic process he ascribes to that instinct the chief part in human events, "in real life and in the neuroses." . . . I am unable to assent to this view, and indeed I regard it as a misleading generalization. I cannot bring myself to assume the existence of a special, aggressive instinct alongside the familiar instincts of self-preservation and of sex, and on an equal footing with them.

But in that the same crucial year in his career, Adler was not only speculating about a basic drive for aggression. In a short article published in a new educational monthly that Freud might well have missed, Adler was also asserting that we all have an innate need for affection, whose early manifestations

> are sufficiently striking and well known. Children want to be fondled, loved, and praised. They have a tendency to cuddle up, always to remain close to loved persons, and to want to be taken into the bed with them. Later this desire aims at loving relationships from which originate love of relatives, friendships, social feelings, and [sexual] love.

Adler was not yet suggesting that we actually have an inborn striving for social feeling; he would arrive at this position several years later. Rather, as with aggression, he was attributing our need for affection to a confluence of biological impulses "to touch, to look, and to listen." In Adler's socially oriented view, educators had a particularly important responsibility to direct this confluence of impulses in a healthy manner:

> A large part of the child's development depends on the proper guidance of this drive complex. . . . Before attaining satisfaction, the impulse should be forced to detour in order to furnish the drive for the [child's] cultural behavior. Thus, the way and goal of the need for affection are raised to a higher level. The derived, purified social feelings awake in the [child's] soul as soon as the goal permits substitute formations: the place of the father can be taken by the teacher, the friend, or the comrade-in-arms. . . . [However], if the child . . . attains only satisfactions of a primitive kind without [learning] delay, his wishes will remain directed toward immediate, sensual pleasure.

In Adler's view, effective education must be able to gratify youngsters' inborn needs for affection. Otherwise, such problems as alienation and delinquency may well result, for "every unsatisfied drive ultimately orients the organism toward aggression against the environment." In subsequent years, Adler would gain international acclaim for his work in Central Europe and elsewhere in unraveling the psychological origins of juvenile delinquency.

━━━━━

Meanwhile, in 1908, Adler was gaining the companionship of another energetic socialist, one who would exert tremendous influence upon the world: Leon Trotsky. Nine years younger than Adler, he was born Lev Davidovich Bronstein to affluent Jewish parents in the Ukraine. After two years of revolutionary activity as a Social Democrat, Trotsky was arrested in 1898. He escaped from Siberian exile in 1902, and went to London, where he first met Lenin. Later returning to his homeland, Trotsky participated as a leader in the abortive Russian revolution of 1905. He was again jailed, but escaped once more, and finally made his way to Vienna three years later.

He was twenty-nine-years old at the time, and married to his second wife, Nathalia Sedova, who had been an art student at the Sorbonne when they became acquainted in 1903. With two young sons, Leon and Sergei, the couple was renting a shabby apartment while Trotsky took over editorship of the exile newspaper *Pravda*. Among his small staff was a fellow emigré journalist named Adolf Joffe. He had become addicted to morphine through a recent illness and, suffering from depression, had sought out Alfred Adler for expert treatment. Joffe, who would later become a key Bolshevik diplomat in the Lenin government, spoke very highly of Adler, much to Trotsky's curiosity.

Socially, the Trotskys were becoming well acquainted with Samuel Klatschko's lively salons for the Russian-socialist emigré community in Vienna. Klatschko was apparently just as warm and generous with Trotksy as he had been several years earlier with his future son-in-law, Furtmüller. Before long, Nathalia became friends with Furtmüller's wife, Aline, and with Aline's confidante, Raissa Adler, as well.

By 1909, the Trotksy and Adler families had developed close ties, mainly through the growing friendship between the two wives. Although Nathalia had grown up in a Greek Orthodox rather than Jewish household in Russia, she and Raissa shared much in common. They had both been raised in affluent families and studied abroad; they were also longtime advocates of revolutionary socialism, although Nathalia had been much more of an activist. As a youth, she had been expelled from her Russian boarding school for urging her classmates to read socialist works instead of the Bible, and was later jailed for participating in the 1905 revolution. Both women were raising young children in a foreign land and were married to brilliant and charismatic men.

During the five years that the Trotskys resided in Vienna, Nathalia and Raissa spent considerable time together. Often their husbands joined them for dinner conversations and recreational outings. Kurt Adler later recalled one such occasion: "On a sunny day when I was about six, our respective families got together in Vienna's Stadpark. It had a huge open area for children to play, but footballs for soccer were prohibited. Trotsky was already there with his two sons, playing ball. A policeman suddenly appeared and demanded to confiscate it from Trotsky, who immediately engaged him in conversation. Much to everyone's surprise, he actually convinced the policeman to let us keep playing with the football."

More interested in ideas than in soccer, Trotksy found Adler's psychological notions extremely interesting. After the October revolution, Trotsky would urge Russian physicians to be open-minded about psychoanalytic precepts. His own cure for the emotionally frail Joffe, though, consisted of patiently encouraging his talent, promoting his self-confidence, and, especially, giving him a sense of mission in aiding the socialist revolution.

Yet another Russian revolutionary whom the Adlers knew well was M. I. Skobelev, who served with Joffe and Trotsky on *Pravda*'s staff. His wife had two young sons, and like Nathalia Sedova, became especially friendly with Raissa. During the fateful year of 1917, Skobelev would become a member of the duma (Russia's prerevolutionary parliament) and of the Soviet Executive Committee, where he would fight Lenin's antidemocratic policies.

Involved at least peripherally with such leading Russian revolutionaries, Adler, in March 1909, felt moved to offer a presentation before the Vienna Psychoanalytic Society titled "On the Psychology of Marxism." At the time, he was its only member belonging to Austria's Social Democratic party. Although planning to articulate these same ideas in a published paper, Adler never did so, perhaps due to the coolness that his lecture received from Freud and other attendees that evening.

As recorded in Rank's almost telegraphic notes, Adler's position is difficult to follow. He clearly began by praising Marx's intellectual achievements and then argued that "class consciousness" among the proletariat always involves a psychologically instinctual sensitivity to debasement and degradation. Later, he asserted that while in neurosis the aggression instinct is inhibited, "class consciousness liberates it. Marx shows how [the aggression instinct] can be gratified in keeping with the meaning of civilization: by grasping the true causes of oppression and exploitation, and by suitable [political] organization." Adler's final pronouncement was that "Marx's entire work culminates in the demand to make history *consciously.*"

Freud was not impressed. He insisted that Adler had failed to show any evidence of psychoanalytic insight within Marxism, but he felt moved to offer his own idealistic view of human progress, involving not class struggle but "the enlargement of consciousness [that] . . . enables mankind to cope with life in the face of the steady process of [psychological] repression." One attendee derided socialism as "a substitute for religion," and Freud mildly encouraged Adler to pursue the topic for professional publication.

Nine days after Adler's fourth and final child, Cornelia, was born on October 18, his long socialist isolation within the society was ended when Furtmüller was accepted into membership. From the very beginning, he was an articulate and outspoken participant who sought to bring a Marxist perspective to the society's wide-ranging discussions about the emotional problems of children and adults. Thus, in a December presentation entitled "Fatalism or Education?" Furtmüller argued that economic changes affecting the modern family had increasingly separated children from their parents' lives. Consequently, educators now bore a new responsibility to help youngsters develop appropriate social skills. Praising Adler's recent paper, "The Child's Need for Affection," Furtmüller remarked that his friend "has offered remarkable suggestions as to how the child's need for affection can be turned to pedagogical advantage."

Likewise, at a major society discussion devoted to juvenile suicide (subsequently published as a symposium) led by Adler's colleague David Oppenheim, Furtmüller aptly insisted that, "Pupils' suicides can no longer be treated from a purely psychological viewpoint, but must be considered also from social points of view. The school is not so much guilty because of its individual teachers, as it is as a whole institution." Contradicting Freud's mild remark that formal education mirrors society's dictates, Furtmüller acidly commented that, "School is not only like life; it is harsher. Not one of us could endure with equanimity the fact that every half-year, judgment was to be passed on his activity and his general achievement. . . . [We must] remodel the institution of the school as a whole."

Not long after Furtmüller's entry into the society, Adler successfully recruited several more intellectual allies. These included Franz and Gustav

Grüner, Baron Franz von Hye, Stefan von Maday, and fellow socialists like physician Margaret Hilferding, one of the society's first female members. She was married to physician Rudolf Hilferding, who was already a leading Marxist theoretician among the Social Democrats and would later serve as finance minister in Weimar Germany. Margaret would herself become an energetic advocate for women's issues, including abortion rights, in post–World War I Austria.

———

By the winter months of 1910, Freud was feeling increasingly alienated by recent developments within the society. In a letter penned to colleague Karl Abraham in March, he reported no longer receiving any pleasure from the Vienna group and called Adler, Stekel, and Isidor Sadger the "older generation," as well as "a heavy cross to bear [who] will soon be feeling that I am an obstacle."

Such feelings were nothing new. As far back as June 1909, he had described Adler to Jung as "a theoretician, astute and original, but not oriented to the psychological; he aims for the biological." Nevertheless, Freud had characterized Adler as "decent" and added, "We must hold on to him." Apparently, his younger colleague's increasingly divergent approach over the ensuing year had dissuaded Freud from maintaining even this mildly favorable viewpoint.

Matters came to a head on March 30, on the occasion of the second International Psychoanalytical Convention held in Nuremberg, Germany. Acting as Freud's deputy in a speech obviously planned well in advance, Ferenczi startlingly proposed that an international psychoanalytic association be formed: Jung would serve as its permanent president with authoritative control over all publications; his Swiss compatriot Franz Riklin would serve as secretary. The Viennese who heard Ferenczi's recommendation were tremendously shocked; such a step would obviously transfer power from their own organization to Zurich. To add insult to injury, Ferenczi also heaped criticism on the Vienna Psychoanalytic Society.

Representing about a third of the convention's sixty-five attendees, the Viennese group, including Adler, rose in protest and secreted themselves in a private caucus called by Stekel. As they sat in the Grand Hotel's meeting room and debated the best course of action, Freud suddenly appeared at the door. As later recalled by several witnesses, including longtime ally Fritz Wittels, he seemed unusually distraught as he said: "Most of you are Jews, and therefore you are incompetent to win friends for the new teaching. Jews must be content with the modest role of preparing the ground. It is absolutely essential that I should form ties in the world of general science. I am getting on in years, and am weary of being perpetually attacked. We are all in danger. . . . The Swiss will save us."

No documentation exists concerning Adler's own reaction to this speech, but after long debate, Freud agreed to a compromise: The president of the international society would be elected for only two years, and would not have censorship power over publications. At the society's next meeting the following week in early April, Freud diplomatically suggested that Adler serve as its new chairperson, as well as chief editor for a new monthly journal, *Zentralblatt,* to supplement Jung's recently established *Yearbook.* Freud also proposed that Stekel assist Adler by serving both as deputy chair and coeditor, alongside Freud himself, of the *Zentralblatt.* Virtually everyone, including Adler's supporters, liked the new plan very much, and by acclamation they elected Freud to the newly created post of "scientific chairperson."

During the spring weeks that followed, Adler exerted an active role as the society's chairperson, appointing Stekel and five others to round out its executive committee. Among the chief items of business was to find a new meeting place for the society's expanded membership. Having grown to about thirty-five, with perhaps half that number attending any given session, the group could no longer be accommodated around the large table placed in Freud's waiting room. Adler investigated two prospective coffeehouses, the Café Siller and the Café Pucher, and Rank, the Café Arkaden, as alternatives, but the membership rejected all three choices and opted instead to rent the austere auditorium of the College of Physicians.

It was probably a poor decision, for the group's social dynamics immediately underwent a change for the worse. Years later, the British analyst Ernest Jones recalled that the relocation had seemingly engendered "a chillier and more formal atmosphere. I observed myself that it was very different from what I had witnessed in the earlier years of the Society." Nevertheless, Freud was initially pleased by the seemingly successful amelioration of tensions between him and the Vienna Psychoanalytic Society's members. Although possibly engaging in wishful thinking, he wrote to Jung that "I am satisfied with the outcome of my statesmanship. Fair competition between Vienna and Zurich can only benefit the cause. The Viennese have no manners, but they know a good deal and can still do good work for the movement."

Freud would not offer such cheerfulness for long, for Adler was rapidly developing a very different and competing psychological viewpoint. Published that year in a major medical journal, his seminal article was entitled "Psychic Hermaphroditism in Life and in the Neurosis." Now abandoning his earlier notion about the existence of an innate aggression drive, Adler shifted his emphasis to the subjective, emotional state of inferiority. Looking back on his own intellectual development decades later, he reminisced that, "In 1908, I hit upon the idea that every individual really exists in a state of permanent aggression, and I was imprudent enough to call this attitude the 'aggression drive.' But I soon realized that I was not dealing with a drive, but with a partly conscious, partly irrational attitude toward the tasks which life imposes."

This 1910 paper on psychic hermaphroditism (the phrase reflected Adler's notion that everyone has both masculine and feminine traits) was a crucial conceptual breakthrough, and one that clearly contradicted Freud's basic outlook. In *A Study on Organ Inferiority,* Adler had suggested only implicitly that people with inferior organs experience a striving that leads to compensation or overcompensation. Now, three years later, he was making the notion explicit and the lynchpin of his emerging psychological system:

> These objective phenomena frequently give rise *to a subjective feeling of inferiority* and thus hinder the [child's] independence, increase his need for support and affection, and often characterize an individual throughout life. . . . *The starting point . . . is the child's feeling of weakness in the face of adults.* From this arises a need for support, a demand for affection, a physiological and psychological dependency and submission. In cases of early and subjectively felt organ inferiority, these traits are intensified. Increased dependency and the intensified feeling of our own littleness and weakness lead to inhibition of aggression and thereby to the phenomenon of anxiety.   (emphasis added)

At the time, Adler called this sense of inferiority *masculine protest,* since in European men it seemed associated with such culturally tagged masculine ideals as assertiveness, ambitiousness, aggressiveness, and defiance. Adler believed that European women who felt inferior likewise suffered from masculine protest, since they typically devalued culturally defined feminine ideals like sympathy, compassion, and acquiescence. He suggested that such disturbed emotional functioning could be successfully treated, for "it is the goal of education and psychotherapy to uncover these dynamics and to make them conscious. Overgrowth of masculine and feminine traits then disappears . . . and the patient learns to bear the tensions from the environment without losing his equanimity."

It is vital to understand that Adler regarded such formulations as part of psychoanalysis's evolving quest for scientific truth about the human mind. He certainly knew that by deemphasizing the sexual drive, Freud's entire theory of personality development and neurosis was being undercut. Yet Adler seems to have believed, naively in retrospect, that Freud would acceptingly alter his theory once all the facts were objectively presented. Thus, in the society's *Symposium on Suicide* completed in June, Adler clearly expressed satisfaction with the Viennese association's accomplishments. By all evidence, he viewed himself as a loyal and effective exponent; for in his view, the science of psychoanalysis was far broader than Freud's notion of infantile sexuality. In the symposium's preface, Adler happily recounted that:

> For about seven years, a circle of medical men and psychologists interested in the study of psychoanalysis have been meeting every week to discuss their experiences. This circle, which arose out of the work of Freud and Breuer, is primarily responsible for the development of psychoanalytic methods and [ideas]. Since then, centers of psychoanalytic study have been formed all over the world; the number of collaborators, already quite considerable, is increasing rapidly.

It is hardly surprising that Freud would feel alarmed by Adler's sentiments. With the appearance of his new article on psychic hermaphroditism emphasizing the sense of inferiority, and not libido, as the basis for neurosis, Adler had clearly arrived at a wholly unacceptable position for Freud and his sympathizers. For more than a decade since *The Interpretation of Dreams* had been published, Freud had been carefully erecting a formidable structure of theory and clinical evidence to buttress his notion that infantile sexuality was the key to human personality. He was not about to allow an upstart like Adler, however intelligent, to overturn this structure and replace it—even if still glibly calling it psychoanalysis.

The essential battle between Freud and Adler, therefore, was not over power or personality, but intensely different ideas. It was a sharp conflict, and Freud's emotional letters to Jung and other foreign colleagues during the months of 1910 reveal his growing conviction that Adler was "paranoid" and a threat to the entire Vienna society and to the international psychoanalytic movement as well. He had to be removed before his assertive influence could become steadily more powerful and damaging. But how? After all, Adler was the Psychoanalytic society's chairperson and was well respected by most members. He had also succeeded in recruiting his own loyal faction of Social Democratic educators and physicians.

Soon Freud cleverly contrived a plan that would force the issue immediately, before Adler could amass greater support. In mid-November, Freud's protégé, Hitschmann, suggested at a society meeting that "Adler's theories be for once thoroughly discussed in their interconnections, with particular attention to their divergence from Freud's doctrine." Hitschmann disingenuously commented that such a presentation might lead to a profitable fusing between the two viewpoints; Freud then amended the motion to request that Adler specifically explain his notion of masculine protest, and he genially agreed to do so.

The first lecture, broadly entitled "Some Problems of Psychoanalysis," took place on January 4, 1911. Adler praised Freud for his ground-breaking insights on the role of sexuality in neurosis, but then quickly shifted to his own perspective in recounting a recent clinical case, namely, that "sexuality is aroused and stimulated through organ inferiority, and it is felt by an intensified masculine protest as gigantic." Then, in what the Freudians must have perceived as blasphemy, he added that, "In general, it is not possible to regard the sexual stirrings of neurotics—or those of civilized men—as genuine enough to take into account" in understanding human sexuality.

During the highly critical discussion, Freud did not participate at all. Allies like Paul Federn, Eduard Hitschmann, and Rudolf Reitler took up the cudgel for their mentor and swung it solidly at Adler. The most potent was Federn, who declared that, "if sexuality is not the center and cause of the neuroses . . . then Adler's views represent a real danger . . . he has done regressive work and aligned himself with the opponents of Freud's teachings." In response to such comments, Adler mildly noted that he had "never wanted to dispute the fact that the germ of his views is to be found in Freud's teachings," but nevertheless affirmed that "there is no principle more generally valid for all human relationships" than the drive for assertion, not sexual gratification.

On February 1, Adler offered his second and more detailed lecture, "The Masculine Protest as the Central Problem of Neurosis." Once more, he began by praising Freud's insights and then quickly shifted to elaborating a very different outlook on personality development. Quite specifically, Adler explained that the basic "ego instinct"—what enables us to function in the social world—involves "a wanting to be more important, a striving for power, and for dominance." Each child's particular milieu helps determine how this impulse will be expressed in his or her relationships, including those that are sexual.

As for the key issue of how neuroses are formed, Adler identified two separate forces: "The budding of a feeling of inferiority connected with the inferiority of certain organs; and, unmistakable indications of an actual fear of a feminine role. When these factors support each other . . . [then] emotional life becomes falsified."

For more than three years, Adler had been emphasizing to the society that children who have inferior organs are at greater risk to develop neurotic problems. Now, he was also saying that society's values were another major factor in neurosis: specifically, the all-pervasive influence of gender roles. "That woman is devalued by man is clearly expressed in our culture; indeed, it can even be regarded as a driving force in our civilization."

If only by omission, such comments were clearly ignoring the whole basis of Freudian theory in infantile sexuality. But Adler then declared explicitly that with regard to treating neuroses, "Whether and how much libido is involved makes no difference. . . . There are patients who have known about their Oedipus complex and yet did not get better. One can no longer speak of a complex of libidinal wishes and fantasies; *even the Oedipus complex will have to be understood as one component phenomenon of an overstrong psychic dynamic, as one stage of the masculine protest.*" (emphasis added)

This time when Freud opened the discussion, his mood was not genial or conciliatory. He described feeling resentment over Adler's way of claiming credit for alleged discoveries that were actually quite familiar to his own approach, but simply given different names like masculine protest or psychic hermaphroditism. Then, more scathingly, Freud attacked Adler's viewpoint for the danger posed by its "antisexual tendency":

> All these teachings of Adler's are, in [my] judgment, not without importance; and [I] would make the following prediction about them: They will make a deep impression and will, at first, do great harm to psychoanalysis. . . . It is evident that a significant intellect with a great gift for presentation is at work on these matters; however, the entire doctrine has a reactionary and retrogressive character.

With obvious bitterness, Freud predicted that by downplaying the true importance of sexuality in the human psyche, Adler's superficially alluring approach would gain many adherents:

> Instead of psychology, it presents, in large part, biology; instead of the psychology of the unconscious, it presents surface ego psychology. Lastly, instead of the psychology of the libido, of sexuality, it offers general psychology. It will, therefore, make use of the latent resistances that are alive in every psychoanalyst, in order to make its infuence felt. . . . This is ego psychology, deepened by the knowledge of the psychology of the unconscious.

Permitted to respond immediately to Freud, Adler insisted that he too saw sexual problems present in neuroses. He tersely reaffirmed, however, that "behind what one sees as sexual, there are concealed far more important relationships, which merely take on the guise of sexuality. . . . The 'purely' sexual is nothing primary . . . it is a confluence of drives."

Stekel was permitted to respond by mildly praising Adler's presentation, and then Freud concluded the meeting. Less heated than before, he conceded having always "acknowledged the worth of Adler's characterological studies" and having "found fault with them only insofar as they are meant to replace the psychology of the unconscious."

Later that month, the society devoted two entire meetings to continuing its reaction to Adler's presentation. At the first of these sessions, Freud's supporters became overtly hostile. Hitschmann resorted to an ad hominem attack by sarcastically commenting that because of Adler's "personal relations with academic psychology, as well as with pedagogy, socialism, and the feminist movement, [he] has come to interpret everything—even what is most obviously sexual—as masculine protest."

Two weeks later, dermatologist Maximilian Steiner remarked that since Adler's "valuable study on organ inferiority, [he] has deviated more and more from Freud's doctrine," and then crudely compared Adler's "anachronistic" viewpoint (denying sexuality as the primary psychological drive) to that of the early Christians. For those like Adler, Freud, and virtually all others in the society who prided themselves as enlightened secularists, few insults could have been more derisive.

The most conciliatory figure that evening was probably Stekel, who aside from Reitler, had been the only one to work with both men since the Wednesday Psychological Society's first session nearly nine years before. Stekel praised Adler as having importance secondary only to Freud for showing "the most important disclosures about the dynamics of dreams" and then commented that, "Adler's views are not incompatible with [Freud's] . . . but [are] simply a structure built on Freud's foundation."

Freud, of course, was not interested in conciliation at all. Rather, as the minutes indicate, he sarcastically noted that, "While Stekel does not see any contradiction between Adler's views and Freud's doctrines, one has to point out that two of the persons involved do find this contradiction: Adler and Freud."

Whether Adler had decided his response before the meeting is unknown, but the barrage of insults he experienced, coupled with Freud's apparent acquiescence, could hardly have left him much choice: Later that evening, he resigned as society chairperson because of the "incompatibility of his scientific attitude with his position in the society." Stekel immediately declared himself in complete agreement with his longtime colleague, and resigned his own position as deputy chair.

At the society's next general meeting on March 1, it was obliged to choose a new chairperson. To no one's surprise, Freud was elected by acclamation. Adler's friend Furtmüller thereupon succeeded in gaining, over Freud's objection, a majority vote to resolve that the body find no incompatability of beliefs between the two protagonists. Nevertheless, a relatively pleased Freud wrote to Jung later that night and summarized recent events within the society. Still wary of Adler's remaining influence, he remarked that, "I must avenge the offended goddess Libido [and make sure] that heresy does not occupy too much space in the *Zentralblatt*. . . . I would never have expected a psychoanalyst to be so taken in by the ego. In reality the ego is like the clown in the circus, who is always putting in his oar to make the audience think that whatever happens is his doing."

Adler continued to serve as editorial director of the *Zentralblatt* and attended meetings actively as usual. Outwardly, relations between him and Freud seemed less acrimonious, and it seems unlikely that he was eager to sever further ties with the society. Freud, however, saw matters differently. During the summer recess, he cleverly initiated a second and final step to eliminate his rival from all influence within the Vienna Psychoanalytic Society. Freud wrote to the *Zentralblatt*'s publisher and announced that he could no longer serve as coeditor with Adler: The publisher would have to choose between them.

Clearly, Freud was deliberating raising the ante for a confrontation he felt confident about winning. To his colleague Jones, Freud vituperatively revealed that, "as for the internal dissension with Adler, it was likely to come and I have ripened the crisis. It is the revolt of an abnormal individual driven mad by ambition, his influence upon others depending on his strong terrorism and sadismus."

Even for the customarily trenchant Freud, such remarks leveled against his longtime associate in the Vienna Psychoanalytic Society were extremely harsh. They also suggest that he was quite affected emotionally by Adler's insistence that sexuality is not the decisive force in human personality, but of only secondary importance. Freud had labored for more than fifteen years to emphasize infantile sexuality as the fundamental drive, and regarded his theory as still far from academically respectable. Yet, he had become increasingly hopeful in the last few years that psychoanalysis would indeed attain worldwide influence and acceptance. Perhaps Freud actually believed that through his sheer intellect and persuasive ability, he could triumphantly unify all of modern psychology into his approach.

Adler's intellectual position itself probably did not arouse such animosity in Freud. Certainly, he felt capable of refuting his younger colleague's theoretical arguments, however superficially alluring they seemed to be. But what must have caused Freud such distress was the irrefutable evidence that his basic system was going to be challenged, and rejected, by other cogent explorers of human personality. There would be no universal applause after all. Freud must have sensed at least intuitively that Adler's break would not be the only one, and that others would certainly follow.

Thus, Adler was the first to shatter Freud's optimistic vision of a world paying grateful homage to his work; and perhaps inevitably, we feel most embittered toward those who destroy our earliest Olympian dreams of accomplishment. Although many would eventually quit their association with Freud, including formerly close colleagues like Stekel, Jung, and Rank, none would arouse such lifelong implacable enmity as Adler.

When *Zentralblatt*'s publisher relayed Freud's ultimatum, Adler spared him the embarrassing choice and resigned his editorial position and his membership from the Vienna Psychoanalytic Society as well. Confiding to faraway Ernest Jones during the summer months, Adler condemned Freud's "fencer's postures" and lamented that, "I have always stayed within moderate limits in that I could wait and never begrudged anyone being of a different opinion." In a subsequent letter, he announced that Freud was planning to perform a "nonsensical castration" upon him.

Except among Freud's closest allies in the society, news of events at the *Zentralblatt* elicited dismay. Many expressed sympathy for Adler and deplored Freud's tactics. When the necessity for making a choice between the two opponents became clear, however, declaring open support for Adler seemed less palatable to the majority.

Nevertheless, twelve society members (out of about a total of thirty-five), led by Furtmüller, signed an open letter dated July 26. They formally protested Freud's manipulative action and declared their readiness to help achieve a fruitful reconciliation for the benefit of all:

> Upon learning of the impending leadership change of the central periodical, the undersigned have turned to Dr. Adler for more detailed information. At their request, he produced the letters pertaining to this matter, and from these, they have gathered that Dr. Adler, one of the two founders of the periodical, is

being pressured out of his editorial position under the guise of publishing and financial reasons.

The matter at hand is not an isolated incident; rather, this conflict is merely the latest in a whole series of unfriendly acts directed against Dr. Adler's person and scientific works, the implications of which have only recently become clear to us.

Although in our view, the Society and the periodical should be power structures organized against the opponents of psychoanalysis while instigating free discussion within the psychoanalytic community, these actions make more and more obvious a tendency to struggle for control even within the community—and to defend this control with all the irresponsibility characteristic of any power struggle. Our senses revolt against such a state of affairs. We are convinced that both the inner life and the outer reputation of psychoanalysis will suffer from them.

Therefore, we greatly regret that Dr. Adler's withdrawl from the Psychoanalytic Society was formally provoked and declare emphatically that we condone his actions. We obviously attribute the greatest importance to remaining in a steady scientific dialogue with him and we will find an appropriate form for this continuous discussion.

Two reasons drove us to make this declaration. First, we see it as our duty, in a matter of such importance, to remain fully honest and open with regards to the Society. Second, although we value most highly our continuing position as active members of the Psychoanalytic Society, we wish to remain members only in so far as we are welcome. Should the leadership of the Society, therefore, decide that our views and performance of duties in any way harm the Society, we beg them to call a general meeting of all members in order to come to a decision on the matter.

Like these signatories, Adler refused to be quiescent in the face of Freud's machinations. He could have chosen to say nothing and simply allow his name to vanish silently from the *Zentralblatt*'s masthead. Or he could have decided to offer a vaguely euphemistic explanation. But temperamentally, Adler had always been assertive and uncompromising when it came to important principles. Clearly, he also possessed a tremendous sense of self-confidence that enabled him to challenge Freud's powerful personality so directly. Undoubtedly, Adler had by now decided that, in the long run, he was better off disassociating himself entirely from Freud and his loyalists. Thus, he pointedly announced in the August issue that:

Herewith, I would like to notify the readers of this periodicial that as of today I have resigned from [its] editorship. The editor-in-chief of the periodical, Professor Freud, was of the opinion that between him and myself there are such large scientific differences that a joint editorship would appear unfeasible. I have therefore decided to resign from the editorship of this periodical voluntarily.

It is not precisely known how Adler spent the remaining summer weeks, but he seems to have already begun organizing his own independent Society for Free Psychoanalytic Study. The name suggests that Freud's method though not his theory still appealed to Adler. But clearly, their nine-year professional relationship was now completely finished. For the rest of their respective lives, the two men would remain bitter foes.

The first Vienna Psychoanalytic society meeting of the 1911–12 academic year took place on October 11. At the special plenary session held at Café Arkadan's club room, Freud served as chairperson. After revealing that Adler and three other members had resigned from the society, he pointedly declared that, speaking for the society's board of directors:

> he confronts those members who also belong to Dr. Adler's circle with the fact that its activities bear the character of hostile competition, and calls upon them to decide between membership either here or there. . . . Those members whose position is not yet known [must] present their decision no later than Wednesday.

Freud certainly knew that the thinly veiled ultimatum would immediately lead to more defections from the society. But to rid himself of Adler's remaining supporters was precisely his goal. Writing to a colleague before this meeting, Freud had cynically predicted that only "a few rather useless members" would emulate Adler's resignation.

Perhaps Freud was thinking of those like the firebrand Furtmüller, who led the Adlerians' battle that evening. Voicing shock and dismay concerning the board's decision as conveyed by Freud, he demanded an immediate full meeting vote on the question: Is Adler's position incompatible with membership in the Vienna Psychoanalytic Society? The next three speakers, all pro-Freudian, affirmed the board's viewpoint. It is not clear how the speakers for that evening were chosen by chairperson Freud, but none of Furtmüller's five sympathizers took the floor. Stekel still pressed for a continuing effort to reconcile the two opposing camps, but no one seemed to support this approach anymore—not even Furtmüller, who finally called for an open ballot. He asserted that the key issue was not the accuracy of Freudian or Adlerian notions, but whether the Vienna Psychoanalytic Society was to be intellectually "free" to arrive at its own conclusions independent of Freud's biases.

Twenty-one members were present for the voting. With five abstentions, the tally was eleven to five in favor of Freud's motion that membership in Adler's new group was incompatible with membership in the Vienna Psychoanalytic Society. The tabulation certainly shows no sweeping mandate for Freud: Only eleven of his twenty colleagues backed him that evening, and three others had already quit beforehand in allegiance to their former chairperson, Adler.

When the final voting yielded its expected result, Furtmüller announced that he and his five losing colleagues were hereby resigning from the society. Rising en masse, they thanked the group for its past stimulating years of joint endeavor, and then walked out. Together they headed for the Café Central to meet with Adler for a late-night celebration.

CHAPTER SIX

The Birth of Individual Psychology

Individual psychology starts with an
understanding of the child's inferiority
feeling. Its stimulation arouses all
powers, the entire psychological
movement, to force compensations,
or to push in that direction.

ALFRED ADLER

Adler's decisive departure from the Vienna Psychoanalytic Society in the fall of 1911 immediately unleashed an extremely productive period in his life. Undoubtedly, he had long felt uncomfortable, if not utterly stifled, by the society's predominantly partisan atmosphere and devotion to an increasingly dogmatic Freud. With an intense drive for accomplishment almost rivaling that of his older colleague, Adler was liberated and inspired now that he was truly on his own.

During the next few months, Adler began energetically organizing his fledgling Society for Free Psychoanalytic Study. His name for the group was hardly accidental; at the time, he still regarded himself as a loyal psychoanalyst (that is, a practitioner probing the hidden workings of human personality), but one seeking scientific truth rather than conformity to the particular teachings of one man, Sigmund Freud. The nucleus of Adler's own group comprised most of those who had vigorously supported him as fellow members of the Vienna Psychoanalytic Society. These included Furtmüller, the Grüner brothers, Hilferding, Hye, Maday, and Oppenheim; several other professionals, including philosopher Alexander Neuer, and physicians Otto Kaus and Erwin Wexberg, who soon followed suit.

Meanwhile, Freud was gratified by his own seeming triumph. Immediately after Adler's faction had felt obliged to quit the society, Freud spread the slanderous rumor that his foe had been "driven mad by ambition" and was now "paranoid." Thus, Freud defended his recent maneuvers by confiding to Stekel that, "Adler isn't a normal man. His jealousy and ambition are morbid." All his writings were pronounced worthless and wholly unacceptable to any true psychoanalyst. Before long, Stekel too would quit the society for its dogmatism, and would later rationalize his initial refusal to challenge Freud's malicious behavior toward their longtime colleague by claiming that, "My first impulse was to join [the Adlerians]. . . . But I was partly dependent [financially] on Freud for my practice. Also, I was so fond of the Journal that I did not want to give up [co-editorship] if I could help it."

At least initially, most remaining members of the Vienna Psychoanalytic Society and its foreign supporters went along with Freud. They concurred that Adler was an overly ambitious man who had veered sharply from psychoanalytic truth by denying the reality of infantile sexuality and its vast impact on human personality and social life. Some had long felt disdain for Adler's impassioned socialism, and were glad to be rid of his Social Democratic clique, which they regarded as muddying the scientific purity of psychoanalysis with irrelevant political concerns.

Initially, Adler's Society for Free Psychoanalytic Study met at his new medical office-residence at Dominikanerbastei 10 in Vienna's fashionable Inner City (First) district. Like many affluent families of Jewish heritage, including the Freuds, the Adlers had decided to leave the ethnically dense and working-class Leopoldstadt area for more genteel surroundings. There were really only two choices for Jewish Viennese in business or the professions: either the Alsergrund (Ninth) district, where Freud had long dwelled, or the Inner City, enclosed by the elegant Ringstrasse.

The Adler family's new residence was a spacious, second-floor apartment on a main boulevard successfully defended centuries earlier against Turkish invaders. The quiet but central locale appealed to Adler, and he would make it his Viennese home for nearly twenty-five years. As poetically recalled by a frequent visitor, it was a neighborhood of "courtyards and sheltered alleys, and trellis-covered cafés. Here and there through a break in the houses flashed the shining roof of the Stephansdom. Medieval signs still swung in front of tradesmen's shops . . . [and] lamps still burned before age-old madonnas in dark stone niches. The old University, opposite the post-office, had long been out of use, but its ghosts still seemed part of the moonlight lingering upon its cobbled square and in the shelter of its ancient walls."

It was against this charming Old World backdrop that the Society for Free Psychoanalytic Study held its early meetings. Surviving minutes from sessions during the fall of 1912 and early 1913 reveal a broad range of topics, including "Clinical Observations on False Self-Accusation in Cases of Hysteria," "The Psychology of Pascal," "The Psychology of Fear," and "The Neurotic Life of the Individual." Unlike the sedate Martha Freud, whose sole function at the Vienna Psychoanalytic Society meetings was to serve coffee and cigars, Raissa Adler functioned as recording secretary for her husband's new group and often participated in discussions.

One evening in late November 1912, Stekel attended as a guest, and announced after hearing Kaus's lecture on neurosis that, "having listened in Freud's society to empty debates [on this topic]," he was "delighted to see such substantial and sensible work going on here." Although Stekel was already on the verge of breaking with Freud (who was now privately describing him as "an unbearable human being"), this cordial visit with the "enemy" camp could hardly have improved relations. Soon after, a caustic Freud characterized Stekel as one who had degenerated into a preacher "in the pay of Adlerism."

Not only in native Vienna, but throughout Europe as well, Adler was rapidly gaining supporters for his new group. After initiating correspondence, he received expressions of strong interest from medical colleagues in such countries as France, Germany, Serbia, and Russia. Among these were the Moscow psychiatrists I. A. Birstein and N. A. Vyrubov. The latter figure was editor of *Psikhoterapia,* a bimonthly periodical that had recently begun operating. During the year of 1912, Vyrubov eagerly published several of Adler's latest articles and book reviews, as well as information about his fledgling group's professional activities. Sensing an intellectual compatibility, Adler eventually joined *Psikhoterapia*'s editorial board, as did his Viennese associates Kaus, Stekel, and Wexberg.

With such growing professional commitment, in addition to his increasing clinical specialization in neurology-psychiatry, Adler was busier than ever in his life. Raissa, however, began feeling increasingly burdened by domestic demands involving the four children and rather stifled in her role as a "doctor's wife" in bourgeois Austria. In addition, Alfred's new Society for Free Psychoanalytic Study was growing to a size that could no longer be comfortably accommodated at Dominikanerbastei 10. When his group was therefore obliged to shift its meetings to various club rooms around Vienna, Raissa maintained much less regular involvement and felt herself steadily distanced from her husband's expanding career.

Nevertheless, Adler's children all seemed to have regarded him as a devoted father. "When we were growing up," later recalled Alexandra, "he was very busy. But he always spent time with us if we ached or cried. My little sister Nelly [Cornelia] would sometimes go to his office and bang on his door if something needed his attention at home. Then he would come out from his office, and go with her."

At mealtimes, the Adler children often had to share their gregarious father with friends visiting for lively discussion. "We children, who always joined the grown-ups at meals, were permitted to remain as long as we wished," Alexandra reminisced, "and we were encouraged by our parents to use our own judgment about when to leave and go to bed. The only condition was that we should be able to be in school on time the next morning. I remember our listening with rapt interest and disappearing, one by one, as sleep [overtook] us."

Alexandra also remembered her father as unequivocally opposed to physical punishment. "He would never, never hit us. My mother hit me only once, and I never forgave her. It was out in the country while he was at work. I didn't dare to tell him about it, but perhaps he knew already: He seemed very disturbed about something that day."

Of the four children, both Alexandra and Kurt later became psychiatrists, and Valentine, the oldest, received a doctorate in sociology; only Cornelia would opt for a nonacademic vocation as a stage actress. Nevertheless, their prolific father was never insistent upon dictating their career choices; nor was he domineering in his intellectual expectations for them. When the Adler family moved to the more affluent Inner City District, however, the shift to a more challenging school initially proved frustrating for ten-year-old Alexandra. "I found at once that I was having difficulty with mathematics. I actually skipped the first test and went home because I felt I couldn't do it. My father said, 'What is it? Do you really think those stupid things that anyone else can do, *you* can't do? If you try, you can do all of it.'"

After receiving such encouragement, Alexandra recollected that, "In a very short time, I became the best in mathematics. My teacher told me, 'You see, Adler, if you try, you can do it.'"

Similarly, during the same period, Kurt recalled that he was experiencing problems in the second grade. "My father was not at all impressed with the teachers we had, although we went to a so-called progressive school." One day, Kurt's teacher insulted him in class about his ability. Upon aggrievedly relating the episode to his father that evening, the lad was startled to hear the unexpected reply: "Your teacher is an idiot." Decades later, Kurt would still smile in remembering how that pithy comment had bolstered his scholastic self-esteem.

━━━

In late March 1912, less than six months after breaking decisively from Freud's association, Adler's small group launched its own monograph series. Entitled "Papers of the Society for Free Psychoanalytic Study," these were intended to advance what Adler considered the budding field of psychology in a manner untainted by dogmatism about sexuality. During the ensuing few years, the monographs would range in topic from the clinical treatment of specific psychiatric disorders to literary analysis and philosophical speculation.

In introducing the series, Adler as editor explained that his goal was not only to improve understanding of human development and mental illness, but also of major principles dealing with morals and ethics, and the "spiritual life of artists, normal people, and those changed by illness." With obvious allusion to Freud, Adler concluded:

> The Society in whose name I publish these *Papers* should continue to be the developmental site of our science. The studies destined for publication are handled there in a communal effort. They will show that we do not contradict the value of other psychological viewpoints and directions. We do, however, claim the right to free ourselves of dogmas and to follow our own way. Everyone who understands the significance of our research orientation is invited to work with us.

━━━

The still-simmering question of whether Adler's approach differed substantively from Freud's would soon be laid to rest forever. In that same year of 1912, Adler's major work, *Ueber den nervosen Charakter* (first published in the United States as *The Neurotic Constitution* five years later), was issued and clearly established his approach as distinct from psychoanalysis. For the rest of Adler's evolving, twenty-five-year career as a thinker of international importance, this book would stand as seminal. Rather technically written in the original German, it has unfortunately never been well translated into English.

In several respects, *The Neurotic Constitution* embraced viewpoints long basic to Freud. First, it emphasized that our adult personality is shaped during early childhood and is thereafter relatively resistant to change. Second, it stressed that our inner world is not quite so hidden from others as we might like to believe; virtually all that we do, say, and even dream can reveal important clues to the knowledgeable about our innermost feelings and desires. Third, it insisted that much of our true personality is often unconscious to ourselves; and fourth, that it is possible to gain greater self-insight through the aid of a trained therapist.

All of these notions were central to Freudian psychology, and it is obvious that Adler was strongly influenced by his older colleague during their nine years together. But what made *The Neurotic Constitution* so different from Freud's system was its emphasis not on infantile sexuality as the key human force, but on our early sense of inferiority. In works like *The Interpretation of Dreams* and *The Psychopathology of Everyday Life,* Freud had depicted sexuality as secretly manifesting itself almost everywhere in daily human life: Our preference for certain foods, forms of art and literature, intimate social relationships, and even professional activities could all be traced to infantile libido.

For Adler, our overriding drive instead involved the struggle for mastery and power: in countless aspects of day-to-day living, we reveal this urge. If neurotic, we will express it indirectly, even sneakily, through an unconscious effort to manipulate others. For example, Adler insightfully described the *sick role* (the person who uses illness as a means of control or domination) as a common example of this tendency. He also indicated that habitual lateness (thereby keeping people dependently waiting) can be seen as a similar, unconscious ploy to dominate.

In *The Neurotic Constitution,* Adler sought to buttress his position with historical as well as literary examples drawn from such diverse sources as the Bible, the *Iliad,* the *Arabian Nights,* Gogol, Strindberg, and Tolstoy. He also cited approvingly some of Nietzsche's philosophical insights about human nature. Certainly, Adler emulated Nietzsche's belief in the importance of will or intentionality as a powerful force guiding individual and social life. Likewise, both thinkers regarded successful people as those who were fully able to express their creative, striving impulses rather than meekly submit to society's dictates. They also shared an aloofness toward religious involvement. Philosophically, therefore, Adler had already attracted to his fledgling group several ardent adherents of Nietzschian thought. Yet, as an idealistic socialist who had long been concerned for the working-class masses, Adler was definitely no Nietzschian exponent when it came to the philosopher's heaping of contempt on ordinary men and women as they pursued their everyday lives. Rather than sympathizing with Nietzsche's ideal of the "superman" unfettered by conventional ethics and religiosity, Adler tended to be mainstream in his social and sexual values.

The Neurotic Constitution was far more influenced by another German philosopher and a contemporary of Adler's: Hans Vaihinger. Born in 1852 to devout parents, he had attended the Theological College of the University of Tübingen and eventually become a philosophy professor at Halle. In 1876, at the age of twenty-four, he began writing a highly creative and innovative work about human life. Finally published in 1911 as *The Philosophy of "As If,"* it exerted a tremendous impact upon Adler's evolving approach. As Adler readily admitted, Vaihinger's intriguing ideas were immensely useful in helping to launch individual psychology as a distinct system of thought.

In particular, Adler embraced Vaihinger's viewpoint that *fictions* (nonrational ideas) rather than objective realities play a key role in our lives. For example, the religious beliefs in a personal God and human immortality have long enabled people to find purpose in a seemingly vast, indifferent cosmos. On a daily level, Vaihinger suggested, persons are guided by similar, unprovable fictions, such as the belief in unhindered free will.

Thus, in *The Neurotic Constitution,* Adler emphasized that during our childhood years we all develop unconscious beliefs or fictions regarding life. Among the most important of these is the outlook we develop concerning our early sense of inferiority. Calling the process *fictional finalism,* Adler insisted that each of us develops a particular life strategy, or life-plan, for effectively overcoming this painful sense of weakness and experiencing instead the satisfaction of mastery. The fictional goal for a particular youngster might be to attain a sense of accomplishment—what Adler termed *superiority*—through intellectual achievement in scholarship or science. The fictional goal for another child might entail gaining superiority through physical prowess as a great athlete. But during adulthood as well as childhood, he insisted, we are all steered unconsciously by such *guiding goals.* As Adler acknowledged later in his career, his own life aim had been to "conquer death" by becoming a physician, and it had originated during early childhood, when he had suffered from various medical ailments and then witnessed his little brother, Rudolf, succumb to diptheria.

━━━━

Immensely pleased with *The Neurotic Constitution,* Adler in July finally felt ready professionally to begin teaching at the University of Vienna Medical School. He submitted the new book, together with a formal application to its voting faculty, in order to receive permission to lecture as an unpaid instructor (*Privatdozent*). The position itself was relatively modest, but it was the essential first rung on the academic ladder leading to a coveted professorship at his alma mater. As Adler undoubtedly knew, competition was extremely intense even for such a modest faculty post, and without political connections, one was was hardly assured of rapid academic advancement. After gaining such a position in 1885 on the basis of his aphasic studies, Freud had patiently waited a dozen years before the medical school's committee recommended him for promotion to the next higher, and far more prestigious (but still unpaid), title of professor extraordinarius. Even then, it was only after Freud succeeded in pulling the right political strings that he actually received the academic appointment in 1901. Certainly, Adler at the age of forty-two must have hoped that his own academic rise would necessitate far less time than Freud's sixteen years: otherwise, he would be close to sixty before attaining professorship rank and status.

Although Adler was strongly hopeful of gaining a teaching position at the university, he was already active and well regarded in one of Vienna's most intellectually stimulating places: the Café Central. Regularly conversing with colleagues and friends there until long after midnight, it became Adler's favorite haunt after the Café Griensteidl was demolished. Raissa sometimes went there as well for a pleasant evening.

Situated on the fashionable Herrengasse near Stephansdom and the Ringstrasse, the Café Central was during the city's prewar years the essential meeting place for its artistic, intellectual, and literary avant-garde. Dimly lit and hazy with cigarette smoke, the large, crowded establishment had high ceilings and gray stone walls. The plentiful fare, served by unctuous waiters eager for lavish tips, included a variety of coffees, pastries, brandies, and other alcoholic drinks. Amply supplied, too, were a plethora of unusual magazines and newspapers for browsing. At the height of the Café Central's prewar reputation, patrons could choose from among two hundred different Austrian and foreign publications listed in a special catalog.

Among the Central's nightly habitués were Adler's longtime friend and now magazine publisher Franz Blei, the Hungarian writer Egon Kisch, the journalist Egon Friedell, the cocaine-addicted anarchist-psychoanalyst Otto Gross, and writers Peter Altenberg, Robert Musil, Alfred Polgar, and Franz Werfel. The Central also regularly drew Austria's leading socialist thinkers, including Otto Bauer, Rudolf Hilferding, and Karl Renner; in later years, all would wield considerable political power. At least every Saturday evening, they would gather to debate Marxist theory and plan strategies for overthrowing capitalism through parliamentary means. Historian Helmut Gruber has commented that, "It is here, in the special ambience of the Viennese *Kaffeehaus*, that the Austromarxists are alleged to have developed their remarkable ability to harmonize and reconcile inconsistencies: to be well integrated in society and zealously to repudiate it in word and print."

Often, Bauer and his fellow Social Democratic leaders were joined for coffee or schnapps by Russian emigré revolutionaries, for the two groups were on friendly terms during these years before the Bolsheviks initiated terrorism as a tactic against their opponents. Among those regularly meeting with the Austromarxists were Adler's former patient Joffe and his *Pravda* boss Trotsky, who would later recall that, "They were well-educated people, and their knowledge of various subjects was superior to mine. I listened to them with intense and, one might almost say, respectful interest in the Café Central."

Like Adler, Trotsky enjoyed the Café Central as an incomparable institution of Viennese life, exotically serving as home, office, and restaurant. When Count Leopold von Berchtold, the Austro-Hungarian foreign minister from 1912 to 1915, was told that a Communist revolution might erupt in czarist Russia, he exclaimed with an incredulous guffaw, "And who, if you please, will make that revolution? Mr. Bronstein [Trotsky] who is playing chess at the Central all the time?" But the Café's famous headwaiter, Josef, is reported to have shown no surprise upon hearing the news in 1917 that the Russian revolution had broken out and that Trotsky was among its leaders. "I always knew that Herr Doktor Bronstein would go far in life," quipped Josef, "but I shouldn't have thought that he might leave without paying for the four coffees he owes me."

Adler enjoyed playing chess as a minor hobby, and may have sparred occasionally with Trotsky. But he was finding himself busier than ever in advancing a new psychological system that was becoming increasingly divergent from the Freudian. Besides speaking at prestigious gatherings such as the International Congress of Medical Psychology and Psychotherapy, Adler in 1913 published several important articles that further demarked his approach. These included "On The Role of the Unconscious in the Neurosis," "New Principles for the Practice of Individual Psychology," and especially, "Individual-Psychological Treatment of the Neuroses."

In these papers, Adler repeatedly emphasized that emotional difficulties in adulthood can nearly always be traced to a faulty life-plan formulated in the preschool years. "It is during this period, from hints thrown out by our makeup, and from the nature of the social environment, that we should look for the first tentative attempts leading subsequently to the ever-impelling goal of superiority," he observed. For this reason, "the most important element in therapeutics is the disclosure of the neurotic's system or life-plan." Once the therapist fully comprehends this plan, the goal is then to help the patient become as conscious of it as possible. To accomplish this, Adler decisively rejected Freud's inviolate technique of requesting the patient to lie down on a couch and "free associate" aloud to an utterly passive, silent, and even unseen therapist. Rather, emphasized Adler, "the uncovering of the life-plan proceeds apace in [face-to-face] friendly and free conversation . . . [with the patient while] always [pointing out] his disturbing 'arrangements' and constructions."

Increasingly articulating such innovative notions, Adler decided that year to disassociate his group completely from psychoanalysis and change its name to the Society for Individual Psychology. It was a logical development from the Adlerians' perspective, and one that Freud found gratifying: At last, he hoped, the public would understand that the respective approaches offered quite different conceptions and techniques concerning the human mind.

In the winter of 1914, Adler's third book, with Furtmüller as coeditor, was published. *Heilen und Bilden* (To Heal and To Educate) was an anthology of articles the two had written during the past decade. The contributors to the interdisciplinary work encompassing psychology, medicine, and education included several other persons who had been active with the Society for Individual Psychology. All but one of Adler's own sixteen papers had appeared before, and some dated back a decade. But the new volume possessed the important virtue of bringing these together in one place for the first time.

During the same productive winter of 1914, Adler and his colleagues succeeded in launching the first issue of their new *Journal for Individual Psychology* (*Zeitschrift für Individualpsychologie*). Adler served as editor in chief and entrusted the key position of managing editor to Furtmüller, whose literary skills were well suited to the demanding task. In the quarterly journal's premier issue, he both explained and defended its important title:

> The name of Individual Psychology intends to express the conviction that psychological processes and their manifestations can be understood only from the individual context and that all psychological insight begins with the individual.
>
> We certainly know that a thorough understanding of an isolated individual case is impossible. But this must not deter us from viewing the expressions of a

personality in their appropriate historical context. In each case, we must ask . . . 'Whence?' and, most importantly, 'Whither?' Personality is not revealed in its totality to the questioner; we are pressed to work more and more with personality-*models*. Precisely because of this situation, we are insured against being stuck in the study of the isolated case, and can progress to generalize laws of behavior governing human inner life.

Writing in the same preface, Furtmüller hoped that the new approach might prove beneficial for the fields of psychological theory, psychotherapy, and education. Sounding the rallying cry for all potential supporters, he declared:

> We do not aim at a one-sided dependency, but at equal exchange and reciprocal support. . . . This journal will give individual psychological research a focal point and an organ for discussion. It will also try to nourish interest in individual psychology in those scientific circles that are not yet associated with it. Our group of permanent co-workers would therefore be only too happy to admit new members to its circle.

Undoubtedly, the most prominent American thinker to heed the call was Professor G. Stanley Hall of Clark University. Since William James's death a few years before, Hall, at the age of seventy, was probably the country's leading and most influential psychologist. In the half decade that had elapsed since Hall had hosted Freud's visit in the fall of 1909, relations between the two men had been cordial. But Hall, an independent thinker, had become increasingly attracted to Adler's evolving system in place of psychoanalysis, and had recently begun planning to sponsor him for an American lecture series.

Thus, in an article on fear published during April, Hall praised Adler's conception of compensation as a "key" insight "for both abnormal and normal psychology." Explicitly rejecting Freud's emphasis on sexuality as the driving force of personality, Hall insisted rather that, "Sex anxieties are themselves only symbols of this deeper sense of abatement of the will to live, to be powerful. . . . Sex anxieties are only parables . . . of a larger general law."

During the same month, Hall eagerly initiated correspondence with Adler, and praised his new anthology, *Heilen und Bilden,* as a work that Clark University's graduate students were finding quite stimulating. "To my mind, there is very much in it that bears upon normal psychology, and it has suggested to me what I believe is a new theory of attention." Hall then requested Adler's opinion on several specific points raised in the new book, including the personality traits of only children and women's reactions to midlife aging. Responding in early May, Adler delightedly sent Hall additional articles, as well as the new *Journal for Individual Psychology*. In the accompanying detailed letter, he commented that, "Your sustained interest in our work does us great honor. I believe indeed that I can agree with you: our Individual Psychology is really a philosophy and psychology of attention and . . . interests. . . . The cooperation of your school would be a significant advancement for us."

Not all were pleased by the growing international appeal of Adler's psychological approach. Back in Vienna, Freud was disgusted to learn that his nemesis might actually gain the prestige of lecturing at Clark University, and sarcastically wrote Ferenczi that, "Presumably, the object [for Hall] is to save the world from sexuality and base it on aggression." Nearly three years after their bitter break, Freud was adamant that Adler represented an utterly regressive and destructive influence upon modern psychology. Indeed, during the spring, Freud was vigorously at work on a monograph that would powerfully and decisively express this viewpoint. In letters to supporters, he joyfully referred to the work in progress as his "bomb" directed against both Adler and Jung. The iconoclastic Swiss psychiatrist had also finally broken with Freud for his same relentless stress on sexuality as the fundamental force in human personality.

Completed quickly by Freud in mid-July, *The History of the Psychoanalytic Movement* was not intended as a conciliatory work. Nor was it very objective or even attentive to important detail from any reasonable historian's viewpoint. But then its highly motivated author was hardly writing a dispassionate account of long-past events. He regarded himself as recounting a momentous and ongoing struggle of which he was the prime figure—a struggle that permitted no compromise, sentimentality, or nostalgia.

Thus, Freud failed even to mention his initial invitational postcards in the fall of 1902 to Adler, Kahane, Reitler, and Stekel, but paternalistically described the Wednesday Psychological Society's creation twelve years earlier as involving several physicians who "gathered around me with the expressed intention of learning, practicing, and spreading psychoanalysis." No longer tolerant of Stekel's divergent viewpoint either, Freud refused even to mention his name in relating how "a colleague who had himself experienced the benefits of the analytic therapy" had provided the impetus for the society's founding.

Devoting several ensuing pages in the volume specifically to his key rival, Freud remarked that, "I had the opportunity of studying Dr. Adler many years and have never denied him the testimonial of having a superior mind, especially endowed speculatively." But he then ridiculed Adler as a pathetically ambitious figure who had once lamented to Freud, "Do you believe that it is such a pleasure for me to stand in your shadow my whole life?"

On the value of Adler's school of individual psychology, Freud was unremittingly hostile. He branded it as "radically false" and insisted that it had failed to contribute even "a single new observation" to science. Either deliberately misrepresenting individual psychology, or else revealing his own ignorance of Adler's evolving approach since he had left the Vienna Psychoanalytic Society, Freud declared:

> The view of life which one obtains from Adler's system is founded entirely upon the impulse of aggression. It leaves no room at all for love. One might wonder that such a cheerless aspect of life should have received any notice whatever; but we must not forget that humanity, oppressed by its sexual needs, is prepared to accept anything, if only the "overcoming of sexuality" is held out as bait.

In essence, Freud was still bitterly pronouncing the same prediction he had made after hearing Adler's lectures in the winter of 1911 before the Vienna Psychoanalytic Society: that by offering a competing and nonsexual view of human nature, he would gain many eager adherents. Dismissing Adler's basic concepts as unredeemably simplistic and mistaken, Freud with characteristic sarcasm concluded that, "these [scientific criticisms] "have not prevented Adler's own followers from hailing him as the Messiah, for whose appearance waiting humanity had been prepared by . . . so many forerunners."

Freud's exponents would soon adopt *The History of the Psychoanalytic Movement* as their official stance toward Adler. For the rest of his life in Austria and later the United States, nothing Adler would do or say would significantly alter their perception of him as a distastefully ambitious man who had constructed a false psychological system of human nature based on aggression rather than sexual love.

But psychiatric thinkers and their supporters were not the only ones in the Austro-Hungarian Empire planning battle that summer. Following the assassination of military commander Archduke Francis Ferdinand and his wife, Sophie, in the provincial capital of Sarajevo in Bosnia-Herzegovina, Europe's nations were rapidly escalating charges, demands, and threats against one another. Soon the clashing field of psychology would be subsumed by a far bloodier war that would irrevocably change Adler's own life and subsequent career.

CHAPTER SEVEN

The Great War

*I felt throughout the war
as a prisoner feels.*

ALFRED ADLER

T he early summer of 1914 was a season of dazzling beauty throughout Europe, or so it seemed to millions in retrospect. Certainly,
few could have imagined the swift series of events that unfolded after the assassinations at Sarajevo on June 28. Although its own investigatory
commission two weeks later could find no evidence that Serbia's provincial
regime had shared complicity in the terrorist act, the Austro-Hungarian
government decided otherwise. On July 23, it presented the Serbians with
a ten-point ultimatum to prevent and eliminate all nationalistic challenges
to the Dual Monarchy's sovereignty over the Balkan region. Much to the
surprise of many, Serbia agreed to all but one of the demands; but eager
for a potent retaliation, or "punitive expedition" as many Austrians called
it, the empire declared war on Serbia on July 28, and began shelling its
capital, Belgrade, the same day. Within the week, all of Europe's major powers with the exception of Italy were at war: Germany joined with Austro-
Hungary against England, France, and Russia.

The scale of military movement was historically unprecedented. Across
Europe, approximately six million men received orders in early August and
began mobilizing for active duty. Within Vienna as most elsewhere, the
popular mood was almost euphoric with patriotic excitement. The spirit
engulfed many intellectuals like Freud, who confided to a colleague that,
"for the first time in thirty years, I feel myself to be an Austrian and feel like

giving this not very hopeful Empire another chance." Except for the fact that England seemed to be "on the wrong side," Freud gleefully related, "All my libido is given to Austro-Hungary." Even the Social Democrats, long opposed to Emperor Franz Joseph's regime as imperialist, immediately supported the war once he pronounced his declaration. Several of its leaders volunteered for military service, and Friedrich Austerlitz, editor of the Social Democratic newspaper, *Arbeiter-Zeitung*, wrote jingoistic editorials. Austria's Social Democrats were not unique in this regard; virtually all their socialist counterparts throughout Europe abruptly abandoned their internationalist slogans and ardently worked for national victory.

But not so Alfred Adler. Perhaps it was because he took his socialist idealism more seriously than party leaders; possibly, it was because his wife was Russian and therefore a potential "enemy" citizen of the Austro-Hungarian Empire. In any event, shortly after the Sarajevo assassinations were publicized, Adler had an ominous intuition that a long, disastrous war was in the making and would greatly affect civilians as well.

Having completed required military service in December 1912, Adler felt in no personal danger of conscription. But he did have a pressing problem: In the late spring, Raissa and their four children had left to spend a long vacation with her wealthy relatives in Smolensk, Russia. Although she had vacationed in Russia before, her current visit marked their longest separation in fifteen years of marriage, and he was lonely. Others in Vienna seemed to have felt Raissa's absence as well. In a letter penned in late June, a half-dozen friends jointly wrote: "Dear Mrs. Adler, we are all here in the Café Dom and miss you very much. Hope you are enjoying yourself in Russia and that you and the children are well."

As Raissa's own letters revealed, all were indeed relaxed and happy, especially with frequent outings into the countryside. A photo-postcard she sent Alfred shows the five of them warmly posed together, peering out a rustic cottage doorway, and smiling broadly into the camera.

But sensing the likelihood of a major war, Adler knew that such idyllic moments were illusory. As international tensions began mounting during July, he telegrammed Raissa to bring the family home immediately. Failing to see the urgency, Raissa viewed her husband's request as unreasonable, and telegrammed back: "Shall wait." Seemingly overnight, though, Austro-Hungary and Russia had became mortal enemies, and her precious family was trapped far from home. "It was initially a harrowing experience, and my mother especially felt very endangered," later recalled Kurt.

True to his striving temperament, Adler did not wait passively for events to unfold. Enlisting the help of a Vatican prelate (a former patient) preparing to leave Vienna, together they boarded a train for Rome. It was Adler's plan to contact Raissa from the capital city, since Italy was still officially neutral in the raging war between Russia and Austro-Hungary. During the harrowing trip, the train suddenly stopped in the mountainous region of the Dolomites. It was the middle of the night, and the conductor slowly made his way while carrying a lantern. "What's the matter?" the prelate worriedly asked him.

"I don't know," was the conductor's honest reply.

"So at least bring me a glass of water!" demanded the prelate. For Adler, who later recounted the episode to his family when all were safely back in Austria, the priest's incongruous request revealed with unwitting humor a psychological axiom: that people almost always need to feel some sense of control over external events.

Fortunately, the remainder of the train ride proved uneventful for Adler. After reaching Rome, he attempted to initiate negotiations with Russian officials to effect his family's release. But Raissa played the instrumental role. She managed to gain an audience with the Czar, and surrounded by a cordon of armed police, declared herself a loyal Russian citizen who had been forced to marry Adler and bear his children. The Czar thereupon granted her return to enemy Austria. After a tense train ride to Finland, she and the four children secured ship's passage to Sweden, and from there, traveled to Germany and then back home to Vienna in December 1914. As Kurt later reminisced, "These were exciting and educational days. To see the caricatures of Kaiser Wilhelm and Kaiser Franz Joseph and all the stories about their ridiculousness, and then to come back to Vienna and see the caricatures of the Czar, King George, and the French Prime Minister [offered us] a good lesson not to believe anything just because authorities stated it."

Nevertheless, the unremitting war with its tremendous casualties on all sides made life very uneasy for the Adlers. Politically, Alfred and Raissa had long been internationalist and socialist; privately, they also sympathized more with the Allied democracies of England and France than with the monarchist regimes of Germany and Austro-Hungary. To complicate matters considerably, however, Raissa's native Russia was ruled by a reactionary czarist regime that she and her revolutionary friends like Trotsky despised.

As for individual psychology, the fledgling movement had quickly fallen into abeyance after war erupted. Many of Adler's most active associates were drafted into military service, including his close friend and coeditor Furtmüller. Their lively weekly meetings ended; organized activity on the monograph series and journal was reduced to almost nothing. Adler recruited physician Charlotte Strasser to serve as the journal's third coeditor, but after August 1914, only one more quarterly issue would be published for over two years.

━━━━━

It was in January 1915 when Adler finally received the long-awaited decision of the University of Vienna Medical School committee regarding his application to lecture as an unpaid instructor. Nearly two and a half years had elapsed since he had proudly submitted *The Neurotic Constitution* as evidence of his professional expertise. It is not clear why so much time was involved, but administrative matters at the university were never known for their alacrity. Unfortunately for Adler, the twenty-page report could not have offered worse news: an unequivocally negative response. Its author was the fifty-seven-year-old Julius von Wagner-Jauregg, well-respected head of the neurology department that also included psychiatry and psychotherapy. Although the two men were hardly friends, they were not complete strangers: In the small world of Viennese medicine, Wagner-Jauregg had presided over Adler's third *Rigorosum* (qualifying examination) twenty years earlier, in 1895, as well as the ceremony awarding his medical degree.

Wagner-Jauregg began his report by remarking that Adler's application marked the first time that a member of the "psychoanalytic school" had applied for *Dozentur,* and that a thorough evaluation was therefore appropriate. He then provided a rather terse description of Adler's academic achievements: "According to him, he was active during the four years following his medical degree in the Vienna General Hospital and in the Poliklinik in the fields of psychiatry, internal medicine, and opthamology, in which institutes and in which position is not said." Perhaps this somewhat flippant phrasing suggests that Wagner-Jauregg was not altogether convinced of the veracity of Adler's references.

Immediately after that, Wagner-Jauregg declared that Adler's extensive writing was marked by a consistent failure to offer empirical evidence. He explained that all other candidates for the *Privatdozent* position had presented quantifiable data as part of their research in such specialties as anatomy, histology, experimental physiology of the nervous system, and clinical investigation into the nature of nervous diseases; Adler's writings provided nothing scientific of this kind, however, only "explanations of a purely speculative nature." In this sense, Wagner-Jauregg accurately observed, "Adler has remained faithful to the school of Freud in method, although not in substance; actually, with regard to the latter, he has completely renounced it."

Wagner-Jauregg conceded that the notion of organ inferiority as a factor in the etiology of neurosis was "interesting and reasonable." But he criticized the concept as too vague, since it included entire physiological systems, like the digestive or cardiovascular, and not merely specific impaired organs.

The Neurotic Constitution prompted an even harsher assessment from Wagner-Jauregg. Acknowledging its basic theories of fictious life aims, masculine protest, and the sense of inferiority as intellectually "ingenious," he nevertheless condemned the work as lacking supportive validation. To Wagner-Jauregg, Adler's approach was rooted in intuition and conviction; it therefore contained fanciful elements "as grotesque" as Freud's.

Clearly, Wagner-Jauregg held animosity toward psychoanalysis as a purportedly scientific system and had little respect for its founder, his junior colleague at the university. In attacking Adler's work so vehemently, he was probably interested in driving away other potential faculty applicants who similarly espoused a humanistic orientation in personality study and psychotherapy. In this regard, not all of his criticism of *The Neurotic Constitution* was even aimed specifically at Adler; vaster quarry, including those allied with Freud, was his goal.

Labeling *The Neurotic Constitution* as an unacceptable work of psychoanalysis, Wagner-Jauregg rhetorically asked, "Is it desirable that Adler teach at the Medical School? Since it is to be assumed that [he] will never teach anything else, my answer must therefore be a definite *no*." Following this damning appraisal, the faculty committee of twenty-five repudiated Adler's candidature unanimously.

The rejection came as an emotionally crushing blow for Adler, who at the age of forty-five must have fully realized that his dream of a professorship at the university was now gone forever. The report's harsh and decisive tone, coupled with the faculty's unanimous agreement, made it virtually impossible that he would ever be reconsidered for a position at Austria's most prestigious educational institution. The faculty's vote was doubly humiliating, since his rival Freud had enjoyed a professor's status there for nearly fifteen years.

At the time, some of Adler's friends felt that his ardent socialism was the actual reason for the rejection. This supposition seems rather unlikely, however, especially since an even more prominent Social Democrat, anatomist Julius Tandler, had already held a faculty appointment for twelve years.

Conservative-minded colleagues might certainly have viewed Adler's politically tinged articles with disdain, but their chief objection was probably just what Wagner-Jauregg had stated: that *A Study of Organ Inferiority* and *The Neurotic Constitution* were unacceptably speculative and ungrounded in conventional medical research.

Indeed, decades later, Vienna medical school psychiatrist Otto Pötzl explicitly commented that, "Had Freud brought us *The Interpretation of Dreams* as a thesis, I am quite sure we should have refused him his Professorship upon it, in precisely the same manner that we refused Adler his, for *The Neurotic Constitution*. Psychology was, and still is in our academic circles, not considered to be a science in itself; nor should it be given a philosophical handling such as Adler's [second book] presented. Freud received his professorship from a specialized thesis upon aphasia."

Support for Pötzl's recollection can be indirectly found through another historical source; for in 1914, the Russian journal *Psikhoterapia,* on which Adler was serving as a contributing editor had similarly criticized the absence of empirical data in his intriguing writings: "People sometimes say that Adler's theory of guiding ideas is philosophical, not psychological. And that is true. [His] teachings might be termed a Philosophy of the Ego."

═══════

If Adler was badly upset by the university's rejection of his accomplishments, he had little chance for further achievement in the immediate future. The Austro-Hungarian Empire was beginning to suffer serious losses against the Allies (Italy had joined England, France, and Russia in May 1915) and although the United States under President Woodrow Wilson was still two years away from military intervention, Austrians increasingly viewed the "war of attrition" (as it had come to be called) as an unmitigated disaster. Amidst the mounting, staggering casualties in the trenches, few could recall their country's initial euphoria about entering the battle against Serbia and its blustering supporters. But like every major European combatant, Austro-Hungary was unwilling to end the slaughter: For its elder statesmen to seek peace talks would be tantamount to admitting that tens, even hundreds of thousands of brave soldiers had died in vain. And so the war ground on.

Austria's own military regulations were revised so that many men previously exempted from service could be mobilized. Among these was Adler, who in 1916 was drafted as an army physician and initially sent to work in the neuropsychiatric department of the military hospital in the mountain-

ous village of Semmering, some fifty miles southwest of Vienna. With a resigned attitude about participating in such military work, he closed his
private practice after entrusting ongoing cases to collegial members of the
Society for Individual Psychology. These included twenty-six-year-old psychiatrist Erwin Krausz, who was surprised and gratified by Adler's confidence in his ability.

As virtually all medical participants would later recall, conditions in Austria's military hospitals were appalling. Similar to their counterparts elsewhere in Europe, these institutions were dominated by one primary goal:
to treat physically or mentally wounded soldiers so that they could be returned to the battlefield as quickly as possible. For those anguished young
men with broken or missing limbs, army physicians generally had a clear
path to follow: some injuries were obviously minor and others were completely incompatible with combat duty. But for soldiers exhibiting psychiatric symptoms, the matter was far more muddled: How to determine who
was truly disabled emotionally and who was only malingering? And what was
the most effective approach for restoring soldiers' normal psychiatric capacity for combat activity?

Long before Adler arrived in Semmering, his fellow army psychiatrists
throughout Central Europe had already established the key issue: convincing their hospitalized patients that it would be less painful to perform their
patriotic duty in the trenches than to maintain their symptoms of anxiety,
confusion, and fear. To accomplish this task, military physicians experi-
mented with a variety of shock "treatments," including subjecting patients
to repeated cold showers, performing mock surgery upon them, and lock-
ing them naked in isolation chambers for extended periods of time.

Perhaps the most common technique was to employ sudden, acute electrical shock. It was originated by German psychiatrist Fritz Kaufmann, who
emphasized in 1916 that, "Success can only be achieved through inexo-
rable obstinancy in the execution of the treatment." As psychoanalyst Max
Nonne observed at the time, the choice of a specific method was not so
much a medical issue as one of the physician's personal taste. All such techniques were intended to make the patient feel completely powerless and
therefore submissive about returning to the battlefield. But despite the violence of these "therapeutic" methods, they rarely succeeded. Most psychi-
atrically hospitalized soldiers never recovered sufficiently for combat, and
at best were fit only for reserve, garrison chores.

In Stekel's postwar autobiography, he recalled having served in the same
military hospital at Semmering shortly after Adler's tour of duty there, and

found that his longtime colleague had done excellent work, that his examinations had been thorough and his case histories faultless. Stekel expressed disgust for other physicians there, however, "who, as slave-drivers for the war mongers, forced half-recovered soldiers to go back to the trenches. . . . Convalescents, still in pain, their wounds unhealed, were marched off to their regiments. In many hospitals, they were tortured with a faradic [electrical] brush, so that they preferred the terrors of war to the terrors of the hospital. Each week, the chief of the hospital, a major and former dentist, came into the ward and shouted, "We must evacuate! Send fifty percent of the patients away! A new transport is coming!"

It is hard to imagine how Adler could have been intellectually inspired by such an atmosphere, but he did find occasion to discover something new about the human personality. While making nightly rounds of the neuro-psychiatric ward, he eventually noticed a fascinating link between the soldiers' sleeping positions and their waking personalities. For instance, those who slept in a tight fetal position were usually more frightened in daytime interactions; others who slept with outstretched arms seemed to need greater nurturance. After the war, Adler would frequently discuss this previously unreported aspect of expressive behavior:

> By comparing the sleeping postures of patients in various hospitals with the reports of their daily life, I have concluded that the mental attitude is consistently expressed in both modes of life, sleeping and waking. . . . If an adult is accustomed to sleep in a certain position and suddenly changes it, we may assume that something is altered in his mental attitude. . . . All sleep postures have a purposive nature. Restless sleepers, who keep moving at night, show that they are dissatisfied and want to be doing something more than they are. . . . The quietest sleepers are those who are most settled in their attitude toward the problems of life. Their lives being well organized by day, they can use the night for its proper purpose of rest.

Adler found such observations interesting and further validation for his notion that one's personality can always be discerned through subtle gestures and movements. But he knew that psychological theory was only incidental to his real purpose at Semmering's military hospital: curing emotionally stricken soldiers sufficiently so that they could be returned to combat in a senseless, protracted conflict. Two years later, while the war still raged, he would curtly write that, "The treatment of neuroses among the civil population in times of peace had as its unexpressed but self-evident object the patient's cure or at least freeing him of his symptoms so that he might be able to find himself again and pursue a course of life dictated by himself. Military neurology had as its object naturally enough not the desire to cure a man for his own sake, but for the sake and the advantage of the army and the 'state.'"

Refusing to regard his military service as a patriotic virtue, Adler soon began feeling personally responsible for sending his young patients to their potential deaths. He found especially unnerving, even traumatizing, the necessity for making selections among them for renewed battlefield participation. Such painful decisions were antithetical to his idealistic nature and two decades of medical work devoted to safeguarding human life. Years later, Adler would remember long, sleepless nights in which he agonized over his role in prolonging the endless suffering. But he seems to have kept such unpopular sentiments to himself, and by early 1917, had gained reassignment to a far more appealing setting: Austria's Garrison Hospital Number 15 in Cracow, Poland.

For a common army physician like Adler, lacking military rank, to have gained such a comfortable position in a university town was rather unusual, and suggests that he may have benefitted from a high political connection; among his patients was the wife of a leading Austrian general, who may have intervened. Little information has survived about Adler's activities at Cracow, however. It is known that in November 1916, he lectured army physicians there on "war neurosis." His numerous postcards (probably censored) to family members merely expressed chatty solicitude about their health and well-being in the midst of massive food shortages. On at least one memorable occasion, he managed to send them a large canister of honey. In mid-July, Adler penned a more elaborate, fatherly letter congratulating his oldest child Valentine upon her graduation from the University of Vienna:

> Your telegram reached me at the hotel yesterday evening. How I wish I could have been with you, laughed and sung with you, and helped you make jolly plans for the summer and for the more distant future.
>
> But we'll make up for it—sometime—somehow!
>
> Now you are entirely free and you must build your own life in your own way.
>
> There are no more special rules and regulations to restrict you, and there are many paths that are worthwhile for you to follow.
>
> It is not, you know, ever a question of what you choose to do, but how you do what you have chosen, and the level that you have set yourself to reach. . . . Now you have to deal with the demands of your own ideals, which you must not misuse by turning them into excuses and pretexts in order to evade realities . . . . Try also to acquire a really good relationship with our dear Ali [Alexandra] and with our boy, for you *can* do this.

Some time between August and November 1917, Adler was transferred once again, this time to Vienna's northern, vine-laden district of Grinzing, where he was apparently responsible for treating soldiers stricken with typhus.

By now, Adler had been devoting considerable thought to the psychological causes of war. Impelled to new theorizing by the destruction he had witnessed, he clearly saw no answer in conventional religion. Adler had been an agnostic since his youth, and now certainly saw no evidence of divine intercession as Europe's battlefields continued to fill with the corpses of young men.

Nor did modernist philosophy provide Adler with any satisfying answers. Though he had long admired Nietzsche's bold emphasis on individual will as the highest value, it now seemed indisputable that what civilization needed was not more individualism but more *social feeling:* compassion, altruism, and selflessness. Such qualities, of course, were deemed ethical; but they were ultimately psychologically rooted, Adler was sure. Drawing upon his earlier work, he became convinced that so many people lack this vital cluster of traits because they feel inferior and inadequate. In contrast, emotionally healthy people possess social feeling in strong measure and are also able to encourage it in others. If men and women, and particularly children—who had most of their lives still ahead of them—could overcome their sense of inferiority, then they could truly begin helping others. It was up to science and not religion, specifically, the modern science of psychology, to seize the initiative and foster this key personality trait throughout the world.

During military leave, upon visiting friends at the familiar, high-ceilinged Café Central on the Herrengasse, Adler first revealed his new concept; it would appear in print the following year. With Austria in the throes of war and suffering from severe food shortages, the famous coffeehouse had a very different, subdued atmosphere. All the Russians expatriates like Trotsky, Joffe, and Skobelev were now gone and actively involved in the October revolution. Initially, Adler seemed the same jovial figure to his friends: portly with twinkling eyes, pince-nez, and an easy smile. But to their uneasy suprise, he now began zealously promoting the importance of social or community feeling (*Gemeinschaftsgefühl*). In German, the term carried an ethical, almost religious connotation that seemed at odds with the iconoclastic physician they had long known.

It would not be many months before several members of the Society for Individual Psychology, including such Nietzschians as E. Froeschel and Paul

Schrecker, would therefore resign, more in disgust than in anger. As one dissenting colleague later reminisced, "This sudden missionary idea of *Gemeinschaftsgefühl,* how could we deal with it? The medical profession must keep its science above the crowd. Adler should, as a scientist, have known this, and he should have known that if he insisted on spreading this sort of religious science through the laity, we as a profession could not support him."

As Adler began to speak in 1917 about the trait of social feeling as the latest underpinning of individual psychology, he undoubtedly felt buoyed by the growing international respect for his work. During that year, *A Study of Organ Inferiority* was finally translated (after a decade) into English by Smith Ely Jellife, a distinguished New York neurologist and friend of William Alanson White; the two men had met while working at the Binghamton State Hospital in upstate New York. Jellife and White had founded the *Journal of Nervous and Mental Diseases* in 1902 and *The Psychoanalytic Review* in 1913. It was White who wrote the introduction to the American edition of *The Neurotic Constitution,* cotranslated by psychiatrists Bernard Glueck and John Lind, and likewise published in 1917. With his two major works now available to English-speaking professionals for the first time, Adler must have gained a badly needed jolt of esteem since his humiliating rejection by the Vienna medical faculty two years earlier.

It seems that Adler spent much of the ensuing year in Switzerland, possibly involved in transporting sick or wounded prisoners. Such military work seems to have left him considerable time for new professional endeavors, and he finally resumed the prolific output that had marked his recent career before the war. Adler had published nothing new in 1915, and only three new pieces in the next two years. The *Journal for Individual Psychology,* which he edited, had issued only one volume by late 1916. But the year 1918 witnessed the appearance of six new articles, including those on such wide-ranging topics as war neurosis, obsessive-compulsive disorders, the life of Dostoyevski, and individual-psychology education.

Published in January of that year, Adler's paper on war neurosis criticized governmental policy for subverting "medical ideas and purely medical considerations" into serving military goals. But he espoused no pacifist or anti-conscription stance, and instead, attributed war neuroses to those men who already possessed emotional difficulties. "The enormous amount of data gathered by the Cracow *Nervenzentrale* [Neurological Center] gives the same result . . . clear-cut and easily discernible cases of war neurosis are relatively rare among officers. This seems to indicate that only wavering natures and those exhibiting timidity when faced by their social obligations, become afflicted with neurosis."

Thus, Adler contended that psychiatric combat disorders offered new evidence for his view that "behind every neurosis [is] the existence of a weakling whose incapacity for adapting himself to the ideas of the majority calls forth an aggressive attitude taking on a neurotic form."

More significant as a marker of Adler's evolving approach that year was his lecture in November before a Zurich association of neurologists. In discussing treatment of what today we would call *obsessive-compulsive* disorders like repetitive handwashing, Adler stressed the importance of understanding the patient's total personality, and not simply focusing on the isolated symptom. "Attempts should be made to obtain information about him, to penetrate into his nature, his purpose in life and his attitude toward the demands of family and society. . . . The examination . . . should include [such] decisions in life [as] love, marriage, and the selection of a profession."

Adler also devoted specific attention to the importance of birth order in forming the obsessive-compulsive personality, specifically, growing up as the second-born son or as the only girl in a family of boys. In coming years, Adler's prescient ideas about birth order as a key determinant of adult personality would have considerable impact upon the field of psychology. As for effectively treating individuals with obsessive-compulsive difficulties, he explained that the key was to improve their social maturity: "If we were to put the question to the patient, '*What would you do if you were quite well?*' he would almost certainly name the particular [societal] demand . . . that it might be assumed he was trying to evade [by his symptoms]."

Much broader in scope, and far more revealing of Adler's own philosophical outlook by the war's close, was his lecture on a longtime favorite author: Fyodor Dostoyevski. Speaking in Zurich's architecturally renowned townhall, Adler admiringly described the nineteenth-century Russian author of *Crime and Punishment, The Brothers Karamazov,* and other acclaimed novels as having achieved a "great synthesis of uniting heroic life with love of neighbor." He also remarked approvingly that Dostoyevski had found "the richest fulfillment of human worth in the form of fellow-love" and summed up Dostoyevski's ultimate message in the precept that, "Man must look for his [inner] formula and he will find it in a willingness to help others, in a capacity for sacrificing himself for his people." Before long, Adler would become widely known throughout Europe and abroad for espousing this notion in psychological rather than literary terms.

"[Dostoyevski's] achievements as a psychologist have not yet been exhausted," Adler declared. "[He] must be hailed as our teacher even today, as the teacher Nietzsche hailed him to be. . . . His idea that no one acts or thinks without a goal or a final climax coincides with the most modern results of students of the psyche. . . . His creations, his ethic, and his art take us very far in an understanding of human cooperation."

There was a buoyant, almost strident optimism in Adler's presentation that would soon become his hallmark as a popular lecturer and writer. Perhaps he was joyfully anticipating the war's imminent end, for in the preceding months, Austro-Hungary's participation in the four-year-old conflagration had begun disintegrating at a quickening pace. In March, Adler's former acquaintances Trotsky and Joffe, now leaders of Russia's new Leninist government, had succeeded in removing their country from hostilities by signing the Treaty of Brest-Litovsk with Germany. But with the United States committing millions of troops to the European front, Russia's withdrawal had come too late for the Germans and their military collaborators. By the early fall, as defeat by the Allies' combined forces appeared certain, the Austro-Hungarian Empire had begun collapsing into an array of small independent nations, including Czechoslovakia and newly formed Yugoslavia. The end lay in sight.

It was against this political backdrop in November that Adler presented a speech on "Individual-Psychological education." Speaking before the Zurich Association of Physicians, he began by quoting the dictum of nineteenth-century German medical reformer Rudolph Virchow that, "Physicians will eventually become the educators of humanity." Adler particularly stressed the vital importance of training youngsters "so that they may become individuals actuated by ethical principles [and] the utilization of their virtues for the good of the community." Such a challenging task also belonged to parents and educators, Adler declared; but he praised physicians for their special expertise concerning human personality and development.

Expanding upon sentiments expressed in his prewar socialist articles, Adler emphasized that not only childhood illness and congenital weakness can cause emotional problems during adulthood, but so too can harmful influences in our early emotional-social environment. Thus, "a man whose childhood has been spent in a loveless atmosphere shows, even in old age, indication of this upbringing. He will always suspect that people desire to be unkind to him and he will shut himself off from others."

Then, expressing a theme that would soon catapult him to national and then international acclaim, Adler insisted that: "It is, of course, an extremely disagreeable task to pursue every individual who has gone wrong or who is afflicted with a neurotic illness or a psychosis. This would constitute a tremendous waste of energy, and it is about time that we turn our attention more definitely to prophylaxis. . . . We have constantly been trying to work toward the goal by educating both parents and physicians. . . . [But now we must] disseminate the ideals derived from [the insights of] . . . individual psychology, [and] then apply them so that all can aid us with their strength and in every possible manner."

This was an extremely optimistic pronouncement to a civilization torn by the greatest mass destruction of its history. But Adler was seized by the vision of promulgating his psychological system throughout the world. In this sense, he shared the revolutionary zeal of his wife, Raissa, and her Bolshevik friends, but he believed that true change could occur through psychology rather than violent political action.

On November 11, the "silence heard around the world" took place as Germany surrendered to the Allies. The fighting that had claimed over fifteen million military and civilian lives was over. The same day, Emperor Karl I abdicated his throne in Vienna, and the Austro-Hungarian Empire was no more. The first Austrian Republic was declared the next day. For a war-weary Adler, the time was finally at hand for tremendously expanding his dormant psychological movement.

CHAPTER EIGHT

A Psychological Revolutionary

*Artists, geniuses, thinkers, inventors,
discoverers: they are the real leaders of
humanity. They are the motive power
in the history of the world.*

ALFRED ADLER

W hen the republic of Austria was proclaimed on November 12, 1918," recalled novelist Manes Sperber, "everyone knew what was ending on that day but not what might be beginning. The Hapsburg Empire had crumbled some time previously, and the royal and imperial army had dissolved; no one was interested any longer in what it had fought for, against whom and for what reason. Stray remnants of regiments roamed the streets of the former capital . . . at times the soldiers resembled marauders who had lost their way or homeless beggars."

The aftermath of military defeat and the collapse of the Austro-Hungarian Empire devastated Austria. For centuries, Vienna had been the nexus of a sovereignty that, by the start of World War I, had come to number 54 million inhabitants. It was the second largest European power in territorial size and the third by population. Now Vienna was the oversized capital of an impoverished nation that would soon be reduced, by the Allies' imposed peace settlement, to only one eighth of its former geographical area. Almost a third of the shrunken country's entire population of 6.2 million were Viennese residents. To the mocking alpine provincials who had always distrusted the sophisticated capital, it had become an absurd, hydrocephalic head perched on a dwarf's body. To make matters worse, the former imperial city had long been located near the center of the Dual Monarchy; now it stood on the new Austria's eastern periphery, isolated geographically and culturally from its mountainous areas.

Almost overnight, once-glittering Vienna had become just another city in a minor country. Throughout Austria, a mood of gloom was pervasive. Re-entering from Switzerland immediately after the war, novelist Stefan Zweig recollected that, "Hardly was the train out of sight when we were obliged to change from the spruce, clean Swiss cars into the Austrian. One had but to enter them to become aware beforehand of what had happened to the country." The train guards were haggard and shabbily dressed; many looked half-starved. The trains themselves were filthy and dilapidated. Alongside tattered immigrants and weary soldiers returning from prisoner-of-war camps or the military front, local beggars were competing for alms.

After four years, international peace reigned in Europe, but it brought no economic benefit to Austria. An intense famine gripped the country and was especially pernicious in Vienna, where residents depended on outside sources for food. "The famine was unrelieved and people froze in the wet cold," recalled Sperber. "There was a shortage of everything. Everyone said that the victors were not keeping their promises. The bread was now worse than ever; it smelled rotten and tasted like sawdust. 'There is no end to the end'—that is what people kept saying as a joke, but their faces were drawn and angry."

Austria's financial situation was possibly the most desperate in all of im-mediately postwar Europe, and the hard times were especially difficult for children. Sick youngsters in overcrowded hospitals were treated with paper bandages, and in the absence of medicine were given acorn coffee and boiled carrots. For a short time, no chloroform could be obtained for sur-gery. In the summer of 1919, large numbers of malnourished Viennese chil-dren were sent to neutral countries, especially Holland or Switzerland, where relief organizations placed them with families or in improvised camps.

Although living in central Vienna, Adler's family fared better than most. He and Raissa had never lived beyond their means. As his son, Kurt, re-called humorously, "We never had much money anyway, so things didn't seem so bad for us after the war. We adapted." To help keep Adler's large family well-fed, his provincial patients paid him in foodstuffs from their farms or large estates. As for Raissa's relatives in Russia, they had recently lost all their savings in the Bolshevik takeover; her rich grand-uncle Efim had been allowed emigration to Paris with his large family only after turning over his assets to the Communist regime. In Vienna, Adler's wealthy older brother, Sigmund, assisted them financially as needed, although relations between the two remained strained.

The long famine was straining many political relationships, adding to the tension between Vienna and the provinces. Long accustomed to ridicule by the better educated and more cosmopolitan Viennese, Austria's rural residents now drove hard bargains when approached by city dwellers virtually begging for food. When international relief help began arriving in Vienna, those in the hinterlands were envious. The longstanding alienation between the Viennese and their fellow rural Austrians would soon accentuate and help sustain an air of political crisis for years to come.

Contrary to the naive hope of many Austrians like Freud that United States President Woodrow Wilson would personally insure a "just peace," the final terms were unexpectedly harsh. During the negotiation of Austria's peace treaty in the village of Saint-Germain-en-Laye near Paris, French Premier Georges Clemenceau is said to have remarked that when the frontiers of the defeated empire's heartlands were discussed that "Austria is what's left." Four months elapsed before the defeated nation was even allowed to send delegates in June for the treaty making at Saint-Germain. Upon their arrival, they quickly realized that the Allied powers, especially France, were eager to capitalize on their military triumph. They assigned Austria's South Tyrol, where nearly a quarter of a million German-speaking people lived, to Italy. The historic provinces of Bohemia, Moravia, and Austrian Silesia were handed over to Czechoslovakia in their entirety.

The final peace terms left the country with approximately a quarter of the population and territory of the Austrian half of the Dual Monarchy. No less than one third of the German-speaking inhabitants of old Austria were placed under foreign rule; certain areas in the west, where Germans sometimes outnumbered Slavs by almost twenty to one, were given to Czechoslovakia and Yugoslavia. The Austria that emerged from this dismemberment was likened to a "mutilated trunk bleeding from every pore" and a "rump state." Even one of the English negotiators referred to the country he had helped to create as "a pathetic relic."

Nor was the treaty of Saint-Germain economically fair to Austria. Vienna was now geographically severed from the mining and industrial regions of Bohemia and Bavaria, from the lush farming regions of Croatia, Hungary, Slovakia, and Slovenia, and from its maritime supply line by way of Trieste. Austria had lost almost all its coal regions; initially, the country even lacked sufficient coal supplies to transport available foodstuffs to the country's inhabitants. As for agriculture, less than 5 percent of the new Austria's territory consisted of plains and little more than a quarter was arable.

Since Armistice Day in November 1918, Austria's economic viability seemed so preposterous that many citizens and political leaders had immediately sought *Anschluss* ("union") with Germany as the only sensible course. Not only did the conservative Pan-Germanists in the provinces favor this merger, so too did the Social Democrats concentrated in Vienna. Under the political direction of Otto Bauer, they confidently awaited an imminent Marxist revolution in Germany that would welcome Austria into a mighty socialist union. But such hopes were decisively dashed by the final terms of the completed treaty, which one Austrian negotiator bitterly called a "death warrant" and which the country's parliament was forced to ratify in September 1919: *Anschluss* with Germany was explicitly forbidden.

Not only was Austria's economy in a state of utter collapse, but a virulent epidemic of influenza also broke out in 1918. Mere hours before the first republic was proclaimed, the Social Democratic party's beloved leader Viktor Adler became the latest statistic. Lying on his Armistice Day deathbed, he said, "I don't mind dying. But I am so curious."

Thanks partly to the legacy of Viktor Adler's political acumen, the Social Democrats gained tremendous power just a few months later, in mid-February 1919, in Austria's first parliamentary election as a republic. Garnering over 40 percent of the national vote, the Social Democratic party was catapulted into dominant popularity. But lacking a majority, they were forced into a Grand Coalition with the Christian Socials and the smaller party of Pan-German Nationals. Reflecting their newfound and unprecedented political muscle, the Social Democrats secured the key positions of chancellor, foreign minister, and war minister. The more conservative Christian Socials agreed to such appointments in part out of fear that Austria's government might be toppled by more militant left-wing forces, as was occurring in neighboring Hungary and Bavaria.

Previously, the Social Democrats had been mainly a party of industrial workers led by a small intellectual elite. Before the war, the party had approximately ninety thousand members in all Austria. But by 1922, the Social Democrats would expand more than fivefold and include many influential middle-class citizens, such as lawyers, physicians, white-collar employees, business people, and even some small entrepreneurs. By 1924, fully one out of five adults in Vienna would hold membership in the Social Democratic party.

Among Vienna's largely assimilated Jewry, the ratio of Social Democratic membership was probably even higher. According to one Austrian historian, "Eighty percent of the intellectuals who joined the labor movement in Vienna were Jews. They made up the bulk of the Socialist students' organization, formerly 3,000 strong. The 200 lawyers who were organized Social Democrats, the 400 members of the Socialist Jurists' Association, and the 1,000 members of the Social Democratic physicians' organization in Vienna were almost exclusively Jews."

They were also disproportionally represented within the Social Democratic party's apparatus, especially among its higher echelons. It has been estimated that nearly a third of the most prominent Social Democrats were of Jewish origin. Viktor Adler had been the party's founder and its leader until his death in 1918. Otto Bauer served as Austria's foreign minister immediately after the war and then led the party for sixteen years after Viktor Adler's demise. Other key Social Democratic party leaders of Jewish background included Hugo Breitner and Julius Tandler, Vienna's municipal finance commissioner and health and welfare commissioner respectively. The Austrian Communist party, which remained tiny and politically insignificant during the postwar years, also included a disproportional number of Jews among its active supporters.

Although the Social Democratic party's leadership was heavily Jewish by birth, they were hardly pro-Jewish in sentiment. At best, many shared Alfred Adler's viewpoint that Judaism was thoroughly outmoded and that its most valuable, ethical ideals should now be expressed through social and political action. Some Social Democrats like Viktor Adler converted outright to Christianity; others like Bauer and Tandler merely distanced themselves completely from their ancestral religion.

Indeed, the Social Democratic leadership was not above anti-Semitic stereotyping, partly to offset often vicious conservative-clerical criticism that their party was dominated by selfish Jewish interests. For example, in one booklet entitled *The Jewish Swindle,* the Social Democrats railed against Jewish capitalists and denounced the Christian Social and German Nationalist parties as "the bodyguards of Jewish capitalism." The Social Democrats' newspaper, the *Arbeiter-Zeitung,* to which Alfred Adler contributed several articles over the years, frequently published cartoons depicting hooked-nose Jews as exploitative capitalists. As Leopold Plasehkes, Austria's Zionist leader wryly noted, one could generally identify the country's major political parties by the types of Jews they depicted as caricatures in posters: the Christian Socials with Jews as artisans, the Pan-Germans with Jews as usurers, and the Social Democrats with Jews as bankers.

While Alfred Adler was probably appalled by such crudities, he remained completely aloof from Vienna's Jewish community. In sharp contrast to Freud, who proudly maintained membership in Vienna's B'nai B'rith and came to value (if privately) his ethnic identity, Adler had absolutely nothing to do with Jewish religious or fraternal involvement. As organized anti-

Semitism would steadily mount in Central Europe during the 1920s, Freud felt moved in his books to denounce it. Adler did not. In this respect, he was far from atypical among Austria's leading Social Democrats, who at no time would issue a full-scale rebuttal of anti-Semitism. Adler had other battles to fight.

═══

Amidst Austria's widespread suffering and confusion, Adler became increasingly radicalized. Certainly, he had regarded himself as a committed socialist since his student days, and, in his numerous articles, had frequently praised Marxist insights. Yet, the nitty-gritty of political organizing had never seemed very appealing in comparison to working therapeutically with patients and expressing his ideas through writing. But now times were different, and perhaps encouraged by Raissa, Adler decided to become politically active for the first time in his life. He was particularly excited by the prospect of instituting educational reform as the newly elected vice chairperson of the Workers Committee of Vienna's First District, where he resided.

During the turbulent period of 1918–1919, workers committees had suddenly sprouted throughout Austria and were especially energetic in Vienna, where a fledgling Communist party was newly active. These committees, representing wealthy organized workers and demobilized soldiers, were strongly influenced by the Russian Bolsheviks and their newly triumphant allies (though only temporarily) in bordering Bavaria and Hungary. Although Austria's workers committees never gained enough strength to actualize specific policies, their leadership was generally aimed toward building the nation on revolutionary socialist, rather than democratic capitalist, lines.

For many serving on the workers committees, personal opportunism proved their motivating force: to gain a foothold for a political career involving a seat in the city council or parliament, or perhaps to secure a major administrative appointment. With a strong interest in intraparty strategy and policy making, Raissa may have hoped that Adler would finally follow suit, but his close friend Furtmüller, quite active with the Social Democrats, recollected that "Adler's ambition never faced in this direction. He was not the person to work under the conditions of party discipline, and he felt in the long run that he should give all his time and energy to the field where he could not be replaced by anyone else."

In any event, wider events in Austria soon aborted Adler's nascent political career. The Social Democratic party leadership, fearful of losing their own clout, adroitly maneuvered Vienna's various workers' committees into accepting the principle of proletarian democracy. This stratagem allowed the more numerous Social Democrats to bind the communists and other radical groups alike to decisions governed by majority rule. The successful and relatively peaceful parliamentary election in February 1919 signaled to major, participating parties that competing sources of power were weak, and by the fall, an anticommunist counterrevolution was victorious in Hungary. As a result, the Austrian workers' committees found themselves pushed to the political sidelines and were soon disbanded.

Throughout early 1919, the Austrian communists and their Red Guard tried putsch attempts to seize power. Seeking to force a pro-Moscow regime, Russian and Hungarian agents kept busy in Vienna, but the Social Democrats foiled all such plots. The last effort at a coup occurred in June, when twenty people died in street fighting. After this debacle, Austria's Communists never again tried revolutionary action in Vienna. Although Raissa would long work hard as a Trotskyite loyalist, Austria's communist movement was destined to be small and politically insignificant.

Her husband, however, almost immediately rejected the Bolsheviks once they asserted power in Russia and neighboring states. Adler had prided himself as an intellectual Marxist, but had never embraced Lenin's elitist and antidemocratic advocacy of violence to establish a dictatorship of the proletariat. Outraged by the terrorism unleashed by Lenin and his cohorts, Adler published a scathing article for a Swiss periodical in December 1918. In "Bolshevism and Psychology," he wrote:

> The rule of Bolshevism is based on the possession of power. Thus its fate is sealed. While this party and its friends seek ultimate goals which are the same as ours, the intoxication of power has seduced them. Now the terrible mechanism is automatically released in the unprepared minds of men whereby attacks are answered with counter-attacks, without regard for the goal of society, only because the mutual will to power is threatened. Cheap reasons are given to justify action and reaction. Fair becomes foul, foul becomes fair! The Bolsheviks must reply by reinforcing their power positions. There can be no reduction in violence, but only further increases, as is always the case when power has the decisive word. If there is any means to call a halt, it can only be the remembrance of the miracle of community feeling, which we must perform and which will never succeed through the use of power. For us the way and the tactics are determined by our highest goal: the cultivation and strengthening of social interest.

In appealing to former Bolshevik acquaintances like Leon Trotsky and Adolf Joffe to halt their ideologically driven mandate of force in the vague name of "social interest," Adler was perhaps willfully naive. But to his credit, he never retracted or altered this trenchant criticism of the Bolsheviks' contempt for peaceful, democratic change. In this regard, he may have exacerbated marital tensions with Raissa, who viewed the October revolution sympathetically and for many years would remain on closest terms with the Trotsky family. Indeed, as late as 1931, she would publish an article praising Soviet education for its liberating insights.

In 1919, Adler published a new article on child rearing for an Austrian educational journal. In this forum, he took the opportunity once more to blast bolshevism as "the enforcement of socialism by violence" and "a Hercules who strangles not the snakes but his own mother. What a useless expenditure of spirit, strength, and human blood!" Rejecting the Leninist justification for using force as a pragmatic means to advance socialist revolution, Adler argued that, "Human nature generally answers external coercion with a counter-coercion. It seeks its satisfaction not in rewards for obedience and docility, but aims to prove that its own means of power are stronger. . . . When in the life of man or the history of mankind has such an attempt ever succeeded? . . . No blessing comes from the use of power."

Despite Adler's fervently anti-Bolshevik view in the early postwar years, he generally wrote from a radical perspective. Thus, in 1919 in the same Swiss newspaper, he published a broadside entitled "The Other Side" that dealt specifically with the issue of collective guilt. At the time, many political commentators were seeking to fan the flames of ethnic resentment by blaming those who had fought in the Great War. In Adler's view, such efforts to blame combatants, even those who had voluntered for military duty, were severely misguided. "Now, [some people] want to burden the people with the guilt of the war," he observed angrily. "If one has lived among this people, one will acquit them of any guilt. They were immature, had no guiding lines and no leader. They were pushed and driven to slaughter."

Depicting Europe's elder statesmen and their servile journalists as the real culprits, Adler insisted that, "It is not the people who should be asked to do servitude and penance; but those who thought up this degradation, materialized it, and participated in it with foresight." With bitterness, he still recalled his own role as a conscripted military physician: "Herded together, with blinkers on, this is how we all received the merciless call to die. There was no way out, no protection from the bullet or the court-martial. And so the people acted in a way that would at least make their situation more bearable; they made virtue out of necessity." Thus wrapping themselves in patriotric fervor, "they were no longer whipped dogs exposed against their will to the rain of bullets, but heroes and defenders of the Fatherland and of their own honor."

═══

With Austria's future as a democratic republic reasonably secure by 1920, Adler began addressing immediate social problems troubling his country. These included widespread incidence of both prostitution and juvenile delinquency. Of course, since Adler's days with the Vienna Psychoanalytic Society more than a decade before, he had addressed such topics as the psychology of prostitution and the spread of venereal disease. Indeed, Adler, Freud, and other Viennese psychological pioneers had devoted considerable attention to these issues, for they affected nearly everyone. As novelist Stefan Zweig would later recall, "The present generation has hardly any idea of the gigantic spread of prostitution in Europe before the World War. . . . Then the sidewalks were so sprinkled with women for sale that it was more difficult to avoid than to find them. . . . To this was added the countless number of 'closed houses,' the night clubs, the cabarets, the dance parlors with their dancers and singers, and the bars with their 'come-on' girls. . . . It cost a man as little time and trouble to purchase a woman for a quarter of an hour, an hour, or a night, as it did to buy a package of cigarettes or a newspaper."

With Austria's heightened economic misery after the war, the practice of sex-for-sale steadily increased. When Adler wrote his essay in 1920, eight thousand arrests for prostitution were made in Vienna alone. He viewed the key question simply: Why does a society that tolerates and facilitates this behavior nevertheless consistently condemn it as disgraceful, or even seek to punish it? Alluding to historical, social, and psychological factors, Adler identified "the well-fed, self-satisfied bourgeois [man who practices] legitimate marriage tempered by prostitution" as its chief supporter. In Adler's perspective, such men are often outwardly solid citizens. But they feel contempt for women and are likely to treat their own wives in a brutalized, degraded manner.

With a lust to dominate women, most men who frequent prostitutes are aided by two groups, Adler suggested, brothel keepers and the prostitutes themselves. Revealing his new emphasis that individuals with an early sense of inadequacy fail to develop appropriate responsiveness to others, Adler depicted pimps as possessing a "deficient social feeling, an inclination to obtain easy success, the idea of using women as a means to an end, and a tendency toward effortless gratification of their will to power." As to why certain women consistently plied their bodies in exchange for money, Adler insisted that poverty was not a tenable explanation; most impoverished women never prostitute themselves, and only a few of those who do so ever make it habitual. Rather, the origins of female prostitution are found among those who regard their gender as "a stigma and a reproach" and who seek, with deep feelings of inferiority, to gain esteem through sex in a male-dominated society. "This explanation may not strike us as correct," Adler commented. "But ask the prostitutes and the brothel-keepers!"

In April 1920, Adler offered a public lecture on another major social problem of postwar Austria, that of alienated, predelinquent youth. In this address, Adler clearly foreshadowed the social concerns that would come to dominate his attention during ensuing years, such as child and adolescent personality, educational reform, and the treatment of juvenile delinquency and criminal behavior.

"Of the 'blessings' that came in the wake of the Great War," he noted sarcastically, "perhaps no one thing is of such importance as the tremendous increase in the demoralization of youth. Everyone has noticed it and may have taken cognizance of it with horror." Remarking that youthful alienation often takes place slowly and silently before exploding into obvious criminal activity, Adler identified certain types of books and movies for their destructive social influence. But his strongest criticism was leveled against Austria's educational system. "We know the demerits of our schools. The crowded classes, the insufficient training of many of the teachers, occasionally their lack of interest, for they suffer intensely from cramped economic conditions and more is hardly to be expected of them. Primarily, however, the greatest drawback of the school is the *prevailing ignorance about the psychic development of the child* (Adler's emphasis)."

Adler called for a variety of specific changes in how Austrian society could better deal with alienated, predelinquent youth. He emphasized the importance of changing their outlook before it became ingrained and then criminally oriented. He insisted upon the necessity for choosing school administrators based on the principle of merit rather than on political patronage. Adler also recommended new university courses in teacher training and "curative pedagogy," which would disseminate research findings on the best methods for treating and preventing juvenile maladjustment. He likewise advised that an innovative model school be founded to train teachers and clinicians on how to work more effectively with troubled youngsters.

Adler ended his address on a stirring note for societal change. Seeking to dispel among his audience any false nostalgia for prewar life under the Dual

Monarchy, he declared that, "Even in times of complete peace, our civilization was not able to gain effective control over demoralization and crime. She could merely punish, revenge herself, frighten people, and never solve the problem. The influential point of my argument is this: in a civilization where one man is the enemy of the other—for this is what our whole industrial system means—demoralization is ineradicable, for demoralization and crime are by-products of the struggle for existence known to our industrial civilization. . . . The correct and proper thing is to act immediately."

Countless others in Vienna were seemingly feeling the same way. On May Day 1920, hundreds of thousands of blue-collar and white-collar workers—much of Vienna's workforce—streamed from all city districts to the Ringstrasse, the boulevard that encircles the Innere Stadt, the First District. Carrying flags and pennants, the demonstrators—men, women, and children, with the smallest perched on their fathers' shoulders—all made their way to city hall. They wanted a new and better society, and they wanted the Social Democrats to help build it now.

═══

Postwar Austria had become highly politicized, even in the seemingly lofty field of psychiatry. Weeks after Armistice Day, the country's provisional parliament had passed a law providing for "the determination and prosecution of neglect of duty in military authorities during the war." Not long after, a special fact-finding commission was launched by Social Democrats to investigate possible cases of psychiatric malpractice by those serving in the military. In early 1919, serious charges of physical abuse, including torture, were leveled against the esteemed University of Vienna professor who had decisively rejected Adler's application four years before: Julius von Wagner-Jauregg. As titular professor of psychiatry and neurology, and director of the Department of Psychiatry at the Vienna General Hospital, the sixty-two-year-old Wagner-Jauregg was the foremost representative of Austria's psychiatric establishment.

The official inquiry took place in October 1920, and Wagner-Jauregg testified that during the war he had volunteered, out of patriotic fervor, to treat those soldiers deemed "neurotic" for refusing to fight. Wagner-Jauregg affirmed that at the time he had regarded such men as emotionally disturbed and in need of "treatment" for placing their own self-interest above loyalty to the beloved empire. Although assembled court evidence could not implicate Wagner-Jauregg directly, it confirmed the appalling reports of former Austrian soldiers.

Physicians without any neurological or psychiatric background had indeed been put in charge of field hospital departments where "nervous illnesses" were treated. Their practices included cold showers, straitjackets, isolation cells, public humiliation, naked exposure, burning cigarettes on patients' bodies, and applying deliberately painful electrical shocks to their nipples and genitals. Such brutal practices were found to be especially common in German field hospitals, and fatal in at least twenty cases.

Recruited as an expert witness for the commission, Freud submitted a written "Memorandum on the Electrical Treatment of War Neurotics." He argued that such psychiatric brutality had not been based on well-meaning and mistaken theory, but that physicians had adopted these practices out of political expediency to stop soldier malingering. In particular, Freud singled out the compulsory military draft of the Great War as "the immediate cause of all war neuroses."

Diffusing the issue of Wagner-Jauregg's responsibility by emphasizing the broader, inhumane backdrop of the war, Freud emphasized that, "The physicians had to play a role which turned them into something like machine guns behind the front, of driving fugitives back. This certainly was the intention of the War Office. . . . But then, this was rather an unsuitable task for the medical profession. The physician should act as the patient's champion." In short, Freud offered a general condemnation of military psychiatry, but carefully rejected any notion that his respected colleague had done anything deserving retrospective punishment. The two medical professors had never been close, nor had Wagner-Jauregg even showed much respect for psychoanalysis. But ever mindful of university politics, Freud most likely felt it prudent to refrain from uttering any direct criticism of his department's influential head.

As later recalled by one of Freud's in-laws visiting Adler that day, the founder of individual psychology was enraged to hear about Freud's testimony. Astutely sensing that Wagner-Jauregg would probably be exonerated as a result, Adler was furious and declared that he would have behaved quite differently in Freud's place. Freud should not have spared Wagner-Jauregg from the consequences of his immoral conduct during the war; to defend him nobly was inappropriate. "This kind of generosity," declared Adler, "is out of place when faced with such enemies."

———

By the early 1920s, Adler, in his role as impassioned psychological thinker, had begun exerting a major influence on Austria's new, postwar generation.

Disillusioned with Europe's elder statesmen who had been unable to stop the fighting that had killed tens of millions and bankrupted entire nations, this youthful generation looked eagerly toward new ideas about human nature and the mind. They were especially contemptuous of organized religion, as church leaders in every combating nation had pronounced their respective blessings upon the battlefield carnage. With his forceful social criticism and confident optimism in the science of individual psychology, Adler seemed a promising figure indeed, especially to idealistic men and women.

In the fall of 1920, he offered the first of many psychology courses through the auspices of Vienna's Volksheim (People's Institute). Established nearly twenty years before by socialist educators like Adler's friend Furtmüller, the People's Institute was expanding substantially due to the efforts of the Social Democratic party now firmly controlling Vienna's municipal government. With a strong belief in education as the bulwark of a worker's democracy, the party's leaders were encouraging a wide variety of lectures and courses on topics ranging from politics and history to culture, women's issues, and the "new psychology."

The iconoclastic People's Institute had several branches throughout Vienna. Its most widely attended forum was in the heavily Jewish Leopoldstadt where Adler had spent part of his boyhood. Of course, the institute hardly compared in academic prestige to the University of Vienna. Nevertheless, the institute was attracting well-regarded writers and scholars as interested in sharing their work with a receptive adult audience. Although ostensibly aimed at the working-class masses, many classes of the People's Institute instead attracted mainly university students and graduates. This situation certainly seems to have been the case with Adler's psychology lectures, which especially appealed to those seeking to transcend their bourgeois Victorian upbringing and help create a better society through activity in education, social work, or medicine.

Among those attending Adler's People's Institute lectures in the early, postwar years was a precocious teenager destined to become a major European novelist and to play an important role in individual psychology, Manes Sperber. Born in 1905, he was raised in an Orthodox Jewish milieu and fled the Ukraine with his family during the Great War. As refugees, they arduously made their way to Vienna in 1916, where young Sperber joined the Zionist youth movement Hashomer Hatzair (Hebrew for "The Young Guard"). Idealistic and interested in social action, he saw in Zionism rather than traditional religious piety the means to enhance Jewish life.

In the summer of 1921, Sperber developed tuberculosis and was obliged to convalesce in a countryside sanatorium administered by a Jewish-American relief agency. Fortuitously, his roommate was a well-read university student and the two youths spent many hours together in spirited discussion.

Before long, their conversation turned to Nietzsche's work, and Sperber revealed his great admiration for the philosopher's writings. Then the roommate excitedly recounted his own exposure to Nietszche through inspiring seminars taught by Adler at the People's Institute. After leaving the sanatorium in September, Sperber followed up his roommate's recommendation, and one evening went to a large classroom filled mostly with young adults, to meet the founder of individual psychology.

Like many who later recalled their first encounter with Adler, the sixteen-year-old Sperber was not impressed, "for nothing about him was striking or special. What he said [about the striving for power] was formulated cleverly but artlessly. . . . [I felt that his] extemporaneous presentation was not really improvisation but repetition; he had probably presented similar material frequently in earlier courses." Nevertheless, Sperber decided to return for Adler's next Monday-evening lecture and soon became a regular participant in class discussions. In retrospect, he found himself most affected by Adler's charismatic debating style.

Genially, Adler would typically fence off in debate by expressing warm agreement for the spirit—if not wholly the content—of the questioner's remarks. Then, while still voicing praise, admiration, and even flattery for the speaker's acuity, Adler would forcefully reassert his own position. Often, the would-be critic was so touched by Adler's disarming and effusive compliments that the debate was over.

Adler liked to encourage those enrolled in his course to offer their own presentations before classmates, and eventually Sperber volunteered to prepare a talk on "The Psychology of the Revolutionary." Several weeks later, Sperber, with strident praise for the Bolsheviks headed by Lenin, defended the earlier, unsuccessful revolutionaries of Russia's past as lonely heroes. After Sperber's impassioned talk, Adler offered a friendly, gentle rebuttal and commented to the earnest teenager that, "You spoke like an individual psychologist who doesn't know yet that he is one."

In a quavering voice, Sperber replied that, "I'm not an individual psychologist, but perhaps I ought to become one."

"Certainly," Adler answered. "I shall help you. All of us will help you."

Not long afterward, Sperber was pleased to receive an invitation from

Adler to attend a meeting of the Society for Individual Psychology; sessions were held regularly at the Whiff of Tobacco coffeehouse off St. Mark's Square. At the time, Adler was not well-known internationally; most of those in attendance were local Viennese acquaintanted with him since before his break with Freud or at least since before the war. As Sperber entered the room, he suddenly felt self-conscious of his youth in the presence of Adler's circle of well-established physicians, educators, and writers. Older and more sophisticated than the young adults who attended the People's Institute, most present at the meeting tried making an obviously uncomfortable Sperber feel at ease. Nevertheless, it would be more than a year before the inquisitive teenager would again venture to draw close to Adler.

Another idealistic young man attracted to individual psychology in this period was Rudolf Dreikurs. In decades to come, he would gain acclaim in the field of child psychiatry and especially as one of Adler's key popularizers in the United States. Born in 1897 to affluent, assimilated Viennese Jews, Dreikurs was completing medical training at the university. He was interested in psychiatry and socialism, and became friends with Otto Fenichel and Wilhelm Reich. (Both men would later become important figures in the "Freudian Left.") They informed Dreikurs that he could not attend the meetings of Freud's society as an observer, but would first have to undergo extensive psychoanalytic treatment before admittance to its proceedings. To attend a session of Adler's group "was simple," however, reminisced Dreikurs many years later. "You just went. No one was excluded, and the door to the weekly Monday meetings was characteristically left wide open."

With an abrasive personality that mellowed little in later years, Dreikurs soon antagonized Adler's group. One evening during 1923, the founder of individual psychology was expounding before his gathering a particular critique of psychoanalysis when Dreikurs suddenly rose and demanded, "How can you treat Freud so shabbily? A man with an international reputation has to know what he's doing, and cannot be so easily dismissed." Immediately, one of Adler's associates took Dreikurs aside and scolded him for his naiveté and audacity. Mortified by this treatment, Dreikurs would not return to Adler's group for some time.

Although Sperber and Dreikurs quickly became enamored of Adler, a young intellectual Austrian whose reaction remained negative was Wilhelm Reich. Like his friend Dreikurs, Reich was born in 1897 to assimilated Austrian Jews and attended medical school at the University of Vienna. As a psychiatric student in March 1920, he heard Adler lecture on "Foundations of Individual Psychology" at the Society for Social Medicine, chaired by the psychoanalyst Heinz Hartmann. By this time, Reich had already become personally acquainted with Freud and had organized a discussion group among his medical peers interested in sexology.

Reich wrote a letter to Adler soon after the lecture in which he expressed disagreement on several major issues. For one thing, he felt that Adler had badly minimized the potent influence of sexuality in human life. For another, Reich rejected Adler's gender-role egalitarianism and insisted that, "In contradistinction to your view, the passive and subordinate are inherent in the nature of the female." Finally, Reich argued that Adler's theory of *masculine protest* (feminine gender-envy) was misplaced. As Reich explained, most women did not envy the economic or social power of men, but rather their greater *sexual* freedom. "It is far more logical to interpret the traditional complaint of girls during puberty and later, 'I'd give anything to be a boy!' to mean: 'Then I would have all the [sexual] freedom I want!', rather than: 'Then I could do great things!' [You imply] that sexuality is subordinated to the will to power," concluded Reich, "but sexuality is demonstrably subordinated to the sexual drive which strives solely for *pleasure, and nothing else,* and not for power."

It is not known what Adler replied to Reich, but the two men never became friendly. By the late 1920s, Reich had broken strongly with Freud over political issues and moved to Germany to become involved with the Communist party. By historical coincidence, Adler's only son, Kurt, lived for a while in the same Viennese apartment building as Reich. The two young men developed a nodding acquaintance and even spent one pleasant skiing trip together before Kurt's interests took him elsewhere.

═══

Not only was Adler gaining greater visibility through his public lecturing, but his earlier, prewar writings were now also steadily reaching a wider audience. In late 1920, Adler's first major anthology since 1914 was published. Initially appearing in German, *The Practice and Theory of Individual Psychology* was comprised of twenty-eight essays dating from 1911 through his most recent pronouncements on such contemporary social problems as prostitution and juvenile delinquency. Many of the chapters had previously appeared in professional journals; others were edited versions of public lectures he had presented. Well received in Austria and Germany, the substantial volume helped promote Adler's psychological approach among educational and health professionals in the postwar world.

Then, in the fall of 1922, Adler's first major anthology, *Heilen und Bilden*

(To Heal and To Educate), was reissued in a new edition. When the book was originally published eight years before, Adler's friend Furtmüller was the co-author and had done much of the planning and editing. Now, however, his attention was dominated by the demands of initiating far-reaching reforms as a key administrator for Vienna's Board of Education. Consequently, the task of preparing the new edition of *Heilen und Bilden* fell to Erwin Wexberg.

Unlike many of Adler's close associates, who had backgrounds in education, literature, or the arts, Wexberg was a fellow graduate of the Vienna medical school and a practicing physician. Completing the new preface to *Heilen und Bilden* in May 1922, Wexberg confidently observed, "The World War hindered not only international scientific relations, but also interest in peaceful research in European countries. It may have deprived the first edition of *To Heal and to Educate* of the response it would otherwise have elicited. . . . Now, eight years after the appearance of the first edition, we can fulfill the promise we made in its preface. We can appear before the public, strengthened by an enlarged circle of new colleagues."

In presenting *Heilen und Bilden*'s new edition, Wexberg briefly highlighted the growth of individual psychology. But clearly, his main intent was to demark sharply the Adlerian approach from the Freudian. "It is no coincidence that the word and title of psychoanalysis, which still played a considerable role in the first edition, is treated more as a kind of historical reminiscence in its new incarnation. We do not wish to undervalue the many-sided stimulation and fertilization which modern psychology owes to psychoanalysis," Wexberg remarked somewhat disingenuously, "nor do we wish to ignore that the historical source of individual psychology lies in psychoanalysis. Nonetheless, we are convinced that, with the progressive development of the two, the divergence between psychoanalytic and individual psychology . . . has become quite large. . . . Just as we do not want to identify individual psychology with those parts of psychoanalysis that we believe are mistaken—and there is hardly an idea of Freud's which we would want to call our own—we would not want to burden the psychoanalytic school with discoveries which must appear heretical."

Wexberg ended the new preface to *Heilen und Bilden* optimistically. "The ideas of individual psychology found their way beyond the close circle of Alfred Adler and his friends and colleagues long ago. Slowly but surely, we are beginning to receive the international attention which we have counted on from the beginning."

In that same year, Adler was pleased to write a new preface for the third edition of *The Neurotic Constitution*. This was the 1912 volume that he had unsuccessfully submitted in seeking faculty appointment to the medical school of the University of Vienna. Now at the age of fifty-two, Adler commented with mild bitterness that, "By this decision, I have up to the present been prevented from giving lectures to university students and physicians. Those who know, understand how difficult the dissemination of my views became. Yet today this has been accomplished. . . . The watchword of Individual Psychology is the fellowman, the fellowmanlike attitude toward the immanent demands of human society."

During the next few years, Adler in vigorous middle age would find his optimism well placed. As never before in his career, individual psychology would gain new adherents and visibility, not only in Austria but throughout Europe and the entire globe.

CHAPTER NINE

≡

Red Vienna

*Socialism is deeply rooted
in community feeling. It is the
original sound of humanity.*

ALFRED ADLER

Although Adler was becoming influential as a psychological revolutionary, after the war his chief reputation soon became established in the applied field of child psychology. In Austria and Germany, and eventually throughout Europe and abroad, Adler became best known for his innovations on behalf of children's mental health through interdisciplinary effort involving education, medicine, psychology, and social work. He also pioneered in promulgating clinical insights to numerous lay audiences, including parents and teachers. Unlike Freud and Jung, who remained identified primarily with issues of adult personality, Adler's name became more closely linked with child guidance in family and school.

Certainly, Adler had long expressed an interest in education. As early as 1904, he had written a series of articles for a medical newspaper advocating "The Physician as Educator," and throughout his nine-year association with the Vienna Psychoanalytic Society, he had emphasized the importance of schooling reform. Yet, it was not until after the war, when Adler was already in middle age, that he became most strongly committed to the emerging fields of child guidance and educational psychology. In the early 1920s, Adler seized on these new disciplines as the most worthwhile way to disseminate the teachings of individual psychology to a conflicted and demoralized postwar Europe. Indeed, for the rest of Adler's life, he would argue that, in the long run, educational reform provides the most reliable means for peaceful world improvement.

Undoubtedly, Adler's influential work in child psychology was aided immeasurably when his Social Democratic friends gained decisive political power in Vienna. In the municipal election of May 1919, the Social Democratic party captured 54 percent of the vote, thereby producing the world's first socialist mayor of a major metropolis. Although the Social Democrats lost national power when the Grand Coalition broke up the following year, they greatly increased their hegemony in Vienna, especially after the city gained semiautonomous status in late 1921. Optimistic that Austria's future belonged to socialism, party leaders patiently awaited a return to national power. At the same time, they focused their efforts on creating a new society in what would become known for about a dozen years as Red Vienna.

Almost overnight, the Social Democrats embarked on an ambitious program of public health and welfare. Enjoying an overwhelming majority on the municipal council, they enacted under commissioner Julius Tandler an unprecedented array of social services funded by sharply increased taxes on the middle class and wealthy. One year older than Adler, Tandler had grown up in a poor Jewish family and had received his medical degree from the University of Vienna in 1895. He was a highly respected anatomy professor there, and committed to social medicine. In his view, government rather than private religious agencies had the true responsibility for helping citizens. Soon, the city was providing free dental and health care, establishing child and youth clinics, and even building public swimming pools and sports facilities. Tandler also greatly expanded the role of social workers in providing services to impoverished families and investigating child welfare. By the mid-1920s, Red Vienna was likewise the site of massive, government-built housing projects for working-class residents. Provocatively named after socialist heroes like Karl Marx, these "super-blocks" were intended to create an entire new culture for its residents.

Indeed, Social Democrats like Adler were not simply aiming at economic reform. Under the Marxist banner of *Kulturkampf* (cultural battle), they sought to create what philosopher Max Adler (no relation to Alfred Adler) was calling *Neue Menschen* (new human beings) through youth organizations, adult education programs, lending libraries, bookstores, newspapers and magazines, theaters, festivals, and other cultural events. As one Austrian historian later noted: "On a given day, a worker might hear a worker's chorus, read a socialist newspaper, or attend a lecture on the socialist implications of the theory of relativity. The creation of a culture to counter the bourgeois, Catholic, conservative influences represented by the Christian Social Party was one of the most original features of Austrian Socialism in the First Republic."

Central to the Social Democrats' conception of Red Vienna was their commitment to transforming public education. In this venture, their much admired leader was Otto Glöckel, who had served briefly as Austria's minister of education. Born near Vienna in 1873, Glöckel was the idealistic son of a teacher and early decided on a similar career. By the age of nineteen, he was already working in a Viennese slum district; politically active, he joined with Karl Seitz (future mayor of Vienna) and other liberal teachers to found an organization called Die Jungen (The Young Ones). Their chief goal was to improve educational conditions for Vienna's poor, and they soon joined forces with the Social Democratic workers' movement.

As a dedicated teacher, Glöckel rose to leadership within The Young Ones. Then one morning in 1897, he learned from the newspapers that he had been summarily discharged for political radicalism. Without the slightest due process of formal charges and a hearing, conservative Mayor Karl Lueger had fired and banned Glöckel and four young colleagues from further educational activity. Initially, Glöckel found alternative employment in an insurance agency, and politically undeterred, continued his efforts for The Young Ones. In 1898, Glöckel copublished a manifesto on educational reform and later helped establish a socialist educators' group called The Free School Society. Meanwhile, he entered politics as an organizer for the Social Democrats, eventually serving under their banner as a member of Austro-Hungary's imperial parliament.

During the Great War, Glöckel found himself jailed for his political activism. But he was released undaunted, and in early January 1917, addressed The Free School Society meeting with an impassioned speech entitled "The Gateway to the Future." This speech became Glöckel's platform for his subsequent work as Austria's minister of education during the country's Grand Coalition immediately after the war.

Few were surprised when Glöckel appointed Carl Furtmüller to serve as a key administrator for the ministry's new Reform Division. For more than twenty years, he too had been battling for educational change from a socialist perspective. Working at the Reform Division under Glöckel, he strongly contributed to formulating its "Guiding Principles," which defined its goals for restructuring Austrian education. When Glöckel became president of Vienna's school council in 1922, he named Furtmüller as official inspector for Vienna's experimental schools.

With Vienna a semiautonomous state and Glöckel in charge of its educational system, the Social Democrats lost little time in authorizing a sweeping new set of educational regulations. Women teachers were finally granted rights equal to their male colleagues. Their celibacy requirement for employment was abolished, and female students were allowed to study law, engineering, and agronomy. General salaries were increased significantly so that Viennese teachers were now the best paid in Austria. After thirty-five years of service, each teacher would receive a pension equal to fully 90 percent of his or her salary at retirement time. In addition, a series of regulations was mandated for providing due process in supervisors' evaluation of teachers.

The municipal council instituted a variety of other educational reforms. These included providing free schoolbooks and related materials for all pupils regardless of need, creating school libraries for students and an educational library for teachers, establishing parents' associations in each local school district, and abolishing corporal punishment. To help provide for children's health, funds were created for the hiring of some fifty physicians and 210 social workers, and for the establishment of eleven dental clinics.

Such reforms were unquestionably worthwhile and long overdue. Glöckel and his aides were planning a far more ambitious educational program, however. They intended to revamp compulsory education in Vienna completely, so that working-class youngsters would acquire equal access to higher education. With Furtmüller given major administrative duty for implementation, Glöckel authorized that new middle schools be created for all students between the ages of ten and fourteen. The curriculum would provide common, enriched core subjects (mathematics and German) for everyone, yet simultaneously be flexible enough to permit the study of specialized subjects required by the traditional *Gymnasium* and the *Realschule,* the gateways to higher education. The tremendous innovation of this proposal was that it would delay tracking students until they finished compulsory education at age fourteen.

Glöckel knew that to carry out such a radical restructuring effectively would require new curricula and teaching methods. As he later remarked, the elementary "drill school" of their grandparents' generation had served to instill the authority of church and crown plus a smattering of the three R's. The "learning school" for older pupils had prepared the masses for manual work and an elite few for skilled technical jobs and the professions. But the new "work school" that he envisioned would base its curriculum on the life experiences of students, replace rote learning with independent study and self-discovery, supplement intellectual with manual learning, and make the city as well as the classroom a true learning environment. More broadly, Glöckel envisioned the work schools as incubators of worker democracy, embodying comradely cooperation among youngsters, teachers, and parents.

=====

As part of this atmosphere of idealistic reform, Adler established several informal child guidance "clinics" in Vienna in the years 1919 and 1920. With Glöckel approving Furtmüller's modest request for his friend, Adler was allowed to make himself regularly available on an unpaid basis to teachers seeking advice on how to handle various students in their classes. Such psychological training was virtually unprecedented in Austria, and indeed, throughout the world. The fields of personality study and psychotherapy were still quite new and poorly understood. Having felt his own schooling extremely stifling decades earlier, Adler must have felt a special pride in helping Vienna's teachers to apply psychological insights in their daily classroom. Essentially, his goal was to end the educational authoritarianism he had personally known, and to help all children be seen as unique individuals with specific emotional and intellectual needs.

At the time, "there were no trained clinical psychologists connected with the Viennese school system," educator Regine Seidler reminisced, "no counselors, no guidance workers. The only special service was given to the graduating students who were interviewed, examined, and advised by specialists in vocational guidance. The economic and psychological conditions in a country demoralized by defeat, crushed by hunger and cold, swept by inflation, called urgently for counseling and guidance."

For classroom teachers struggling to help their students, Adler's sessions were extremely informative. As Seidler recollected, "[These] served as much for the education and training of teachers as for the immediate benefit of the children and parents who attended." Typically, a teacher would recount a troublesome case—perhaps, a shy, fearful six-year-old boy, or a defiant and truant teenage girl—before an audience of colleagues. After asking the teacher pointed questions to elicit a fuller description of the child, perhaps concerning peer relations or self-esteem, Adler would offer his general impressions. Thereupon, the parents and child were brought into the classroom and interviewed by Adler before the teachers. Once the family members left, Adler would initiate another and final discussion of the case. "The findings were generalized," recalled Seidler, "and many of Adler's most profound lectures were given in connection with practical case work before the teacher audience of the child guidance clinic."

Soon, however, Adler's free public consultative sessions attracted the interest of many parents, and a new site was found where they too could obtain advice about their offspring. By 1922, a regular format involving "treatment teams" had evolved under Adler's direction. The teams were all led by a psychiatrist or psychologist knowledgeable about individual psychology. Serving without compensation from the Vienna Board of Education, the teams varied considerably from district to district within Vienna; but their help was always free to families.

Typically, the teams would meet in a school district's empty classroom one or two evenings per week. After first obtaining parental permission, they would discuss the case with the classroom teacher making the referral, as well as with other invited professionals such as social workers. After the case was reviewed, the parents and child would be called in. The order of appearance varied. Some teams preferred to meet initially with the parents to affirm their authority. Others wanted to interview the youngster first in order to gain a direct impression unbiased by parental comments. Adler's own preference was to meet initially with the mother and then with the child.

Thereupon, the team would discuss the case again and offer its recommendation to the parents. Clinical members deemed a medical evaluation vital in order to rule out organic factors, such as a hearing or visual impairment, that might be contributing to the child's academic difficulties. After the initial visit, some families returned for a follow-up consultation. Sometimes, the youngster might be given special tutoring at no cost to the family. Most of the children were between the ages of six and thirteen, although preschoolers were sometimes included.

During this period, Adler and his colleagues also helped provide lectures on child guidance for Vienna's new parent associations. Under Glöckel's encouragement, each school had established a monthly meeting for all interested parents. Some school districts were more eager than others for organized sessions; the Leopoldstadt, which housed the chief People's Institute where Adler regularly lectured, was particularly hospitable to his colleagues' presentations on individual psychology. Such lectures carried a dual purpose. As psychiatrist Olga Knopf reported at the time, "It is well known that many parents refuse to bring their children to the guidance clinic because they believe that the child, and hence they themselves, are being arraigned here, or because they think that no one can understand their child as well . . . and that guidance is therefore useless. To remedy this situation, it is important to win the parents over . . . [such as] in the monthly meetings of the parents' associations."

Yet another important outgrowth of Adler's child guidance work during these years lay in actual classroom activity with middle-school youngsters. He had long been contemptuous of the antiquated methods that dominated Austria's public schools, allowing minimal opportunity for students to express their own values and opinions. In this regard, little had changed in curricular methods since Adler been a bored pupil more than forty years earlier. Now, with his socialist-minded friends like Furtmüller revamping Viennese education, a younger generation of teachers were eager for innovation. Among the most influential of those who studied personally with Adler was Oskar Spiel.

Expanding upon his mentor's dictum that childhood feelings of inferiority form the basis for virtually all antisocial behavior, Spiel wrote that, "Children who are impudent, vicious, annoying, and lazy are . . . discouraged [and expend] their energy on the side of the useless . . . It is necessary to [help them] through individual psychologic treatment outside the classroom, through private conferences in free periods, and after hours."

In a direct effort to encourage students to become more creatively autonomous, Spiel gained Adler's encouragement in creating a method known as the class council. A president and two assistant group leaders were elected; these students led discussions on matters that affected the group. All had the opportunity to voice their viewpoints and help establish a consensus to be communicated to the teacher. The three class leaders were also entrusted with the responsibility of assisting peers with academic problems.

Around this time, Adler's own children, particularly Alexandra and Kurt, began attending individual psychology meetings on a frequent basis. As young adults with inquisitive minds, both found themselves excited by the lively discussions, and enjoyed the opportunity to be with their father, for by the early 1920s, he was seldom home. Adler's rigorous pace involved frequent lecturing and a busy medical practice, coupled with writing, supervising, and nightly café camaraderie with friends and colleagues. Raissa had long ceased to join Alfred in his meetings and other professional activities; and it seems likely that their marriage began to suffer significantly during this time. Intellectually well-read and skillful in French, German, and Russian, Raissa kept active with translation projects involving articles and books. Outgoing and sociable, she also found satisfaction through political friendships, especially her longtime dedication to the Trotskyite movement yet powerful in Europe. While Raissa respected her husband's psychology work, she believed that revolutionary activity was ultimately more important.

═══

During the early 1920s, Adler was also active in promulgating individual psychology throughout nearby Germany. His chief associate there was psychiatrist Leonhard Seif who, in 1922, established the first similar program in Munich. That year, Seif also helped organize there the First International Congress for Individual Psychology and its follow-up three years later in Berlin. For many years, he assisted in leading individual psychology through-out Germany and lecturing about it abroad. Especially after Adler shifted most of his own activity to the United States in the late 1920s, Seif would offer therapeutic training to professionals throughout Europe interested in becoming individual psychologists. His chief colleagues included psychologists Johannes Neumann and Paul Rom.

Before long, Adler became a frequent traveler from Vienna to Germany for both consultations and speaking engagements. One evening, he was scheduled in Berlin to present a lecture on child psychology. Traveling by train to hear Adler, one clinician later recalled sitting beside a young mother and her increasingly restless, moody five-year-old son. As the boy began to whine with crankiness, his mother became distraught. Despite her admonitions, the boy became increasingly disruptive and his mother finally threatened a beating. Suddenly, a stout middle-aged man resembling a civil servant smilingly approached the boy and revealed a toy horse in his palm. Drawn into friendly conversation with the man, the five-year-old calmed down quickly. That evening, as Adler was introduced in the lecture hall, the clinician was startled to discover him to be the kindly, rotund man seen earlier on the train that day.

By the early 1920s, Adler's ground-breaking work in child guidance was garnering increasing attention. Professionals from all over Europe and abroad were coming to Vienna to study firsthand how clinicians and teach-ers were helping children with emotional problems. Undoubtedly, Adler gained an important boost for his growing movement when the *Journal for Individual Psychology* was reestablished in late 1923, replete with a presti-gious international editorial board that included the venerable American psychologist G. Stanley Hall. Yet not only through writing was Adler gaining increased foreign attention. That same year, he visited England for the first time and presented in untranslated German a paper at a Cambridge con-ference. Also in 1923, he began the first of many subsequent lecture tours in Holland.

Despite such international receptivity to individual psychology, Adler found that locally, in Vienna, his efforts were not without criticism. For one thing, the public nature of his school-guidance clinics was often attacked as inappropriate. Some professionals insisted that it was harmful for children and parents to be interviewed before an audience of up to twenty strangers, however well-meaning. In response, Adler and his associates argued that youngsters seemed to enjoy the attention and to benefit emotionally from the sense of importance it gave them. Adler's colleagues also pointed out that a private consultation was always conducted if parents requested it or if their child seemed overanxious. Perhaps more sensibly, some Adlerian physicians avoided the whole issue by holding clinic sessions in their private offices and permitting an audience of no larger than three.

Another reasonable criticism voiced about Adler's child-guidance work was his failure to keep rigorous statistics. Dating back decades to elementary-school days, he had never much liked mathematics. As a young physician interested in publishing his ideas, Adler had likewise shunned experimental or statistical work. Partly for this reason, the medical faculty of the University of Vienna had, in 1915, rejected his application to teach there. They had praised his speculative talents in *The Neurotic Constitution,* but had severely criticized his lack of empirical effort. Unfortunately, Adler throughout his career never really responded effectively to such criticism.

As late as 1935, even a sympathetic observer would report about the Adlerian child-guidance work in Vienna that, "Their records are at once too summary (since parents and children attend too irregularly) and too incomplete (one cannot always tell whether those who have ceased to attend did so because they think all is well now or for the opposite reason). Parents rarely seem to think it worthwhile to inform the psychologist of their reasons for ceasing to present themselves."

In a related criticism, some professionals argued that Adler and his associates never provided a systematic follow-up of their interventions. How was it possible to determine if individual psychology had truly helped an academically slow or disruptive youngster if an organized follow-up was never carried out in the schools? Unlike his colleagues Charlotte and Karl Bühler at the Pedagogical Institute, established by Vienna's municipal government, Adler simply was uninterested in painstaking and methodical research. Certainly, he was not philosophically averse to such activity. At times in his writings, he specifically cited the findings of individual psychologists like Alice Friedmann. Nevertheless, Adler's own indifference to experimental work would eventually come to hinder his reputation.

Finally, Adler's zealous optimism about children's responsiveness to psychological intervention evoked criticism. Certainly, his philosophy was a useful antidote to the often thinly veiled racism and ethnocentrism associated with the eugenics movement of the 1920s, both in Europe and the United States. Yet, not all who studied hereditary factors in childhood learning and behavior were racists, and they rightfully objected to Adler's overarching emphasis on environmental factors. As a result, he would eventually feel almost defensively obliged to explain that his motto, Anyone Can Learn Anything, was not to be taken literally: that he was merely trying to instill more optimism among educators and clinicians when working with problem children.

Ironically, this same debate continues today, seventy years later, in the fields of medicine and psychology. On the op-ed pages of major American newspapers and in professional journals, arguments still rage back and forth over whether hyperactivity, or learning disabilities, or attention deficit disorders are real biological impairments, or, as Adler would have claimed, are predominantly false labels imposed on children who are failing due to emotional causes.

Although Adler was now focusing increasingly on child guidance, he continued to address wider issues. Both in public lectures and popular articles through the mid-1920s, Adler expressed a strong political outlook infused with socialism. Thus, in the fall of 1922, his People's Institute course highlighted the lives of historically important figures, including the founders of the French Revolution: Danton, Marat, and Robespierre. In an article based on his lecture notes and published in the Social Democrats' *Arbeiter-Zeitung* in late 1923, Adler clearly attempted to synthesize Marxism with individual psychology. In his view, the political behavior of each of these three key revolutionaries could be traced to their childhood experiences and their subsequent attitude toward life:

> The rapid economic development of France with the urbanized growth of an industrial proletariat and exploitation of the peasants, had brought the country into chaos. The exclusion of the most capable men from many public functions irritated them. Voltaire and Rosseau gave expression to feelings of the masses and helped to create a 'revolutionary line.' A critical point came when the first attempts to introduce urgently needed reforms were checked by the government. This set into motion the revolutionary tide and paved the way to its great leaders . . . Marat . . . offered himself as a victim, the more so because his health was ruined. . . . Danton, an inordinately ambitious man, had given an early indication of his lifestyle when, being a schoolboy, he escaped in order to watch the King's coronation. . . . Robespierre had been a 'model pupil,' always at the head of his class. His predominant passion was self-conceit. . . . His tactic was to keep himself as much as possible in the background to slowly and methodically [crush] his enemies.

Since soon after the war, Adler's friend Furtmüller had been seeking to actualize his own socialist ideals by spearheading educational reform in Vienna's middle schools. Although his notions seemed workable, he eventually saw the necessity for offering training to teachers in the new and noncoercive methods favored by Adler and like-minded innovators. Administrators at the University of Vienna refused to become involved in this effort, however. Instead, they disdainfully insisted that the general "masses" of Austria's youngsters did not require college-trained teachers for their classrooms.

Led by Tandler and Glöckel, Vienna's municipal government therefore established its own Pedagogical Institute. In 1923, educator Viktor Fadrus was entrusted with the task of organizing it. After a teaching career with the hearing impaired, he had been appointed director of Austria's elementary school reform by Glöckel in March 1919, and had held the post until after Glöckel's departure for Vienna's administrative school leadership. In his role as director of the Pedagogical Institute, Fadrus recruited from Germany the husband-and-wife team of Karl and Charlotte Bühler. Teaching psychology at Dresden's Polytechnical College, they were well regarded in their field.

In close association with the Pedagogical Institute and the University of Vienna, the Bühlers founded the Institute of Psychology. Hugely successful from the inception, it emphasized the new disciplines of developmental and educational psychology. The Bühlers' Institute of Psychology attracted many young scholars who later achieved recognition in the social sciences. These included Rowena Ripin Ansbacher, Bruno Bettelheim, Egon Brunswik, Else Frenkel (Brunswik), Marianne Frostig, Marie Jahoda, Paul Lazarsfeld, Fritz Redl, and Rene Spitz. Before long, Anna Freud also joined the Pedagogical Institute faculty.

In 1924, Adler was recruited as professor at the Pedagogical Institute's Division of Remedial Education. As he later recalled, supportive teachers had gone to the Vienna Board of Education without his knowledge and insisted that he be hired for the faculty. Adler's first course was entitled "The Difficult Child." In another, nonrequired course entitled "Problem Children in School," he explicated individual psychology through case reports given to him by teachers in the audience.

Having already been lecturing at the People's Institute for several years, Adler had perfected a warm, down-to-earth style. As foreign visitors would later remark, it was the complete antithesis of the stereotypical, ponderous Germanic professor. Adler instead kept technical terms to a minimum and emphasized actual situations involving problem children faced by Vienna's classroom teachers. In this way, he would demonstrate how individual psychology might regard various facets of child development and treatment. Certainly for its time, Adler's approach was unprecedented in stressing how emotional, physical, and familial factors affect each child's ability in school.

In particular, he never ceased emphasizing that difficulties exhibited by children can almost always be treated effectively. As Furtmüller later recalled, "[Adler enabled the teachers to] make at least a fair guess at what was happening in the child's mind, a guess which would be tested in the child's reactions to the teacher's further handling of him." In Adler's optimistic view, teachers should never become resigned about a child or attribute a difficulty to heredity. Anyone Can Learn Anything therefore became his famous educational motto during this period.

In the first three years, Adler drew more than six hundred Viennese teachers to his course. Reportedly, he did not miss a single lecture. These would later form the basis for his (German) book *Individual Psychology in the Classroom*, aimed at revealing what he and associates "have for many years been striving for in the Educational Counseling Centers: to improve the lot of the children, the teachers, and the family."

The Pedagogical Institute proved a thriving enterprise, and in 1925, it expanded its mission to include the training and certification of elementary and secondary teachers, as well as special instructors. It also continued to offer teachers post-graduate courses in what today would be called special education, that is, classes that focused on children with cognitive, emotional, or physical deficits. In addition, closely connected with the Pedagogical Institute's course offerings were two new educational journals, *Die Schulereform* (School Reform), which was largely theoretical, and *Die Quelle* (The Source), which dealt mostly with practical, methodological issues. The Institute of Psychology also published its own journal devoted to educational psychology, edited by Charlotte Bühler and Fadrus. Beginning in 1927, the city under Glöckel's initative would hire only those teachers who had graduated from the Pedagogical Institute.

While the Pedagogical Institute justifiably gained international respect for its excellent faculty, it is hard to determine just how effective the school was in affecting daily education within Vienna itself. For one thing, most classroom teachers had been trained in earlier times, when a more traditional authoritarian approach had prevailed. In retrospect, it also appears likely that relatively few of the new "progressive" teachers actually found positions, for a drastic decline in the Viennese pupil population between 1915 and 1923 would produce a surplus of teachers until 1929. To Glöckel's

155

credit, he tolerantly retained all teachers rather than dismiss the old-timers in favor of their younger, more progressive colleagues. Unfortunately, as Adler and his colleagues probably realized, this humanitarian decision left Vienna's teaching staff heavily balanced against democratization and the other new reforms. Thus, by 1930, the Social Democrats would claim an affiliative teacher's organization comprising five thousand members, while the more traditionalist Pan-German Austrians and Christian Socials each boasted teacher association memberships of double that number.

It would therefore be inaccurate to suggest that everyone embraced Adler's psychological approach to education. Conservative Christians especially felt antagonism toward the Social Democrats' staunch opposition to religion in public schooling. Indeed, Austria's powerful Catholic church had been vigorously opposing the Social Democrats' educational reforms since Glöckel had first gained power in April 1919. At the time, he had struck an important blow for secular education as Austria's deputy education minister by decreeing the return to the principles of the 1869 reform law, which abolished religious practices in all public schools. Glöckel's edict, however, merely reduced—and did not eliminate—the church's potent influence on public education.

Because compulsory religious attendance still existed throughout Austria's public schools, the priests remained an active force in combating Social Democratic reform efforts. That is, without receiving a passing grade in religion, a student could not be promoted to the next grade. The only pupils exempted were those whose parents had officially renounced religious affiliation before their child was seven years old. Church officials made sure that religious instruction was vigorously enforced: One afternoon a week, a Catholic priest would visit each classroom for instruction, and "minority" students (usually Protestants and Jews) were sent elsewhere.

The political battle for control of Vienna's public schools would continue for over a decade. Ultimately, with the triumph of Austria's fascist government in 1934, the Christian Socials would be granted power to liquidate all educational reform efforts dating back to 1919. Much to the dismay of Adler and his ardent colleagues, these would include his entire array of internationally acclaimed programs in child guidance, parent education, and teacher training.

But the Catholic church was not the only opposition to the Social Democrats' ambitious social and educational efforts for Vienna. On economic grounds, many locals viewed *Kulturkampf* as carrying an excessive and unjustifiable price tag for a city still struggling to recover from the Great War.

They argued that the Social Democrats were imposing heavy taxes that were victimizing more than just businesses and the wealthy. There were taxes on opera tickets, restaurant meals, telegrams and telephone services, and even on windows and staircases. With the Austro-Hungarian empire gone and Hungary now an independent country, most Viennese companies and wealthy individuals could no longer threaten a relocation to Budapest. They could do nothing but pay the levies.

Feeling especially hard hit were Vienna's real-estate owners, for the Social Democrats increased the already high property taxes of the prewar era. Simultaneously, the Social Democratic administration led by Finance Commissioner Breitner imposed strict rent controls on residential properties. During Austria's hyperinflation, the price of a single dinner in a good restaurant thus became roughly equivalent to the cost of renting a luxury apartment for a year. Then, as real-estate values plummeted, the administration was able to purchase real estate for its own housing projects at rock-bottom prices.

A strong backlash was perhaps inevitable. In 1927, a group claiming to represent "intellectual Vienna" would declare in a manifesto that the mounting political campaign against city hall's tax policy must not dissuade anyone from ignoring its "great social and cultural achievements." This endorsement of Red Vienna included such well-known signatories as Alfred Adler and Sigmund Freud, writers Robert Musil and Franz Werfel, and composer Anton von Webern. Emotions on both sides of the Viennese tax issue must have been running high, for the manifesto marked one of the few occasions that Adler and Freud would publicly agree on anything.

Yet, outside the capital, many affluent Austrians were just as disgruntled as local Viennese about the Social Democrats' economics. For decades, conservative-minded provincials had uneasily viewed the cosmopolitan, polyglot capital as something rather alien. Rural churchgoers had viewed sophisticated Vienna as an irreligious, decadent, even sinful place. Now after the war, these same people were shocked to find themselves indirectly paying for the Social Democrats' ambitious programs in Vienna, as the city's steep taxes increased the costs of virtually all goods and services flowing through Austria.

Nevertheless, Social Democratic leaders ignored such criticism and hailed their social achievements in glowing terms. In their view, tax increases were a minor price to pay for developing an unprecedented system of valuable human services. Certainly, in fields like child guidance and welfare, these innovations were attracting admiration from around the globe. Thus, as early as 1923, School Superintendent Glöckel praised his city as a modern-day mecca for its new educational accomplishments. Five years later, in sentiments that Adler certainly shared, Glöckel would declare "that today Austria stands in the front rank of civilized countries in educational innovation and that Vienna can claim the proud title of 'city of school reform.'"

CHAPTER TEN

Beyond Austria:
International Prominence

Most of the methods employed today
to solve pressing [social] problems
are . . . obsolete and inadequate. . . .
Individual psychology might be
developed into a most powerful
instrument for ridding nations
and groups of the menace of their
collective inferiority complexes.

ALFRED ADLER

By the mid-1920s, Adler had become increasingly recognized in Central Europe as a leading figure in the field of child psychology and family relations. Reflecting this newfound influence, in 1925 he was invited to contribute a chapter to a new anthology on marriage. Edited by the prolific Count Hermann von Keyserling, *The Book of Marriage* was initially published in German and then translated into English the following year. Its impressive list of contributors included psychiatrists and authors like Havelock Ellis, Carl Jung, Thomas Mann, and Rabindranath Tagore. Popular mores about sex and marriage were in a state of rapid flux. As never before in modern times, many Europeans and Americans were questioning the traditional notion of marriage as a lifetime, monogamous union.

In this regard, Adler was no revolutionary, however. While readily conceding that contemporary matrimony was often unsatisfying, he was interested in providing advice to improve rather than overturn marriage. In Adler's view, society's treatment of women was the major culprit; too many husbands demeaned their wives, who in turn felt chronically resentful about their second-class status. Perhaps thinking of his parents' forty-one years together ended only by Pauline's death, Adler insisted that marriage was "a task for two," and that the greater the mutual cooperation and respect between partners, the happier and more fulfilling their bond. He praised matrimony rooted in monogamy as the highest, and perhaps therefore the most challenging, form of human social feeling.

Even after coming to the United States several years later, Adler would consistently express this viewpoint. Unlike many popular thinkers of the time, such as behaviorist John Watson and philosopher Bertrand Russell, Adler never suggested that monogamy was obsolete or replaceable by a new, more satisfying style of adult relationship. For him, what was definitely obsolete and irrelevant was the traditional male attitude: the infamous double standard with respect to extramarital sex and the equating of wife as a husband's servant or property. With true equality between spouses, modern marriage required no substitute.

From all accounts, Adler practiced what he preached. Despite the difficulties in temperament and outlook that would eventually mark their separation for several years, there is no evidence that he was ever unfaithful to Raissa or even showed romantic interest in other women. He apparently exhibited so little flirtatiousness for a successful man of his background that his European friends would later feel impelled, almost apologetically, to defend his virility.

A rare formal photograph taken of the couple during these years reveals a standing Adler, proud and with a self-satisfied, almost jaunty smile; he seems to be privately savoring a pleasurable memory. A stiff Raissa sits beside him and stares tensely into the camera.

Surprisingly, Adler's own marital strains did not sour his sentiments toward the institution itself. Although living alone and as an apparent celibate for most of his late fifties through mid-sixties, he continued to extol monogamous marriage. As evidenced by Raissa's midlife letters to her adult children, she was a concerned and doting mother. Despite the fact that she continued to be active as a Trotskyite revolutionary, phrases like "Are you feeling well?" "Be sure to dress warmly," and "Are you getting enough to eat?" were ever-present themes in her correspondence with Alexandra, Valentine, Kurt, and Cornelia, even into their thirties. When the latter was experiencing marital tensions that would eventually culminate in divorce, Raissa urged her daughter to avoid vindicativeness. Since Adler's correspondence with family members was likewise solicitous in tone, it seems likely that parental emotions helped strengthen his bond with Raissa.

In Austria, most Social Democrats embraced Adler's position concerning monogamy. Similar to Adler, party leaders had generally been raised in solidly middle-class Viennese families during the Victorian era. Like Adler, too, many came from ethnically Jewish households that traditionally revered marital fidelity and sexual compromise. Although such Social Democrats might rhetorically call for overthrowing world capitalism, their sexual morality was conservative and they viewed Freud's sexual theories with alarm. Privately, party figures like Vienna's health and welfare commissioner Tandler might well enjoy the company of a mistress; but they would never publicly attack conventional morality or advocate a sexually liberated society as later Reich did.

As one Austrian historian has noted, "The socialist reformers showed little concern for sex as a source of pleaure and as a normal and important part of everyday life. In its 'pure' form, sex was an embarrassment and was treated obliquely. Most frequently, it was dealt with in party publications as a problem of moral control in which women and youth were the primary objects of concern."

Thus, one of Austria's most widely read socialist writers was the novelist Johann Frech, whose pamphlets on marriage extolled female chastity and denounced premarital experimentation. Although there is no evidence as to whether Adler and Frech were friendly, they did share the ideals of marital fidelity and monogamy. Nevertheless, Adler adopted a decisively more radical stance than his Social Democratic colleagues on another important social issue, namely, abortion.

At the time, Austria had a stringent antiabortion law known as Paragraph 144 of the national penal code. For a woman even to attempt an abortion was a crime punishable by a prison term of six months to a year. A successful abortion was punishable by a term of one to five years, and implicated midwives and physicians were subject to the same penalties. In the absence of sex education in the schools and of readily available and inexpensive birth control devices (both of which the Catholic church vigorously fought), however, abortion was a prevalent form of birth control among Austria's working class; one researcher at the time estimated that between 20 percent and 40 percent of all pregnancies were aborted. Therefore, a law of leniency existed, that allowed judicial disgression in reducing or canceling prison sentences.

Against this legal backdrop, the Social Democratic party held a series of ambiguous positions on the abortion issue. In 1920, a national conference of women members demanded that Paragraph 144 be revised to permit abortions during the first trimester of pregnancy. Due to parliamentary maneuvering, however, the Christian Socials prevented the issue from being formally debated. Over the ensuing years, the first-trimester guideline was supported by the Social Democratic party, but its leaders refrained from pushing the issue vigorously.

Then in May 1924, a conference of Social Democratic physicians on abortion and population politics was held. The participants endorsed the conservative position of Julius Tandler, who had argued that under no circumstances should abortion be peformed on demand, because society, not individual women, needed to retain ultimate control over sexual reproduction. As a compromise gesture, Tandler had proposed a complex arrangement by which abortions would be decided on an individual case basis by a panel of experts, including a judge, a physician, the pregnant woman, a lawyer representing the fetus, and a societal representative.

Tandler's recommendation was never incorporated into the Social Democrats' party platform. But it aroused considerable discussion among reformers, and in 1925, Adler felt moved to address the issue publicly in an article published in his *International Journal for Individual Psychology*. "When we examine the anti-abortion law," he commented at the outset, "we find that only from the viewpoint of Individual Psychology can all sides of the problem be seen in proper illumination and be recognized in their true significance."

At first, Adler suggested that many of the arguments advanced by pro-choice advocates were spurious. For example, he noted from his own twenty-seven-year medical experience that many young women who initially feel ambivalent about their sudden, unplanned pregnancy become secure and happy once their baby is born. Also, many originally unplanned children grow up quite adequately, argued Adler, and learn to compensate well for any early disadvantage.

Nevertheless, Adler viewed these examples as unessential and rhetorically asked, "Should one force . . . a woman who so strongly rejects the idea of having a child to give birth against her will? For the legislator, the problem may end with the birth of the child. But we know that the problem only begins at birth, [for] what kind of mother will she be to the child?" Emphasizing his opposition to bringing unwanted babies into the world, Adler concluded that, "Alone in the interests of these children, I am in favor of telling every woman plainly: 'You need not have children if you don't want to.' . . . Compared to this argument, all others take a secondary place: Only a woman who wants the child can be a good mother."

Adler's position on abortion was definitely too "hot" for the Social Democrats' leadership to support. Indeed, the year after the article was published, delegates at the party conference, held that year in Linz, refused even to back Tandler's more conservative position and instead recommended that abortions be performed in public hospitals only under the following conditions: danger to the mother's health, the event of a deformed birth, or danger to the mother's economic existence or that of her children. In the ensuing years of the first Austria Republic, the Social Democrats never went beyond their Linz stance.

Ironically during the 1920s, several Marxist-feminist activists joined with racists and anti-Semites, like the Nazis, in arguing for abortion on eugenic grounds: that the "biologically unfit" comprise a burden and threat to society, and should be "weeded out" through legally easier abortion. Among these feminists was Adler's longtime medical colleague Margaret Hilferding, the first woman to be admitted as a member of Freud's Psychoanalytic Society. Her husband, Rudolf Hilferding, was a well-known Marxist theorist for the Social Democrats. In her book entitled *Birth Control,* published in 1926, Hilferding reprinted Adler's article on the abortion issue. Adler never again raised the issue publicly, however, either in Austria or later in the United States. Perhaps he timidly feared a conservative backlash against individual psychology; for while friendly with America's leading birth-control advocates like physician Ira Wile, Adler refrained from publicly endorsing any position on this similarly controversial issue.

———

In 1925, Adler experienced the most significant rupture in his growing individual psychology movement since well before the Great War. Many of Adler's intimates had long seen the event as inevitable, but with his genial and inclusive manner, he may have avoided the necessary confrontation until too late. In essence, it involved a long-simmering tension between Adler's younger, more Marxist-oriented admirers and his older, more conservative professional colleagues in the Society for Individual Psychology.

As recalled nearly fifteen years later by participants, the catalyst for the rupture was a recently published book on psychopathology by Oswald Schwarz, a respected physician and member of Adler's circle. Armed with a hidden agenda, several of the younger figures in the society politely asked Schwarz to present his new work at the next meeting. When he cordially did so, he found himself suddenly attacked as a reactionary by the younger, more politically minded Adlerians. Schwarz defended himself and then criticized severely this younger faction, led by Manes Sperber and Viktor Frankl. Joining Schwarz in his criticism was psychiatrist Rudolf Allers, who read from prepared notes. At this point, the twenty-year-old Sperber angrily leaped to his feet and tore Allers's paper to shreds.

Allers reacted with quiet composure to Sperber's crude behavior and then turned to Adler for defense. To the surprise and shock of the entire society, he stood up and said, "But perhaps the boy is right!" and abruptly sat down without further comment. There was a tense and seemingly interminable pause, and then Allers, Schwarz, and several sympathetic colleagues walked out of the building, never to return. Though several well-respected scholars like Oppenheim and Wexberg continued to publish in Adler's journal, they would never again feel as close to their former mentor. Nearly fifteen years later, Oppenheim commented bitterly and perhaps a bit self-righteously that, "He gave us up for a little frog, a nothing! Adler forgot how powerful we were, and that it lay in our hands to spread or retard the science of individual psychology."

What made Adler act in this way to alienate some of his most influential colleagues? It is possible he identified unconsciously with Sperber's position in the group as an idealistic, young dissident striving to express his view before a more conservative, entrenched majority? After all, more than fifteen years before, Adler had painfully found himself in almost the identical situation with the Vienna Psychoanalytic Society dominated by Freud's coterie. It also seems clear that Adler long felt a special affection for "the little frog" of Sperber, who either consciously or not adopted the role of dutiful child to a benevolent parental figure. Coincidentally, Sperber was exactly the same age as Adler's only son, Kurt, who at the time seemed to be veering away from a psychological career. Decades later, Kurt would tersely recall that, "I never quite trusted Sperber in those years." Soon after the breakup within his society, Adler decided to make individual psychology even broader in its general appeal, and less oriented toward narrow, medical-psychological work. Thus, at the People's Institute, he began offering a monthly lecture demonstration of family interviewing and also initiated a major change in editorial directorship of the *Journal for Individual Psychology*.

Although Adler's actions may have temporarily strengthened the Marxist faction among his Viennese following, his motives had more to do with personality clashes than with international politics. For by 1925, Adler seems to have been clearly moving away from Marxism and even from what was only a minimal involvement with the Social Democrats. His last article for the party newspaper, the *Arbeiter-Zeitung*, would appear that year. More significantly, after hearing a lecture by the influential socialist philosopher Max

Adler (no relation either to Alfred or Viktor Adler) at the Society for Individual Psychology, Alfred Adler felt moved to write a rather critical response in his *International Journal for Individual Psychology*.

Much beloved by the Austro-Marxists, Max Adler was born to Viennese-Jewish parents in 1873. He received his law degree from the university in 1896 before entering legal practice. A scholar rather than a politican, Max Adler edited a Marxist journal from from 1904 to 1922, and at the same time contributed many articles to Otto Bauer's *Der Kampf* (The Battle). In 1907, Max Adler cofounded the Vienna Sociological Society with several key Social Democrats, including Rudolf Eisler and Karl Renner. When the party burgeoned after the war, Max Adler served in parliament for a few years. But he found intellectual activity preferable to political maneuvering, and since 1920, had been most influential as a sociology professor at the University of Vienna.

In 1904, Max Adler had published his first major work, calling for a sociology focusing on human attitudes and values. In later writings he rejected the historical materialism of Lenin and other Bolsheviks, and accused them of fatalism by regarding the individual as a mere tool of economic forces. In Max Adler's caustic view, Lenin had falsified Marx by identifying his philosophy with materialism. By the mid-1920s, though, Max Adler was advocating dictatorship of the proletariat—not to vindicate Stalin but to proclaim a new, more individualistic type of socialist citizen.

Although the content of Max Adler's speech before the Adlerians is not known, it seems to have been fairly critical of their movement. In his view, individual psychology was probably politically naive, overly pragmatic, and lacking a firm foundation in socialist theory. Thus, Alfred Adler's article defensively rejected the charge that individual psychology was merely utilitarian folk wisdom, an accusation that would follow for years to come in Europe as well as the United States. "We hold to the stodgy moral formula that 'Honesty is the best policy!'" he declared. "We hold that 'Giving is better than receiving!' And, as painful as it may sound . . . we believe that these views are correct. We represent the view that Individual Psychology strengthens, secures, and can, and often must, help explain that which is lasting and eternal in human morality."

Alfred Adler went on to deny vigorously that his movement was pragmatically opportunistic. "The raising of spiritual standards—and this teaching: *to make oneself useful*—is found in every great achievement. Individual Psychology attempts to make this often intuitive and creative force—the unconscious, as Freud would say—more open and effective. With this task before us, we do not aim an educated caste to forge new weapons, but rather to serve the general good. If this caste wishes to rid the world of its neurosis and raise individual and social consciousness, it must dedicate all its knowledge and power. [This involves] the services of the physician, the educator, the parent, and the school."

Adler concluded by offering praise for socialist theory. "I find the studies of Marx exceptionally valuable. His work aims at a focus on continuity and context as perhaps no other work does. I agree that Marx's thoughts were born of the strongest social feelings and could lead to the strongest social feeling as well. I must go even farther and emphasize that in hindsight, Marx's scientific achievements, as well as those in other areas, possess a wonderful view toward connections close to Individual Psychology." But in a manner that most Social Democrats and certainly Bolsheviks undoubtedly found distressing, Adler then added: "Of course, we should not forget that these contributions exist in other places, especially in poetry and religion."

Consistent with Adler's conciliatory approach, he ended his brief article on a positive note: "That Max Adler recognized and described the importance of social tendencies in human behavior a long time ago is a pleasant and valuable enrichment of the development of Individual Psychology. We strive to become acquainted with all our predecessors and to acknowledge their contributions fairly. Our most important job is an alliance with all forces that share the same goals. May the future pass its judgment over the troublemakers and the opponents."

═══

The year 1925 also saw Adler's second anthology, *The Practice and Theory of Individual Psychology,* made available to English-speaking audiences for the first time. Published initially in England, it was brought out the following year in an American edition. By this time, Adler's innovative work in psychology was not only drawing major international attention among professionals, but was also beginning to attract popular interest. Thus, Adler was first featured in the *New York Times* in September 1925. The article comprised a major interview whose headline proclaimed "Inferiority Sense Held to be Our Chief Enemy" and which carried a subtitle that stated, "Dr. Adler, founder of 'Individual Psychology,' claims war can be eliminated and love problems solved by attacking this foe—at variance with Freud."

In this piece, the *New York Times* described the tremendous impact that the "new psychology" was having on American as well as European culture. Then, using an oddly theological metaphor, the article explained that,

146

"One of the most important schools of this new science of the soul is individual psychology, founded by the Viennese scholar and neurologist, Dr. Alfred Adler. Laymen sometimes make the mistake of regarding individual psychology as a mere subdivision of the psychoanalysis of Freud. It is no more that than is Protestantism a subdivision of Catholicism."

The *New York Times* was mainly interested in whether Adler's intriguing system of individual psychology could be applied to social and political matters. Adler, of course, answered in the affirmative and insisted that two factors affected all human relations: the inferiority complex and the striving for social feeling. Recalling his 1919 broadside entitled *The Other Side*, Adler commented that he had "shown how the imperialistic tendencies of the great financial powers" had heightened feelings of inferiority among Europe's masses. "The young men who murdered the Austrian heir to the throne . . . the crowds which subsequently clamored for war as a solution, and the still larger crowds which accepted war as a solution, consisted . . . of individuals at odds with themselves."

In a manner hardly calculated to gain supporters on the political left, Adler then added that, "Motives of hatred appear most clearly in the economic disturbances of our time. The class struggle is carried on by crowds made up of individuals whose quest for an inwardly and outwardly balanced mode of life is thwarted. . . . These mass movements produce further disturbing motives in the individuals [and] always proceed with a firm and resolute step toward their destructive aims."

Adler described how individual psychology regards the craving for power as a reaction to deep feelings of inferiority. Then, affirming the value of his approach in fields as diverse as child development and political psychology, Adler spoke of his system almost messianically: "Most of the methods employed today to solve pressing problems in the lives of people or groups are obsolete and inadequate. They are mostly based on stimulating nationalistic and religious passions and lead to oppression, persecution and war.

"Individual psychology could rally all the latent forces for good which are inherent in groups, just as it is already rallying such latent forces in individuals. Wars, national hatreds and class struggle—these greatest enemies of humankind—all root in the desire to escape, or compensate for, the crushing sense of their inferiority. Individual psychology, which can cure individuals of the evil effects of this sense of inferiority, might be developed into a . . . powerful instrument for ridding nations and groups of the menace of their collective inferiority complex."

147

It may be no surprise that Adler, so eager to pin the label of inferiority complex upon individuals, social groups, and even entire nations, evidenced a bristling sensitivity whenever his association was Freud was mentioned. Decades later, his young devotee, Manes Sperber, recalled that during the mid-1920s, "I divined that the hurt which Freud and his followers had inflicted upon him in the months preceding the break still affected him, as though it had happened only recently. . . . In his conversations with me he repeatedly reverted to those intrigues and attacks, deliberate misunderstandings, and insidious accusations. I listened to him in fascination. Usually it was late at night, an hour after we had left" the Café Siller.

Elsewhere, Sperber remarked that, "To me, he was an exemplary teacher, and in those years I promised myself that I would be grateful to him for the rest of my life. Yet I suspected early on that this would not always be easy, for in my presence he sometimes spoke unfairly and with almost cruel severity about friends and adherents whom he had suddenly began to distrust. In such cases he was incapable of listening calmly to even the mildest intercession on behalf of those . . . expelled [for their deviancy from individual psychology]. Then he would suddenly be transformed and give me such a hostile look that I had an oppressive feeling that I was facing a stranger." In years to come, other young associates of Adler would similarly recall the tendency of their usually genial and solicitous mentor to flare suddenly into heated anger when he felt his authority challenged on an important matter.

Often, the two men continued their late-night conversations together over glasses of dark beer in Griechenbeisl, Vienna's oldest restaurant, or in a café with extended closing hours. Eventually, Sperber found enough material to complete a short biography of his mentor, which was published in July 1926. Written in German, *Alfred Adler: The Man and his Work* is not well-known today. The small volume has never been reprinted or translated into English, but it was among the first biographical works devoted to Adler's career.

Laudatory in tone and prominently incorporating his mentor's personal reminiscences, Sperber expected an enthusiastic response from fellow members of the Society for Individual Psychology. But not all were pleased by its appearance that fall. "I was stupid enough not to discover until much later," recalled Sperber, "that my little book had netted me the carefully concealed and thus all the more implacable enmity of many Adlerians—particularly some of Adler's early *compagnons de route*. I had no idea that they would interpret my failure to mention their names in my monograph as an insulting provocation."

Although Sperber never specified precisely whom the book had offended, it is not difficult to guess. It contains not a single mention of such longtime intimates as Carl Furtmüller, Alexander Neuer, or Erwin Wexberg. Decades later, in memoirs like *Masks of Loneliness,* Sperber would vaguely blame such figures for "poisoning" Adler against him and his later communist activism. But, as we shall see in Chapter Nineteen, historical evidence does not support Sperber's interpretation.

Indeed, by the winter of 1926, Adler had already begun mentoring another, idealistic and energetic young devotee destined to serve as a far more productive collaborator: Walter Beran Wolfe. A twenty-six-year-old American psychiatrist of Austrian parentage, he had specifically come to Vienna to study with Adler. A bright Ivy League graduate, Wolfe must have appealed immediately to Adler, for he soon became the first American member of the Society for Individual Psychology in Vienna, and more significantly, he was entrusted with associate editorship of Adler's international journal. In addition, Adler chose Wolfe to edit and translate his upcoming popular book, *Understanding Human Nature* (*Menschenkenntinis* in German), for the English-speaking world.

Buoyed by the growing international interest in his work, Adler began preparing in the early fall for an upcoming lecture tour of Great Britain and then the United States. He was not adept in English, and spent weeks immersed in solitary study to improve his proficiency before traveling to London in early November.

━━━━━

During Adler's visit to England, only the second of his career, he was pleased that psychological services for children were finally beginning to make headway. Only the previous year, in 1925, a London magistrate had visited several child-guidance clinics in the United States. Impressed with the interdisciplinary approach involving clinicians and educators, she formed a professional interest group in London to help build similar programs throughout Great Britain. Among those working most actively toward this end was psychologist Cyril Burt, whose new book, *The Young Delinquent,* had advocated precisely for the establishment of such clinics.

Not only was Adler promoting individual psychology to medical colleagues, he was also eager to establish a lay branch of his society in London. Not long after arriving, he was introduced to a charismatic Serbian philosopher named Dimitrije Mitrinovic. Nearly forty years old, he was a brilliant conversationalist who had acquired a loyal following among the artistic and intellectual avant-garde living in Bloomsbury. The two men spent hours together in conversation, and Adler was intrigued by Mitrinovic's colorful life.

Born in Herzegovina in 1887, he was the oldest of ten children. As a youth, he had developed strong nationalistic feelings and clandestinely organized a lending library in opposition to Austro-Hungarian governmental repression. When the empire annexed the provinces of Bosnia and Herzegovina, Mitrinovic and three colleagues, acting in protest, began a secret society that they called Rad ("Work"). Its purpose was to spark culturally a nationalistic outlook among the south Slavs. In this way, Mitrinovic quickly developed a reputation as a leader of the "Young Bosnian" movement. At the age of eighteen, he had gained additional visibility through poems and critical essays published in Serbia's leading journals, as well as those in the Austrian-controlled provinces of Bosnia, Croatia, and Slovenia.

In 1914, Mitrinovic enrolled at the University of Munich, where he studied art history. There he became acquainted with the expressionist artist Wassily Kandinsky and his Blaue Reiter group. By now, Mitrinovic had become a fervent advocate for radical cultural change, based on ideas he had derived from European folklore, mythology, and nationalism. Early that year, he gave a public lecture in the Great Hall of the University of Munich entitled "Kandinsky and the New Art: Taking Tomorrow by Storm."

Meanwhile, political tensions in the Balkans had escalated. Serbian nationalists had loosely divided into two political factions: those favoring violence as a tool for liberation from the Austro-Hungarian Empire, and those seeking a peaceful alternative. Mitrinovic was recognized as a leader for those advocating peaceful change, since by political outlook he was a pan-European with liberal sympathies.

Then came the assassination of Austria's Archduke Francis Ferdinand and his wife, Sophie, in Sarajevo. Feeling endangered both by the Austrian police and the Serbian terrorists whom he had opposed, Mitrinovic fled to England, where he was befriended by the Serbian Legation. By early 1915, he was already publishing and lecturing in English, and soon became friendly with London's avant-garde group of artists and intellectuals. These included A. R. Orage and later Philip Mairet, both men well-regarded editors of iconoclastic cultural-political periodicals like *The New Age* and *The New English Weekly*. By the war's close, Mitrinovic's vision had shifted from creating the nation of Yugoslavia to wider concerns: Europe and the entire world. During the 1920s, he dabbled in metaphysics, philosophy, psychology, and pan-European radicalism.

Although his writings were often dense, Mitrinovic had a brilliant and captivating style of debate. It is likely that Adler was impressed with his sheer intellect as well as his commitment to progressive social change based on the "new psychology." In any event, Mitrinovic soon was installed as director of the new London branch of the International Society for Individual Psychology. Editor Philip Mairet and several young literary figures eagerly became active assistants. An independent medical group interested in Adler's system was likewise established; its head was the well-respected psychiatrist Francis Crookshank.

On November 9, a seemingly delighted Adler wrote to Raissa in English: "I have passed my two lectures yesterday free speaking and without preparation. They applauded me strongly. I must remain in Grosvenor Hotel. This of course is expensive. I am invited for Oxford and Cambridge. Here is a very nice letter. I hope you [*sic*] all healthy and thinking of me."

Nevertheless, Adler was feeling worried about his impending trip to the United States. On his last night in London, he experienced a vivid and anxious dream. He was on board the ship as planned, when suddenly it capsized and sunk. All of Adler's worldly possessions were on it and were destroyed by the raging waves. Hurled into the ocean, Adler was forced to swim for his life. Alone he thrashed and struggled through the choppy water. But through the force of will and determination, he finally reached land in safety.

The next day, Adler boarded the ship at its dock in Southampton and began his first transoceanic voyage. The dream was not hard for him to interpret. Fifty-six years old, and not without a little trepidation, he was ready to begin the next, momentous phase of his life.

Part Two

═══

The United States is like an ocean. An individual has infinite possibilities for development in such a country, but he also has greater difficulties to overcome. The incentive to ambition is great but the competition is also very keen. In Europe, they are still swimming around in a bathtub; life is circumscribed, opportunities are few, and the need for [psychological] knowledge is limited.

ALFRED ADLER

CHAPTER ELEVEN

A New World in Social Upheaval

Never in recent generations have human beings so floundered about outside the ropes of social and religious sanctions. . . . Sensationalism finds in new manners of life subject for five-inch headlines. . . . People will act—and then a new code will grow up. But along the way guidance and interpretation are deeply needed.

FREDA KIRCHWEY
OUR CHANGING MORALITY

I f Adler was experiencing a rare bout of self-doubt and anxiety on the eve of his first trip to the United States, such feelings were understandable enough. Having long prided himself on being an adroit public speaker, the prospect of shifting to his awkward and heavily accented English could hardly have been encouraging. And although at least a few sympathetic colleagues and supporters would be attending his talks, essentially he would be alone for the entire four-month visit. But perhaps more significantly in heightening Adler's tension, the United States was a country quite different in many ways from his native Austria.

Certainly, America's sheer size had no counterpart in his experience living in Vienna and traveling in Central Europe. His homeland was geographically miniscule by American standards: The entire country of Austria was little more than half the size of Illinois and roughly equal to that of New England's rocky Maine. In total population, America's ethnically diverse and geographically scattered 115 million people represented more than twenty times the number of Austria's inhabitants.

Economically, Adler's homeland had only recently begun to recover from its disastrous military defeat and its subsequent hyperinflation, destroying the life savings of many citizens. National employment was still far from high, and there seemed little possibility for major improvement. As Adler well knew, the United States, however, was in the midst of an unprecedented economic boom. Both he and his old nemesis Freud had been personally benefitting from the foreign presence of dollar-rich Americans eager for therapeutic treatment and study in Vienna.

But alongside American economic changes were social changes of enormous import. These would prove crucial in creating a climate of opinion highly receptive to Adler's confident advice on how to adapt and live in a more fulfilling way. Outside the home, greater leisure time was opening up for millions through a steady reduction in the workweek. As recently as the 1890s, even high-level business executives enjoyed no paid vacations. Everyone worked six days a week except for the handful of national holidays like Christmas and the Fourth of July. By the 1920s, however, the paid vacation—a week or two long—had become increasingly common for white-collar workers. Between 1900 and 1930, working hours would eventually decline by 15 percent. The old twelve-hour, six-day workweek was gone, replaced for most workers by a standard ten-hour workday and a half-holiday on Saturday. Most Americans were using Saturday afternoons for chores and had Sunday entirely free for leisure. It is estimated that the massive new leisure time ran to a national aggregate of two billion person-hours per week and, of course, had tremendous impact upon the society. The economy benefitted enormously, for the huge vacation industry was created.

Culturally, most Americans were spending their increased leisure time on entertainment and hobbies, rather than on religion or self-improvement. The year 1924 witnessed the emergence of mah-jongg as a national craze. The following year, crossword puzzles became immensely popular and helped catapult two publishing partners named Simon and Schuster into sudden wealth. That same year of 1925, contract bridge was invented and soon achieved huge popularity.

Although most Americans were not avid readers, the boom years of the 1920s were stimulating many new publishing ventures and a steady expansion of titles were issued. Adler's major American publisher was established during this period, and the year of his first American lecture tour witnessed the founding of both the Book-of-the-Month Club and the Literary Guild. Artful novelists including F. Scott Fitzgerald, Ernest Hemingway, and Sinclair Lewis were doing well financially. But for two and a half years, the bestselling volume was entitled *Diet and Health;* Bruce Barton's *The Man*

Nobody Knows, portraying Jesus Christ as an astute businessman and self-promoter, had sold almost as many copies as Lewis's highly praised *Main Street.*

Nevertheless, organized religion was a clear casualty of the time. Generally, clergy no longer commanded the respect they had enjoyed before the war. Religious attendance declined substantially, and church and Sunday school enrollments failed to keep pace with America's population growth. Not more than 60 percent of Americans attended church or synagogue regularly in most places, and in the West the figure was closer to 25 percent. Although a fundamentalist revival grew in the South, religion held little appeal for most young Americans.

Side by side with the decline in organized religion went an upheaval in social values with regard to marriage, romance, and sexuality. American cultural historians have long debated the precise cause for this tremendous shift during the early to mid-1920s. To at least some degree, World War I exerted a definite impact. Two million men, and not an insignificant number of women serving as nurses and clerical workers, were sent to Europe, where they witnessed a culture with very different social practices. In France brothels were legal and taken for granted, while premarital and extramarital sex were treated with a casualness that astounded many American soldiers furloughing in Paris or in other cities on the Continent.

Besides exposing many young Americans to foreign mores, the Great War and its mass sufferings helped to instill a sense of disillusionment with traditional values. Writing as early as 1930, historian Frederick Lewis Allen noted that especially among Americans stationed in France, "there had been a very widespread and very natural breakdown of traditional restraints and taboos. It was impossible for this generation to return unchanged when the ordeal was over. . . . They found themselves expected to settle down into the humdrum routine of American life as if nothing had happened, to accept the moral dicta of elders who seemed to be living in a Pollyanna land of rosy ideals which the war had killed for them. They couldn't do it, and they disrespectfully said so."

Another contributor to changing sexual morality in the United States was the increasing usage of the private automobile among unmarried teens and young adults. In their famous Middletown study, the Lynds found that car ownership not only carried prestige for high-school students eager to impress their peers, but also permitted an unprecedented freedom from adult supervision. Prior to the automobile's advent, young people were far more likely to socialize in public groups for community dances, picnics, or skating parties. Now for the first time in many small towns, they were able to pair off as independent couples.

Throughout the 1920s, a car became "a portable living room, and could be used for eating, drinking, smoking, gossiping, and sex." Among a Middle-town group of thirty young women charged with committing "sex crimes," nineteen of them were accused of acts occurring in cars. The attendant juvenile court judge declared that the automobile had become a "house of prostitution on wheels."

Certainly another cause for the liberalization of American sexual mores lay in Hollywood. Early in the establishment of the film industry, its execu-tives had discovered that women as well as men enjoyed watching attractive stars in glamorous settings. Although film fare commonly included West-erns, adventure epics, and lighthearted comedies, the most enticing adver-tisements promised "brilliant men, beautiful jazz babies, champagne baths, midnight revels, petting parties in the purple dawn all ending in one terrific smashing climax that makes you gasp." Another movie touted its "neckers, petters, white kisses, red kisses, pleasure-mad daughters, sensation-craving mothers . . . the truth—bold, naked, sensational."

Not surprisingly, many social observers blamed Hollywood for promoting irreverence and hedonism among young people. Such criticism had long been raised. As late as 1913, no motion-picture theater was allowed within two hundred feet of a church. But after World War I, vocal opposition to Hollywood's film content mounted steadily and surged after the lurid, highly publicized sex scandal involving the comic actor Roscoe "Fatty" Ar-buckle. Accused of manslaughter in the hotel-room death of actress-model Virginia Rappe, the five-thousand-dollar-a-week comedian was successfully acquitted in 1922 after three separate trials. That same year, the immensely popular actor Wallace Reid publicly underwent drug and alcohol rehabili-tation, and yet another major Hollywood scandal broke. This one involved the trinity of sex, suicide, and narcotics, and splashed the names of such famed actresses as Mabel Norman and Mary Pickford onto the front pages of newspapers. In an anxious defensive maneuver to ward off possible pub-lic boycott or governmental intervention, Hollywood's magnates recruited Will Hays to head their new "morals office." An influential member of President Harding's cabinet and a Presbyterian elder, Hays understood that his new job was essentially for public relations rather than decision making, and, in this capacity, he played his role well.

"The potentialities of motion pictures for moral influence and education are limitless," Hays preached. "Therefore its integrity should be protected as we protect the integrity of our children and our churches, and its quality developed as we develop the quality of our schools. . . . This industry must have toward that sacred thing, the mind of a child, toward that clean virgin thing, the same responsibility, the same care about the impressions made upon it, that the best clergyman or the most inspired teacher of youth should have."

Despite such high-sounding reassurances, virtually all perceptive observers soon realized that a revolution in America's marital and sexual values was truly underway. As early as 1925, editor Freda Kirchwey aptly noted in her anthology of essays entitled *Our Changing Morality* that, "Men and women are ignoring old laws. In their relations with each other, they are living according to tangled, conflicting codes. Remnants of early admonitions and relationships, the dictates of custom, the behavior of their friends, their own tastes and desires, elusive dreams of a loveliness not provided for by rules—all these are scrambling to fill the gap that was left when Right and Wrong finally followed the other absolute monarchs to an empty, nominal existence somewhere in exile. . . . Much has been written about sex— and everything remains to be said. Largely, new conclusions will be reached through new processes of living. People will act—and then a new code will grow up."

Kirchwey modestly saw only a limited role for writers or intellectuals in affecting social values, but in this respect, she was probably in the minority. Over the next few years, American society became inundated with countless magazine articles, interviews, and books all touting their particular viewpoint on how men and women could better cope with changing mores about marriage and sexuality. For those today who cling to the erroneous belief that popular interest in such matters first arose among those who came to adulthood during the Vietnam War, it can be startling merely to skim the titles of articles and books appearing during the mid- to late 1920s.

Even the most mainstream American periodicals, such as *Good Housekeeping, Forum, Harper's, Literary Digest,* and *Outlook and Independent,* gave a great deal of attention to the twin topics of matrimony and sex. Some articles were analytic or philosophical in tone, and bore such titles as "The Breakdown of Marriage," "The Chaos of Modern Marriage," "Does Society Mock at Marriage?," "Marriage Today and Tomorrow," and "Our Changing Monogamy." Other magazine pieces sought to offer their readership specific advice, and included "The Christian Ideal of Marriage," "The Job of Being Married," "Model Marriages," "If Your Wedding Ring Were a Wishing Ring," "Can You Be Married and Free?," "The Secret of Being Happily

Married," and "How Can You Hold the Man You Love?" Still other magazine articles were more frankly confessional in tone. Although extremely tame by contemporary literary standards, these included "How I Would Make My Wife Over," "I Would Rather Be Married than Single," "I Have the World's Best Husband," "So This is Marriage, and "I Married the Wrong Man." As their titles would suggest, most of these confessional pieces were written specifically for women, and generally appeared in widely circulating women's magazines. As for books on the same popular topic, those receiving serious attention during the same period included *The Bankruptcy of Marriage, A Short History of Marriage, Marriage and Morals, Motherhood in Bondage, The Woman a Man Marries, Women in Soviet Russia, Wholesome Marriage,* and *The Marriage Bed.*

With such a plethora of books and magazine articles, no one viewpoint predominated. Opinions ran the social gamut, from religious conservatives who railed against even the suggestion of granting easier divorce to self-proclaimed radicals demanding a heightened pace to the sweeping changes in sexual attitude and behavior. But most middle-class Americans of the 1920s rejected both extremes. Enjoying a way of life fueled by material affluence and mass entertainment, they were generally pleased with new developments around them.

Especially in the fast-growing cities, few were interested in returning to what journalists derisively called the "old rules" about male-female relations and larger moral dicta. In these years after the war, it was science—and not organized religion—that now commanded greatest credibility and respect. To be sure, not all Americans felt this way. But perhaps for the first time, those championing traditional pieties about daily living were placed on the intellectual defensive. As perhaps never before, those who spoke instead with scientific authority held powerful and unprecedented appeal.

Largely for this reason, the timing of Adler's first and subsequent visits to the United States was most fortuitous. By international reputation, he was a highly original thinker whose work was rooted in medical science. His ideas about sexuality, marriage, and child rearing therefore carried great legitimacy. Also, for a vast country that still looked toward Europe for intellectual and artistic leadership, Adler as a famous Viennese possessed a special aura of erudition and evocative charm. Such factors helped to arouse initial interest in his pronouncements. But it was Adler's personal traits of geniality, optimism, and warmth coupled with an intensely ambitious drive that soon catapulted him to American prominence as a psychological expert.

Of course, Adler's message was also persuasive for the times: He generally embraced the changing social mores, but with gentle and cautionary advice.

As readers of Von Keyserling's newly translated anthology, *The Book of Marriage,* could readily see, Adler was interested in offering helpful, practical guidance. Thus, in his chapter entitled "Marriage as a Task," he had nothing hostile to say about matrimony as an institution, but instead constructively focused on how men and women might enhance it. In his view, our capacity for a loving relationship derives greatly from early personality development. Without a strong sense of self-esteem gained from having supportive and nurturing parents, as children we experience difficulty in forming close bonds with others. If reaching adulthood with feelings of inferiority (which today psychologists might call shame or guilt), we are likely to find it hard to develop lasting friendships, and certainly the intense intimacy required for satisfying marriage.

Adler also saw much of the prevailing marital unhappiness as related to the harmful influence of sex-role myths and stereotypes. Women were constantly demeaned by the dominant culture, and consequently tended inwardly to deprecate their abilities—as well as to feel resentment for the masculine domination. "The man, through a long-outworn common tradition, possesses an . . . advantage which he attempts to preserve, selfishly but to his own detriment. For [those who share our viewpoint] the master of the family is a thing of the past. He sees marriage as a duality in which both parties make a united effort to perform a common task. . . . Marriage is not a constructed edifice which one approaches . . . but a . . . creative performance in time. . . . Always one will find in marriage only that which one has created in it."

While Adler's chapter in *The Book of Marriage* was critical of many marital relationships, far more radical in perspective was *Companionate Marriage.* Its senior author was Judge Benjamin Lindsey of Denver's Juvenile and Family Court, and his book was published in December 1926, the date that coincidentally marked Adler's arrival for his first American lecture tour. Judge Lindsey argued that his professional work in divorce law had convinced him that traditional marriage was unworkable and obsolete. He therefore proposed that two distinct legal categories be established: companionate (childless) marriage and family marriage, involving the presence of children. Lindsey insisted that companionate marriages should be allowed to terminate in an easier and more humane way than current state laws were mandating. For this reason, he outlined new legislation of a three-pronged nature: first, that childless couples be permitted to divorce based on mutual consent; second, that alimony be abolished in such cases, except with reference to each spouse's economic position; and, third, that medical and scientific boards be permitted to enable couples to remain childless if they wish.

Although Judge Lindsey was calling for legalized birth control, he was no revolutionary. Indeed, he clearly rejected the popular concept of trial marriages and insisted instead that most couples would experience companionate marriage as merely a way station to the fulfilling life of parenthood. Lindsey's chief point was that companionate marriage had already become a social reality in the United States and that it ought to be made more conventionally respectable and legally valid.

Interestingly, from our own historical vantage point, the mainstream American press of the 1920s expressed ambivalent praise for Lindsey's popular work. Perhaps to counter the strident attacks of religious fundamentalists, nearly all major newspapers and magazines declared the author of *Companionate Marriage* to be an eminently reasonable fellow. "You will find no demagogic oratory in this book, no anti-social argument," the *Outlook* reassured its middle-of-the-road readership, "You will find wise, sane, documented exposition of the ideas of a man of wide experience, sympathy and intelligence." Likewise, the *Saturday Review of Literature* praised Lindsey "for the extraordinary value of his services, for his realism, his courage, and his charity."

Yet, most mainstream reviewers were unwilling to endorse Lindsey's key notion of mandating a separate legal category for childless marriages—and to make these easier to dissolve. Even with such arrangements, "there are problems of human and social relationships for which neither the dissemination of scientific birth control information nor divorce by mutual consent would offer a panacea," observed a critic in *Survey*. A lengthy *New York Times* review disparagingly remarked that Lindsey's viewpoint was basically an advocacy for "temporary marriage [which] can be no contribution to our knowledge of a phenomenon whose ideal essence is permanency. . . . A marriage entered upon with a view to the practice of childlessness has precisely nothing to teach you with regard to marriage *cum* children."

Speaking more broadly about the rising rate of marital unhappiness and divorce, the same *Times* reviewer suggested that young adults of the 1920s lacked earlier generations' capacity to accept compromise and adversity as basic to everyday life relationships including marriage: It was their misguided emphasis on self-gratification and their unrealistic expectations about marriage that needed changing, not the matrimonial institution itself.

During the late 1920s, Adler, in his role as a popular lecturer in the United States, would vigorously expound the same viewpoint. To the general public intrigued by the "new psychology" but uneasy with radical social ideas, his message about the viability of conventional marriage was optimistic and reassuring. With his appealing emphasis on improving marital relationships through psychological insight, Adler would gain considerable popularity in coming years.

=======

It was a confluence of many emergent forces after the war that generated the sweeping changes in mores occurring in America during the 1920s. But in the important realm of ideas it was Freud whose influence was powerful and persuasive, and vitally contributed to Adler's own success in the United States. For this reason, it is crucial to understand how Freud's notions gradually gained adherents in American culture beginning with its intelligentsia. For those whose saw themselves fighting an uphill battle to overturn restrictive Victorian values, Freud was an impressive figure. With his aura of intellectual courage and integrity, he acquired a devoted following. Starting before Freud's sole American visit in 1909, and greatly accelerating afterward, he gained a steadily growing number of zealous adherents in professional and lay circles.

In particular, two articulate psychiatrists helped promulgate Freud's notions effectively within the New World. Of all American analysts during this period, Abraham A. Brill undoubtedly stood closest to Freud. Born in 1874, he had left Austro-Hungary as a teenager and grown up on New York City's Lower East Side, a neighborhood teeming with other Jewish immigrants. After graduating from medical school at Columbia University, Brill studied psychiatry with Eugen Bleuler, who had introduced Freudian ideas into his Zurich clinic. In 1908, Brill met Freud in Vienna and arranged to translate his works into English. Thus began an enduring friendship that Brill proudly described as "the greatest experience of my life."

Returning to the United States later that year, Brill began assertively championing Freud's work in academia as well as the wider culture. "I was full of enthusiasm about the prospects of psychoanalysis . . . and I started at once to inform and convince others," Brill later recalled. Wasting little time, he founded in his living room in 1911 the New York Psychoanalytic Society and was elected its first president. (That same year, Britisher Ernest Jones established the American Psychoanalytic Association, a separate organization designed to include all those in North America interested in Freud's work). Until after World War I, Brill served as Freud's sole translator and dutifully sent all royalties back to his mentor. With fierce determination and interest, Brill frequently provided interviews for New York City newspapers and wrote prolifically to defend his mentor against all attacks. He would remain implacably hostile to Adler upon his increasing American professsional activity.

William Alanson White operated more as a summarizer and integrator for the American press. As a young man, he turned to psychiatry, and served from 1903 through 1937 as superintendent of the federal government's largest psychiatric institution, St. Elizabeth's Hospital in Washington. With consummate political skill, he carefully tended his connections among the wealthy, the politically powerful, and the press. He cultivated the image of a benevolent scientist-healer who stood above partisan strife.

In 1911, White authored what was probably the first book on psychoanalysis by an American, and cofounded in 1913 with his psychiatric colleague, Smith Ely Jellife the Freudians' first English-language journal, *The Psychoanalytic Review*. White's role as a well-reasoned advocate for Freud eventually climaxed politically in 1924, when he was elected president of the American Psychiatric Association. During the next few years, White would come to offer Adler moderate though short-lived support in the latter's efforts to plant the flag of individual psychology within the United States. More diplomatic than the caustic Brill, White provided numerous stories on psychoanalysis to the capital press corps, as well as to national wire services utilized by newspapers large and small throughout the nation.

With such key figures as Brill and White spearheading the psychoanalytic drive in the United States, it soon broke through the relatively narrow confines of Freud's own medical community. Intellectuals, writers, and artists found in psychoanalysis a fascinating new way of looking at human life. In Greenwich Village during the early teens, Freud's ideas became a popular springboard for literary and artistic discussion. Such interest in the dark recesses of the human personality represented the first stirrings of what would manifest in the 1920s as a major cultural upheaval.

In the Progressive Era, most socially interested Americans viewed their milieu rather benevolently. Generally, they felt little estrangement from their country or politics, except for specific forms of injustice deemed correctable through concerted citizen action. Indeed, some threw themselves into public affairs with an almost religious fervor. But to the alienated who flocked to Greenwich Village, Freud seemed to be confirming through modern science their suspicion that instead of attempting to reform society, the creative individual should be cultivating his or her "self." As a result, such devotees began to see Freud as a fearless advocate for sex as liberation and freedom. Without the right to behave spontaneously in matters of love and art, they interpreted Freud to be saying, irrevocable emotional crippling would occur.

Probably the most well-documented activities took place at the home of Mable Dodge Luhan, a wealthy socialite aspiring to intellectual status. Only a moment's stroll from the Washington Square arch, her elegant residence drew "Socialists, Trade-Unionists, Anarchists, Suffragists, Poets, Psychoanalysts, I.W.W.'s, Birth Controlists, Newspapermen, Artists, and Modern Artists."

Visitors like the novelist Floyd Dell, the political philosopher Max Eastman, the young magazine editor Walter Lippmann, and the journalistic muckraker Lincoln Steffens frequented her salons where Freud's name was touted. As Dell later recalled, it seemed that everybody in the Village began talking psychoanalytic jargon, playing parlor games of word association, and attempting to analyze dreams through purportedly Freudian methods. More broadly, intellectuals like Lippmann saw in psychoanalysis a brilliant beacon for throwing light on a variety of challenging social problems in the United States. Becoming editor of the influential *New Republic* in 1914, Lippmann forcefully applied Freudian notions to such issues as labor unrest and the feminist movement.

Dodge underwent psychoanalysis with Brill, who clearly saw the need to expand its influence beyond bohemian Greenwich Village. He astutely encouraged Dodge to write regular columns for the Hearst newspapers and thereby spread Freud's ideas to the working-class masses. Soon, the *New York Journal*, which then had the largest circulation of any newspaper in the country, was running her byline under such headlines as "Mabel Dodge Writes about Mother Love." In 1915, Max Eastman (also psychoanalyzed by Brill) helped popularize Freud in mass-circulation magazines like *Good Housekeeping* and *Everybody's Magazine*. Depicting psychoanalysis as a miracle cure, Eastman declared that, "Every case of nervous invalidism not arising from a physical cause has its origin in some maladjustment of the sex life. . . . This dangerous maladjustment has its beginning in the experiences of the child before its first five years are past."

In years to come, such intellectuals and literary figures would remain indifferent, if not openly hostile, to Adler's approach. They found immensely liberating Freud's apparent message that society thwarts its creative individuals through sexual inhibition. In contrast, Adler seemed to be promoting a conventional attitude toward sexuality, and emphasizing instead a vague appeal to altruism. Although he would gain great popularity in the United States, Adler would never win the support of its avant-garde intelligentsia.

Despite the fact that by the mid-teens artists and intellectuals like Eastman were already celebrating Freud's genius, most academic psychologists certainly were not. They were almost unanimous in condemning his approach to the mind as lacking in scientific objectivity, and surrounded by overblown, unverifiable claims. The prominent R. S. Woodworth of Columbia University sarcastically wrote for *The Nation* in 1916, "That there will found in the end to be something in the views of human nature which the followers of Freud and Jung are now erecting into an uncanny religion it is not necessary at this time to deny. . . . But there is no question that Freud and his followers over-work these concepts to an enormous degree, and by failing to take account of countless other motives and mechanisms in mental life, produce a wholly one-sided psychology. They accept Freudism as a religion. They will not admit any qualification to the least of its tenets, and scarcely any limitation to its scope and usefulness in understanding human activity in all fields, from myth to agriculture."

For more than a generation to follow, most experimentalists in psychology expressed the same sentiment. Seeking to make their rather fledgling field as scientifically prestigious as physics or chemistry, they could not abide the subjective nature of psychoanalysis. Especially abhorrent was the claim made by Freud's followers that being psychoanalyzed was necessary in order to understand what the complex system was truly all about. As one historian has noted, "What united experimental psychologists more than anything else was a distrust of personal experience, a sense that feelings in particular were dangerous and had to be held carefully in check lest they flood in and destroy the very foundations of the work. They were willing to make a number of sacrifices to protect psychology from this threat, including a radical narrowing of the field to include only phenomena that could be studied 'objectively.' "

In this same regard, most American academicians of the teens and twenties held little interest in Adler's work. They usually associated his approach with psychoanalysis, and rarely taught his ideas in college courses. There were exceptions, of course, like G. Stanley Hall of Clark University. But generally it was not until the thirties, with the rise of such applied fields as social work, child guidance, and educational psychology, that Adler truly gained academic respectability and influence in the United States.

Despite opposition from academia, Freud enjoyed increasing attention in the popular American press. As early as 1916, the *New York Tribune* highlighted Freudian ideas by reviewing a satirical new Greenwich Village play entitled *Suppressed Desires*. Quoting the play's Freudian disciple, the reporter explained that "psychoanalysis . . . removes [your mind's] obstruction

[and] brings into consciousness the suppressed desire . . . psychoanalysis is simply the latest scientific method of preventing and curing insanity." Two years later, the *Tribune* interviewed A. A. Brill and solicited his responses on such questions as: What is psychoanalysis? Is it supernatural? Does it have any value for normal people? What sort of man is Freud personally? Answering the questions clearly and at length, Brill helped the *Tribune* reporter present a story replete with reader identification. That same year, the *New Republic* noted that an avid American public had seized upon Freudianism for the "satisfaction of thwarted curiosity and the orientation of personal behavior."

By 1920, popular novels by writers like F. Scott Fitzgerald were mentioning Freud by name and the *Tribune* was referring to psychoanalysis as the "latest intellectual fad." In 1921, the *Brooklyn Eagle* sent a reporter to interview Freud directly in Vienna. Describing Freud as a famous advocate of sex and hunger drives, he told readers that the primary reason any American would want to visit Freud would be to have his dreams analyzed.

The press, of course, was not entirely uncritical regarding psychoanalysis. During that same year, the *New York Herald* devoted nearly an entire page to a disparagement of Freudian dream interpretation. Under the streamer headline "Dreams and their Meanings Wholly Natural," a New York neurologist scorned that, "The extraordinary symbolism ascribed to dream life by the new psychology is clearly the invention of the psychoanalysts. There is more to be learned from the interpretation published of the psychology of the analyst than of the psychology of the dreamer." Several weeks later, the *Herald* gave similar space to a prominent Philadelphia neurologist who likewise attacked the psychoanalytic method of dream interpretation as uselessly subjective.

As the 1920s progressed, Freud became an increasingly well-known figure in the popular media of the day. The millions who read *Good Housekeeping, Ladies' Home Journal, McClure's,* and other mass periodicals learned of Freud as a daring medical practitioner who had developed a new, scientific method for emotional cures revolving around sexual openness and freedom. Most of these popularizations offered their readers a few basic terms like *Oedipus complex* or *repression* and some overly simplistic, even distorted, explanations. Often these writers jumbled Adlerian, Freudian, and Jungian ideas in a confused manner. Generally, they attributed anything called a complex (including Adler's inferiority complex) to Freud, who was infuriated by such shallow accounts. He therefore granted few interviews to American journalists, whom as a group he intensely disliked.

167

In Sherwood Anderson's 1925 novel *Dark Laughter,* one character re-counts, "If there is anything you do not understand in human life, consult the works of Dr. Freud." Indeed, in 1925, a Tin Pan Alley song was entitled, "Don't Tell Me What You Dreamed Last Night, for I've Been Reading Freud."

In a very real way, this intellectual confusion would both help and hinder Adler when he first began lecturing throughout the United States. Certainly, he benefitted from the entire Viennese mystique and the impression that, like Freud, he could offer sensual mysteries about the human mind. Most journalists knew only of Adler's former association with Freud, and still believed him to be a loyal exponent—if not a trusted friend—of the psychoanalytic founder. For the first two or three years of Adler's public tours in America, many newspapers and magazines continued to depict him as Freud's "right-hand" and emissary, seeking to spread the gospel of sexual freedom. Such erroneous descriptions would infuriate Adler, and frustrate his efforts to advance his own psychological system. In time, though, virtually all journalists would accurately see individual psychology as quite different from the Freudian.

———

Despite the growing popularity of psychoanalysis in the United States during the 1920s, Freud took meager comfort in developments there and categorically opposed any suggestion that he make even a brief return visit. In this regard, his hostility toward America stood in stark contrast to Adler's upbeat and favorable attitude. Not only had Freud in 1924 declined a lavish *Chicago Tribune* offer of $25,000 if he would psychoanalyze the teenage killers Leopold and Loeb, but he had also rebuffed movie mogul Samuel Goldwyn's incredible $100,000 invitation to come to Hollywood and help develop a "really great love story" for the screen. Freud had likewise repeatedly rejected enticing offers from major magazines interested in publishing his byline on sex.

If anything, such financial blandishments only intensified Freud's long-standing dislike for the New World. Indeed, in the seventeen years since he had briefly set foot on its soil, his irritation and sarcasm about American culture had continued unabated up to the time of Adler's first visit in 1926. As historian Peter Gay has aptly noted, anti-Americanism runs through Freud's voluminious correspondence "like an unpleasant, monotonous theme." Another psychoanalytic historian has similarly observed that "Freud had an antipathy toward the United States that in many ways was prejudicial and irrational."

It was apparently not always this way. His sister Anna recalled that during Freud's childhood "he knew a lot about America and its culture." He enjoyed reading Mark Twain and, as a teenager, eagerly visited the American pavilion at Vienna's World Fair of 1873. According to Anna, her brother already spoke and read English by then. He felt inspired by various historical documents at the pavilion, including an exhibit of President Lincoln's letters in facsimile, the Gettysburg address, and the American Constitution.

Thirteen years later, Freud as a young physician even contemplated emigrating to the United States. Reminiscing to his colleague Ferenczi in 1919, Freud commented that, "Thirty-three years ago today, I stood as a freshly minted physician before an unknown future, resolved to go to America if the three months my supplies would last did not start out promisingly." How psychoanalytic history would have been altered had Freud made the major relocation in the 1880s is fascinating to speculate. Indeed, he too wondered in this same letter how matters would have changed "if fate had not smiled so amiably then."

Freud's early infatuation with cocaine may have been the turning point in tilting his attitude negatively toward the United States. When in 1884 he began his investigation into the alleged benefits of cocaine usage, Freud found himself swayed by the numerous, glowing medical reports coming from the New World. In contrast, European researchers were more cautious about interpreting findings. By initially extolling the addictive drug, and later rather shamefacedly modifying his opinion, Freud may have felt deeply betrayed by his faith in the United States. In any event, he eventually began expressing a haughty sarcasm toward the vast nation.

As early as 1902, Freud cynically compared his own Old World, "governed by authority," with the New, governed "by the dollar." This stereotype, that Americans are an uncouth, money-grubbing lot, became Freud's catechism for the rest of his life. Thus, while negotiating in January 1909 with Clark University for travel expenses concerning his upcoming visit, Freud found G. Stanley Hall's allocation "too American," that is, overly concerned with materialist issues. He commented to Ferenczi that "America should bring in money, not cost money."

Freud, though, was generally pleased during his nearly month-long sojourn in the United States later that year. He and Jung were friends at the time, and when both lectured at Clark University, they seemed to be in full agreement about psychoanalysis. Freud's visit had clearly enhanced his reputation and influence on the North American continent, and his reception had generally been quite cordial. Key figures in American psychology, including the celebrated William James, had come to Worcester especially to meet him.

Nevertheless, Freud soon came to view the entire experience quite negatively. The causes were manifold. For one thing, he complained that American cuisine with its heavy food combined with ice water had given him chronic indigestion. Although he had suffered from this condition for several years before the visit, after 1909 Freud always called this condition his "American dyspepsia." Other complaints included his inability to find a barber who could properly trim his beard, as well as the unavailability of public lavatories. He even blamed the deterioration of his handwriting on the United States.

At Clark University, Freud had presented his lectures in German as he feared that he could not understand Americans' English nor they understand his. Indeed, he claimed that "these people cannot even understand each other." Sharing the sentiment of many Europeans, Freud also felt displeasure for the "free and easy manner of the New World." He particularly disliked the relatively higher status of its women as compared with their European counterparts. In contrast, Adler during these early years was already an ardent backer of feminism who condemned masculine dominance in Europe's social mores. Years later, Freud went so far as to tell Ernest Jones that, "America is a mistake; a gigantic mistake, it is true, but nonetheless a mistake."

In the Freud household, the phrase *Echt Amerikanisch* ("It's American-like") thus became synoymous with the gaudy and superficial. Especially after the war, Freud's anti-Americanism seems to have become closely interwoven with his own financial strains. Like many other Austrians worried over their military defeat before the Allies, Freud had hoped for the just peace that President Woodrow Wilson had vowed Europe. The grim, postwar reality for Freud, however, was that he lost most of his life savings in Austria's nightmarish hyperinflation. Thereafter, he experienced considerable economic tension and specifically blamed Wilson for failing to keep his promise. To remain solvent, an embittered Freud was required to treat many American patients since they would pay him in valuable dollars. Indeed, for many years, American and British patients would comprise the bulk of his medical practice.

Not only was Freud resentful about his financial dependency, he was also chagrined about his inability to attract rich American backers as his former associate Jung had accomplished so successfully. The Swiss psychiatrist had gained several wealthy Americans as admiring patients who provided large financial donations, thereby enabling him to establish his Bollingen Foundation and an international training center in Zurich. "All its popularity in America," a rueful Freud complained to Ferenczi in 1922, "has not produced [for psycho-] analysis the benevolence of just *one* of the dollar uncles." Ironically, Adler in the United States would precisely gain such philanthropic support by virtue of his altruistic emphasis on social improvement.

As the 1920s progressed, Freud perhaps justifiably resented the fact that many Americans proclaiming their admiration for psychoanalysis had never even bothered to attempt its study or to understand what it really taught. In Freud's view, most Americans preferred crass popularizations of his painstaking work because they lacked the patience and diligence for intellectual effort. Freud leveled such criticism even against professionals in the American mental health field and several years later would comment that, "Psychiatrists and neurologists make frequent use of psycho-analysis as a therapeutic method, but as a rule they show little interest in its scientific problems and its cultural significance. Quite particularly, often we find in American physicians and writers a very insufficient familiarity with psychoanalysis, so that they know only its terms and a few catch-words—though this does not shake them in the certainty of their judgments."

No doubt alluding to Adler's popularity in the United States, Freud went on to declare that, "These same men lump psycho-analysis with other systems of thought, which may have developed out of it but are incompatible with it today. Or they make a hotch-potch out of psychoanalysis and other elements and quote this procedure as evidence of their broadmindedness whereas it only proves their lack of judgment."

"Many of these evils which I have mentioned," concluded Freud, "with regret no doubt arise from the fact that there is a general tendency in America to shorten study and preparation and to proceed as fast as possible to practical application. There is a preference, too, for studying a subject like psycho-analysis not from the original sources, but from second-hand and often inferior accounts. Thoroughness is bound to suffer from this."

Freud was certainly correct in this regard, for his actual writings in the United States were being read by only a few. His most popular book in translation was *The Interpretation of Dreams,* of which only 5,250 copies were sold in Great Britain and the United States between 1910 and 1919, and only another 11,000 would sell between 1920 and 1932. In contrast, Adler's down-to-earth works like *Understanding Human Nature,* with advice for parents, would sell in the hundreds of thousands.

Resenting America's often crude popularizations of psychoanalysis, Freud saw the New World as chiefly having only one virtue, its wealth. When his close associate Otto Rank prepared to embark for therapeutic work within the United States in 1924, Freud felt obligated to offer some fatherly advice: The only way to endure a "sojourn among such savages [is] to sell one's life as dearly as possible." Rank's American patients were mostly psychiatrists who had already been analyzed by him or Freud and who now wanted more treatment. A sardonic Freud therefore wrote to Rank in May 1924 that it was "nice that you now have nearly all of my former analysands whose analyses I recall without any satisfaction. It often seems to me that analysis fits the American as a white shirt the raven."

That same year, Freud expressed such similar sentiments as "What is the use of Americans if they bring no money?" and that "America is useful for nothing else but to supply money." In coming years, Freud also resented the fact that most of his book royalty income was coming from the United States. "Is it not sad," he later exclaimed, "that we are materially dependent on these savages who are not better-class human beings?"

A pensive Adler at the age of fifteen. (Beth Hatefutsoth Photo Archive, Israel.)

Adler about the age of forty, shortly before his decisive break with Freud. (Jewish National University Library, Jerusalem.)

"Dear A(lfred), I wanted to surprise you with this photograph. . . . With us all is well," Raissa Adler wrote while vacationing with their four children in the Austrian countryside one weekend in 1910. From left to right: Kurt, Raissa, an unidentified nanny holding Cornelia, Valentine, an unidentified domestic, and in foreground, Alexandra. (Courtesy of Dr. Kurt A. Adler; Alfred Adler Collection, Manuscript Division, Library of Congress.)

While lecturing in Sweden, Adler takes time to bandage a girl with a minor injury. (Beth Hatefutsoth Photo Archive, Israel.)

Adler relaxing in his rose garden at Salmannsdorf, outside Vienna. (Courtesy of Dr. Kurt A. Adler.)

Based in Germany, author-lecturer Alice Rühle-Gerstel sought to unite Adlerian psychology with revolutionary Marxism. She is seen here with her husband, socialist theorist Otto Rühle. (Courtesy of Dr. Stephen S. Kalmar.)

The wealthy and powerful businessman Charles Henry Davis was Adler's key American benefactor. (*Cape Cod Magazine.*)

London psychiatrist Francis Crookshank was a leader of Adlerian psychology in England. (Elliott & Fry.)

New York pediatrician-psychiatrist Ira Solomon Wile helped Adler gain professional allies in his new homeland. (University of Rochester Library.)

English novelist Phyllis Bottome became an ardent supporter of Alder and his semi-official biographer. (Vanguard Press.)

This group photograph of the Freudian "Secret Committee" was taken in September 1922 in Berlin. (From left, rear) Otto Rank, Karl Abraham, Max Eitingon, Ernest Jones; (from left, front) Sigmund Freud, Sandor Ferenczi, Hanns Sachs. They viewed Adler as a renegade who denied the primacy of sexuality as the key to human personality. (Courtesy of A. W. Freud, *et al.*, by arrangement with Mark Paterson.)

The Russian revolutionary Leon Trotsky was friendly with the Adler family, especially Raissa Adler, for many decades. (AP/Worldwide Photo.)

Viennese educator/socialist Carl Furtmüller was long one of Adler's closest
friends. (Courtesy of Heinz L. Ansbacher.)

Boston merchandiser/philan-
thropist Edward L. Filene was
one of Adler's most prominent
American supporters. (Coward
McCann, Bettman Archive.)

CHAPTER TWELVE

━━━

Planting the Flag

*Above all in America, blatant
ambition—not only in sports—
presides over everything....
Competition, the drive for validity, is
considered a virtue. To be first is
everyone's goal.*

ALFRED ADLER

ven to sophisticated Europeans, the United States of the raucous,
booming mid-1920s loomed as a formidable and alien place. But
unlike the disdainful Freud who bore little but caustic animosity
toward the New World he had visited once in 1909, Adler was quite excited
by his impending lecture tour to several major American cities. In a way, he
had been patiently waiting twelve years for this triumphant event, ever since
G. Stanley Hall of Clark University had suggested a visiting lectureship in
early 1914. The ensuing international war, however, had changed everyone's plans for a long while.

The elderly and esteemed Hall was now dead, and Adler was not even
scheduled to appear at Clark University on this trip. But this was of little
concern. Having been so decisively rejected for a junior faculty position
at the University of Vienna, he must have felt gratified by the array of prestigious American lecture invitations, including Harvard, Brown, and the
University of Chicago. Even more importantly, he saw an unprecedented
opportunity to promote his system of individual psychology before a potentially vast and receptive American audience.

Despite Adler's anxiety dream the night before he left England from
Southampton in late November 1926, his voyage on the luxurious S.S.
Majestic was uneventful. The British-owned ship was the world's largest
oceanliner afloat and replete with such amenities as a first-class lounge and

dining room. While on board, Adler spent some of his leisure hours diligently practicing his English, for it remained a difficult tongue that he would soon be obliged to speak effectively before a variety of American gatherings.

Arriving without press fanfare in New York City's harbor, Adler spent his first weeks lecturing at such Manhattan institutions as Beth Israel Hospital, the Unitarian-oriented Community Church, the Cooper Union Institute, and Mt. Sinai Hospital. Years later, attendees would recall these early talks as marked by a genial mood and a heavily accented English with occasional malapropisms whose meaning was nonetheless generally clear.

Convivial and outgoing, Adler had long enjoyed the knack for making enduring friendships that would benefit his career. Among the most prominent of his new acquaintances during these weeks was the pediatrician-educator Ira Solomon Wile. Seven years younger than Adler, he had served as New York City's educational commissioner before initiating, in 1919, the country's first child-guidance clinic attached to a general hospital's pediatric service. Beginning with a clinical staff comprised of only one physician and a social worker, the program at Mt. Sinai Hospital slowly expanded to encompass ten professionals around the time of Adler's arrival in the United States. By then, approximately fifty-two hundred children had been treated and some eight hundred were on its active list. Similar to Adler's child-guidance efforts in Vienna, Wile's program emphasized a interdisciplinary rather than narrowly medical approach.

Wile was also a prolific writer. He held editorial posts on several major journals and his books included *Blood Examinations in Surgical Diagnosis, Sex Education,* and *The Challenge of Childhood.* In this latter volume, published in 1925, Wile explicitly rejected the psychoanalytic approach to child development as overly confining. "The Freudian psychologists reduce all human activity to terms of the sex instinct," he insisted. "The contributions of Freud to dynamic psychology are real . . . and basic, but nevertheless this does not serve to place the seal of verity upon every conclusion he has reached. All of life is not an Oedipus or Electra complex."

Like Adler, Wile was a liberal on social issues affecting women's rights. As a founding director of the American Birth Control League, he had long been active in the movement spearheaded by his friend Margaret Sanger, and would later testify before Congress on her behalf. Soon after meeting Adler in New York City in the winter of 1927, Wile began collaborating on a popular book entitled *Marriage in the Modern Manner;* by the late 1920s, he had begun to parallel closely Adler's effort to apply professional knowledge in psychiatry to societal betterment, and in coming years the two men maintained close cordial relations. Wile was extremely well placed in New York

City's public health and educational networks, and may have helped Adler at least initially to cultivate important connections for his subsequent career in the United States.

During these weeks while first meeting Wile and other leading New York professionals, Adler found comfortable quarters for himself. Although still an idealist at heart, he was hardly a self-effacing ascetic, and his residence was the new and fashionable Gramercy Park Hotel. Created out of a private land donation to New York City in 1846, the lower-midtown Manhattan area comprised a large square of elegant townhouses and homes facing the historic enclosed Gramercy Park; on a tall flagpole within it, an American flag fluttered in the wind. Later known as the American Bloomsbury for its genteel, London-like ambience, the leafy, oasislike neighborhood was much to Adler's liking.

Completed only two years earlier, the hotel itself was already attracting a glamorous clientele. Humphrey Bogart had held his lavish wedding there a few months earlier, with hundreds of guests from Hollywood and the arts, and the bombastic Babe Ruth and his entourage were regulars at its well-stocked bar. For much of Adler's subsequent decade living in the United States, a residential suite at the Gramercy Park Hotel would be his most permanent home.

Although he initially attracted no media attention upon entering the United States, this situation soon changed decisively. During Adler's first few weeks becoming comfortable at the posh Gramercy Park Hotel, he granted a lengthy interview to the *New York World,* which was specifically interested in his views on Benito Mussolini. The year before, Adler had been interviewed by the *New York Times* for his intriguing perspective on European foreign affairs, including communism.

Published the day after Christmas, the *World*'s detailed article featured a prominent sketch of Adler absorbed in thought. The banner headline read "Mussolini Spurred to his Fight for Power by Pique Over Inferiority as a Child, Says Dr. Alfred Adler." At the time, the forty-three-year-old *Il Duce,* ("The Leader") as he was known, had been Italy's controversial premier for several years. After a journalistic career as a jingoistic socialist, he had founded in 1917 the first political party to be called fascist. Appealing initially to dissatisfied veterans and nationalists, Mussolini had gained enough power in 1922 to force King Victor Emmanuel III to ask him to head the nation. Since then, the diminutive *Il Duce* had transformed Italy into a dictatorship. He had abolished all political parties except the Fascist party and seized control of the country's major industries, newspapers, police, and schools.

Although Mussolini claimed to be reducing poverty and effectively modernizing Italy, his regime was marked by threats and violence against opponents. As perhaps the most troubling example of rising, postwar European authoritarianism and remilitarization to date, Italy's dictatorial situation was arousing considerable concern in the United States.

In Adler's perhaps overly reductionist viewpoint, both *Il Duce* and the country he ruled were suffering from an intense sense of inferiority. "I quite agree with H. G. Wells that socialism is an expression of the inferiority complex of the disinherited," he told the *New York World,* "The more intense the inferiority, the more violent the superiority. This is the equation. Mussolini's life shouts it. So does the history of modern Italy. And it accounts for the threat to the peace of the world."

Alluding to Mussolini's recent saber rattling on the Continent and the Mediterranean region against Corfu, England, and France, Adler observed that, "Men and nations cannot bear to feel inferior. Strife for power [eventually] develops. . . . In addition to the blackshirts, Mussolini was supported by the sons of feudal lords, by thousands of men of the upper classes of Italy, by thousands of officers who found nothing to do after the war. . . . Mussolini offered them a place in a big movement—his opponents made the mistake of not offering something to do to those who had nothing to do."

Taking renewed opportunity in condemning the Soviet Union's rulers who had once been his social acquaintances, Adler remarked that, "In Russia, no usual reformers could have satisfied that suppressed people. The chaos of Russian common life was seized by extremists who thought themselves supermen. . . . It is a law of every revolutionary movement to find places for . . . persons who cannot find their own place and to give them something to do. Is Soviet Russia ruled today by workers and peasants? Did workers or peasants make the revolution there? Men and women of the hated bourgeoisie made the revolution, and are even now at the heads of most departments of the Bolshevik state. Even [former] Czarist officers command regiments."

Finally, in a statement that would become central to Adler's popular message in coming years, he declared that, "The behavior pattern of persons can be studied from their relation to three things: to society, to work, to sex. The feeling of inferiority affects a man's relations to [these]. . . ." He then added that, "Mussolini's behavior patterns are clear in two things—society and work. Of what is generally whispered of his 'superiority complex' in sex, I have nothing to say at this time. We should watch closely any sign of failure in Italy to achieve economic success," he presciently warned, "for in that moment disillusionment may come, and along with it, a return to the despondency of inferiority and violence."

To professional as well as popular audiences throughout his lecture tour, Adler emphasized the concept of inferiority as central to understanding human nature. Typical of such presentations was his January 11 lecture on "The Feeling of Inferiority and Its Compensation," before the prestigious New York Academy of Medicine. Echoing his recent newspaper comments, Adler tersely declared that, "In life, you can find three fundamental questions: the social questions (friendship, comradeship, social behavior) the question of occupation, and the question of love and marriage. Everybody gives his individual answer to these questions by his behavior, and this answer is also an expression of his action-line or style of life."

In the same presentation, Adler described neurosis as an emotional disturbance manifesting itself "before a difficult problem and [causing] a loss of courage, so that the individual begins to hesitate or stop." Depicting such troubled persons as basically conflicted in their *achievement motive* (what today is aptly called the fear of success and fear of failure), Adler commented that the neurotic "fears a defeat even more than [risking success] and escapes to the useless side [of life]. . . . He is not really the conqueror, but he is satisfied with the presupposition . . . that he could be the conqueror if he did not have [the particular] hindrance. He hides from himself and others his real feeling of inferiority."

Three days later, Adler traveled to New England to offer his first lectures outside New York City. In the ensuing weeks, Adler's reception in such locales would prove enthusiastic. His initial and well-publicized talk in the area was held on January 14, before a standing-room audience at the Plantations Club of Providence, Rhode Island. Several weeks before, the city's local newspaper had proudly announced that Adler's upcoming visit was being organized by Sophie Lustig. The Russian-born wife of a wealthy Hungarian-immigrant textile manufacturer, she had long been prominent among the city's cultural and philanthropic elite. Having graduated from St. Petersburg's university during czarist times, Lustig was a colorful figure who wrote detective stories and whose published memoirs later became a local best-seller.

Traveling through Europe in 1926, Lustig had decided to meet briefly with each of the famous triad of Viennese analysts: Freud, Adler, and Stekel. Of the three men, Adler had proved so unexpectedly fascinating that she abruptly cancelled her return-trip plans and spent the next three months studying with him. As Lustig admiringly told readers of the *Providence Jour-*

nal, "There, in a cosmopolitan, democratic group, rich and poor, patient and pupil, famous physicians and internationally known psychiatrists sat together [in Adler's classes] and listened [to him]. . . . Each evening, he draws the crowded café assemblings around him, much as in old days of ancient Greece, the Athenian population sought Socrates."

Illustrative of the epigraphs that Adler received throughout his first American lecture tour, the *Providence Journal* recounted that he was a "famous Viennese psychologist and neurologist" and "popularly known as 'the father of the inferiority complex.' " The newspaper reported excerpts from his Plantations Club speech, particularly that, "Every individual from birth struggles against a feeling of inferiority to [an unseen] goal" and that "The three great questions in life that require answers by each individual have to do with occupation, society, and love. [They] are interlocked in an endless circle." With a practical emphasis, Adler described mothers and teachers as the key figures in "helping the child [to] create a style of life that is profitable for himself, for society, and for posterity."

During the next few days, Adler maintained an extremely busy lecture schedule. His audiences included Brown University's faculty and students, Butler Hospital's medical staff, and the Providence Medical Association. He also gave several private lectures for local residents gathered at the Lustigs' attractive home on tree-lined Elmgrove Avenue. In coming years, Adler would gain a virtually unparalleled reputation in the United States for his ability to speak effectively about psychology before diverse civic, professional, and religious groups. In a manner unthinkable for the intellectually aloof and rather condescending Freud, Adler not only tolerated but actively welcomed the opportunity to talk about his ideas to even the most unpolished audiences. In his optimistic view, they all offered occasions to help build a better world through psychological knowledge.

While lecturing in Providence that January, Adler gained the acquaintance of an important local educator, Mary Helena Dey, with whom he would subsequently become friendly in his American career. Director of the private Mary C. Wheeler School for girls, she had studied under John Dewey at the University of Chicago and become devoted to his progressive educational philosophy. As a high-school administrator affiliated with the university before coming to help direct the Wheeler School, Dey believed strongly in the "whole-child" approach to learning. It is hardly surprising, therefore, that she found the Adlerian emphasis on nurturing children's esteem and emotional well-being to be appealing. To Adler, democratic thinkers like Dewey and his supporters represented the best of American idealism, and the two men would ultimately correspond about education. In later New

England lecture tours, Adler would rely upon the Wheeler School to provide a sympathetic forum for his ideas on effective teaching and parenting.

After leaving Providence, Adler spent several days lecturing in the Boston area. Hosted by the venerable psychiatrist Morton Prince, he spoke at Harvard and its mental health affiliate, the Judge Baker Guidance Center. There his sponsor was the equally influential William Healey, whose innovative directorship since 1920 had helped gain the center national acclaim as a model in the growing field of child therapeutic treatment. Healey was particularly interested in uncovering the psychological causes of juvenile delinquency and had already studied Freud's sexually oriented viewpoint. Undoubtedly, Adler offered the Judge Baker staff a rather different way of thinking about youthful crime, for he had long traced delinquency to a deep-seated sense of inferiority, particularly in social relations.

During this trip to Boston, Adler also found himself invited to address a group with another set of concerns, the Daughters of the American Revolution. It is not clear what they hoped to learn from him, but he was dutifully housed in an elegant hotel. Meeting him in the lobby before his lecture, several of the society's leading members introduced themselves, and then their chairlady announced proudly, "Dr. Adler, our ancestors came over on the *Mayflower!*" She awaited his deferential reaction, but the boast was completely lost on him. Reflecting his Viennese education, he had never heard of the Pilgrims' ship and also misinterpreted the English word "ancestors" to be a synonym for "relatives." But always eager to maintain a cordial demeanor, Adler was at no loss for a suitable reply to the seemingly trivial comment. "Yes, yes?" he said pleasantly. "And I came over on the *Majestic!*"

Addressing more formal gatherings, Adler's English-language struggles could sometimes be embarrassing. Several weeks later in New York, he was explaining concepts in child guidance to an eager audience of mostly educators and physicians. His thick Viennese accent was hard enough to understand; but several were startled to hear him, in describing a specific case, denounce a well-behaved, studious boy as a "veritable *monster* child." After the presentation, a friendly German-speaking psychiatrist named Anthony Bruck (later to teach individual psychology) decided to ask about the odd choice of words. "Adler was incredulous," recalled Bruck. "He had selected his term [in confusion] of the French word *monstrer* (to show) and the German ecclesiastical term *monstranz* for the elevated, consecrated vessel in the Mass." He had wanted to describe the youngster as being so wonderful so as to be worthy of being "held up" before everyone's admiration.

Despite such occasional difficulties with the English language, Adler's lecture tour was becoming a clear success. On February 10, he offered a talk before the well-regarded Child Study Association based in New York City. Published in the *New York Times* the next day, the reporter found particularly intriguing his remarks about children's sleeping positions as a personality indicator:

> "If your child sleeps with his head beneath the covers, don't give him courageous tasks, for he's afraid," Dr. Alfred Adler, Docent of the Pedagogical Institute of Vienna, told the Child Study Association in an address here.
>
> Dr. Adler, who has been associated with Freud, thus urged parents to watch for attitudes in children's sleep. Physical defects caused inferiority complexes, he said, but children frequently overcome them to the degree where liabilities became assets. But he admitted also that some children's complexes drove them to efficiency along useless and detrimental lines as they strove to shake off the feeling of inferiority. . . . Dr. Adler advocated watching a sleeping child to determine his complexes and influence him toward the right goal.

Staying at the Cambridge Hotel on Manhattan's West Sixty-Eighth Street, Adler penned a jovial letter to Raissa the following day. He described his talk as "very exciting" and boasted that "I am terribly spoiled and loved here." But he also felt hurt by his wife's seeming indifference to his new success and commented, "I can't remember when I last got a letter. Has something happened to you? My thoughts are already constantly directed at Vienna."

Raissa's failure to write her husband may have reflected growing marital strains. An active member of the Austrian Communist party, she was perhaps sensing more acutely in his absence their growing differences in outlook and life-style. It is not known whether she had the opportunity to accompany Adler on this first trip to the United States; but unlike their adult children, Alexandra and Kurt, she persistently refused to do so on Alfred's subsequent visits.

Although an ocean away from Vienna, Adler in New York City that first winter was not entirely removed from psychoanalytic politics. One day while hurrying through the bustling, multitiered hub of Penn Station, he was startled to see the familiar face of Sandor Ferenczi nearby. Adler motioned to Freud's longtime Hungarian associate in friendly greeting, but Ferenczi deliberately snubbed him and walked on. During this same American visit, Adler learned from the Viennese emigré psychoanalyst Clarence Oberndorf that Freud had recently broken with Otto Rank, now lecturing at the New York School of Social Work.

Upon learning this unexpected news about the man whom he had introduced to Freud, Adler is said to have responded, "That is the will of God! The little fellow [Rank] always tried to set the old gentleman [Freud] against me!"

═══

On February 13, Adler left Manhattan for a six-week lecture tour of the American Midwest. Undoubtedly, his most enthusiastic reception took place in Chicago, where the city's board of education had invited him to present six lectures for teachers and administrators. Although Adler's was hardly a household name at the time, it seems that he was already well-known to school professionals: more than twenty-five hundred applications for tickets had to be turned down due to space limitations. On February 22, the *Chicago Tribune* reported that the Art Institute had proven too small for Adler's talks, which were being henceforth moved to the larger theater of the city's Field Museum.

The following day, the *Tribune* admiringly recounted in detail Adler's speech "before as many Chicago teachers and principals as were able to force their way into Fullerton Hall at the Art Institute." Offering as subtitle the slogan that "Instilling of Courage Makes Success," the *Tribune* was excited by Adler's seeming message that achievement and success are only a matter of proper mental attitude. After all, it was a perspective that closely meshed with the sprawling midwestern city's ethos in the booming 1920s:

> Children need optimism.
> Give the child the idea he is getting along well and that he is able to do a lot better, and nine times out of ten he will. Impress him with the belief that everything he does is wrong, that other children are his superiors, that his little mistakes are mountainous failures and right there you sow the seeds for him becoming just like that—a failure.
> Like the grownups whose emotional counterpart he is, the child must be imbued with self-confidence and courage to succeed, Dr. Albert [sic] Adler believes. He doubts you can make a child too self-confident and too courageous for his own good.
> "Only courage is able to develop all the potential faculties and capabilities of the child: lack of courage spells retarded development."

Not only did Adler expound upon child psychology before thousands of school personnel, but he also gained administrative backing to initiate an exchange program with his Viennese associates. In addition, Adler lectured at the University of Chicago and spent a week demonstrating techniques of child-guidance work at the city's Institute for Juvenile Research. Both in his own lifetime and afterward, Chicago would constitute one of Adler's most important bastions of professional interest and support. Writing from Cincinnati in early March, Adler commented to daughter Valentine that, "Tomorrow, I will give my last presentation here and at night I will go to Chicago." He was disappointed by her failure to write at all during the preceding weeks, but added that, "Here, again, great acclaim and great success. As you already know, the invitations to universities are becoming serious . . . probably to Chicago."

Later that month, Adler traveled four hours eastward to begin a new series of lectures in the Detroit area. Similar to the response he had received in Chicago, his various presentations on individual psychology were hosted by a variety of professional groups, hospitals, and child-guidance centers, including the influential Merrill-Palmer School (as it was then known). Such sectarian organizations as the Detroit Federation of Jewish Women were also involved. As reported by the *Detroit News* the next day, March 21, Adler expounded before some three hundred medical professionals gathered at McLaughlin Hospital that:

> Every child is naturally dependent and defenseless at birth, and from this insecure position may develop a feeling of helplessness and inferiority. Becoming adult, most children slough off this feeling, though some carry it over into later life as an inferiority complex.
>
> Success and happiness are largely a matter of goal. If the child has socially helpful ambitions, he will become contented and happy. If his goal is inimical to society, he probably will come to grief. Teachers and parents should see that the child's goal is a proper one.

Speaking before students at the University of Michigan in the picturesque college town of nearby Ann Arbor later that day, Adler was gratified by the interest shown in his work. Similar to later developments in Chicago, Detroit-area educators would provide him with a highly receptive audience for years to come. The American Midwest was already internationally renowned for its pragmatic rather than theoretical emphasis in psychology, and undoubtedly Adler's optimistic and practical approach appealed to professors and schoolteachers alike far more than Freud's dark, mythologically rich system centering on infantile sexuality.

After still more lectures around Chicago, Adler finally returned to the Northeast in early April for a few remaining speaking engagements. He also began laying the groundwork for what he hoped would become solid organizational structures to advance his approach across the United States. To this end, he appointed professor S. D. House of Columbia University to head a new organization devoted to educational psychology; for its medically oriented counterpart, he chose the young psychiatrist Walter Beran Wolfe, who had recently returned from intensive Viennese training with Adler. At the time, neither figure was well known, but both would come to be quite helpful personally in coming years.

Amidst these promising developments, the *Boston Globe* published a lengthy article about Adler on April 10. Similar in tone to the highly favorable attention he had been receiving all through his four-month lecture tour, the newspaper piece was rhetorically entitled "What's Your Peculiar Inferiority Complex?"

> What is an inferiority complex? What causes it? How does it show itself? And how can we cure it?
>
> People have been asking these questions for years, and we have had all sorts of answers—some sublime, many ridiculous.
>
> At last we can get an answer backed by the authority of the one man who knows, because he discovered the inferiority complex 20 years ago and has been figuring it out ever since.
>
> Dr. Alfred Adler of Vienna, Docent of the Pedagogical Institute, inspirer of 22 child guidance clinics, founder of his own school of individual psychology, popularly known as the father of the inferiority complex, is here in America to tell us about it.

The detailed and laudatory piece explaining basic concepts of individual psychology must have been immensely gratifying to Adler. Shortly after its publication in the *Globe,* he embarked from New York's harbor for his return voyage to Europe. Less than four months before, his arrival in the United States had gone unnoticed. Now, happily climbing on board the S.S. *Leviathan* on April 11, he had gained so much popular attention that even his vague plans for the upcoming months were now dutifully noted by a *New York Times* reporter. As he had sincerely told the *Times* journalist, "American interest in psychology was highly developed" and was both "keen and remarkable."

Thinking ahead to his family and associates in Vienna, Adler could hardly wait to recount—and further—the tremendous interest in individual psychology that seemed to be burgeoning throughout the world. As Adler would delightedly tell his Austrian friends and colleagues, he had clearly succeeded in planting his movement's "flag" on American soil.

CHAPTER THIRTEEN

Coming Home

*Give everyone who opens new paths
for individual psychology a free reign,
and support them most warmly.*

ALFRED ADLER

After a relaxing week on board the luxurious S.S. *Leviathan,* Adler returned home to Vienna on April 17. Although glad to be back with his family and friends after a long absence, he lost little time in resuming his active public life there. Only eight days later, he lectured before a large and enthusiastic audience in the auditorium at the University of Vienna's Histological Institute. It resembled a homecoming celebration for Adler, who was introduced by Professor David Oppenheim, a friend and longtime associate from the days when both men were dissenting members of Freud's Vienna Psychoanalytic Society.

Sponsored by the International Society for Individual Psychology, Adler's lecture focused mainly on America's burgeoning mental hygiene movement. He expressed admiration for all the dedicated physicians, psychologists, and educators seeking to found programs for variant children and their families. "Due to the incomparably higher material resources in America," Adler remarked, "the whole area of social welfare is far more developed than in most European cities." He also praised American universities for their educational openness and accessibility to general citizenry.

Adler did criticize certain aspects of America's mental hygiene movement, however. He disparagingly noted that its "leadership and most important institutions . . . lie in private hands," unlike in Vienna, where public educators trained in his approach dominated child-guidance work. Proudly, Adler summarized his extensive schedule of lectures that had helped promote the teachings of individual psychology throughout the United States. Specifically mentioning the anticipated teacher-exchange program he had initiated between the Chicagoan and Viennese school systems, he informed a delighted audience that, as a result of his efforts, they could expect "a substantial number of American visitors to Vienna during the next months. They will want to study the educational work of individual psychology and our counseling sites, as well as Viennese schools and welfare developments."

During the spring of Adler's return to Austria, he often spoke animatedly with friends about life in the United States. He also published interviews on this topic with several popular Austrian and German periodicals, including *Allgemeine Zeitung, Neue Wiener Abendblatt, Morgen,* and *Abend.* Adler was struck by how strongly American mores differed from those of his homeland. In particular, he saw the American character of the mid-1920s as a strange mixture of competitive individualism and social conformity. "It is very rare for someone to sit alone at a table; the American habitually prefers to act in groups. . . . The servant question is also significantly different. [Unlike in Europe] servants in America are an exclusive luxury of the rich." In this regard, America's "working population has won a particular right for itself and sticks to it, facilitated by immigrant restrictions."

With Adler's own intensely competitive nature, it is not surprising that he was fascinated by the paradoxical quality of American competitiveness. "The social tendencies of [the individual] are particularly obvious when his competitive drive has succeeded," he remarked. "Once an American reaches his goal and receives his money, he does not rest until he has founded some social institution. It becomes important to do something for the general good, so he founds or subsidizes public service programs, hospitals, or universities."

Adler was also favorably impressed with women's rights in the United States as contrasted with those of Central Europe. Because of their comparatively wider exposure to higher education, American women played a "much greater role in cultural and social life" as compared with their Austrian counterparts. "They take part in all scientific questions. They have much more educational opportunities than European women. They are stronger and more assertive than our women," Adler commented with admiring sentiments unthinkable for Freud or Jung. Yet, Adler was not naive about the economic situation of American women. "Although [they] are active in almost every profession, they are still paid badly; in a larger sense, then, they are only superficially accepted. The privileges of men, who try to distance themselves from the ever advancing rights of women, remain intact."

American parents, in Adler's view, seemed far more concerned about adequate child rearing than their European counterparts. He expressed satisfaction with the sizable funds and resources that the American government was committing to education, but sardonically commented that, "In most cases, the wrong educational methods are employed and the institutions are often led by ignorant people." Finally, in these interviews, Adler observed that American children tend to be "more spoiled than in Europe, play a greater role in their parents' lives, and periodically bring them to desperation through angry conflagrations." Because Americans daily seemed to run "a constant race," they often appeared to Adler too busy to care for their youngsters adequately. He expressed hope that through the growing influence of individual psychology, the United States would witness improved child rearing both at home and at school.

━━━

During the summer, Adler led a well-attended educators' conference in Locarno, Switzerland. En route, he stopped in the scenic south Austrian village of Kitzbühel for several days, having been invited to renew acquaintanceship with a tall, mild-mannered Scotsman, Ernan Forbes-Dennis. Adler's host was interested in establishing with his English wife, Phyllis, a private school for foreign-language study. The couple were in early middle age and childless. Forbes-Dennis had been in combat during the Great War and critically wounded on the western front. Soon after recovering physically, he married his sweetheart, Phyllis Bottome, and through political connections attained a coveted diplomatic post in Vienna.

A slender, sensitive-looking woman in her mid-forties, Bottome was the daughter of a country parson. A member of a wealthy American banking family, she had grown up in both Sussex, England, and the New York City area. Bottome had been drawn to the theater as a teenager and had planned an acting career. But while caring for a sister stricken with tuberculosis, she developed a severe case of the dread disease and was confined to a sanatorium for several years. There, she began to write fiction to keep her active mind creative, and published her first novel at the remarkable age of seventeen. She was a prolific writer whose novels were distinctive for their vivid character portrayals and evocation of continental Europe. Under her maiden name of Phyllis Bottome, she would eventually become one of England's most popular interwar novelists and her friends would include Eleanor and Franklin Roosevelt, Sinclair Lewis, and Ezra Pound. Bottome would later become Adler's semiofficial biographer.

In the Vienna of the early 1920s, Ernan and Phyllis enjoyed an active social calendar with literary and artistic friends. They began to plan for parenthood when, in 1923, Phyllis suffered another serious bout of tuberculosis and was forced to spend months recuperating in a Swiss sanatorium. Deciding to settle in the healthful mountain village of Kitzbühel, the couple made plans to set up a school for high-school students interested in foreign-language training. But lacking a formal background in education, they felt it wise to obtain the consultation of Alfred Adler. His name had been celebrated among their Viennese social circle for penetrating insight about children's educational needs.

During the previous year, Forbes-Dennis had met with Adler in Vienna several times and avidly studied the textbooks recommended to him. Meanwhile, Bottome had eagerly anticipated meeting the famous founder of individual psychology. But, like many others for whose Adler's lofty reputation had preceded his actual presence, she felt "profoundly disappointed" when they first met in Kitzbühel. "I had expected a Socratic genius who would plunge us all into the depths of psychology. [Instead, I found him to be] "a kindly and considerate guest who talked about nothing in particular and to everyone in general. To look at, Adler was stout, considerably further into middle-age than we were, sallow and with unremarkable features. [He] had a benevolent and genial air, but his eyes were inscrutable, sometimes veiled as if he had altogether withdrawn himself; sometimes, and when you least expected it from his bland and casual air—piercing."

But several days later at a village cafe, she felt her opinion change decisively. Sitting in a small group, Adler was casually asked about his wartime experiences as a physician. "He spoke with horror of the wicked waste, the senseless futility of all wars, and with biting scorn of the Austrian statesmen who had unleashed the 1914 war," Bottome later recalled. When a Viennese woman in the group immediately rebuked Adler for criticizing his homeland before Englishmen—Austria's wartime enemies—Adler gently replied that, "We are all fellow men. Those of common sense in every country felt the same—organized murder and torture against our brothers—how should it not be unwanted?" He proceeded to describe the medical horrors and suffering he had witnessed and the Austrian government's repeated lies to keep its citizens supporting the continued fighting. "In those hours," commented Adler's future biographer, "I ceased to think of Adler as ordinary; I knew that what I was looking at, and listening to, was a great man."

═══

By the year 1927, many Austrians, like Adler, were pleased that their country was prospering and forging a new, progressive era. The majority of Social

Democrats believed that before long the entire nation, not just Vienna, would be led by peaceful socialist ideals. Unfortunately, unforseen political events early that winter suddenly cast a very different light on the country.

As almost all Austrian historians agree, the trouble began with a specific episode. On January 30, the Social Democratic party was about to hold a public meeting in the politically progressive village of Schattendorf, situated in the pastoral Burgenland province where Adler's father had grown up. Suddenly, before the meeting even began, members of the rightist Front Fighters sitting in a nearby tavern fired unprovoked shots into the crowd. Two people, including an eight-year-old boy, were killed and five others, among them a six-year-old boy, were injured. The three snipers initially escaped unhindered, but were eventually caught by police and put on trial.

Almost immediately, Austria's Social Democrats reacted in a strong but disciplined manner. That same week, they successfully shut down several large factories in protest and held a symbolic, fifteen-minute general strike throughout the country. In national parliamentary session, the Social Democratic party demanded a vigorous prosecution of the Schattendorf killers and the dissolution of the Burgenland's veterans' organizations. Nothing concrete emerged from parliamentary debate on the January 30 episode, however.

In the eight-day trial that began several months later, the Front Fighters were vigorously defended by right-wing lawyer Walter Riehl. It took the jury less than four hours to emerge with their verdict on July 14: All three men were acquitted on the grounds of self-defense. Even the prosecutor's fallback charge, that the Front Fighters had employed excessive force in self-defense, was rejected. The very next day marked the beginning of Austria's slow, seven-year slide into a civil war that would culminate in fascism. A wildcat protest strike of Vienna's powerful national Workers' Union spontaneously erupted that morning and sent thousands of enraged demonstrators marching toward the municipal complex. At the same time, young workers seized control of the Palace of Justice, which soon began burning. In self-righteous excitement, the occupiers started hurling governmental documents out the windows, where crowds below eagerly set them aflame.

Wilhelm Reich, a politically oriented physician who personally witnessed much of the street action, later remembered that, "An armed police contingent was marching to the Palace of Justice . . . groups of people of every age and vocation were everywhere. . . . Thousands upon thousands were still merely nonparticipating onlookers. I walked on to the Rathaus Park. Suddenly, shots rang out nearby. The crowd dispersed in the direction of the [city's inner] Ring [to hide as] shooting continued in the park. Mounted police rode into the crowds. Ambulances with red flags arrived and drove off bearing the dead and wounded. It was not a riot per se, with two antagonistic factions, but simply tens of thousands of people, and groups of policemen shooting into the defenseless crowd."

Before order was finally restored the next day, the Palace of Justice burned to the ground. Nearly ninety people were dead and hundreds more were wounded. Pockets of sporadic gunfire continued in the northern suburbs through July 16 and resulted in additional deaths and casualties. Early in the morning of the third day, Vienna's streetcars began to run again and the newspapers resumed publication. "The everyday appearance of a large city was restored as if nothing had happened. However, a great deal occurred from that time onward," recalled Reich.

Indeed, neither Adler's native Vienna nor Austria was ever the same again politically. In particular, the calamity made visible the inherent weakness of the Social Democratic party under Otto Bauer's vacillating leadership. Many of its members felt betrayed by his inability to take any decisive action during the two days of extensive rioting and police gunplay: specifically, to authorize the party's well-trained *Schutzbund* (private militia) to aid the unarmed protesters. In disgust, some Social Democratic sympathizers like Reich decided to embrace Austria's more militant communists. Many on the political left who had never quite trusted Bauer's optimistic vision of peaceful democratic triumph over capitalism began moving in the same direction. These would include several important, left-wing supporters of Adler in Austria and Germany. Still other progressive Viennese, bitterly disillusioned with the Social Democratic party, withdrew altogether from political involvement and support.

Simultaneously, parties on the political right sought to capitalize on the July 15 debacle. They shrewdly saw the opportunity to pin the blame for the deadly rioting on their longtime foes. In national parliamentary debate, the Catholic prelate and Christian Socialist Federal Chancellor Ignaz Seipel immediately took the offensive. He announced that he supported the Schattendorf acquittals and criticized the Social Democrats for having attempted to politicize the trial, both before the verdict and afterward. In sarcastic reply, Bauer commented that, "Shooting is popular nowadays, and shooting at citizens seems to awaken [among those like Seipel] feelings of gratitude." At the party congress that summer, Vienna's socialist mayor, Karl Seitz, declared with gusto that, "We are so convinced that democratic

189

developments will lead to our goals that we do not need to assist them with violence."

Yet, such words of sarcasm and bravado had little power behind them. During the ensuing months, the Social Democratic party suffered a series of significant political losses, both on local and national levels. As early as August, the Christian Socialist–controlled parliament succeeded in passing—without prior debate—several new school laws aimed at reversing the reformist achievement of Adler's friend and educator, Carl Furtmüller. In place of the common, obligatory, enriched middle school permitting pupil tracking only at age fourteen, dual tracks were now mandated with a compromise proviso allowing a select group of gifted *Hauptschule* (main school) pupils to take examinations for college preparatory admission. This federal law effectively ended Vienna's steady trend toward school reform so vigorously championed by Adler and his associates. Thereafter, the Social Democratic party made no sustained attempts to deepen or extend their efforts in educational reform.

Later in August, an election for Vienna's police force representatives shifted control from the Independent Trade Unionists into the hands of the Christian Socials, who had justified firing into the crowds of protestors. In September, the national parliament defeated Bauer's proposal to grant amnesty to those accused of rioting on July 15. At a gathering of union metalworkers in October, he publicly acknowledged that Austrian social democracy was weakening. But the Social Democratic party head nevertheless urged the unionists to continue their valiant struggle for "peaceful democratic development."

Such was Adler's own viewpoint. For nearly a decade, he had completely rejected the Bolshevik notion of violent revolution as a justifiable means toward achieving humanitarian ends. In various articles and public interviews dating back to Lenin's ascension of power in the name of the Russian prolitariat, Adler had condemned the concept of "class warfare" as a "hateful" ideology promulgated by the discouraged and embittered. Soon after July 15, Reich discussed its momentous events with Freud and recalled that, "It seemed to me that he lacked all understanding of the revolt and viewed it as a catastrophe similar to a tidal wave." Adler had a more sophisticated political understanding of the forces that converged on that bloody day, yet he did not alter his belief in the long-term viability of peaceful democratic change.

Unfortunately for Adler and his tireless effort to promulgate individual psychology, not all of his Central European followers were so optimistic.

They saw that Hungary, Austria's neighbor to the east, had already established a fascist regime. Under Mussolini, Italy had followed suit in the 1920s, and in Germany, several far-right groups, including the extremely militant Nazis, were steadily gaining strength and aiding their Austrian sympathizers with arms and money. Indeed, the Schattendorf verdict had greatly emboldened Austria's homegrown fascist Heimwehr (paramilitary organization), which had steadily been gaining influence since 1920. Such ominous worrisome developments had begun to convince Adler's more leftist associates that the time had come for him to declare, unequivocably and decisively, his allegiance to revolutionary Marxism.

———

Undoubtedly, the most zealously influential of this group was Alice Rühle-Gerstel (née Gerstel). Born in Prague in 1894, she was the daughter of a wealthy furniture manufacturer of German-Jewish background. With a maverick personality and a very poor relationship with her mother, Alice had sought activity outside the family home. As a teenager, she became active in Prague's literary circle, where she met such well-known writers as Willy Haas, Egon Kisch, and Franz Werfel.

At the age of eighteen, Alice received state certification to become a music teacher, but broke with her parents' expectations when war erupted. She volunteered for nursing duty at a war hospital during 1914–15, and later, while studying German and philosophy at the University of Prague, she became increasingly interested in politics. Unlike Alice's more conventional brother who took over the family business and became a major factory owner, she chose to become a dedicated socialist.

After World War I ended, Gerstel continued her education in Munich. There she became drawn to individual psychology and underwent analysis with Adler's chief German associate, psychiatrist Leonhard Seif. In 1921, Gerstel completed her university education and married the well-known socialist theorist Otto Rühle.

Almost twenty years older than Alice Gerstel, Rühle had long been an important figure in German politics. Before the war, he had worked for the German Socialist party and published a major sociological work entitled *The Proletarian Child*. In 1912, he was elected to the German Reichstag; two years later, he courageously opposed its almost unanimous decision to enter the war. Dismayed by the prowar sentiments of the Social Democrats, Rühle decided to move further to the political left and helped to found the German Communist party. This association too proved disappointing as well as

191

short-lived for Rühle; he soon accused Lenin of brutal and dictatorial policies and broke off all contact with the Bolsheviks. Thoroughly disillusioned
with party politics, Rühle then began to devote all his energy to writing
about social and economic issues.

Despite their disparate ages, Gerstel and Rühle enjoyed a mutually stimulating marriage. He shared his detailed knowledge of Marxist economic
theory with Gerstel; she taught him about Adlerian psychology. This introduction came at a crucial time for Rühle, for since the early 1920s, he had
been seeking to determine why Weimar Germany's oppressed working class
had failed to rise up in revolutionary fervor. No explanation seemed plausible, until he started reading Adler and discovered a satisfying answer: Most
German workers, raised since early childhood to feel inferior and helpless,
lacked the confidence needed to challenge governmental authority.

Through the mid- to late 1920s, Gerstel and Rühle collaborated on an effort to synthesize Marx and Adler. Their aim was certainly pragmatic rather
than scholarly, for both were trying to find a way to further the cause of political action against capitalism. (Several years later, Wilhelm Reich would
attempt in Germany a similar union between Freudian and Marxist ideas.)
In 1924, the activist couple established a multiregional association in Germany to promote what they called "Education through Self-Awareness." In
this group, teachers and other interested professionals could join with
working-class parents to promote socialist-minded education.

During these years, Gerstel and Rühle also lectured extensively. They offered hundreds of talks and courses on Marxism, history, education, and
women's issues. In particular, Rühle-Gerstel was a zealous exponent of individual psychology and taught its tenets with gusto. Rühle-Gerstel also began
publishing articles in Adler's international journal and, with her husband,
gave active support to a variety of left-wing organizations, including The
Society of Decisive School Reformers, The Friends of the Children, The
Society of Proletariats of Peace, and The Society for Sexual Reform. In
addition, the radical couple founded a publishing company out of their
home and produced various books on socialist theory and a magazine entitled *The Proletarian Child,* aimed at promulgating socialist ideas to working-
class parents.

In 1924, Rühle-Gerstel wrote *Freud and Adler,* a comparison of psychoanalysis and individual psychology. It was a relatively well-balanced work
that presented the strengths and flaws of each approach in a lucid manner.
She inserted minimal Marxist ideology into the volume, emphasizing instead how Freudian and Adlerian notions supplemented each other in bet-

ter understanding the human mind. Rühle-Gerstel clearly underwent a significant radicalization over the next few years, however, for her second book, *The Road to We,* was very different.

Published in 1927, this work was subtitled *An Attempt to Combine Marxism with Individual Psychology* and was dominated by Marxist-Lenist concepts of class struggle, dictatorship of the proletariat, the tactical use of force, and temporary mass impoverishment as the basis of a new, classless society. Not only did Rühle-Gerstel depict communism to be the logical culmination of liberal, "bourgeois" democracy, but she also had nothing to say about actual developments within Russia in the decade since the Bolsheviks had seized power there. In Rühle-Gerstel's viewpoint, Adlerian psychology provided people with a useful tool for self-knowledge in the service of the revolutionary overthrow of capitalism. Men and women would thereby overcome their alienation and join in a true community of "socio-economic order and interpersonal ties . . . the sole goal of [our] movement."

Rühle-Gerstel ended *The Road to We* triumphantly predicting a "new unity" in which "class conflict and courage are freed from their particular spheres" to result in "the activity of real class consciousness. Here Marxism and individual psychology stop being two separate teachings and movements. . . . This human synthesis is the necessary and therefore feasible ideology for that time which must make the leap from the realm of necessity to the realm of freedom. . . . This synthesis of Marxism and individual psychology is not yet extant," she declared, "but it is to be achieved in the final experience of building a society through class conflict."

Rühle-Gerstel's Adlerian supporters in Austria and Germany were delighted with her latest book. As her friend Manes Sperber, only twenty-two at the time, warmly reminisced decades later, "[It] particularly appealed to me. *Wir,* the word and the promise that it had long harbored for me, meant a road and a goal. . . . Circumspectly and courageously, she formulated views on which Marxist Adlerians could agree. Unlike Otto, who sometimes had trouble controlling his impatience with badly motivated objections or pointless digressions, Alice [always] managed to keep her composure . . . She argued like a virtuoso foilsman. . . . She was certainly not homely but not beautiful either, although she seemed to become so when she was analyzing very complex [psychology] cases with a charming mixture of girlishness and luminous lucidity."

Sperber was not the only Adlerian enamored with Rühle-Gerstel, and when the Fourth Congress for Individual Psychology opened in Vienna during mid-September, he helped organize a conclave for all those sharing her rigorous Marxist perspective and her advocacy of political revolution. They looked toward the writings of contemporary Austrian philosopher Max Adler for inspiration, as his call for creating the "new individual" through socialism seemed to complement the therapeutic work of individual psychology. The group sought Alfred Adler's support for their position, but were disappointed by his polite refusal. As Sperber later recollected, Adler tactfully replied, though with a revealing choice of metaphor, that he would "remain just as independent and neutral toward" [their Marxism] "as toward the efforts of Catholic or Protestant psychologists to combine [my] views with religious doctrine."

Adler was clearly being diplomatic with Rühle-Gerstel, Sperber, and others in their cabal of Marxist psychologists. Conciliatory by nature, he had no desire to embroil the well-attended conference that was bringing together virtually all of his European associates and coworkers. Cordial to all, he lectured on a variety of topics pertaining to child guidance, education, and character development. He also described some of his latest ideas and methods for treating psychosis and schizophrenia.

But privately, Adler was quite disturbed by Rühle-Gerstel's decision to publish *The Road to We* so soon after the calamitous events of July 15. For her to mix the teachings of individual psychology with inflammatory slogans celebrating class warfare, dictatorship of the proletariat, and Soviet communism seemed not only foolish, but also a sure way to increase political resistance to all the educational reforms his colleagues had been diligently pursuing in Vienna, Berlin, and elsewhere in Central Europe. But despite his irritation, Adler by nature avoided confrontation and would successfully maintain pleasant relations with Rühle-Gerstel and her supporters for several more years. He also continued to publish their articles, albeit on apolitical topics like contemporary literature and psychotherapy, in his international journal.

Adler believed that it was often necessary—perhaps even inevitable—to join with widely varying people if they seemed to be working for the common good. In contrast to the highly political Freud with his behind-the-scenes machinations, and perhaps too naively, Adler had little concern for the types of individuals proclaiming his sponsorship as they sought to present themselves as spokespersons for individual psychology. Eventually, Adler's casualness—even indifference—about his method for delegating administrative responsibility would come to damage his movement's effectiveness. But this issue prefigured still distantly in the future.

Over the next few months, Adler busily traveled throughout the Continent to lecture, consult, and help create new educational and psychological programs. More personally, he was active in helping Raissa set up the country home they had just purchased for weekend and holiday usage. It was situated in the historic village of Salmannsdorf, about an hour from the Stephan's Platz area of Vienna. Adler had bought the expensive estate against all the advice of his business friends and relatives. The large, many-windowed house had a beautiful garden and orchard, and offered a magnificent view of the countryside stretching away in a series of wooded foothills to distant blue mountains. From the shadowed plains, the dome and spire of the Stephansdom rose majestically above Vienna. For Adler it seemed like a wonderful place for entertaining his growing number of out-of-town visitors, as well as being a good financial investment; he still remembered vividly how worthless bank-account cash, including his own hard-earned savings, had become during Austria's postwar hyperinflation.

With his career thriving as never before, Adler began preparing busily for his second and far more extensive professional tour of the United States.

CHAPTER FOURTEEN

===

Return to America

Do you have an inferiority complex?
Do you feel insecure? Are you
fainthearted? Are you imperious?
Are you submissive? Do you believe
in hard luck? Do you understand
the other fellow? Do you
understand yourself?
Spend an evening with yourself. Try
the adventure of looking inside of
yourself. Let one of the greatest
psychologists of the age help you
to look in the right places, discover
the right things.

ADVERTISING COPY FOR
UNDERSTANDING HUMAN NATURE

Arriving in New York City on a blustery day in early February 1928, Adler immediately gained attention at a press conference held at his hotel suite on East Sixtieth Street. He announced his plans for an upcoming lecture series at the New School for Social Research, to be followed by a tour of major cities, including Chicago and Philadelphia. As the *New York Times* highlighted the next day, Adler presented his view on such topics as "melancholia, pampered youth, and suicide" and "denied that, contrary to popular belief, he ever had been a pupil of Dr. Sigmund Freud."

After discussing his notion of melancholia (what today we would call clinical depression), Adler broadly stated that, "All psychological illness is based on some mistake in early childhood. The child who is pampered always tries later to be the center of society. Things in which he is not the central idea do not interest him. The pampered child is a bad companion in marriage because he always focuses his thoughts on himself. Marriage is a task for two."

Adler went on to offer four vignettes illustrating the importance of mutual helpfulness and sharing for happy married life. He also criticized such popular parlor games as handwriting analysis and palm reading as "rubbish [for] many circumstances in a person's life cause changes in his attitude." Shifting topics, Adler asserted that "every suicide is a cowardly escape" and recounted the importance of learning early in life how to overcome disappointment and frustration. Perhaps somewhat autobiographically, he claimed that succcessful people have invariably mastered this ability and insisted that, "We cannot develop without struggling with difficulties."

Although Adler had long addressed such issues, he was gaining greater recognition in the United States with the appearance of his new book, *Understanding Human Nature.* Published just a few months before, in November 1927, it was Adler's first popular volume for the English-speaking world and was unquestionably more readable than *The Neurotic Constitution* or *The Practice and Theory of Individual Psychology.* By the time of its author's mid-winter arrival in New York, *Understanding Human Nature* had already gone into a second printing, and would eventually sell in the millions.

Based on a year's public lectures presented by Adler at Vienna's People's Institute (Volksheim) for adult education, *Understanding Human Nature* was clearly designed for wide American consumption. As would become the pattern for Adler's many popular books to follow, he had little to do with its actual writing. Unlike Freud, whose prose deservedly won international literary acclaim for its beauty of imagery and expression, Adler lacked any stylistic flair. Aside from dashing off chatty letters to far-flung family members, he derived no pleasure from writing. As a professional activity, Adler regarded writing as only a vehicle by which his ideas could reach an audience wider than the consulting room or lecture hall.

The task of organizing, editing, and translating Adler's Volksheim lectures fell to Walter Beran Wolfe. An American psychiatrist in his mid-twenties, he had studied with Adler in Vienna for the past two years and had come to greatly admire his teachings and therapeutic work. Like others whom Adler would later hire to edit or even ghostwrite his English-language works, Wolfe was an excellent choice. The son of a Viennese physician, he grew up in St. Louis and attended Dartmouth College. Although enrolled in premedical curriculum, he found time to serve on the college's literary magazine, *Jack O'Lantern,* and to publish poetry in several major American newspapers. In 1921, young Wolfe returned to St. Louis for medical training at Washington University and then served as a medical officer in the United States Navy, before deciding to pursue psychiatry and study especially with the famous Adler in Vienna.

Although definitely presented as a work for the layperson, *Understanding Human Nature* is, by today's standards, hardly pop psychology. Written in a semitechnical style, the book includes chapter subheadings like Temperament and Endocrine Secretion and Untamed Instincts as the Expression of Lessened Adaptation. In essence, *Understanding Human Nature* offers Adler's approach to key issues of personality development from birth through childhood and adolescence. There is little mention of adult-related topics such as sex, marriage, and parenthood, which would later figure prominently in Adler's innumerable lectures to American audiences.

At the outset, he explained that, "The purpose of the book is to point how the mistaken behavior of the individual affects the harmony of our social and communal life; further, to teach the individual to recognize his own mistakes, and finally, to show him how he may effect a harmonious adjustment to the communal life. Mistakes in business or in science are costly and deplorable, but mistakes in the conduct of life are usually dangerous to life itself."

In Adler's viewpoint, our personal difficulties stem from erroneous and self-defeating strategies toward life that we develop during our earliest years, almost invariably by age four or five. Striving to overcome natural feelings of inferiority, all children seek ways to maintain a satisfying degree of self-esteem. Generally, our specific method for doing so relates to biological as well as social factors. For example, a thin, weakly muscled child might focus on reading and other solitary cerebral activitites. A muscular youngster might become drawn to sports as a means for gaining a greater sense of competence. Whether in childhood, adolescence, or adulthood, we experience turmoil when a particular strategy for obtaining self-esteem stops working, or even starts becoming counterproductive.

For instance, a successful research chemist finds by his late twenties that he is increasingly lonely and depressed. Working night and day on complex projects is no longer enough; yet he feels helpless about making friends or seeking a love relationship. For Adler, such individuals must first understand their hidden life strategy—in this case, to experience esteem through solitary, intellectual work—and then take the appropriate actions to achieve a more fulfilling existence.

Adler optimistically insisted throughout *Understanding Human Nature* that we all can grow in this way, unlearning and changing our early life strategy when necessary. He did not believe that this process was always easy, but deemed it possible with sustained willpower and effort. Even with very negative factors that might seemingly inflict long-lasting emotional damage,

Adler refused to become fatalistic. In a prescient insight that now dominates current research on life stress and illness, he suggested that, "It is not our *objective* experiences which bring us from the straight path of development, but our personal *attitude* and *evaluation* of events, and the *manner* in which we evaluate and weigh occurrences."

Although Vienna's Volksheim characteristically drew many left-wing students and intellectuals to its public lectures, *Understanding Human Nature* offers little economic criticism. There are a few scattered references to "class injustice" and comments like "class differences . . . have created privilege for one, and slavery for another." In one instance, Adler specifically praises Marx and Engels for their insights on how "the economic basis, the technical form in which a people lives, determines their . . . thinking and behavior. . . . Our conception of the 'logic of human communal life,' of the 'absolute truth,' is in part an agreement with those concepts."

In later books predominantly written for Americans, Adler would completely eliminate any reference to Marxist thought. It seems that socialism increasingly lost its appeal for him as the 1920s progressed and his own movement became embroiled in factionalism over wider political aims. Far more impassioned than Adler's critique of capitalism was his attack on male dominance as a socially destructive force. In this regard, *Understanding Human Nature* was only the first of Adler's popular books to insist—quite radically from Freud or Jung—that, "All our institutions, our traditional attitudes, our laws, our morals, our customs, give evidence of the fact that they are determined and maintained by privileged males for the glory of male domination. These institutions reach out into the very nurseries and have a great influence upon the child's soul."

In a lengthy section, Adler went on to summarize historically that "masculine dominance is not a natural thing" and that "[t]here is no justification for the differentiation of 'manly' and 'womanly' character traits." After providing numerous case examples of how sex-role stereotyping—especially concerning the alleged inferiority of women—"poisons" virtually all social relations, including marriage, Adler insisted that, "It is our duty to support [the emancipation-for-women movements] in their efforts to gain freedom and equality, because finally the happiness of the whole of humanity depends upon [it]."

For Adler, the key agent of such all meaningful social change was the public school. "If parents were good educators, with the necessary insight and the ability to recognize mistaken development in their children when it began, and if, further, they were capable of combatting these errors by proper education, we should be happy to admit that no institution was better adapted for the protection of valid human beings.

"Unfortunately, however, parents are neither good psychologists nor good teachers," Adler argued. "Various degrees of a pathological family egoism seem to play the chief role in the home . . . of today. This egoism demands that the children of one's own family should be especially cultivated, and should be looked up to as being extraordinarily worthwhile, even at the cost of other children."

Adler conceded that the typical public school "is not adapted to this task. There is hardly a teacher today who is . . . prepared for [it]. It is his business to retail a certain curriculum to his children without daring to concern himself with the human material with which he works. . . . [Overcrowding] in each class further militates against the accomplishment of his task."

Nevertheless, Adler concluded that only the institution of public education—based on the progressive, scientific principles of individual psychology—could create effective social change. With a fervor undoubtedly flamed by memories of his own stifling schooling, he declared, "Up to the present time, it has always been . . . [that] the individual who got a school into his hands fashioned it into an instrument for his own vain and ambitious plans. We hear clamorings today that the old authority should be re-established in the schools. Did the old authority ever achieve any good results? How can an authority which has always been found harmful suddenly become valuable? We can speak of a good school, only when that school is in harmony with the necessities for [children's emotional] development. Only with such a school shall we ever be able to consider a school for social life."

Understanding Human Nature was inarguably an original book for the American public of the 1920s. Adler spoke about personality development in a helpful, pragmatic manner relatively free of technical jargon. While he lacked Freud's dark, powerful use of imagery, Adler had a knack for offering concrete examples from everyday family life that many found appealing. Yet it remains unlikely that *Understanding Human Nature* would have achieved its phenomenal publishing success—greatly eclipsing all of Freud's combined American books sales through the 1920s—if not for the shrewd, aggressive marketing of Adler's publishing house, Greenberg Publisher.

Its owner-president was Jae W. Greenberg, who had founded the company only three years before. A graduate of Columbia University, he had been involved in the New York publishing scene since working as a college student part-time for Dodd, Mead & Company on their *New International*

Enyclopedia. Finding the work stimulating at the time, he confided to owner Frank H. Dodd his desire for a publishing career. "If you want an interesting life, and don't care about getting rich, I'd recommend it" was Dodd's laconic reply.

Sixteen years later, in 1924, Greenberg Publisher was launched. It was a good time for American publishing, and the young company's first season yielded a surprise best-seller, *Tony Sarg's Book for Children*. Lauded as an "epic" in a full-page *New York Times* book review, Sarg's work soon appeared in a special limited edition issued at fifty dollars, the first copy of which was bought by President Coolidge for his grandchild. In 1925, Greenberg bought out the Adelphi Company, and soon achieved another huge success by publishing R. F. Foster's *Contract Bridge* during the height of the game's craze.

It was Greenberg's acumen to market *Understanding Human Nature* as a self-help rather than philosophical or scientific book. In strikingly contemporary style, the following full-page advertisement appeared in the January 1928 issue of *Publishers Weekly*, weeks before Adler's arrival in the United States:

> Do you have an inferiority complex . . . do you feel insecure . . . are you faint-hearted . . . are you imperious . . . are you submissive . . . do you believe in hard luck . . . do you understand the other fellow . . . do you understand yourself?
>
> Spend the evening with yourself. Try the adventure of looking inside of yourself. Let one of the greatest psychologists of the age help you look in the right places, discover the right things.

Jae Greenberg had accurately read America's pulse. Within six months, *Understanding Human Nature* went through three more print runs and would soon total over one hundred thousand copies. *Understanding Human Nature* immediately catapulted Adler to national recognition, and would help generate for Greenberg Publisher a variety of significant works in the fields of psychology and education, including five additional books by Adler, several by Joseph Jastrow, and even a popularization of psychoanalysis rather luridly entitled *Freud: His Dream and Sex Theories*, which likewise became a big seller. No wonder Freud was bitterly sarcastic about American interest in his work.

But the huge success of *Understanding Human Nature* can hardly be attributed solely to effective marketing. Most reviewers were quite favorably impressed by its originality and lucidity. The mainstream *Survey* admiringly commented that, "Adler demands that the knowledge of human nature be made available to all, not reserved for a few scientists. For only by understanding can we live on satisfactory terms with ourselves, our community and our world."

Likewise impressed was psychologist S. Daniel House of Columbia University, an influential reviewer of psychology books for the general public. In *Bookman,* House stated that, "To understand human nature in the Adlerian sense is to be possessed of a social philosophy that honors cooperation rather than competition, to see in the young child a plastic and creative personality, to regard the home and the school as the two most promising centers for inculcating in the child self-confidence and self-dependence, to view life as a series of problems of equating the ego with a variety of social environments. . . . Dr. Adler's work teaches us that psychology at the service of life is the only kind of psychology worthy of our serious attention as humans urgently in need of a realistic insight into the dynamics of behavior and of misbehavior."

Writing in the *Saturday Review of Literature* that same month, House commented more lavishly that, "The Adlerian approach to the problems of disharmony and maladjustment resident in human nature constitute a new chapter in psychology and, what is more important, a fresh beginning in education. . . . We might refer to Adler's work as educational sociology and compare him in his general social philosophy and creative attitudes toward education with John Dewey. Or, if one thinks of his enlightening contributions more medically, he might be referred to with considerable accuracy as the pioneer in the comparatively new field of educational psychiatry."

House went on to observe that, "[Adler's] philosophy is colored by the Nietzschean wisdom, humanized by an enormous respect for the superiority of the principle of cooperation to the reigning ethic of competition. His psychology also has affinities with the so-called Gestalt psychology. . . . Therapeutically, Adler therefore never stops emphasizing the need on the part of parent and teacher to stimulate in the child a sense of confidence, to evoke his cooperative dispositions, to socialize and humanize his ego. Communal fellowship, an affectionate attitude toward children, a genuinely humble comradeship with them, an appreciation of their inner life, are the impressive doctrines that constitute the Adlerian basis for understanding human nature.

"It is a pleasure to find a psychologist writing so humanly and thoughtfully," lauded House, "avoiding the technical sterility of [both] the academician . . . and the speculative luxuriance of the dogmatic psychoanalyst . . . about problems that concern us all so intimately. The translation of a very difficult German into an eminently readable English is the work of Dr. Walter Beran Wolfe, Adler's most important American disciple."

In the academic world as well, *Understanding Human Nature* generally met with high praise. The *American Journal of Sociology* declared that, "Of all psychiatrists, Dr. Adler seems to be most akin to sociologists in spirit and perspective. In earlier works, he has shown a keen appreciation of the role of social relations in personal development; in the present book, which is constructed out of a series of popular lectures, we have the simplest and clearest picture of these views."

Delighted by the stunning public response to *Understanding Human Nature,* Greenberg quickly capitalized on his new publishing "find" by signing Adler onto producing two more popular psychology books within twenty-four months. Dated February 15, the finalized contracts referred to *The Style of Life* (actually entitled *The Science of Living* upon publication) and *The Education of Children.*

Eager to spread his psychological message before a seemingly ever-widening American audience, Adler probably acted too quickly in signing these and later publishing agreements. As had been true for *Understanding Human Nature,* Adler would find himself relying increasingly upon free-lance editors to transform his transcribed lectures into a readable format for virtually all of his subsequent English-language books. Unfortunately, with little interest in literary writing, Adler tended to allow such ghostwriting work to be done hastily under deadline pressure, and sometimes even shoddily. Eventually, even once-friendly reviewers would begin to turn on Adler for seemingly abandoning his careful, scholarly approach to human problems.

But at this time, the book paved the way to even greater American recognition than he had previously enjoyed. Within days of arriving in New York City, Adler was already busy with a full lecture schedule. Representative of his presentations was an all-day conference on child treatment that he led on February 10 for members and friends of the local parents' council. In the morning, Adler extemporaneously commented on an unfamiliar case concerning a five-year-old boy with behavioral problems at home and school. "Robert's" difficulties included thumb sucking, frequent uncooperativeness, withdrawing from social play, and producing silly behavior such as baby talk.

Steering clear of sexual interpretations, Adler analyzed the boy's conduct as emanating from a lack of sufficient attention. Besides emphasizing that the father—and not just the mother—ought to spend more time with Robert, Adler's approach was innovative for stressing the youngster's strengths and interests. Specifically, Robert showed an aptitude for artistic and musical activity, and was already beginning to carry tunes melodically. He also demonstrated prowess with mechanical toys and blocks.

"When you see such an interest in the life of this boy," Adler remarked optimistically, "you can be sure that he is not lost. He can gain more power. [The parents] must only be convinced that he is also able to [advance] in other things. . . . Everybody can accomplish everything. This must be the motto of every educator."

Adler recommended that the boy's parents encourage such endeavors while simultaneously building up his self-confidence for more sociable activity. "Perhaps we can find a way to bring up children so that they will be courageous and also a poet or musician," he mused aloud at the morning's close.

In the afternoon, Adler commented upon the case of an eleven-year-old girl with hyperactivity, moodiness, and academic problems. The younger of two children adopted during infancy, "Sally" had aggressive tendencies as well. After reviewing aloud the case information about the girl's interests and activities, Adler once more expressed optimism. "It is not necessary for the parents to feel worried," he gently asserted. "The child is striving but does not believe she is able. She must be encouraged, and explained [when] she makes mistakes. . . . She feels like she is in danger. If I would believe I am in danger, I [too] would be more interested in my own person [than in schoolwork]. . . . Free her from her fear and anxiety, and you can be sure that she will [improve] in school. I like this girl."

Through such presentations in New York City and elsewhere that winter, Adler began to exert long-term impact on the American mental-health field. Among those inspired by his approach was the young Carl Rogers, who would later pioneer in the fields of counseling and humanistic psychology. "I had the privilege of meeting, listening to, and observing Dr. Alfred Adler . . . in the winter of 1927–28, when I was an intern at the then new Institute for Child Guidance in New York City," Rogers recalled late in life. "The Institute perished in the Depression. Accustomed as I was to the rather rigid Freudian approach of the Institute—seventy-five page case histories, and exhaustive batteries of tests before even thinking of 'treating' a child—I was shocked by Dr. Adler's very direct and deceptively simple manner of immediately relating to the child and the parent. It took me some time to realize how much I had learned from him."

In mid-February, Adler began his first academic position in the United States, teaching a course on individual psychology at the New School for

Social Research. Founded nearly a decade before in 1919, it comprised a set of brownstone mansions in Manhattan's Chelsea area, southwest of midtown and north of Wall Street. From the beginning, the New School had been created to provide a haven for radical or controversial thinkers, and it boasted such distinguished faculty as historian Charles Beard and sociologist Thorstein Veblen. The famous behaviorist John Watson had been teaching psychology there part-time until recently, along with such leading mental-health figures as Adler's new friend Ira Wile.

Nearly all of the New School's course offerings lay in public affairs, social science, and social work. Most of its students were college graduates seeking additional credits for job-related study. Despite its academic competence, the New School had suffered major financial problems during its early years and had been forced to curtail its activities drastically in 1922, until a massive reorganization could take place. That year, Alvin Johnson, a gifted and farsighted young academician, took over as director. He had been a board member and journalist at the *New Republic* magazine and a professor at several prestigious universities. Under Johnson's able administrative hand, the New School began to stabilize and grow financially, and by 1927, plans were underway to relocate the facility into a building of its own.

Adler greatly enjoyed his first opportunity to teach individual psychology to American professionals over a sustained period. His class met on Tuesday and Thursday evenings for an hour and a half, coincidentally overlapping with a course on juvenile conduct disorders taught by Wile. Over the twelve-session course, Adler covered the basic concepts of his system. These included such topics as "individual psychology and its significance for science and life; the feeling of inferiority as the basis of the development of mind and psyche; the superiority complex; the style of life; problem children in family and school; the problems of life as social problems; love and marriage; and dreams and the art of interpretation."

In conjunction with Adler's course at the New School, he also established a discussion group for those seeking a more detailed understanding of his approach. Assisting Adler in this endeavor were several close American associates, including social worker Sibyl Mandell and the young psychiatrist Walter Beran Wolfe, who had just translated *Understanding Human Nature*. Undoubtedly, Adler was hoping to build the small conclave into the nucleus for a formidable movement within the United States.

Among the short handouts that he prepared for the discussion group was an outline entitled "A Brief Comparison of Individual Psychology and Psychoanalysis." In this unpublished and little-known piece, Adler describes seven major differences between the two perspectives. The most fundamental according to Adler "does not lie in the fact that I, according to [the Freudians] see the 'striving for power' as the only motivating force. . . . not in the 'power doctrine' I once conceived of, but later set aside as inadequate. The real difference lies in the notion that, "Freud takes as premise the fact that man is so constructed by nature that he wishes only to satisfy his drives but that culture or civilization . . . is antagonistic to such satisfaction. . . . [However], Individual psychology claims that the development of the individual, because of his bodily inadequacy and his feeling of inferiority, is dependent on society. . . . Hence, social feeling is inherent in man and bound up with his identity."

After the New School course ended in mid-March, Adler spent the next six weeks lecturing throughout the Northeast and Midwest. As always, his goal was to promote individual psychology as vigorously as possible. He enjoyed public speaking tremendously and felt no intellectual embarrassment about sharing his ideas with the academically unsophisticated. Thus, in a manner unthinkable for his European colleagues like the aloof, reclusive Freud or the aristocratic Jung, Adler eagerly spoke before a wide variety of professional and lay audiences. His extensive lecture itinerary not only included Boston, Chicago, and Philadelphia, but also smaller cities like Cleveland and Cincinnati. Aside from county medical societies, Adler energetically addressed parent-teacher groups and chambers of commerce in cities as small as Columbus, Ohio and Flint, Michigan. Typically, he lectured to these lay audiences on such popular topics as child rearing and marriage.

Before departing for Austria later that week, Adler made a special visit to Wittenberg College in Springfield, Ohio. In mid-October 1927, the school had hosted a widely publicized international Symposium on Feelings and Emotions. The occasion was the dedication of the college's new chemistry-psychology building, and some two dozen of the world's leading psychologists had been invited to attend, including Alfred Adler, Karl Bühler, James Cattell, Pierre Janet, Joseph Jastrow, William McDougall, and William Stern. More than four hundred psychologists—a sizable number for that era—had come to the small Lutheran school, founded on a rolling hill in 1845. Residing back home in Vienna at the time, Adler had been unable to attend, but instead sent a new article prepared especially for the occasion.

Covered by major midwestern newspapers and *Time* magazine, Adler's paper, read by proxy, received considerable media attention. Emphasizing the importance of the early maternal-child bond—rather than heredity—for later personality development, Adler insisted that "social feeling is what enables human beings to survive in this world. . . . We can now understand why all actions on the useless side of life among problem children, neurotics . . . and criminals . . . are caused by a lack in social feeling, courage, and self-confidence." In a comment quoted by many newspapers, he declared that, "Criminals are made, not born."

Adler likewise suggested that the most important single factor in personality development is the relative presence of the "inferiority complex. . . . This feeling of inferiority forms the background for all our studies. . . . It ultimately becomes the stimulus among all individuals, whether children or adults, to establish their actions in such a way that they will arrive at a goal of superiority." Ironically, most accounts of the international symposium followed *Time*'s lead in describing Adler doubly erroneously as a medical professor at the University of Vienna and as a "friend and old pupil of Dr. Sigmund Freud."

Now seven months later, in early May, Adler was making a solo appearance at Wittenberg College to receive an honorary doctorate of laws degree. Looking out at the cap-and-gowned assembly of faculty and administrators, he discussed his experiences in helping to establish Vienna's twenty-two child-guidance clinics and then broadly highlighted his view of education. According to the brief account that appeared the next day in the campus newspaper, "Dr. Adler indicated that the mind is stimulated from the beginning of life for life itself, and that it is necessary to understand the parts of life to understand the whole. . . . [We] must fight back the inferiority of the physical by [our] mental states."

One of Adler's last and most intriguing presentations during his second American lecture tour was held before a small gathering of Chicago psychiatrists. Adler tended to be more informal and jovial with colleagues, and the unpublished transcript of his talk reveals a levity—almost a playfulness—relatively absent in his writing, but which his former patients often described. Certainly, too, Adler may have been feeling especially happy about the prospect of his impending voyage home.

In this seminar, he concentrated on the pragmatic, nitty-gritty aspects of child therapeutic work. His colleagues posed questions on such topics as how they should interact with family members, what value to place on intellectual testing, and how to structure therapeutic sessions in terms of their length and frequency. Focusing mostly on matters involving family therapy, Adler remarked that, "You will never find a neurotic [child] in which you do not find other neurotic persons in the family. It is very necessary to find this other person. . . . I [generally] try to make independent the child I treat but do not antagonize the mother."

Adler explained the importance of establishing what today we would today call a *therapeutic alliance* with other family members. After citing Benjamin Franklin for insight into character development, Adler advised a colleague, "Tell the mother that, 'You have understood everything rightly and you are on the right way. Now I would like to add something. Would you like to try this? Perhaps we can accomplish something.' I speak always as if [the parent] were my companion. I try to avoid all dogmatic expressions. [Otherwise] the [parents] might believe that they are accused and feel it is a [judicial] court."

If the parents demand to know whether their viewpoint is correct, Adler confided that his approach was tactfully to reply, "To a certain degree, you are right." For those family members unwilling to participate in sessions, "I propose always to tell them that I am a teacher for occupational advice and I would like to speak . . . about [to] what occupation [they are] really best adapted. . . . It is not good to have the patients [receive] the impression that they are sick."

Yet, Adler conceded that his attempts at a therapeutic alliance were not always successful. "The mother notices that the child is slipping away [from her] and you must count with it that [she'll] be against you. Therefore, it is best to communicate with the child and tell her the mother is sick."

In relating how to speak with patients, Adler emphasized the importance of building up their confidence. Astutely perceiving that the therapeutic relationship often involves a hidden power struggle by the patient and thereby anticipating what is today called *paradoxical therapy,* Adler observed that, "Do not fight with him. You must give him the idea that everything is a good sign; he must never worry. . . . Sometimes, he begins in an indirect manner to attack you. He will say, 'I feel worse. I could not sleep. . . . I [may then] propose that, 'If you cannot sleep, then collect all your thoughts and bring them to me tomorrow so we can take advantage of your sleeplessness. If you ask him on the next day, 'Have you collected your thoughts?' he will probably say, 'This night I have slept well.' You see, what I do is to give him the responsibility [for improvement]. I try to bring him into a trap and make him think that whatever I do . . . can be used for his health."

Adler also highlighted his use of humor for effective psychotherapy. "I cannot deny that I tease my patients," he conceded, "but I do it in a very friendly way and I like to show what happens in a case always [through] a joke. It is very worthwhile that you have a great collection of jokes and that each neurosis has a joke as a companion. You cannot find a neurosis that does not resemble a joke. . . . Sometimes a joke [can help the patient] see how ridiculous his sickness is."

After sharing several illustrative jokes with his medical colleagues, Adler concluded the seminar by stressing the importance of placing responsibility for improvement solidly upon the family itself, even in cases of severe childhood disturbance like schizophrenia. "I never promise to cure. I say, 'I will try.' If I am asked whether the patient has improved, I tell the family to judge for themselves."

CHAPTER FIFTEEN

The Great Popularizer

*"It is probable that Alfred Adler is the
most accurate and original foreign
psychologist now in America. . . . He
shares, as by birthright, most of our
virtues and frailties. . . . He bubbles
over with courage and energy.
Scientists of today are either hard,
cold, efficient machines like Freud,
or palpitating human beings—no
less efficient—like Adler."*

NEW YORK HERALD

Before returning home to Austria, Adler made a brief stop in London. Flushed with the success of his second American lecture tour and the immense appeal of *Understanding Human Nature,* Adler was eager to bring out a new book explicating individual psychology, based on his English lectures. Although psychiatric consulting and public speaking continued to prove satisfying, Adler had minimal interest in writing as a personal activity. To choose an appropriate free-lance editor for the project was not particularly difficult, for during that same year of 1928, the first popular English work about his approach had just been published.

The author of *ABCs of Adlerian Psychology* was Philip Mairet. Editor of the iconoclastic *New English Weekly,* he had met Adler in London two years before and had been immediately excited by the insights, social optimism, and political progressivism of individual psychology. With his friend Dimitrije Mitrinovic as director, Mairet had energetically helped to establish the English branch of the International Society for Individual Psychology and was currently head of its sociological group. With strong ties to London's literary and intellectual avant-garde, Mairet was intrigued by the "new psychology" emanating from Vienna and particularly by Adler's approach. He was especially entranced with Adler's pioneering efforts to build a humanistic science of the mind, and eagerly negotiated the agreement to perform the necessary editorial work for *Problems of Neurosis,* to be published by prestigious Routledge and Kegan Paul Limited. Once Mairet actually received the manuscript's disorganized raw material, his enthusiasm probably waned, for he recalled decades later that, "Some of [the papers] were Adler's own notes from which he spoke. Others were reports stenographed [sic] or written up by enthusiasts who heard the lectures. . . . They were all in English, which Adler spoke fluently enough, but not an English one could well print."

Not only was Adler's material poorly organized and stylistically weak, but many of the sections offered ideas that seemed to Mairet inadequately developed. During the next few months, he worked valiantly on the challenging editorial assignment, which encompassed "rewriting the whole of the material entrusted to me, very much to Adler's satisfaction." Halfway through the work, Adler "saw what I had done so far, and wrote to me saying: 'Do not fear to elaborate or extend *in our sense.*'"

Mairet was both startled and flattered by Adler's willingness to entrust the expression of his ideas to a lay outsider like himself. But he resisted the temptation to do any more "glossing" than necessary in order to finish the work. Years later in retrospect, Mairet could not recall whether "Adler made any corrections to my final manuscript," but mused intriguingly that, "He was never a very interesting *writer,* whereas Freud was a brilliant one and Jung very fascinating to read. Adler didn't *want* to be a writer—didn't much believe in it. To his mind, every fresh spark of universal human understanding has to be struck out between human beings conversing on these things man-to-man. And ultimately, perhaps, we shall have to admit this as *truth.*"

During the fall, while busily lecturing, training therapists, and helping to establish additional child-guidance clinics in Austria and Germany, Adler received an unexpected letter from the Soviet Union. Erroneously addressing him as a "professor of the University of Vienna," he was informed of his election to honorary membership in the Leningrad Scientific-Medical Child Study Society. Written by Professor Griboedov, vice president of the Soviet's Psycho-Neurological Academy, the letter went on to request information about Adler's latest work and to declare the society's interest in mutual cooperation for future research.

Though Adler's reaction to this specific honor is unknown, he was unquestionably aware of professional Soviet interest in individual psychology. Sixteen years earlier, in 1912, several of his most important articles to date had appeared in translation in *Psikhoterapia.* These included papers on dream interpretation, the role of the unconscious, and the treatment of neurosis. After the October revolution, of course, Adler had written quite negatively about Leninist ideology and bolshevism. It seems likely, therefore, that these writings had escaped Soviet attention at the time of his 1928 award; for much later under Stalin's rule, Adler would be attacked in the *Great Soviet Encyclopedia* as as a "reactionary" whose interpretation of Nietzsche was used as the "psychological basis of the ideology of imperialism."

Yet as his reputation grew internationally, Adler maintained an enthusiastic local following in Vienna. His well-received presentations in cities like Boston, Chicago, New York, and Philadelphia during the previous two visits had been instrumental in bringing many eager professionals and would-be patients to him in Austria. As always, Adler tended to be informal and accessible for those interested in his work.

As recounted by visiting American journalists, his daily schedule in Vienna was rather consistent. Adler would typically arrive at his consulting room early in the morning, long before patients were scheduled for their appointments. After working alone until about eleven o'clock, Adler would invite friends, students, and colleagues to assemble around his desk and hear him expound about whatever during the previous twenty-four hours had most interested him, whether in clinical, educational, or public matters.

Following lunch, Adler was ready to begin seeing patients at two o'clock. Meanwhile, his waiting room had begun to fill with what one reporter described as "a polyglot mixture of paupers and millionaires waiting to see him. Adler's charges are so low—for one with an American reputation— that one may finally be sure that he practices for the pure fun and power of his profession. He makes the ordeal of consultation a quite unterrifying experience."

Typically, Adler's loosely organized society met in a special private room upstairs at the Café Siller on Postgasse. Adler rarely led the evening discussions, but rather served as chairperson and genially appointed at each session a particular member to prepare a specific topic for sharing at the next meeting. The subject matter for a given presentation was wide ranging, from a current criminal case making newspaper headlines to the latest psychiatric theory about delinquent or schizophrenic children.

In the long discussions that followed the reports, Adler preferred initially to be quiet and receptive. He allowed nearly everyone to comment as they wished, sometimes quite rhetorically, before finally taking the floor. Then, with a few short sentences expressed with an air of finality, he would dispose of the case. Only on rare occasions would Adler allow himself to become drawn into serious debate, and if so, his genial manner could become sharply argumentative and tenacious.

"[The spectacle of] Adler's debating in the Postgasse is entertaining as well as instructive," wrote one American journalist on assignment in Vienna. "Nightly there is at least one passage of Freud-baiting. One evening, some one asked for the essential difference between psychoanalysis and individual psychology. This launched an extensive discussion. 'Twisting the lion's tail' was turned into 'twisting the lion's theory.' Adler promptly translated the dark triangular problem of the father, the mother, and the son from terms of psychoanalysis into terms of individual psychology. He claimed that the child's jealousy of its parent was due less to a precious instinct than to an inborn thirst for dominion, which resents the father's control of the household and aims to usurp his place."

In an idiosyncratic rhetorical style that some reporters found amusing, Adler also showed a tendency to use the inferiority complex label upon individual people, social classes, and even entire nations. Like Freud, it seems that Adler was not above resorting to ad hominem attacks against his intellectual adversaries, sometimes, for instance, claiming that they suffered from inferiority complexes that obstructed their ability to accept his theories.

Adler was colorful and he made for good newspaper copy. American journalists typically portrayed the founder of individual psychology by employing such adjectives as optimistic, down-to-earth, and pugnacious. Knowing if only simplistically that Freud emphasized sexuality as the key human drive, such reporters were quick to quote Adler's vigorous and seemingly contrasting opposition to sexual libertarian ideas like companionate or trial marriage. "Love is the basis of all our culture," Adler had insisted to one visitor, "and without it, our present civilization would collapse. Monogamy is the highest form of love. I have no patience with the movements to make love easier. If it is made too easy, it degenerates into cheap pleasure."

Although individual psychology had obviously diverged from psychoanalysis since Adler's break in 1911, Adler continued to be incensed by popular references to his having once been a "disciple of Freud." In 1928, when *The Neurotic Constitution* went into a fourth German edition, Adler took the occasion to publish his most explicit denial to date about their nine-year relationship as recounted by Freud in his 1914 monograph, *The History of the Psychoanalytic Movement*.

Mr. Freud has bad luck with [the interpretation of] my spoken word. . . . My mild rejection, 'it was no pleasure to stand in his shadow'—i.e., to be made an accomplice to all the absurdities of Freudianism, because I was a co-worker in the psychology of the neuroses—he at once interprets as a confession of my revolting vanity to put before unsuspecting readers. Since to date none of those who know wanted to admit this bad luck of their teacher—not mine, as is often erroneously maintained—I see myself forced to destroy the formation of a legend.

═══════

Adler arrived in New York City in early January 1929, hopeful that his third American tour would be enhanced by the publication of his new book. Issued in Germany the year before, it was entitled *The Technique of Individual Psychology, Volume 1: The Art of Reading a Life-and-Case History*. Flush with the overnight success of *Understanding Human Nature,* publisher Jae Greenberg, in early 1928, had hired a husband-and-wife team of Adler's associates to translate the new work into English, which would be called *The Case of Miss R.*

The book's format was unusual. It essentially involved the autobiographical narrative of a Viennese patient, Miss R., who had grown to womanhood during the Great War and its aftermath. Interspersed with her memories of childhood, family upbringing, social life, and dreams and fantasies are Adler's comments and interpretations. Miss R. was not his patient and was unfamiliar to him. At the outset, Adler therefore explained that, "The art of individual psychology is based on knowledge and common sense. . . . In this book, I proceed as I do in my office when I listen to a patient's story for the first time. . . . With every sentence, with every word . . . I consider: What is the real meaning of what she is saying?"

By American standards of the time, *The Case of Miss R.* was strikingly frank in its autobiographical account of a young woman's sexual awakening. Raised in working-class Vienna, Miss R. at an early age was exposed to neighborhood prostitution and to brothels. She recounts episodes of her teenage masturbation and voyeurism, her first romantic stirrings, and her conflicted feelings about rebuffing attempted seductions by older male neighbors, and more direct efforts by sailors interested in a quick liaison.

With clear, simple language, Miss R. vividly evokes the working-class world of early twentieth-century Vienna from a young woman's standpoint. Adler's running commentary offers brief discourses on such topics as childhood pampering and life goals, the inferiority and superiority complex, the nature of dreams and early memories, masculine protest and female sexuality. Surprisingly for one who had explicitly written about underlying power issues in male-female relations, Adler was often silent as Miss R. described the various attempts of much older men to engage her in casual sex. Adler ended the book optimistically but rather abruptly, inviting the reader to "divine how" his colleague cured Miss R. "from her compulsion neurosis."

Undoubtedly, Greenberg was hoping for another Adlerian blockbuster and marketed the book aggressively. After making the German title more commercial, he explicitly tied the new volume to *Understanding Human Nature* and took out a full-page advertisement in *Publishers Weekly* that February, proclaiming that, "because of its unique subject, [*The Case of Miss R.*] will probably have an even more popular appeal and wider public audience." The accompanying advertising copy has an unusually contemporary ring:

> A young girl tells the actual story of her life. No detail is spared. No word is changed. Every phase of her inner life is laid bare. Dr. Adler takes this dramatic story, just as she tells it. He interprets the meaning and significance of every detail of the story. His analysis is the form of a running commentary. The result is both a life story as interesting as any tale of fiction and an analysis of authority by one of the greatest living psychologists. A remarkable human document! The book is original in form, and in subject matter. It will hold the reader's interest from first page to last, both for its dramatic story and its superb analysis.

Although Greenberg certainly tried, *The Case of Miss R.* did not fare well and failed to attract anywhere near the popularity of *Understanding Human Nature*. Why this was the case is difficult to say precisely. A publishing truism suggests that Americans are uninterested in reading about life abroad, especially among ordinary folk rather than glamorous celebrities like royalty. Miss R. was certainly nondescript. The frequent sexual anecdotes she describes may also have rendered the book distasteful for many readers. Perhaps even more disappointing for Adler, the book was not even reviewed by most important newspapers or professional journals. Soon forgotten even by Adlerian sympathizers, it probably remains to this day his most obscure book published in English.

―――――――

During the publication of *The Case of Miss R.* in mid-winter 1929, Adler made his first of two trips to America's West Coast. His lecture tour began in early February at the University of California's branches at Berkeley and San Francisco. His talks included "Understanding Human Nature" and such broader issues about American society as its competitiveness and its controversial experiment with Prohibition.

Twice that week, Adler received major coverage from the *San Francisco*

Chronicle for remarks in which he contrasted Austria's continuing financial woes with his buoyant assessment of the American character. He noted that his homeland had been suffering from high unemployment for almost a decade and that despair gripped many of those chronically out of work. While praising Vienna's educational and medical achievements despite meager governmental funding, Adler was enamored of the new country he was now visiting for the third time. With a striking choice of metaphor unthinkable for many proud Europeans, Adler declared that, "The United States is like an ocean. An individual has infinite possibilities for development in such a country, but he also has greater difficulties to overcome. The incentive to ambition is great but the competition is also very keen. In Europe, they are still swimming around in a bathtub. Life is circumscribed, opportunities are few, and the need for [psychological] knowledge is limited."

The following week, feeling in high spirits amidst the Bay Area sunshine, Adler underwent perhaps the most humorous mishap of his California tour. He had been invited to speak at Mills College, a liberal arts institution for women. The school was situated in Oakland, across the bay from San Francisco. Adler was scheduled to present two lectures, on Friday and Saturday respectively, sponsored by the psychology department. On Saturday evening, a special faculty dinner in his honor would be held. College interest in the visit was running high, abetted by the school paper's front-page feature about Adler published two weeks before the anticipated event.

Decades later, Mills College graduate Margaret Barlow recalled that, "In the mid-afternoon of the day before the dinner, the switchboard operator received a call from Dr. Adler, who asked if someone was coming to meet him . . . at the train station." Apparently, he had misread or forgotten the date of his scheduled visit! "There was a great deal of confusion on the campus. The dinner had to be rearranged, guests informed, etc., and who had a car and the time to get him?"

Selected to chauffeur Adler because she had a car, Barlow was commanded to fetch him and then "keep him away from the campus as long as possible in order that they achieve some sense of order." Expecting the renowned physician to be furious over the college's seemingly disorganized reception, Barlow "was not prepared for the smiling, charming, and totally calm little man patiently waiting at the station." Following faculty instructions to keep Adler removed from Mills College as long as possible, she drove him in "a loop around the campus and then up into the hills along the skyline, hoping he had a bad sense of direction. In a remarkably short time, he turned to me and said, 'Why are we going in circles?'

"I discarded all the evasive statements I had carefully prepared and blurted out, 'They were expecting you tomorrow and all the VIPs who intended to meet you are hurriedly changing plans. I was told to keep you away as along as possible, so please just enjoy the view.' We had a good laugh and while we continued our drive, he outlined plans [for his upcoming summer courses in Vienna]. . . . At the dinner that night, I was invited to sit at the head of the table—a startling honor. As we entered the dining room, he gave me a wicked and amused smile."

Pleasant and jovial, Adler made a good impresssion on other students likewise expecting a stern European academician. The Mills College newspaper thus appreciatively reported the next day that Adler "is far from preposessing in appearance and attitude. He explains his theories in the simplest of classroom lectures, in words of one syllable, illustrated with gestures and extempore [sic] blackboard diagrams, genially and encouragingly answering showers of questions. His table-talk is clever and sparkling and he can listen as well as tell a good story. He likes American food but longs for a chance to show his superiority as a coffee-maker. (It must *not* be made on the stove, and from his description, must be quite able to 'stand alone.')"

As always in such public situations, Adler had virtually perfected his persona of professorial cordiality. Rather astutely, therefore, the Mills College reporter stated, "The most revealing glimpse he permitted me occured during a lull in the dinner. Campus celebrities had momentarily stopped plying him with food and questions, and [I found that] he was absorbed in listening in on a nearby conversation. His eyes were shrewd and kindly."

———

In early March, Adler returned from his invigorating California trip and eagerly began teaching again at the New School for Social Research. This time, he offered more than forty lectures through two separate courses that spanned four nights per week. For the introductory course, Adler's focus was "on the bearing of the system of Individual Psychology on human nature, culture and education" and "the importance throughout life of the striving for superiority [and] the nature of individuality, common sense, and intelligence." He also lectured on "the psychological influence of occupation and of various plans of life and action." These included "love, marriage, and family life; the effect of organic deficiencies; and the problems originating in family discipline, such as those of the pampered or neglected child."

Adler's more advanced course was meant for those already familiar with the basics of his approach and interested in exploring more specific, wide-ranging issues. These included "problems in behavior" such as "misadjusted childhood, neuroses, crime, perversion, suicide, the masculine protest" and "psychological aspects of politics, religion, philosophy, and the woman's movement." With an interdisciplinary perspective, he also addressed "the nature of nationalism and national mentalities."

For the first time in the United States, Adler was also able at the New School to provide extended "live" demonstrations of his method for interviewing children and their parents. Typically, he was referred cases from his New School students, such as psychologists, psychiatrists, social workers, and teachers. After reviewing their case reports, Adler selected the most interesting ones for his class demonstrations. During the typical evening session, he would first comment extemporaneously upon the written case—perhaps, of a bright but highly anxious ten-year-old girl failing in school. Next, the youngster would be ushered into the classroom, where Adler would conduct a brief interview, usually in the parents' presence. Adler would then offer advice, and after the family's departure, he would finalize his clinical impressions with the class.

Those who attended such sessions were often particularly impressed with Adler's ability to establish an immediate, friendly rapport with children and parents seen for the first time. Not only did he teach the importance of presenting a warm, down-to-earth therapeutic style of relating, but he also practiced what he preached. Certainly for the 1920s, Adler's approach to child guidance and family work was pioneering. There was little formal training or printed matter available for those specializing in the new field. Perhaps for this reason and that of his international reputation, he quickly secured a contract for publishing the content of his New School lecture-demonstrations.

As with virtually all of Adler's books, *The Pattern of Life* was derived largely from transcribed talks and involved extensive outside editing. To accomplish this work, Adler relied upon his young friend, Walter Beran Wolfe, who had performed so admirably three years before in the similar task of producing *Understanding Human Nature*. Wolfe now had a growing private practice in Manhattan and a desire to launch his own various book projects, which would eventually culminate in a self-help best-seller. Although *The Pattern of Life* presented Adler's New School lectures clearly and included Wolfe's detailed introduction to individual psychology, it would mark their last collaboration.

"Readers of this book," Wolfe explained, "should realize that it is not a comprehensive treatise on psychotherapy, but rather an outline of childhood neuroses and a key to the art of reading case histories. Its chief value lies in acquainting all those who deal with children and adults with the dynamic patterns of human conduct. The technique of cure can no more be taught by such a volume," he argued a trifle defensively, "than the art of etching can be taught by a treatise on the various physical and chemical processes that comprise the technique of preparing and printing a copperplate. The book will have fulfilled its purpose if it succeeds in [depicting] human beings not as static machines designated by labels, but as moving, living, purpose-fulfilling entities striving for significance and security in a perplexing world."

The Pattern of Life presented twelve different cases requiring professional intervention. These included children manifesting such problems as hyperanxiety, school failure, overpassivity, juvenile delinquency, serious physical illness, and congenital mental retardation. Organized only by particular case and lacking both an index and chapter subtitles, *The Pattern of Life* appears to have been hastily assembled. To be sure, Adler's freewheeling comments on the various cases are often quite intriguing. He addresses such topics as the nature of childhood dreams, the limitations of standardized intellectual tests, the importance of children's friendships in healthy emotional development, the impact of continual marital strife on youngsters' social skills, and the destructive effect of repeated parental punishment on youthful self-esteem.

Interestingly from our contemporary perspective, Adler viewed many of the children as especially suffering from a weak relationship with their fathers. Quite differently from most Freudian adherents of the day, Adler regarded the father-child bond as extremely significant.

Thus, in a case involving an eight-year-old boy already exhibiting delinquency, Adler recommended that the father take him for a daily walk "so that Carl will feel honored and appreciated." For an eleven-year-old boy evincing signs of hopelessness about schoolwork, Adler observed that, "It is a common situation among pampered children who spend the greater part of their time with their mother, that the father cannot compete. . . . As long as the mother is present, Robert will always turn to her. The father should [therefore] take the boy away on a trip, show him a good time, and become his 'pal'. . . . Our treatment should begin with the reconciliation of the boy and his father."

In yet another case concerning a boy with an overzealous desire for independence, Adler advised the father "not to whip him, but to make a companion out of him. It would be a good thing for them to take a trip together and try to understand each other."

In other instances, Adler recommended that a particular child be more actively involved in an after-school play group and advised the mother that, "The less you have him in the home with you, the better it will be for his development." Likewise, Adler often suggested summer-camp participation to help improve children's social maturity, but warned parents against developing unrealistic expectations about what the camp might accomplish.

Throughout *The Pattern of Life,* Adler criticized the tendency of many adults to badger or threaten their offspring into submissiveness. "It is never desirable that a child should obey like a dog," he remarked. "There should be a comradely relationship between parents and children. I have seen too many parents who insisted on blind, unreasoning obedience. . . . Very often, if one child in the family is disobedient, the conduct of the other child is held up as an example. The obedient child is not necessarily kind and good by nature, but may be merely an opportunist who has learned the advantage of propitiation."

Perhaps the most striking theme of Adler's New School case discussions is his optimism about human nature. At times ironically humorous, he observed that, "Individuals who have no social interest like to believe that people are naturally bad. Most egoistic philosophers have sponsored such theories. Socially interested individuals are usually tolerant and kind, and try to understand the factors which make people bad.

"Moreover," Adler noted sardonically, "Stories of good people are really not very interesting to read. Nobody would be interested in [hearing about] a good man who always got up smiling in the morning, said kind words to his family, went to work with a laugh, brought home presents to [everyone], and was always kind, sweet, and gentle. But if you tell a story of a bad man who is cruel and thoughtless, you can get people to read it."

———

Adler was hardly a cruel, thoughtless bad man, but he was sparking considerable American interest. Teaching at the New School, lecturing widely around the East Coast, and now with a second new book being vigorously marketed, Adler was beginning to achieve the status of a scientific celebrity—apart from his former association with Freud. Amidst the economic boom that was helping to fuel America's tremendous optimism about itself and its future, the small, buoyant figure of Alfred Adler was extremely appealing. His self-confident emphasis on scientific childrearing, better adjusted family life, and educational reform as the keys to peaceful social progress seemed sensible to many people interested in the new psychology. But not everyone was enamored of him.

To the Freudian loyalists, Adler was still persona non grata, an unrepentent heretic. No psychoanalyst in good standing would dare to quote Adler for risk of being professionally ostracized. In a telling anecdote, Adler was lecturing about individual psychology one evening at New York City's German Club. As Adler's friends sat entranced with his oratorical power in his native tongue, they were startled to see the figure of Abraham Brill, Freud's chief American exponent, standing intently in the doorway. Before the discussion began, Brill scowlingly turned to his associate and was heard to mutter as they exited, "Let's go. It's no use to debate with this man."

Nor did America's intellectual and artistic avant-garde find Adler very interesting. Throughout the 1920s, their dominant mood was one of pessimism, alienation, and disgust with American mass culture. Widely read novelists like F. Scott Fitzgerald, Ernest Hemingway, and Sinclair Lewis depicted the United States as a land of shallow glad-handers, boorish materialists, and moral hypocrites. To them, Freud was a true revolutionary, a friend of the artist, and an important ally in their continuing effort to tear away society's false veils. For the intellectuals who wrote for influential, elite publications like *The Nation* or the *New Republic,* Adler's unadorned, upbeat talks promoting social feeling evoked amusement if not contempt. But such figures were among a decided minority of those familiar with Adler's name. A detailed and laudatory article entitled "Father of the Inferiority Complex" that appeared in the *New York Herald* in March 1929 illustrates Adler's considerable popularity. After commenting that he "has an eloquence which gains from his innate sincerity," the interviewer briefly highlighted the seemingly never-ending battle between individual psychology and psychoanalysis. "Even today, [Adler and Freud] are at each other's throats. The war between the two scientists, however, has long since exhausted its heavy artillery, and for years has been relying on poison gases."

As vital evidence that he had never been Freud's "pupil" or "disciple," Adler thrust into the *Herald* reporter's hand a faded postcard dated November 1902. It was Freud's handwritten invitation for Adler to attend what became known historically as the Wednesday Psychological Society. Twenty-seven years later, in 1929, Adler still defensively kept the postcard as material proof of his lifetime, intellectual independence from Freud. In an intriguing character sketch that well portrays popular reaction to Adler in the United States, the *Herald* noted:

> Scientific education has again evolved a very human personality. It is probable that Alfred Adler is the most accurate and original foreign psychologist now in America. This eminent specialist, however, is first, last, and always a mere home-loving and sociable being. His is indeed a constitution quite American.

Although his contacts with our country have been limited to three brief visits, he shares, as by birthright, most of our virtues and frailties. He is a self-made man. His life reads like a testimonial in Smile's "Self-Help." He is optimistic. He is tenacious. He bubbles over with courage and energy. In the field of applied science, his theory of individual psychology is specially applicable to us.

He cherished charming "illusions" which his colleagues have long since cast aside. Like any sophomore, he speaks engagingly of the soul, the individual, happiness, love and progress. . . . Scientists of today are either hard, cold, efficient machines like Freud, or palpitating, human beings—no less efficient—like Adler.

━━━━━

By the end of the late 1920s, Adler had emerged as one of the two key figures who helped to create the field of popular psychology in the United States. The other was certainly John Broadus Watson, the influential founder of behaviorism on this continent. The two men never seem to have met and differed greatly in personality. Yet, representing two very different approaches—clinical treatment and laboratory experimentalism respectively—they helped shape American culture's interest in psychological ideas for daily personal improvement. In this regard, their combined impact continues to reverberate through the present day.

Eight years Adler's junior, Watson was born in rural South Carolina into what would today undoubtedly be called a dysfunctional family. His father was an alcoholic who eventually left the home to live with two women. His mother was an ardent fundamentalist Baptist who encouraged that he pursue a ministry career. She had named him after the most prominent revivalist preacher in the area, John Albert Broadus.

First at Chicago and then after moving to Johns Hopkins University in 1908, Watson emulated Russian neurologist Ivan Pavlov by studying reflexive behavior in animals. Following research on how rats learn mazes, Watson studied imitative behavior in rhesus monkeys and the homing mechanism of Florida terns. His campaign for behaviorism, as he termed it began in 1913 with an academically famous "manifesto," that urged the establishment of a new psychology based solidly on rigorous and objective laboratory methods.

Two years later, Watson initiated a long-term study of children's development. Building a special observation chamber in a Washington, D.C. hospital, Watson analyzed how mothers and their infants interacted from birth onward. In highly influential research, he claimed that babies could be conditioned just like Pavlov's dogs. For instance, Watson could easily make a young child terrified of a rabbit by banging loudly whenever the rabbit was put near the youngster. Triumphantly, Watson demonstrated that he could also reverse this process by reintroducing the rabbit gradually and at a distance, under more gentle circumstances. Such work signaled that a new form of mental "cure" was possible.

Watson's academic career was blossoming, but it came to an abrupt halt in 1920. Caught having an ongoing sexual affair with his graduate assistant, Rosalie Rayner, Watson was forced to resign his position at Johns Hopkins University. His wife sued for divorce, and the next year he married Rayner, eventually having two children with her.

Though expelled as a pariah from the academic world, Watson resourcefully landed a position with the J. Walter Thompson advertising agency in New York City. On the strength of his innovative and successful marketing techniques, Watson quickly rose to executive rank. During the 1920s, mass advertising in the United States was just beginning to be established, and Watson taught an eager generation of business managers that people buy products in order to satisfy emotional rather than utilitarian needs. He achieved unprecedented advertising success through the brilliant marketing of such products as laundry soap and men's shaving cream.

Although Watson enjoyed a level of wealth and power in the advertising field almost unimaginable in academic psychology, he felt intellectually isolated among his business colleagues. He therefore continued to write actively, and in 1924, his popular book, *Behaviorism*, was published. With almost evangelical fervor, he declared, "I wish I could picture for you what a rich and wonderful individual we should make of every healthy child if only we could let it shape itself properly and then provide for it a universe in which it could exercise that organization—a universe unshackled by legendary folk-lore of happenings thousands of years ago; unhampered by disgraceful political history; free of foolish customs and conventions. . . . The universe will change if you bring up your child . . . in behavioristic freedom."

Seemingly rooted in science and with an optimistic tone, *Behaviorism* evoked an enthusiastic response. Over the next few years, Watson received increasing public attention for his wide-ranging magazine articles, newspaper interviews, and even radio appearances. All flowed from his unabashed emphasis that experimental psychology—specifically, behaviorism—had immediate value for the American people and their everyday problems of family life and work.

Perhaps even more so than Adler, Watson possessed a talent for promoting his ideas to lay audiences. A lucid writer whose forceful viewpoint always made for interesting reading, he produced articles for such popular print media as *Cosmopolitan, Harper's, McCall's,* the *New Republic,* the *New York Times,* and the *Saturday Review of Literature.* Regaining an academic foothold, Watson began a series of lectures in 1922 at the New School for Social Research, not far from his executive office at J. Walter Thompson in midtown Manhattan. His course on behaviorism was popular, and also gave him the opportunity to discuss his ideas with professionals in fields like social work and education. Unfortunately, Watson's precarious academic career suffered yet again, this time in 1926, when charges of sexual misconduct were raised against him. Although the circumstances remain murky to this day, Watson became the first faculty member of the iconoclastic New School ever to be fired.

Nevertheless, the indomitable behaviorist continued to write and speak for popular audiences about psychology. Undoubtedly, his most influential essays appeared in a six-part series that *McCall's* printed in 1928. Igniting strong readership interest, these essays were published later that year as a major book entitled *Psychological Care of Infant and Child.*

With marketing acumen, Watson effectively planned and promoted his new book as a companion piece to the American bible on child care, *The Care and Feeding of Children,* by Luther Emmett Holt and his son. Since first appearing in 1894, their manual stressed the importance of children's health needs. In his new book, Watson argued that a baby's health can be safeguarded quickly through proper care, but "once a child's character has been spoiled by bad handling, which can be done in a few days, who can say that the damage is ever repaired?"

Rejecting at the outset the popular cliché that parenting is something natural and intuitive, Watson depicted child raising as a strictly logical science. Although not mentioning Adler by name, Watson likewise insisted that scientific knowledge would soon eliminate forever long-standing myths and superstitions about children's behavior. More broadly, he also expressed a satisfaction with the sweeping social changes occurring in his country during the 1920s.

"I believe that the internal structure of our American civilization is changing from top to bottom more rapidly and more fundamentally than most of us dream of. Consequently today less than ever before, is it expedient to bring up a child in accordance with the fixed molds that our parents imposed upon us." In a manner that would have been unthinkable only a generation earlier, Watson insisted that American parents should no longer seek guidance from religious tradition, but from rigorous scientists like himself. In this sense, he was more anticlerical than Adler, who assured a

New York Times reporter that, "Any religion that helps foster the social sense . . . that teaches him that all men are brothers . . . is good."

Watson also espoused an intensely environmentalist rather than hereditary view of human nature and its development. He characterized adult personality as formed wholly by early parental influences. Like Adler, Watson portrayed child rearing as a formidable undertaking that, if improperly done, could result in lasting damage to youngsters. "Since children are made not born, failure to bring up a happy child, a well-adjusted child—assuming bodily health—falls upon the parents' shoulders. The acceptance of this view makes child-rearing the most important of all social obligations."

But Watson's advice for those involved in child raising differed from Adler's in several important respects. Temperamentally, the ardent behaviorist was both more bombastic and sarcastic than his Austrian colleague. For instance, Watson tended to be condescending rather than sympathetic in describing the efforts of American parents of the time. He caustically dedicated *Psychological Care of Infant and Child* "to the first mother who brings up a happy child" and announced that "The oldest profession of the race today is facing failure. This profession is parenthood. . . . No one today knows enough to raise a child. . . . Rarely does one see a . . . child that is comfortable—a child that adults can be comfortable around."

Perhaps still rebelling against his Christian fundamentalist upbringing, Watson was also surprisingly radical in his social values. In a manner almost resembling the young, psychoanalytic revolutionary Wilhelm Reich, he condemned the modern American family as outmoded and repressive, and one that would ultimately be replaced by a more scientific form of social living. In an icily distant manner antithetical to Adler's warm emphasis on family camaraderie, Watson specifically warned parents against becoming overly close with their offspring.

"There is a sensible way of treating children," he wrote in a famous passage in *Psychological Case of Infant and Child*. "Treat them as though they were young adults. Dress them, bathe them with care and circumspection. Let your behavior always be objective and kindly firm. Never hug and kiss them, never let them sit in your lap. If you must, kiss them once on the forehead when they say good night." Advising parents to build fenced-in backyards where their babies should play alone in order to learn independence, Watson cautioned that "the child should learn to conquer difficulties away from your watchful eye. . . . If your heart is too tender and you must watch the child, make yourself a peephole so that you can see it without being seen, or use a periscope."

He regarded the close maternal-child bond as particulary harmful and destructive. "Mother love is a dangerous instrument. It may inflict a never healing wound, a wound which may make infancy unhappy, adolescence a nightmare, an instrument which may wreck your adult son's or daughter's vocational future and their chance of future happiness." Indeed, Watson went on to observe that, "It is a serious question in my mind whether there should be individual homes for children—or even whether children should know their own parents. There are undoubtedly much more scientific ways of bringing up children which will probably mean finer and happier children."

More akin philosophically to Freud than Adler, Watson also saw contemporary family life as sexually stifling for the young. He commented that, "The old theory was to wait until the child's [sexual] questions came naturally. I don't believe this. It seems to me that we should develop sex knowledge in our children as rapidly as they can take it." In a disregard for the middle-of-the road approach that Adler had always advocated, Watson recommended that, "Every college and university should have a department where sex instruction can be pursued by students. . . . This department . . . should instruct both the young men and the young women in the *ars amandi*; for certainly love is an art and not instinct. To achieve skill in this art requires time, patience, willingness to learn from each other, frankness in discussion and above all knowledge of what to expect."

Whereas Adler extolled marriage and monogamy as representing the highest form of social feeling, Watson expressed contempt for such relations. Writing in *Cosmopolitan* during the same year that *Infant and Child* was published, he cheerfully predicted that within fifty years, men would liberate themselves from their sexually unhappy marriages, and the age-old and outmoded institution of matrimony would then cease to exist. Instead of boring and disappointing monogamy, there would be multiple and satisfying sexual liaisons for all.

With such views, Watson definitely shocked some Americans. Conservative and religious-minded organizations and newspapers were appalled. A representative editorial, published in the *Florida Times,* declared that the "theorist" should be "backed up against the wall and let him have it full force from the shoulder that he is plainly wrong." Nevertheless, Watson exerted considerable impact upon the popular culture of this period. *McCall's* reported that his series of articles had set off a national debate on child care, and within a few months of its publication, *Infant and Child* had sold more than one hundred thousand copies. The newly established *Parents Magazine* declared Watson's book to be a necessity that ought to stand "on every intelligent mother's shelf." The *Atlantic Monthly* called it "a godsend to parents."

Oddly enough for a figure with Watson's radical social stance regarding child rearing, sex, and marriage, he was no political progressive. Rather, he ridiculed those who championed economic reforms and later sneered that Franklin D. Roosevelt's New Deal had made "democracy safe for himself, the non-voting population of the South, and for Mr. Stalin and his Communists." Elsewhere, Watson wrote that, "I have always been amused by the advocates of free speech . . . organized society has as little right to allow free speech as it has to allow free action."

By the early 1930s, Watson's growing wealth and influence in the advertising field led him out of popular psychology. Aside from an occasional radio interview, he stopped advising America's parents on how they could improve the world through more scientific child rearing. As Watson's own children later recalled, he was a distant father who became increasingly cold and self-absorbed as he passed through middle age. Watson eventually withdrew from psychology, especially following Rosalie's death in 1935, and spent the remainder of his years in hermitlike seclusion at his Connecticut estate.

═══

While Watson would be leaving psychology altogether before long, Adler was definitely moving in the opposite direction. Indeed, he would soon begin attaining more prestigious American teaching positions than adjunct appointments at the New School for Social Research, thanks to the influential support of a wealthy New England businessman, Charles Henry Davis.

Born in 1865 to affluent Pennsylvania Quaker parents, Davis came from an esteemed family heritage of moral and social activism. His grandfather Edward Davis was an ardent abolitionist who helped organize the Republican party when it successfully nominated Abraham Lincoln for the presidency in 1860. Charles's most influential relative was undoubtedly Lucretia Coffin Mott, a renowned Quaker activist celebrated for her leadership in both the abolitionist and feminist movements of the mid-nineteenth century.

Davis had graduated with honors in engineering from Columbia University in 1887. When his family moved to Cape Cod soon after, he gained experience as a civil engineer in a variety of firms, including the nascent Westinghouse Electrical Company. He also authored books on economics and engineering, and developed several inventions.

The 1890s witnessed the building of the great industrial infrastructure of the United States. In the mid-Atlantic region, where industrialization was most intensely underway, Davis became a major figure in civil engineering. His ventures included the building of railway lines between New Haven and New York City, the designing and building of the first railroad tunnel under New York City's Hudson River, and designing one of the first railway tunnels under the city's East River.

Those who knew Charles Davis admired his veritable Midas touch. By the turn of the century, he began purchasing considerable land on Cape Cod, and gradually combined adjoining parcels until he had amassed extensive real-estate holdings. At this time, the Davis family and their relations also owned lands in the coalfield area of Kentucky's Harlan County. Separately these Kentucky properties held little value and were being plundered by local strip miners. Unlike everyone else, Davis saw tremendous opportunity. Over several years, he quietly bought real estate there until he finally owned and fully controlled almost all of Harlan County's mining and lumbering rights.

Thereupon, Davis formed the Kentenia Mining Company (an acronym for the states of Kentucky, Tennessee, and West Virginia, where his family owned coal mines) and sold stock to establish mine shafts and large-scale mining operations throughout the county. Connected by roads and railway lines that Davis helped design, a coal-mining kingdom had been created. Within Harlan County, he also amassed a major lumbering operation, for the mountainous region yielded timber that could be processed and shipped by the same transportation that handled the coal.

By the time he was in his mid-thirties, Charles Davis was extremely wealthy and successful. But in 1902, tragedy struck when his wife, Helen, developed tuberculosis and died at the age of forty-one. The two had been childless. Thirteen months later, he married Grace Bigelow, of old New England stock, and over the next nine years, six daughters were born to them: Helen (named after Davis' first wife) in 1904, Martha in 1906, Priscilla in 1907, Annalee in 1908, Frances in 1911, and Lucretia in 1912 (who died in infancy). In later decades, virtually all of the daughters, like their powerful father, would become Adler's patients and then his ardent supporters.

During these years, Davis turned his attention to a new field of opportunity, highway engineering. He was among the first civil engineers to see the incredible potential of the private automobile when it was still regarded as merely an expensive toy or curiosity among the rich. Davis's various projects included designing the Lincoln Highway in Illinois, which was the country's first overhead highway, and the "rotary" (circular) interchange, acclaimed for its time, and still common in regions like rural New England. Before long, Davis made it his mission to help establish, through public advocacy and governmental lobbying, a safe and secure system of roads for automobile travel. Until he met Alfred Adler some two decades later, this cause was Davis's life work.

Around 1907, at the age of forty-two, Davis left engineering practice for executive management. It was at this time that he consummated what would be the most important and valuable business decision of his life. Although public interest in the automobile was clearly growing, most of the fledgling manufacturers were pricing cars much too high for all but the wealthy to afford. Nevertheless, Davis was convinced that a reasonably priced automobile could be built and that it would have tremendous appeal. Precisely how he met Henry Ford is not clear, but Davis had the prescience to present the young Detroit inventor with a compelling business proposition. Knowing of the importance of coal for automobile manufacturing, Davis offered to lease his entire Kentenia area to Ford, whose firm would conduct all its own mining. In this way, his automobile production would be guaranteed freedom from price wars in coal manufacturing and from external labor unrest.

In return, Davis requested an agreed price-per-carload of coal at the mine head, plus a royalty on every automobile that Ford's company produced. A lengthy process of negotiation ensued, and finally, Davis gained a long-term contract renewable at its expiration. This single deal with Henry Ford guaranteed Davis more wealth than he probably could have conceived as a youth growing up in Philadelphia.

It was in 1912 that Davis entered the national political scene for the first time. Supporting the pugnacious White House candidacy of former President Theodore Roosevelt with the newly formed Progressive party, Davis immediately became a key financial contributor and fund-raiser, and was soon appointed to its National Finance Committee. In the 1912 presidential election campaign, Davis successfully inserted a plank into the platform encouraging federal support for highway construction: "We recognize the vital importance of good roads and we pledge our party to foster their extension in every proper way, and we favor the early construction of national highways. We also favor the extension of the rural free-delivery system."

Before long, though, Davis decided upon his guiding mission for many years to come. With his friend and fellow mine-owner Coleman Du Pont (president of the E. I. Du Pont corporation and later a United States senator), Davis founded the National Highways Association (NHA) a major lobbying organization, in Washington, D.C. It was the first national organization of its kind, and preceded what is now the American Automombile Association (AAA) by several years. With his ample wealth and political connections, Davis emerged as perhaps the leading figure in what came to be known as the good roads movement. He effectively promoted the NHA as a civic and reform-minded group whose agenda could help everyone, for who could be against safe and manageable higways? Thus, Davis gained for his NHA the membership of such prominent liberals and socialists as Eugene Debs, Max Eastman, and Helen Keller.

Of course, not all those dedicated to the establishment of good roads were enamored of the powerful Charles "Carl" Davis. Some citizen groups, like the Lincoln Highway Association, specifically refused collaboration on the grounds that his organization was too closely tied to road-building companies and his private interests. In a way, such criticism was valid, for Davis always desired benevolent but complete control over projects to which he was drawn. "In his manic times, he had to be the center of everything," recalled one close relative. "He bought the swimming beach across the river from his property and placed a sign that typified 'Cousin Carl': Private Beach, Public Welcome—in other words, everyone is welcome to use the beach, but don't forget that it's mine."

Or as a relative tersely commented: "He was constantly anxious to help people, but usually in *his* way, so that they ended up feeling not only indebted, but resentful. This he didn't understand."

But Charles Davis paid little attention to criticism about his personality or actions. He was usually convinced of the moral rightness of his conduct, and was seldom given to introspective soul searching. In this respect, he shared much in common with the pugnacious Viennese founder of individual psychology, who would later became his therapist and close friend.

During the 1920s, Davis continued to preside energetically over the National Highways Association. His major goal was to persuade the federal government to enact legislation creating 150,000 miles of federal highways. These were to be coordinated in a fourfold system involving the roads of states, counties, and townships. Eventually, for his efforts to help establish the federal interhighway system, Davis was named honorary chairman of the Institutes for Highway Transportation in Washington, D.C.

A tall, strapping man who was always extremely well dressed, Davis in middle age was nearly bald and sported a thick mustache. He invariably drove a brand-new Hudson, which he liked to propel at speeds of fifty to sixty miles per hour. If stopped for speeding by a watchful police officer, Davis would flash the honorary police chief badge he had been awarded in New York City, and hope for the officer's friendly dismissal.

It is not clear historically when Adler and Charles Henry Davis first met, but the well-known philanthropist had apparently been impressed with *Understanding Human Nature* and then decided to meet Adler in person. Living in an elegant Manhattan townhouse on East Thirty-First Street off Park Avenue, Davis may have heard Adler lecture during the winter of 1929 at the nearby Community Church or possibly at the New School several blocks farther downtown.

The two men were five years apart in age, with Adler the younger at fifty-nine. Davis's interest in psychology was not purely intellectual. His oldest daughter, Helen, who was in her mid-twenties, was suffering from severe depression, and he was determined to find a cure. Impressed with Adler's knowledge and personality as a lecturer, Davis met with him privately and then requested therapy sessions for Helen. The results seemed so dramatic that Davis soon insisted upon attending all of Adler's speaking engagements and helping to promote individual psychology as vigorously as possible. By mid-spring 1929, Adler had become Davis's new focus and he contacted his alma mater, Columbia University, to create an appropriate position. He generously provided the funds for Adler's appointment, as well as for his child-guidance clinic to begin operating in February 1930. Perhaps because the teaching duties mainly involved the University's Extension rather than its regular academic departments, Columbia's administration seems to have quickly approved Davis's offer. In the role of trusted friend during coming years, Davis would not only bankroll a private foundation for Adler's activities, but also serve as his business manager and literary agent and endow a five-year position for him at the Long Island College of Medicine.

What was there about Adler that appealed so strongly to a wealthy entrepreneur and Quaker philanthropist like Davis, coming from such a different cultural background? Did Adler become the younger brother that Charles Davis never had?

For one thing, Adler's genuine therapeutic warmth and skill had long helped him to win zealous followers. Perhaps more importantly, though, his social optimism and dedication to educational reform resonated well with the former Progressive Party fundraiser. In a way, Adler's emphasis on social feeling as a key measure of one's emotional health matched almost perfectly Davis' passionate faith in civic progressivism, benevolent government, and scientific progress.

Undoubtedly, too, it was Adler's impassioned belief that people are happiest when devoted to a cause, for Davis's friends would later recall that Adler had helped him to feel more relaxed and content. "It's a little thing, and will not matter much" was the maxim he offered his wealthy benefactor. Similar to the more recent popularism that, "Ten years from now, it won't seem so important," Adler's comment was designed to aid his American friend take himself less seriously in life. On one occasion, he would observe more pointedly, "Carl, you're like a little boy running down the street and dragging along a rope with clanging tin cans. You want everybody to notice you. Sometimes, the quiet way is better."

Another key question is how Davis would affect his newfound friend and the promotion of individual psychology. Before arriving in the United States in late 1926, Adler had already ceased writing for Austria's socialist newspaper and voiced antipathy for the concept of class warfare. Yet, he had nonetheless praised Marx and Engels for their social insights and went beyond his Social Democratic friends in advocating women's rights. After relocating to America, he would become far more muted in his societal criticism; certainly gone was his anticapitalist rhetoric. It may be quite possible, therefore, that either consciously or unconsciously, Adler would moderate his public statements to accommodate his benefactor, Davis.

But such concerns still lay in the future. Meanwhile, a continent away in Central Europe, Adler was energetically making plans that summer for the new life that Davis was helping to build for him.

CHAPTER SIXTEEN

Relocating to
New York

*The community, which Individual
Psychology invokes, is a goal, an
ideal, always unattainable, but always
beckoning and pointing the way.*

ALFRED ADLER

Soon after returning to Vienna in the summer of 1929, Adler began making plans to move permanently to New York City. To become a professor at Columbia University was a situation that he valued tremendously. Although for decades he had voiced a socialist's contempt for academia's ivory tower, he had personally prized whatever recognition the academic world had granted him. Even with a slight award like the honorary doctorate from Ohio's Wittenberg College, Adler had immediately secured Viennese business cards to announce his new title. The promise of teaching at a world-renowned institution like Columbia University excited him a great deal.

Perhaps it was for this reason, and the sudden opportunity that now loomed to promote individual psychology, that Adler was so willing to leave his family, friends, and longtime colleagues. True enough, he would be lecturing as an adjunct faculty member in adult education; but Columbia's medical school would also be allowing him a visiting professorship to discuss his work. Most likely, too, Adler was hoping ultimately to gain a tenured faculty position at Columbia. With Charles Davis's powerful connections and wealth, such an eventuality was certainly within the realm of possibility.

Nevertheless, Raissa was uninterested in joining Alfred for the move to New York City. Although few written records have survived about their relationship during this period, she was clearly committed in the late 1920s to helping Trotsky outmaneuver Stalin and thereby gain control over the worldwide communist movement. Raissa's active correspondence reveals her efforts to strengthen Trotsky's hand in Austria and Germany, key countries in which he hoped to lead a counterattack against Stalin's growing consolidation of party leadership.

In a typical note penned in early July, Raissa warmly assured an exiled Trotsky in Turkey that, "My husband thanks you cordially for your letter. He will write you comprehensively about his position on the Communist Internationale very soon. He is fairly certain that [his books] will soon be banned [by Stalin]."

Although Adler's biographers later attempted to blur Raissa's political activity and outlook, she was an important figure in the Austrian Communist party. Only a few months after her husband would relocate to New York City for the Columbia position, Raissa would send a fiery and impassioned letter to the party's Central Committee, which had accused her of counter-revolutionary sympathies for promoting Trotskyism.

"There is an acute revolutionary situation in Austria," she would defiantly declare in January 1930, "[and] the order of the day is the establishment of the Soviets. . . . The Party, and especially the Central Committee, could learn a lot from the writings of General Trotsky, particularly from his brochure on the 'Austrian Crisis' . . . Indeed, comrades, I am for cleansing the Party of all opportunistic, bureaucratic elements, from top to bottom, and because I am in earnest about this, I associate myself fully and completely with the leftist [Trostykite] opposition. For it is in the position to lead the Communist Internationale [Komintern] out of the rotten swamp of opportunism and set them on the great, historic way of the fight of the proletarian revolution."

With such political convictions, it seems extremely implausible that Raissa would have been interested in associating with her husband's new-found, multimillionaire friend Davis. He may have been a Progressive party fundraiser and a true liberal, but to Marxists like Raissa, he was still an exploitative capitalist whose riches came from the suffering of factory and mine workers. As a longtime feminist, Raissa may also have taken pride in refusing in middle age to follow her husband to a distant, foreign land for the sake of his career. She had many friends and her grown children in Vienna, and was simply unwilling to accompany Adler for his Columbia position.

How bitterly they fought over this issue is not known. Both Alexandra and Kurt later recalled that their parents' marital separation was amicable; and indeed, in ensuing years, their father would return to Raissa each summer for at least a few weeks. Nevertheless, she did not join him even once in the United States until 1935, when the triumph of Austrian fascism would help induce her to emigrate. For years, Adler doggedly maintained a cordial correspondence, but Raissa rarely replied, much to his disappointment. There is no documentary evidence that either one found a lover during their marital separation. Looking back, some of Adler's American friends felt that he was lonely in this period and missed his wife's companionship.

In any event, Adler severed his professional ties to Vienna in preparation for resettling in New York. He resigned his position as founder-director of the Clinic for Nervous Diseases at the Franz-Joseph Ambulatorium and appointed physician-zoologist Lydia Sicher as his successor, with Franz Plewa as her assistant. He also relinquished his position with the Pedagogical Institute, and successfully lobbied for his colleague Ferdinand Birnbaum, an innovative educator, as replacement. Adler likewise chose Sicher to become director of the Viennese Society for Individual Psychology. She would hold this position for nine years, until the Nazi takeover of Austria in 1938.

Sicher had joined the Society for Individual Psychology in 1923, and, with her formidable intellectual abilities, soon became a leading member. She had already known Adler for several years, having once consulted him about one of her patients. By the late 1920s, Sicher had become increasingly important to Adler in Vienna, for relatively few of his supporters there besides Dreikurs were practicing physicians. It was rumored that of all Adler's associates, Lydia Sicher was the only one who had never undergone analysis with him, because he had deemed it unnecessary. Like Adler himself and most of his associates, Sicher preferred lecturing and clinical supervising to the lonelier act of writing. Many expected her to write the definitive text on individual psychology, but she never did so.

In the early fall, Adler settled into his new residence, a suite at the Windermere Hotel on Manhattan's West End Avenue and Ninety-second Street. Within walking distance of Central Park, the Museum of Natural History and the Haydn Planetarium, the location had a pleasant Upper West Side ambience. It was also convenient, only a ten-minute taxi ride north to Columbia's sprawling Morningside campus. But Adler at the age of fifty-nine had little interest in devoting his days to leisurely parkside strolls. Aside from occasional dinners with colleagues, he rarely allowed himself leisurely pursuits. Virtually his only form of true relaxation was his predilection for

Hollywood comedies, especially those starring Charlie Chaplin or the Marx Brothers. Not only did he immerse himself in teaching courses at Columbia's prestigious Physicians & Surgeons Medical School, but he was also energetically lecturing at the university's adult education institute and at numerous public audiences throughout the New York City area.

At Manhattan's midtown posh Temple Emanu-el (affiliated with Reform Judaism), Adler presented nine weekly lectures in the late fall on such topics as "Educational Views of Individual Psychology," "The Family Life," "The Importance of the Mother in Family and Social Life," and "The Influence of the Father." Before a capacity audience of twenty-eight hundred, Adler in his first talk declared that, "The greatest contribution of independent psychology is a right understanding of the demand for cooperation and a discovery of the means of attaining [it]. The meaning of life must be created by every one for himself, and for us this means a life of cooperation, in the present and the future. There is no virtue in the world which does not come from cooperation. . . . Individual psychology finds the roots of mistakes and [guides in] finding the remedy."

Although Adler had decisively left the Jewish faith more than twenty-five years before, he became a regular lecturer at Reform congregations in New York and elsewhere. Several months later, he would actually speak from the pulpit of the American Synagogue in Manhattan, where he would advocate educational counseling in every public school. During the fall of 1929, Adler also offered a similar series of evening lectures at Community Church, an affluent Unitarian congregation. He had spoken there before, but his new talks evoked such a favorable response that its prominent minister, John Haynes Holmes (a founder of both the American Civil Liberties Union and the National Association for the Advancement of Colored People), devoted his Christmas sermon to "The Religious Significance of the Psychology of Alfred Adler." In coming years, several Protestant theologians in Europe would draw upon his ideas for a new vision of human potential, and Adler would himself collaborate with a Lutheran pastor on such a project.

Never one to adopt a passive attitude toward life, Adler was quick to capitalize on his association with Columbia. He had new business cards specially printed for this purpose (replacing those listing his Wittenberg College honorary degree) and began corresponding with publisher W. W. Norton about a book contract. During the previous months, Adler's German-language volume, *The Soul of Difficult School Children,* had just appeared, and he was eager for an American edition. Based on edited transcripts of Adler's Viennese demonstration lectures with emotionally disturbed children and their families, the volume clearly laid out his approach for teachers. Possibly because Adler already had a similar book (*The Pattern of Life*) scheduled for release in the United States later that year, Norton passed on the offer. The book would not appear in English until nearly thirty-five years later, under the title *The Problem Child*.

Adler was certainly prolific in bringing his work to the attention of American audiences. During that busy fall, he was pleased by Greenberg Publisher's issuance of *The Science of Living*. It was his third popular book for the English-speaking world in three years, and the clever title certainly appealed to the widespread impression that science (rather than religion) could now provide people with true insights for happiness and self-fulfillment. Greenberg may have been an astute marketer in choosing the title, but he was not a very ethical publisher. Although physician Benjamin Ginzburg had edited and translated Adler's writing for the book, his name was credited nowhere. Much worse, Greenberg lifted a substantial section from Mairet's *ABCs of Adlerian Psychology,* published in England the previous year, and printed it as the introductory section to *The Science of Living.* This was done without Mairet's permission or even his prior knowledge. Because international copyright law tended to be lax in such matters, Greenberg felt free to act in this crudely unethical way. It is not known how Adler reacted to the ploy, but he soon ceased writing for Greenberg Publisher.

The Science of Living was organized clearly into twelve chapters with such titles as "Principles of Individual Psychology," "Inferiority and Superiority Complexes," "The Style of Life," "Early Recollections," "Dreams and their Interpretation," and "Love and Marriage." Such chapter topics overlapped considerably with Adler's previous course lectures at the New School, and most likely, Ginzburg had been given these to edit for readability. Although lacking much truly new material by Adler, *The Science of Living* offered his term *life-style* for the first time, replacing such previous expressions as guiding image, guiding line, and especially, life-plan. Originally used by the German sociologist Max Weber to denote the differing ways people live in various subcultures, life-style, as emphasized by Adler, would eventually penetrate the English language and become a countercultural buzzword.

The Science of Living's fundamental thesis is that our adult personality is relatively formed by the age of four or five. Depending on our unique upbringing and family dynamics (over power rather than sexual issues), we each form a particular life-style whose nature, function, and goal is to help us achieve a stable sense of self-mastery and esteem. "Because an individual has a style of life, it is possible to predict his future sometimes just on the basis of talking to him and having him answer questions. It is like looking at the fifth act of a drama, where all the mysteries are solved." As always, Adler insisted that disturbances in life-style exhibited by youngsters or adults are externally induced. "These complexes are not in the germ plasm, they are not in the bloodstream; they simply happen in the course of the individual and his social environment."

With his strong environmental rather than hereditary perspective, Adler depicted education, "whether carried on in the home or at school . . . as the most important question in our present social life." He recounted the steady progress being made in replacing authoritarian schools "in which children must sit quietly, hands folded in their laps" with those where "the children are their teacher's friends. They are no longer compelled by authority . . . merely to obey, but are allowed to develop more independently."

Yet, perhaps more explicitly than in previous books, Adler declared that his approach was now aimed at influencing educators more than parents, who are often "so set in tradition that they do not want to understand [us]." Emphasizing that he wished only to intervene with disturbed youngsters and not "normal children, if there be such," Adler explained his perspective. "The best point of attack is our schools. This is true first because the large numbers of children are gathered there; secondly, because mistakes in the style of life appear [clearer] there than in the family; and thirdly, because the teacher is supposedly [one] who understands the problems of children."

The Science of Living received a favorable response. The *New York Times* quoted Mairet's praise of its author as "the Confucius of the West," and commented that "Dr. Adler, famous Viennese physician and psychologist and Professor at the [Pedagogical] Institute of Vienna, makes a surprisingly clear and simple statement of the fundamental principles of psychology with which his name has long been associated."

During 1929, *The Science of Living* was joined in print by *Problems of Neurosis,* his fourth popular book for the English-speaking world. Published initially in England by the well-respected company of Routledge and Kegan Paul, the volume contained a lengthy introduction by psychiatrist Francis Crookshank, Adler's chief medical exponent in Great Britain. Perhaps less successfully than *Understanding Human Nature* or *The Science of Living,* this new work attempted to present individual psychology's approach to emotional problems during adulthood.

Adler offered many intriguing notions about personality change and treatment. He reported typically asking patients, "What would you do if I cured you immediately?" as a way of quickly uncovering their true resistance to improvement. "The discussion invariably reveals an accented 'if,' " Adler observed. "I would marry *if* . . . I would resume my work *if,* and so on. The neurotic has always collected some more-or-less plausible reasons to justify [himself], but he does not realize what he is doing."

In Adler's view, many common, habitual emotional patterns, such as chronic anger, peevishness, and envy, are "indications of a useless striving for superiority [and] attempts toward the suppression of others." That is, people learn to use such inner states—even sadness—as an effective way to dominate or gain special attention. With an intriguing metaphor recalling his days treating Vienna's carnival entertainers, Adler commented: "In a certain popular music hall, the 'strong man' comes on and lifts an enormous weight with care and immense difficulty. Then, during the hearty applause of the audience, a child comes in and gives away the fraud by carrying the dummy weight off with one hand. There are plenty of neurotics who swindle us with such weights, and who are adept at appearing overburdened. They could really dance with the load under which they stagger like Atlas bearing the whole world on his shoulders."

Problems of Neurosis also offered the therapeutic insight, now gaining increasing empirical support, that our earliest memories provide a vital clue to our chief concerns during ongoing adult life. "We do not, of course, believe that all early recollections are correct records of the facts. Many are even fancied, and most perhaps are changed or distorted at a later time; but this does not always diminish their significance," Adler explained. "What is altered or imagined is also expressive of the patient's goal [and provides] useful hints as to why the life-plan [in the first four or five years] was elaborated in its own particular form."

Although *Problems of Neurosis* contained many worthwhile ideas, it was badly written. Reflecting the disorganized quality of Adler's often meager notes from which Mairet was obliged to do his editing, the book even lacked chapter titles. Rather, each chapter was preceded by approximately a dozen or so unrelated subheadings. Nor were specific cases entitled or even demarcated clearly from one another. Nevertheless, when *Problems of Neurosis* was published in the United States the following year, its reception was mildly favorable. After briefly summarizing its contents, the *New York Times* remarked, "Dr. Adler is well known in America through both his lecturing and his writing. This volume is of particular interest to the lay reader because the cases of behavior which he cites have so much in common with that which each of us displays."

But even with *The Science of Living* and *Problems of Neurosis* appearing that fall, and two other books published in English during the past two years, Adler's ambitious publishing program was hardly over. He had three more separate volumes in production at Greenberg Publisher, and during the same autumn of 1929, successfully negotiated a contract for yet another popular work, to be issued by the Boston publishing house of Little, Brown. With Adler's zealous benefactor and promoter Davis now serving also as his literary agent, an advance of $950 was secured. The next step was for Adler to hire a new free-lance editor (psychiatrist Wolfe had probably become too busy) with a psychology background, and he soon decided upon Alan Porter.

A writer and scholar, Porter was the literary editor of the *London Spectator.* He also published essays and book reviews in a variety of influential British periodicals, including the *Times Literary Supplement,* the *Criterion,* and the *New Statesman,* and edited several books, including the acclaimed *Oxford Poetry.*

Like Mairet and many other intellectuals in London's Bloomsbury circle, Porter was attracted to the new psychology emanating from Austria. Idealistically motivated toward world betterment, he found particularly appealing Adler's emphasis on social feeling as the key sign of emotional health. After visiting Adler in Vienna, Porter cofounded with Mairet and Mitrinovic the London Branch of the International School for Individual Psychology and lectured frequently on Adler's theories. When he relocated to New York City in 1929, he obtained teaching positions at the New School for Social Research and the Rand School, and continued to promote Adlerian principles.

In early 1930, Adler approached Porter about editing his new project for Little, Brown. Intellectually excited by individual psychology and undoubtedly needing funds as a young free-lance scholar during the early Depression, it seems likely that he accepted the offer eagerly. The two men got along well together, and Porter substituted for Adler on several teaching occasions at Columbia. Before long, the Oxford author was energetically serving as Adler's chief ghostwriter for a host of popular articles. Dated April 30, his candid letter to Davis reveals:

> From yesterday, I have begun devoting my full time to the preparation of the book of Dr. Adler's American lectures. When I discussed the work with Dr. Adler, I told him that the preparation would take me three months and proposed that I be paid at the rate of $300 per month, each month paid in advance. He agreed with the suggestion and asked me to submit it to you for your approval. I am writing, therefore, to see if these terms meet with your agreement.

In the same letter, Porter went on to spell out his other editing and translating projects for Adler. These included three long articles already completed: "Seven Men and a House: A Study of the Inferiority Complex," "Love and Marriage," and the "Criminal Pattern of Life." Porter requested a modest payment of ten dollars per thousand words and reported that, "Other articles which I have in hand are: two further [ones] from the Crime lectures, three on Love and Marriage, three on the [School] Advisory Councils. I suggest that these should be considered and paid for separately from the book, as I shall not use the material in the same form."

=====

For Adler to be promulgating so many psychology books and popular articles at the same time may seem quite surprising. But even in the early 1930s, as the United States sank deeper into the Depression, his optimistic ideas for parenting, education, and social welfare found a receptive audience. Aside from John Watson, who was withdrawing from his longtime role as America's psychological pundit, virtually no one else possessed Adler's wide appeal for both professional and lay audiences. In 1930, Adler presented a major address on "The Individual Criminal and His Cure" before the National Committee on Prisons and Prison Labor and also provided an interview about child raising for *Good Housekeeping*. It is no wonder that Freud felt bitter about the popularity of a man whom he regarded as a shallow intellectual renegade.

Perhaps spurred by his friend Davis, who had long been active in penal reform, Adler began lecturing on the subject of criminology. It was not an entirely new interest, for in Austria after the war, he had become involved in efforts to treat juvenile delinquents. Also, during Adler's first lecture tour of the United States three years before, he had been intrigued by its high crime rate despite the general affluence. Now, in popular talks and in articles for professional periodicals like the *Police Journal,* he sought to apply individual psychology's insights.

For Adler, criminal behavior always stems from a faulty life-style originating in early childhood. Dismissing the prevalent theory of heredity as the chief cause of the "criminal personality," Adler identified the problem as societal. He stressed the fact that many criminals are born as unwanted children in chaotic families suffering under the weight of poverty. "It is not hard to understand why the number . . . is so high in the big cities, where there are very noticeable extremes of poverty and luxury." But rather accurately in view of later research, Adler described most criminals, regardless of socioeconomic background, as dominated by a sense of inferiority and a lack of social feeling. Ultimately, he emphasized, they are cowards with "a cheap superiority complex," overcoming their victims through darkness, surprise, formidable weaponry, or sheer numbers.

Quite optimistically, Adler asserted that his approach could "change every single criminal," but acknowledged that such a goal was unrealistic, especially since "we find that in hard times, the number of criminals always increases." Rather, Adler offered several concrete recommendations for preventing a further escalation of crime. These included establishing programs to eliminate unemployment through job training, reducing the ostentatious display of wealth that "can act as a challenge to the criminal," and instituting group sessions with prison inmates to heighten their self-esteem and social feeling. Interestingly, Adler also suggested that the mass media "not mention the names of criminals or give them so much publicity," and commented that, "We should not imagine that criminals can be terrified by the thought of capital punishment, [which] sometimes only adds to the excitement of the game."

Between semesters at Columbia in January 1930, Adler conducted his first extensive lecture tour of Michigan, aiming it predominantly at educators. By now, his friend Davis had established a Foundation of Individual Psychology by which to support Adler's wide-ranging American activities, including publications, lectures and demonstration clinics. In conjunction with his upcoming visit, the *Detroit Educational Bulletin* reported that a major, one thousand dollar prize had recently been awarded the best essay on how the new Foundation of Individual Psychology should spend its ten million dollar fund. While Davis indeed printed stationery with the name of this private foundation, no legal papers verifying its existence have been found. Certainly, the purported ten million dollar figure seems implausible, despite the persistent financial aid that Davis would bestow upon Adler's entire American career.

Anticipatory excitement in Adler's Michigan tour was running high, especially after a *Detroit News* article that appeared ten days before his arrival:

> Ever since it first found a place in the public eye 10 years ago, teachers and pupils have shared the somewhat dubious honor of being most often accused of domination by that popular bugaboo, the inferiority complex.
>
> Speakers at parent-teacher and educational meetings, class valedictorians and commencement orators have from time to time laid everything from hip

flask toting and whoopee hats, on the part of their preceptors, to this same ubiquitous demon.

So if you, reader, have ever gritted your teeth and snarled, "Oh, if I ever lay eyes on this fellow who invented the inferiority complex!"—and who has not?—you would undoubtedly pardon similar manifestations of emotion on the part of Detroit's teachers and students.

Dr. Adler, originally a disciple of Freud, parts from the latter in his philosophy by assigning a lesser place to sex than does Freud. Two tendencies, he holds, influence every human activity in his fulfillment of the three great challenges of life: love, work, and society. These tendencies are the social feeling and the individual striving for domination.

In his first formal lecture on the night of January 13, Adler offered Detroit's teachers a general perspective on individual psychology. He emphasized the importance of helping children cultivate a sense of social feeling and commented that, "I would urge all [of] you to ban entirely the heredity idea. It is too easy to hide behind so-called 'hereditary influences' when we cannot otherwise explain a child's actions. The marked differences we find among children, even among those of the same family, could not have been made by heredity," he added humorously. "Only living humans could make so many mistakes."

Adler stressed that teachers should "always understand how to identify yourself with [the child's] personality, so that you can see with his eyes, hear with his ears, and feel with his heart." Punishment and scolding were ineffective and counterproductive in the classroom. "You should use sympathy in education, so that at least you should insist, 'if I had the same kind of mind and life as this person, I would be confronted with the solving of the same kind of questions, and probably I would answer in a similar way.' Put yourself in his place." Finally, Adler imparted his optimism to an audience whose city was undergoing economic devastation. "We do not know the limits of a person," he declared, "but we are sure that most human beings could go farther than they do."

Well publicized by the press and cosponsored by several civic-minded foundations, Adler's subsequent schedule involved three weeks of lectures and demonstration child-guidance clinics at Detroit Teachers College. During one class, a participant remarked that it seemed virtually impossible to train a child in having *exactly* the right amount of social feeling or courage. Therefore, was it better to err on the side of teaching a youngster to be too meek or too assertive?

Speaking in his heavy Austrian accent, Adler smilingly replied, "Life will correct it if children get too big-headed. But it doesn't do the reverse if they get discouraged. There was an old saying in the Viennese circus: 'It's not terribly difficult to tame a lion, but is there anyone who has learned to make the lamb roar?' "

Undoubtedly, the most important figure in organizing Adler's successful Michigan tour was Marie Rasey. Though of slight build, she resembled in personality Adler's metaphorical lion far more than a meek lamb. An associate professor of research at Detroit Teachers College (later to merge with Wayne State University), she had already begun distinguishing herself in a career that would eventually span more than forty years.

Born in 1887 to a barber in rural Michigan, Rasey as a teenager had become committed to the educational field. The second woman from her hometown ever to acquire a college degree, she supported herself at the University of Michigan by managing a rooming house of seventeen beds. After educational duties including a stint at high-school teaching and research for the Detroit public schools, Rasey in 1921 became research director of the Detroit Teachers College. It was probably during graduate work at Michigan that she first encountered Adler's writings. Greatly inspired by his practical emphasis on child development and education, Rasey proceeded to read all he had published.

In 1928, she traveled to Vienna for assistance on a book she was writing involving educational psychology. As later recalled in her autobiography, *It Takes Time,* Rasey arranged to meet Adler while her friends were occupied with the ongoing Schubert musical festival. Adler cordially recommended a variety of volumes and articles, and then announced to an astonished Rasey that, "Now you will stay here, and we will write this book together!" Swiftly changing her plans, Rasey worked closely with Adler for the next few weeks. She attended ward rounds at the Franz-Josef Ambulatorium, participated in medical staff meetings, and assisted in interviewing patients (especially children) in Adler's own office.

"The summer ended with a long oral [psychiatric] examination conducted in German, and to [my] great surprise [I] was awarded the theoretical diploma granted by the International Society [for Individual Psychology]," Rasey later reminisced. The following spring of 1929, she returned to Adler in Vienna and spent the summer months in a new collaboration. At the time, Rasey was researching specific ways to identify children's hand preference, and proudly recounted the eight techniques she had developed. In reponse, Adler insisted that the issue of handedness was meaningless unless one knew what the particular child made of his or preference.

Upon returning to the Detroit area, Rasey was eager to emulate Adler's child-guidance work and related activities. Besides helping to organize his lecture tours in 1930 and after, Rasey implemented a variety of innovative programs for parents and teachers interested in psychological issues. Partly inspired by Adler's ideas, she also founded the Society for the Scientific Study of Character, which sought to help nurture children's moral behavior at home and school. Throughout her life, Rasey was acclaimed for her humanistic approach to educational psychology.

═══════════

Returning to New York City in late January, Adler resumed his busy schedule. He not only directed a child-guidance clinic at Columbia's medical school every day except Sunday, but also lectured weekly to medical students. His other teaching activities included a thirty-lecture series for graduate psychology students at Columbia, and two separate courses sponsored by the school's Institute of Arts and Sciences that involved seven morning and fourteen afternoon sessions respectively. To these, Adler added a series of special lectures, open to the general public, on the popular topics of crime and love and marriage. In late February, he made the national wire services again, this time because of his comments on the psychology of card playing. According to the Associated Press news bulletin:

> Persons who spend most of their time at bridge, in the opinion of Dr. Alfred Adler, are suffering from an inferiority complex. Lecturing at Columbia University, the Viennese psychologist said: 'Bridge is a great invention. A little of it is relaxation. But a lot of it becomes a mental habit, an attempt to satisfy a striving for superiority. It offers an opportunity to conquer others. If you see a bridge player who has won, you will notice a nice expression of superiority on his face.

With all this lecturing, Adler was gaining new young admirers in psychology and related fields; among those who attended his Columbia lectures was Heinz Ansbacher. He had emigrated from Frankfurt in 1924 and initially spent several unfulfilling years in brokerage work on Wall Street. The breakup of a long-term romance exacerbated his malaise, and, "in my despair, I went to Alfred Adler for help. [His] lectures fascinated me greatly," Ansbacher later recalled, "and I still have my notes. . . . [He offered] a thoroughly humanistic psychology with the concept of man as self-determined to a larger extent than is generally recognized, forward oriented, and guided by values and goals." Some two years later, Ansbacher underwent private therapy with Adler, and following his advice, chose a career in psychology. Thanks to Adler's closely knit social circle in New York, Ansbacher also met his future wife, Rowena, during the early 1930s. In later decades, the Ansbachers would become the most important psychologists in the United States to bring Adler's work to academic attention.

In returning from Michigan that same winter of 1930, Adler resumed correspondence with W. W. Norton on several possible publishing projects, including Rasey's new manuscript on child psychology. Norton's reply is not available, but it was apparently unfavorable. By late February, Adler thanked the publisher for his initial interest and turned his attention to other matters.

Among these was the growing professional interest in Adler's own life and career. The National Child Welfare Association requested an autobiographical sketch for publication, and although always reticent to divulge his personal life, Adler produced the most specific account yet for Americans curious about his childhood and adult years through the break with Freud. In introducing the brief memoir for *Childhood and Character,* its editor remarked: "Dr. Adler is a strong believer in the type of psychology which encourages man rather than discourages him with a philosophy of pessimism. Freud's emphasis on sex was too much for Dr. Adler who broke away from the Freudian meetings to establish his own 'Individual Psychology.' "

Although Adler was pleased that American audiences were finally learning the truth of his disagreement with Freud, his old struggle was apparently not finished and may have been behind the most unpleasant event of his American career to date. Professor Frederick Tilney, director of Columbia's Neurological Institute, had decided to propose Adler's name to the medical faculty for a permanent appointment. Tilney took the initiative without conferring first with Adler, and although university documents no longer exist, it seems that the proposal was quickly rebuffed. At the time, rumors were circulating that psychoanalysts who were lecturing at Columbia's medical school had pressed for this decision. They wanted nothing to do with Freud's longtime foe, not even to allow his activity there.

Feeling humiliated upon his return to New York, Adler immediately closed his clinic on February 5 and resigned his position. Apparently, the event was newsworthy enough for the *New York Times* to provide several days coverage, although with little amplification. Tilney expressed complete shock about the resignation. Adler was absolutely tight-lipped about what had happened, and after his courses ended that spring, he never again associated with Columbia University. As for the child-guidance clinic, Reverend John Haynes Holmes of the Community Church announced six weeks later that Adler's Advisory Council of Individual Psychology, (as his clinic was known) "had been taken over by the [church] as a regular part of its community service work." In the early fall, Adler's longtime colleague, Walter Beran Wolfe, would assume its directorship.

CHAPTER SEVENTEEN

"Books Like Firecrackers" and Mass Politics

If the world is to be saved, obviously
the thing most needed is that man
shall be raised to a level where he shall
no longer, like a child playing with
a loaded pistol, constantly risk
destroying himself by misuse of his
own power. It is difficult to see where
this education is to come from if
not from the new psychology.

ALFRED ADLER

If Adler was upset about what had happened at Columbia, his mood probably soon lifted, for the spring of 1930 saw the release of his three new books, all aimed at a relatively popular audience. These were *The Pattern of Life, Guiding the Child,* and *The Education of Children.* Their nearly simultaneous publication in the United States clearly reflected Adler's own shift in professional emphasis from Europe to his present base of activity.

Based on his demonstration lectures at the New School two years before, *The Pattern of Life* presented twelve cases of schoolchildren with differing types of emotional difficulty, such as conduct disorders or extreme shyness. Many of the youngsters came from immigrant families (Italian, Jewish, or Slavic) populous in New York City during the 1920s and were of decidedly lower socioeconomic background. Yet, similar to Adler's other writings during this period, *The Pattern of Life* had little to say about cultural or economic factors that might be affecting such pupils. It was edited by the young psychiatrist Walter Beran Wolfe, who also provided a lucid overview of individual psychology.

The Pattern of Life presented transcribed accounts of Adler's comments about each case and his brief interviews with family members brought to the New School class. While it illuminated Adler's mode of interpreting specific kinds of childhood maladjustment, *The Pattern of Life* would have been a far stronger work for professionals had it contained a more detailed exposition of how he viewed each type of emotional disorder. Too often, his interesting comments appeared telegraphed, undoubtedly due to the book's transcribed lecture format.

Major reviewers generally found *The Pattern of Life* worth recommending. "Usually on the basis of the circumstantial evidence of the case," descriptively noted the *New York Times*, [Adler] was able correctly to reconstruct the family situation to which he attributed the child's conduct. Afterward, the child's parents were brought in for questioning and advice, and finally, the child himself. The too docile, the rebellious, the neurotic, the feeble-minded and the maternally dominant child are some of the types analyzed."

More critical was the weekly *Outlook and Independent,* which regarded Adler's intense therapeutic optimism as unrealistic. "Dr. Wolfe's preface reveals the aspects of Adler's philosophy which have made some academicians place it in the realm of religion rather than science," its reviewer sarcastically remarked. "Essentially free will appears in a new dress. For the underlying idea of Individual Psychology is that 'Every human being can do everything.' The determinism of heredity, the limitations of environment, the stupidities of society are not, it is declared, insuperable obstacles to one who is facing forward to a goal of social usefulness. The [individual's] job is to understand his pattern of life and if his conduct is unworthy, and his goal useless and selfish, master his fate by turning in the right direction."

In the ensuing years of the Great Depression, many American intellectuals would likewise find Adler's buoyant confidence in individual self-determination as overly simplistic. In this sense, his strong socialistic outlook after World War I gradually shifted to a far vaguer perspective on how people are affected by wider social forces. Even during the heyday of President Franklin Roosevelt's New Deal legislation, rarely did Adler ever provide concrete proposals for actually improving America's social conditions. He instead seemed content in late middle age to offer what many perceived as moralisms instead of empirical findings. Thus, the *Outlook and Independent* archly suggested that Adlerian psychology had begun to acquire the trappings of a religion. "Perhaps that is why [he] is hailed by his followers as a prophet rather than a psychologist. A well known Jesuit priest in Germany has said that if Adler continues to expound his social ideals, although a Jew he will establish the first Christian psychology."

Less moralistic in tone was Adler's second new book issued that same spring of 1930, *Guiding the Child: On the Principles of Individual Psychology.* Published by Greenberg, it was an anthology of twenty-one articles written by Vienna's chief Adlerian practitioners. The translator was physician Benjamin Ginzburg, who had organized and edited Adler's *The Science of Living,* published the year before. Adler himself contributed only one essay, "A Case from Guidance Practice," although his daughter Alexandra (Ali), now a fledgling Viennese psychiatrist committed to individual psychology, provided two. Other contributors included Ferdinand Birnbaum, Alice Friedmann, Arthur and Martha Holub, Olga Knopf, Alexander Müller, Alexander Neuer, Regine Seidler, Lydia Sicher, Oskar Spiel, and Erwin Wexberg. Together with Ali, these men and women had become the most important Viennese clinicians to practice and promulgate Adlerian psychology.

Certainly, *Guiding the Child* was aimed at a professional rather than popular American audience. Its well-integrated chapters had originally appeared as articles in Adler's journal during the preceding year. Most were descriptive rather than theoretical, and showed concretely how Adlerian therapists diagnosed and treated maladjusted schoolchildren. The majority of cases were drawn from either child-guidance or teacher-training sessions that Adler's associates had led for Vienna's public schools in the late 1920s.

Guiding the Child predominantly featured children of lower- or working-class Austrian families. Many of the youngsters had lost a parent to death or desertion, and their health was often poor. With little parental supervision, teenage youths were sexually active and several cases involved prostitution or pregnancy. Yet curiously, not a single contributor to *Guiding the Child* even discussed tangentially how socioeconomic factors like poverty or overcrowding might be relevant to such students' lives.

Nevertheless, Adler's associates offered a progressive view of early maladjustment. They decisively rejected the notion, still advocated by many at the time, that these youngsters represented "genetically inferior stock" associated with specific ethnic groups. Rather, the Adlerians optimistically emphasized that virtually all such cases could be treated successfully through the modern principles of psychology. Emphasizing esteem building rather than coercive forms of discipline, they specifically condemned corporal punishment as an outmoded way of treating children. Generally, though, Adler's collaborators expressed satisfaction with the growing enlightenment of Austria's parents and schoolteachers.

With its sober style and sharp focus, *Guiding the Child* received positive comments from most American reviewers. Typical of these was the *New York Times,* observing approvingly that the book "shows how children are readjusted to school work and home conditions through the application of [Adler's] principles in the Vienna free guidance clinics which now exist in every school district. Initially, some ten years ago, partly by the public school teachers themselves, they have been largely fostered by parents' and teachers' associations."

In what may have set an American publishing record for the time, Adler authored yet another new book that same spring. *The Education of Children* marked his fourth work for Greenberg Publisher, and his sixth for the English-speaking world, in just three years. As was true for all his other volumes appearing in this brief period, *The Education of Children* mainly represented lecture material edited extensively for organization and readability. Combining this challenging task with translation from the German were Friedrich and Eleanor Jensen, a husband-and-wife team of Adler's Austrian associates. They performed their task well, for the book was probably Adler's most lucid since *Understanding Human Nature.* Unlike *Problems of Neurosis, The Pattern of Life,* and even *Guiding the Child,* this volume presented in detail Adler's insights on personality development. *The Education of Children* was too specialized for most parents, and had its widest appeal among those professionals already acquainted with Adler's name.

Arguing that all children suffer from feelings of inferiority, Adler attributed early behavioral problems to their intense desire to gain esteem and power. As he had long argued before, most childhood disorders are rooted not in sexuality but in the drive for mastery. Adler saw many problem behaviors as essentially strategies that youngsters unconsciously use to assert their will against much bigger and more powerful family members. In this sense, parents can start feeling helpless or enraged by a peevish child who will not sleep, who seems to eat nothing, or who continually soils the bedsheets.

"These weapons may be compared to [those] which nature has given animals for their protection—claws and horns. It is easy to see how they [originate] in the child's weakness, and his despair of being able to cope with life without such extraneous equipment. And it is remarkable how many things may serve for such weapons. There are some children who have [none] but their lack of control of stools and urine."

Adler advised parents to be gentle and understanding, rather than harsh, when faced with such problems. To threaten or actually carry out punishments is ultimately useless, and only exacerbates the difficulty. "What is essential is for us to see the child's situation with the eyes of the child himself, and interpret it with his own mistaken judgment. We must not suppose that the child behaves logically—that is to say, according to adult common sense—but we must be ready to recognize that children make mistakes in interpreting their own positions." Thus, for example, a five-year-old girl whose mother works a night shift may begin to develop a sleeping disorder. Its origin might lie in the youngster's fear of abandonment, and her intense desire, therefore, to actually witness her mother walk through the front door.

The Education of Children also offered Adler's rather detailed comments on [parental] sex education for children. Adopting a cautious viewpoint, he commented that, "There are many persons who are . . . insane on the subject . . . want [it] at any and all ages, and play up the dangers of sexual ignorance. But if we look into our own past and into the past of others, we do not see such great difficulties nor such great dangers as they imagine." As in previous writings, Adler stressed that parents should explain sexuality to children according to their degree of interest and intellectual capability.

Typical for Adler's earlier books, he highlighted the important role of schooling in aiding a child's emotional development. "An educator's most important task—one might almost say his holy duty—is to see to it that no child is discouraged at school, and that a child who enters school already discouraged regains his confidence through his school and his teacher. This goes hand in hand with the vocation of the educator, for no education is possible except with children who look hopefully and joyfully upon the future." In keeping with his optimistic faith in psychological progress as the key to social improvement, Adler ended his book by triumphantly declaring, "We are entering a period which is bringing with it new ideas, new methods, and new understanding in the education of children. Science is doing away with old worn out customs and traditions."

Despite its insights, *The Education of Children* offered little that was really new to Americans familiar with individual psychology. It covered ground that Adler himself had fully mapped in numerous earlier works, and to many reviewers who had initially been quite receptive to his writing, he was clearly rushing too many books into print. Rather harshly, the *New York Times* related that, "One finds much good sense in this book, much that is suggestive, and borne out by individual experience, but its form detracts from its value. The style is rambling, and the subject matter essentially unorganized. Juggling the titles of the chapters would not matter much. The book is descriptive and interpretative rather than explanatory in the scientific sense or practical in its effort to teach those responsible for children."

Although its tone was more cheerful, even the sympathetic *Outlook and*

Independent could no longer shrug off the repetitive quality of Adler's recent writing. Conveying a backhanded compliment mixed with an unmistakable touch of sarcasm, its reviewer remarked that, "Alfred Adler's new books come off the presses with the rapidity of exploding firecrackers. *The Education of Children* is a third arrival within as many months. But we are not with those who suggest that Dr. Adler should be persuaded to practice Book Control. Even if he does say the same thing over and over, repetition is a well known educational device."

During that same year, the influential William Alanson White, former president of the American Psychiatric Association, scathingly wrote: "While it has slowly been growing in [my] mind that Adler's other books are becoming stereotyped, [I am] now becoming convinced that they are deteriorating. . . . [I have] tried therefore to be tolerant and considerate and to see the good that was in the works of this author, but it is becoming painfully evident that an adverse note must be struck, and [I] therefore with this last work [cry] 'Enough!'

Why was Adler at the age of sixty inviting such unnecessary criticism at the risk of his formidable reputation? The answer is not altogether clear. Certainly, he had little to gain financially from authorizing the release of these "firecrackers" into the American zeitgeist. Greenberg Publisher's advances were not large, and none of his books since *Understanding Human Nature* had enjoyed sizable sales. Nor was Adler at this stage in his long career in need of professional recognition; his ideas were well known to colleagues throughout the world. From the almost casual manner that he entrusted free-lance editors to organize—even embellish—his books, it hardly seems likely that these works were important sources of ego gratification.

It may be that Adler decided that launching quickly done popularizations would be the most effective way to propel individual psychology into wider public awareness. From this perspective, he may have viewed books like *The Education of Children* as merely extending the seemingly successful approach he had initiated more than a decade before in postwar Vienna. By offering countless lectures to nonprofessionals at the People's Institute and by opening his society meetings to all comers, hadn't he greatly expanded the sphere of influence of individual psychology? Most of Adler's career had developed outside academia's groves, and as a social democrat at heart, he had always taken pride in rejecting the intellectual elitism that the University of Vienna medical faculty had long symbolized for him.

Nevertheless, Adler probably underestimated the extent to which he began to alienate once-sympathetic American colleagues by his unbending effort to democratize his psychological system. Although figures like pediatrician Ira Wile might have cordial feelings for him personally, they would come to distance themselves from individual psychology as a distinct approach worthy of special study.

═══════

Returning to Vienna for the summer of 1930, Adler kept busy with a vigorous pace of professional activity. Having resigned his positions with the Pedagogical Institute and the Franz-Josef Ambulatorium the previous year, Adler focused more predominantly on consultative work than in past summers. Yet, he hardly felt relegated to sideline responsibilities. Austria's unemployment was rising steadily in the economic collapse recently originating in the United States and spreading rapidly throughout Europe. More and more Austrians were being thrown out of work, as the country's major industries of luxury-item sales and tourism plummeted.

Surprising to neither Adler nor his associates was that such economic turmoil was manifesting itself with many new cases of child maltreatment, including neglect and abuse, for Vienna's school personnel. As always, the Adlerians provided their guidance clinics free of charge to parents and teachers, a proviso especially important as Austria's fragile economy began unraveling.

In recognition of Adler's humanitarian efforts, the city council decided to award him the title of Citizen of Vienna in a public ceremony. The honor was to be given "in acknowledgment of the great merits that he acquired in science and on the belated occasion of his sixtieth birthday." Always eager to gain recognition for individual psychology, Adler was excited about the event. Unfortunately, Vienna's socialist mayor, Karl Seitz, knew little about either child guidance or mental health. Before the assembled dignitaries gathered to witness the presentation, he disastrously introduced Adler as "a deserving pupil of Freud's."

Although clearly intended without malice, Seitz's remark wounded Adler deeply, who later admitted to feeling more humiliated than had the mayor concocted a deliberate insult. The usually genial and good-natured Adler had, as has been noted previously, one chronic sorepoint: an utter intolerance for the suggestion, even the implication, that he had ever been Freud's disciple. Even now, after nearly twenty years had passed since their bitter parting, the two remained implacable foes.

Several weeks later, in mid-September, the Fifth International Congress for Individual Psychology was held in Berlin. The event allowed Adler the opportunity to criticize his longtime nemesis before a thousand supporters from Austria, Germany, and elsewhere in Europe. Mostly professionals, they had come to hear Adler, and to attend a variety of presentations on topics in child guidance, psychology, psychiatry, and education.

As keynote speaker, Adler opened the Berlin congress with an impassioned speech that many long remembered. Aside from seeking to energize his supporters for their continued commitment to individual psychology, he intended to refute Freud's gloomy message in *Civilization and its Discontents*. For many years, Adler as a socialist had found Freud's political conservatism to be distasteful. Adler had not only felt this way during their years together at the turn of the century; Freud's public defense of Wagner-Jauregg's medical brutality during the war had been only one of many later instances to irritate Adler. But in his view, Freud's new book on civilization far exceeded his earlier writings in its cold aloofness and political regressivism.

Published two years earlier in 1927, Freud's *The Future of an Illusion* had likewise exhibited a pessimistic outlook. But as one who had long ceased identifying with his boyhood Judaism, Adler had shared Freud's distrust for organized religion and theism. Although Adler valued biblical wisdom far more than Freud, he similarly believed that science would ultimately render all religion obsolete. In words that well expressed Adler's own viewpoint as a proud rationalist, Freud had declared his faith in scientific progress. "In this process, there is no holding back; the more the treasures of our knowledge become accessible to people, the more the defection from religious belief will spread."

For Adler, *Civilization and its Discontents* was far more disturbing, but not in every respect. Freud's dismissal of mystical experience as nothing more than regression to infantile consciousness was hardly offensive, for Adler likewise harbored an intense suspicion of mysticism, whether articulated by contemporaries like Jung or by ancient theologians. Nor did Adler find disagreeable Freud's efforts to depict faith in a loving God or an afterlife as originating in the child's feeling of helplessness before a powerful, indifferent world.

What Adler did find truly dismaying about *Civilization and its Discontents* was its mood of despair that nearly bordered on fatalism. Freud seemed to be insisting that "beyond the pleasure principle" lay nothing—that all our actions are reducible to the instinctual drive for physical gratification, and our aggressiveness to serve that impulse. Thus, he sought to repudiate the notion that people are motivated by higher ideals, such as work, aesthetics, or community feeling. With bitter sarcasm, Freud dismissed the ancient religious moralism of Love Thy Neighbor with the terse comment that, "Not merely is this stranger in general unworthy of my love; I must confess that he has more claim for my hostility and even my hatred."

Citing the atrocities that humans have for millennia committed against one another, Freud emphasized that civilization is needed to keep our innate agressiveness in check. To appeal to our nonexistent "higher nature" through religion or philosophy is to remain a child intellectually, he argued. "The time comes when each of us has to give up as illusions the expectations which, in his youth, he pinned upon his fellowmen, and when he may learn how much difficulty and pain has been added to his life by their ill-will."

Yet, insisted Freud, civilization simultaneously stifles our natural impulse for bodily pleasure. We are made to feel guilty for our instinctual feelings and "the sense of guilt [is] the most important problem in the development of civilization. . . . The price we pay for our advance in civilization is a loss of happiness through the heightening of the sense of guilt."

With an overriding emphasis on human aggression ("It forms the basis of every relation of affection and love among people with the single exception, perhaps, of the mother's relation to her male child"), Freud saw no salvation ahead for humanity. Socialists and communists alike were naive in blaming peoples' suffering on the existence of private property; even if the family were abolished and complete sexual freedom allowed, our innate aggressiveness would still remain "indestructible."

For Adler, such an outlook represented almost a personal challenge. For the past decade, he had rooted individual psychology in the human possibility for social feeling. In countless lectures and in his writings, he had sought to help parents, educators, and professionals to improve children's well-being; ultimately, an ideal society might be created this way. Speaking before attendees of the Berlin congress, Adler therefore stressed that the "meaning of life" comes through helping others and, in this way, leaving an enduring legacy for future generations. So much needed to be done—and *could* be done—in fields like education and child guidance; to complain about humanity's foibles was the mark of a selfish, spoiled personality.

Although Adler's speech at the crowded convention hall proved exciting to most listeners, an ominous backdrop pervaded Berlin and the wider countryside. In the year since the American stock market crash, Germany had been suffering from increasing social unrest and political polarization. Street violence and anti-Semitic sloganeering were becoming commonplace. Even academic settings were vulnerable to such outbursts. In June, the University of Munich had been temporarily shut down after a riotous mob had smashed in the lecture-room doors of a professor in international law. At the University of Heidelberg, a prominent faculty pacifist was the target of similar actions.

More disturbing still to most congress attendees was that Germans had gone to the polls earlier in the month and had cast record votes for Adolf Hitler's National Socialist Workers Party. The Nazis were no longer a bad joke. They had increased their electoral support in just two years from 810,000 to 6.5 million. They had gone from occupying only 12 seats in the national *Reichstag,* to holding 107, and now constituted the second most powerful party in Germany.

Most of their increase had come from new voters who had not participated in the 1928 election, either from dissatisfaction with earlier candidates or from being too young to cast ballots. Some of the new Nazi support also drew upon voters who had previously backed the middle-class liberal and conservative parties. In this same election of September 1930, the Catholic parties had slightly increased their strength, while the Social Democrats, with whom Adler identified, had lost support, mainly to the Communist party. There was little doubt, however, about the German election's main significance: The Nazis had finally achieved the political breakthrough that they had long been seeking.

"After spending a week in Vienna with Dimitrije Mitrinovic and Valerie Cooper and another member of our London Society, where we visited Adler in his home," later recalled writer Philip Mairet, "I visited some friends in Germany, where I at once realized that the Nazi revolution was imminent: you could feel it in the psychic atmosphere like a foul smell. . . . Later, I and Dr. Robb went as delegates to the marvelous Congress of the International Society of Individual Psychology in Berlin. . . . It was held in one of the biggest halls of the city, and full every session. You would have thought that Adler was 'on top of the world.' But at the final dinner to the delegates, one could sense that the impending Nazi revolt had, in advance, split the Adlerian movement in Germany, as it split or wiped out many another international effort."

It is unlikely that many attendees were pro-Hitler, although one of Adler's leading German associates, Leonhard Seif, would dutifully maintain his psychiatric clinic under Nazi rule. Rather, several ardent Adlerians argued at the congress that individual psychology no longer possessed the luxury of time in building its movement. Those active on the German political left like Manes Sperber and Alice Rühle-Gerstel felt that time had run out for Adler: If he did not openly identify himself with the communists, then he was naively playing into Hitler's hands. Those were the choices, and it was no use paying lip service anymore to the ideals of peaceful democratic change. Individual psychology *had* to ally itself immediately with Stalin if it were to survive the coming battle in Europe and elsewhere against capitalist fascism.

Sperber was probably the leading Adlerian who argued for this position. Since moving from Vienna two years before, he had become increasingly active with the German Communist party in Berlin. There, in 1929, he met Wilhelm Reich, who was seeking in his own way to radicalize German youth by synthesizing Freudian and Marxist ideas. "Willi Reich was a stocky man whose frequently flushed peasant face seemed to swell during animated conversation," later recalled Sperber. "He could seem aggressive, for he was imbued with the certainy that his views were so convincing and so un-assailably correct that no one's mind could or should be closed to them. . . . His conclusion was that only an orgasmic mankind could be emotionally healthy."

Like Sperber, Reich taught courses at the Marxist workers' school created by the Communist party, and within its political framework, he led study groups devoted to what he called *Sexpol* (sexual politics). He and Sperber often clashed over Adlerian versus Freudian notions, and especially over the relative importance of sexual satisfaction for personal and societal well-being.

Adler felt Sperber was tainting individual psychology by attempting to blend it with Communist party efforts. At the Congress in Berlin, he angrily told a shocked Sperber to end his communist proselytizing, and that he wanted nothing to do with such misguided activity. But the issue was not simply over Marxist ideology. As late as 1931, Adler would publish a totally uncritical, pro-Soviet article by his wife Raissa in the *Journal for Individual Psychology,* based on a lecture she had given before the Viennese chapter of the International Society for Individual Psychology. Although Raissa had not visited her homeland since before the October revolution and had remained a loyal Trotskyite, she ardently praised the Soviet Union's educational approach as a model for other countries.

"The whole . . . system forms a unified whole, from the cradle to kindergarten to school to university," Raissa remarked approvingly in quoting official Soviet policy. "Its goal [of developing] 'a constant fighter for the ideals of the working class and a conscious builder of the communistic society' must be especially emphasized, since such an educational goal is found in no other country." By way of example, Raissa reported how the Soviet government had begun to undermine the traditional Russian family's coercive style by encouraging children to inform on their parents. Through such methods, Raissa warmly observed, a new society was truly on its way.

Since Adler had long expressed his opposition to bolshevism, it is puzzling why he allowed the piece to be published. The most reasonable conclusion is probably that he regarded its position as at least intellectually stimulating. Also, the piece said nothing about subsuming individual psychology under the communist banner. In contrast, Adler may have come to view young Sperber as simply a hotheaded troublemaker. Eventually, Sperber and his supporters would retaliate for their sense of betrayal.

Organizing themselves into the Expert Group for Dialectical Marxist Psychology, based in Berlin, they would publish an anthology entitled *The Crisis of Psychology, The Psychology of Crisis* two years later. In an essay, "The Role of Psychology in the Social Upheaval," Rühle-Gerstel would condemn Adler for seeking political neutrality between the left and right under Hitler's lengthening shadow. "Today, it is no longer feasible for a school of psychology to declare itself as 'neutral' and to close its eyes to the social realities."

In the same slim volume, Sperber would publish a far more hostile article entitled "The Present State of Psychology." Several years earlier, he had extolled Adler in a biographical work for his visionary brilliance and erudition. Now, Sperber would actually villify his former mentor as a protofascist:

> Here is something to think about: Adler's individual psychology was in fact once the leftist branch of bourgeois/petty bourgeois psychology. In his paper, *The Psychological Movement*, Sigmund Freud bases Adler's views in his socialistic world-view. In fact, Adler in his time searched for the basis of his views in Marx and Engels. But just as the social-democratic leadership in the last decade has steadily developed into the most threatening danger to the prolitariat and the most bitter enemies of the prolitarian revolution, orthodox 'legitimate' Adlerian individual psychology has developed more and more into a social-fascistic system, social in some expressions, fascistic in system: in practice, promoting and supporting fascism.

In later decades, Sperber would bitterly lament in articles and books how his hero Adler had heartlessly ejected him from the individual psychology movement. The above statement hardly supports this historical interpretation, however. Rather, it seems clear that by the early 1930s, Sperber had decisively rejected Adlerian psychology in favor of Stalinism.

Certainly, not all who attended the Berlin congress of 1930 were embroiled in international politics. Many came with a desire to further their professional work with children, and among such attendees was an energetic young educator named Oskar Spiel. He had already been studying Freud's writings and had attended psychoanalytic lectures for a year with increasing dissatisfaction. "I could not find anything I could apply to my work as a teacher," he later recalled. "Freud's theories were too complicated for [students] to understand, and far too sterile ethically to be any use to children, even if they could have understood them." In past issues of the *International Journal for Individual Psychology,* Spiel had been intellectually excited by the writings of two Adlerians: Fritz Kunkel and Arthur Kronfeld. As a result, Spiel decided to attend the Berlin congress.

The decision proved worthwhile, for "the moment I heard Adler's opening lecture, I realized I had found the key to my difficulties. This is what I wanted for my children. I had of course often heard in Vienna of Adler's child-guidance clinics," remembered Spiel, "but I had [previously] supposed that his psychology could only be a help in directly abnormal cases. I had not realized the universal value of Adler's teachings, or that they could be applied to every child and by every teacher. This . . . was a revelation to me. I knew that I must from henceforth be an Adlerian myself, and devote all my powers to mastering this new science."

Upon returning to Vienna, Spiel excitedly discussed his reaction with a fellow educator, Ferdinand Birnbaum, who was initially skeptical about Adler's true relevance. After both hearing him lecture at the People's Institute, they become fully committed to developing a special experimental Viennese school based on his notions for student democracy and self-expression. Eventually, this school would gain international attention both for Adler's collaborators and their educational principles. Certainly, such innovative projects were far more important to him than thrusting individual psychology into the treacherous waters of party politics.

———

Although Adler's work in the late 1920s had clearly blossomed in both Austria and the United States, matters were proving very different in England. There his nascent movement of individual psychology had become increasingly embroiled in extraneous social-political causes and factionalism. To restrengthen appropriate developments, Adler decided to make a special visit in January 1931.

Adler, of course, was aware that mental-health services in the British Isles still lagged behind those in the United States as well as in his native Austria. It had only been as recently as 1927 that British professional interest in child treatment had become organized. That year, the newly formed Child Guidance Council, based in London, had dispatched a fact-finding team to the United States to learn the latest interdisciplinary methods. Two years later, the first mental-health course for English social workers was offered at the London School of Economics. Likewise, the country's first child-guidance clinic and child study center was founded in the late 1920s.

Perhaps deciding that his approach might therefore be relatively unfamiliar to English practitioners, Adler offered a fairly rudimentary lecture to psychiatrists of the Royal Academy of Physicians. Published soon after in the British medical journal *Lancet,* "The Structure of Neurosis" was a formal presentation that emphasized a combination of social interest and cooperativeness as a key aspect of mental health. Summarizing his longtime perspective on personality development, Adler recounted how during our preschool years we each create a unique style of life designed to help us cope best with our powerful surrounding environment. "No two individuals are identical in their conceptions, perceptions, feelings, actions, and thoughts," he declared. "Each of these belongs to the style of life created by the child."

Adler explained that with repeated experiences of failure, children develop feelings of inferiority and subsequent difficulties in relating well to others. While conceding that the trait of cooperativeness probably had a hereditary component, he stressed that it was "not very deep and must be taught like history or geography . . . from the kindergarten onwards." Similar to Adler's prior remarks in books like *Understanding Human Nature,* he urged that mental-health prevention "be started at school [where] teachers look out for faulty styles of life and shrinking social interest."

In the brief question-and-answer period that followed, Adler addressed such topics as criminal behavior and its possible link to poverty, suicide as a form of revenge, and the value of traditional English education. The final questioner somewhat humorously challenged: "At what stage does the semi-sanity of us all become neurosis?"

"No general rules can be laid down," Adler gently replied, "for all individuals differ. The degree of social interest is the best guide to [our] amount of neurosis."

Two days later, Adler offered his next major lecture before the London branch of the International Society for Individual Psychology. This was the lay group founded at Gower Street four years earlier by Dimitrije Mitrinovic and his fellow intellectuals, artists, and writers. Although initially focused clearly on Adlerian psychology, they had become steadily immersed in Mitrinovic's eccentric mixture of occult study and the advocacy of pan-European guild socialism. It must have been somewhat uneasily, therefore, that Adler addressed this audience with a formal lecture entitled "The Meaning of Life." It was published shortly thereafter in the journal *Lancet,* and later formed the nucleus for Adler's well-acclaimed book, *What Life Should Mean to You.*

Unlike his presentation before the Royal Academy of Physicians, Adler's talk was both more philosophical and eloquent. "The problem I want to discuss tonight is a very old one. Probably human beings have always asked such questions as: 'What is life for? What is the *meaning* of life? Perhaps they have said that life has no meaning at all. You hear it still in our own time."

Adler specifically attacked Freud's gloomy assessment of human nature. Without mentioning his former mentor or *Civilization and its Discontents* even once by name, Adler nevertheless declared, "It is often said that human beings are governed by the 'pleasure principle.' Many psychologists and psychiatrists, however, are sure that this is not true." All emotionally healthy people, Adler insisted, "strive for the *happiness* of others; this is the true pleasure principle of the socially interested person." In contrast, to search for physical gratification is "the striving of a person who is only interested in himself and not others."

Adler went on to highlight the difference between the emotionally secure and the neurotic. He identified the latter as tending toward pessimism rather than optimism, seeking transient pleasure rather than enduring happiness, and living selfishly for themselves rather than cooperating with others. Those who grow up with such a negative outlook, Adler emphasized, are "not rightly prepared for life. . . . They always feel irritated and are always irritable, because they are not living [fully] in the world."

How can more people acquire true social feeling? The earlier this emphasis begins in life, the better. "We say that the ability to cooperate can be and must be trained. . . . On all points, we can prove that that meaning of life must be, for the greatest part, cooperation. And now we have to make it [alive]."

The following evening, Adler offered a third and quite different public lecture. It was sponsored by the Medical Society of Individual Psychology and was soon excerpted by the *British Medical Journal.* Later in the year, Adler's medical supporters in England published his presentation as a complete monograph entitled *The Case of Mrs. A.*

In order to demonstrate vividly his particular approach to personality diagnosis, Adler created an unusual and almost theatrical format. He pre-arranged with a few medical colleagues, that a completely unfamiliar psychiatric case history be given to him on the lecture platform. Then sentence by sentence, he read the notes aloud while immediately voicing specific deductions about the woman's life, attitudes, and relationships—all based solely on his thirty years of clinical experience.

In a way, this format resembled that of Adler's book *The Case of Miss R.,* published in 1929. He was now, however, interpreting case material extemporaneously as a teaching device. More broadly, Adler's predilection for a Sherlock Holmes–style analysis of small clues to unmask one's basic personality had long been part of his professional repertoire. Indeed, in later years Adler confessed to greatly admiring Arthur Conan Doyle's most famous literary creation.

"Mrs A." was a thirty-one-year-old married woman with two young children. She had been raised in a working-class family with an alcoholic, physically abusive father. Mrs. A's husband had been vocationally ambitious, but due to a war injury was relegated to menial shop labor. Frustrated and embittered, he had expressed his urge for dominance by the continual bullying of family members. Mrs. A. felt little sympathy for him; in fact, for the past eighteen months, she herself had been suffering from a variety of phobias, anxieties, and violent compulsive thoughts, including suicide and the murder of their two small children. As a result, Mr. A. was forced to be at home constantly with never-ending vigilance, lest his wife or offspring come to physical harm.

In Adler's remarkably contemporary viewpoint, the case could best be understood in terms of family dynamics revolving around the vital axis of power. He declared Mrs. A's life-style a "masterpiece" of creativity, for she had developed a complex of seemingly debilitating symptoms whose end result actually gave her true power in the family. "By her neurosis," explained Adler, "she had given [her spouse] rules which he must obey. He became a husband under command. He was required to assume responsibility for her, and she utilized and exploited him. . . . By this strange route," Adler pointedly concluded, "she had conquered and subjected her husband."

Adler's audience was delighted with his artful demonstration of case analysis. Not surprisingly, they also wanted his thoughts on treating this difficult patient, but the hour was already late, and Adler was quickly off. Within a few days, he had departed for a lecture tour in Germany, but not before making decisive changes concerning the leadership of individual psychology in England. In this regard, Adler viewed as paramount the hand that controlled his organization's power there.

———

Undoubtedly, the chief problem was Dimitrije Mitrinovic himself. Little more than four years before, the charismatic Serbian writer-lecturer had impressed Adler greatly. Upon first meeting in late 1926, the two men had enjoyed hours together in lively discussion of history, philosophy, and human behavior. Like Adler, Mitrinovic had appeared committed to world peace and improvement through a new understanding of the human mind. Although a complete stranger, he had appeared so perceptive and enthusiastic about individual psychology that Adler offered personal support in the establishment of a London branch of his society. With Mitrinovic's subsequent visit with Adler in Vienna, their mutual compatibility had seemed assured. Mitrinovic had quickly succeeded in raising funds among his Bloomsbury following for a comfortable meeting place, and energetically served as official head of Adlerian psychology in England.

In retrospect, Adler almost certainly regretted this decision, but in 1926, he had just begun to venture out of Austria for international allies and had comparatively few potential English backers. In the intervening years, Mitrinovic had become increasingly associated with an odd and politically oriented philosophical system. Central to his new outlook was European pan-nationalism. Recently, he had founded the New Europe Group, whose grand aim was to unite all of Europe, including England, into a single federation, presumably under his direction.

With the onset of the Depression, Mitrinovic and his supporters had begun to promulgate a radical political platform whose tenets comprised monetary reform and the abolition of the English Parliament. Times were hard and discouraging economically, and some of Mitrinovic's admirers had real influence, such as Philip Mairet, editor of *The New English Weekly,* and John Strachey, a young Labor deputy whose later influential books would include *The Coming Struggle for Power* and *The Nature of the Capitalist Crisis.* Less predictable in ideology, Mitrinovic himself had begun to call stridently for a triunity of Aryandom, Christianity, and Socialism as "the Religion of the Aryan Will, the Science of the Incarnate Logos, and the Life Universal of Seraphic Socialism." In his proposed system, the English Parliament would be replaced by three political chambers representing a variety of medievallike guilds and workers' councils. Present organized religion would be replaced by a form of occult Christianity.

Much worse than such unorthodox notions, Mitrinovic had been steadily espousing racist, anti-Semitic, and authoritatian ideas under the protective banner of Adlerian psychology. As early as 1920, in an avant-garde English periodical called the *New Age*, he had recommended that an "organized European Senate or White Council" be created to direct the progress of the world's nonwhite races. Several years later, Mitrinovic wrote that, "The Black, the Red, and the Yellow races are. . . . embryological forms of the fully-developed Man, the White race."

He was especially virulent in his anti-Semitism. In 1920, he commented that, "The world has no direct use for the Jews. Judaism stands condemned." Then, at the same time, he contended that, "We wish to be fair to the Jews. The 'punishment' imposed upon them has been great. . . ." But by the late 1920s, his rambling writings often resembled those of Nazi street pamphlets in Weimar Germany. "Everywhere the Jewish mentality creates problems," he argued in a representative article in late 1928, "and on this account, the Jewish race presents itself as a problem of problems. What is their mystery and the source of their power?"

As if to answer this rhetorical question, Mitrinovic presented three public lectures the following autumn before the London individual psychology association. Certainly, his intriguing titles could not be faulted: "Freud versus Adler," "The Significance of Jung," and "Marx and Nietzsche as the Historic Background of Adler." In the first of these acrid talks, Mitrinovic depicted the elderly Freud as "a monster, not a man from the Western world. He is a man of Semitic race . . . and he has come with his clairvoyant and diabolical understanding to shock and frighten us. . . . He is that satanical censor of being who shocks the Christian world, Europe, and the white race."

In a stylistically similar manner, Mitrinovic offered his insight on Adler. "Now, at the same time [that] Freud has arisen with this vision and . . . aim of shattering Western culture, there has arisen another man of the Semitic race: Adler, who has come to redress the balance of Freud and teach us optimism and humility."

Less coherently in his second lecture, Mitrinovic portrayed Jung as a gnostic thinker whose racial concepts might help liberate Western culture from its present enslavement. "Until mankind understands," he warned, "Israel will remain the leading race in the world. They will govern with the rod of iron; they will control finance. Lenin and Trotsky will manage, destroy, and reconstruct mankind." Urging his audience to remain hopeful in the face of their enemy, Mitrinovic declared that, "Nothing could have penetrated the unconscious of America and this dense island of England . . . but this knife of the perverted genius of the Jew which Freud is."

In his final lecture, Mitrinovic sought to fuse individual psychology and

Marxism into a larger system of thought. Adler, of course, had become infuriated by precisely this approach when launched by former left-wing disciples like Manes Sperber and Alice Rühle-Gerstel in Germany. "The Individual Psychology of Adler is nothing but the theory of Marx applied to individual personality," insisted Mitrinovic, "just as Marx, as an economist and philosopher, is nothing but the anticipation of Adler. It is individual psychology writ large, the individual psychology of capitalist society as a whole, analysis of the capitalist class. There is one concept, one single word, in which both Marx and Adler are contained: 'part,' to be a part of the whole."

With obvious allusion to Nietzsche, Mitrinovic ended his three-part lecture series with the dubious assertion that, "The contribution which Adler has made is the proof that the soul of personality is God; that man with his free will can produce every vision, can draw every power from himself."

Adler, of course, cannot be faulted for Mitrinovic's absurd ramblings. Yet, the Serbian philosopher was not the only one among the London chapter of the individual psychology association to espouse an esoteric political outlook with anti-Semitic overtones. Philip Mairet, who had recently edited Adler's *Problems of Neurosis* and had led the Sociological Division of the English individual psychology association, had his own apocalyptic agenda. Thus, he offered a public lecture in October 1929 entitled "The Family of the Future."

With several laudatory references to Mitrinovic and Adler, Mairet declared Western civilization to be dominated by a suicidal revulsion for capitalism and materialism. He cited the new field of population planning as a key sign of contemporary decadence and called for a huge *increase* in world population to accomplish humanity's glorious destiny as revealed in the modern, interrelated globe. "Comparatively suddenly, the whole world has been opened up to man, all the religions fused together so that they seem to cancel each other out; and we have to find a new idea upon which to base an entirely new method of facing the future."

Condemning the Jews for the "financial parasitism" they had brought upon the world, Mairet urged that a new vision to replace materialism was needed to guide humanity. "That idea must be found; and Individual Psychology must play a great part in its finding. The work of peopling the world will be safe to undertake as [our] understanding deepens."

═══

As a result of his visit to England, Adler decisively removed his name from association with the London group that he had entrusted to Mitrinovic and

associates like Mairet. Such a move is hardly surprising, given Adler's resolute desire for individual psychology to remain "pure" from wider political
or social aims, especially of an authoritarian nature. Most likely, with Adler's
ceaseless schedule of activity in the United States and Austria-Germany, he
had simply been unaware of developments within his main association in
England.

Mitrinovic's group reacted mainly with indifference to Adler's action. As
Mairet later recalled, "Dimitrije would have taken his followers away from
Adler . . . even if the Society had not been dissolved. He had other irons in
the fire. . . . He would now let his pupils do whatever they thought best for
himself and for them," and this would involve the Serbian thinker's increasingly obscure quest for gnostic-political utopianism.

In any event, Adler in 1931 transferred leadership of individual psychology in England to a medical colleague with a reputation for excellence,
Francis Graham Crookshank. At the time, it seemed like an excellent
choice, for unlike Mitrinovic, he was a physician not a literary philosopher,
and absorbed by therapeutic issues rather than political messianism. As
head of the Medical Society for Individual Psychology, Crookshank had
known Adler since late 1926 and had long enjoyed a favorable reputation
among his British colleagues.

Born in Wimbledon, he was three years younger than Adler and had been
educated at University College in London. Receiving his medical training
at University College Hospital, Crookshank had in 1895 graduated with
honors in medicine and a specialty in forensic work. The following year, he
had received his M.D. degree, qualifying for the university's gold medal.
Working in general practice and then shifting to psychiatry, Crookshank
held several hospital appointments, including directorship of units for
medical isolation and forensics. By the start of the war, his interests had
definitely changed to clinical medicine and he had served on staff at the
Prince of Wales General Hospital.

Like Adler and many other physicians on both sides of the hostilities,
Crookshank was drafted into military service. He served in northern France,
where he worked as medical director of the English Military Hospital at
Caen. There, Crookshank's language proficiency in French and German
proved valuable in working with colleagues, as well as in treating prisoners
of war. In 1918, he became one of the first doctors to describe an outbreak
of illnesses with strange, new cerebral symptoms. Later, these were identified with the disease of lethargic encephalitis.

Crookshank's participation in the war, however, affected him far more
than merely presenting new diagnostic challenges. He returned to England

from the battle horrors of Normandy with a different outlook on life. In his own appraisal, he experienced a spiritual transformation that caused him to abandon his previous medical approach of "psycho-physical parallelism, bred by agnosticism out of materialism." After considerable reading and philosophical speculation, Crookshank developed a strong belief in the power of the human mind—specifically, the will—to affect all facets of illness or well-being. He began an outpouring of consistent literary activity with this new philosophical stance. Prior to the war, he had written and edited various medical articles of a conventional nature. But beginning in 1920, Crookshank's approach became iconoclastic and influential for its strong philosophical foundation.

As the *British Medical Journal* later noted in praise, "To him a patient was never 'a clear case of such-and-such,' but always a sick individual, with a sick mind manifesting itself through a sick body as a result of many complicated and interacting problems arising partly from the individual's past and present, and partly from environmental factors of all kinds. This view of 'the whole man' is coming more and more to the forefront today, and has been termed the revival of the Hippocratic tradition. In this revival, Crookshank was a pioneer."

In 1922, his first book appeared. Described as "remarkable" by the British journal *Lancet,* it examined the virulent disease of influenza from a multifaceted perspective. Starting that same year, Crookshank became a prolific contributor to medical meetings, journals, and books. In 1926, he authored *Migraine and other Common Neuroses.* A forceful and erudite speaker in middle age, Crookshank gained an iconoclastic reputation for such lectures as "Theory of Diagnosis," delivered before the Royal College of Physicians in London in 1926. His impassioned emphasis on the need for a philosophical revamping of medical care sometimes seemed rather abstract to colleagues. As *Lancet* later recalled, "In argument, Crookshank was too ready to blame [his audience] for failures to perceive what he had failed to explain."

After meeting Adler in London late that year, Crookshank turned increasingly in his writing to individual psychology for fresh insights. With Adler's encouragement, Crookshank established an English medical society interested in this approach, and perhaps wisely, kept his distance from the lay association headed by Mitrinovic. In 1929, Crookshank authored a lucid introduction to Adler's *Problems of Neurosis,* edited by Mairet; the following year, he wrote *Individual Diagnosis,* strongly influenced by Adlerian concepts.

Like Adler's pediatrician friend Ira Wile in the United States, Crookshank valued individual psychology for its professional utility and humanism. Although strong in his beliefs and often argumentative, he was no political or social revolutionary. Rather, Crookshank's primary aim was to promulgate Adler's ideas within England's conservative medical establishment and, in this way, create a better society. Certainly, he was far more conventional in his social values than the Bloomsbury group of writers, artists, and intellectuals that had congregated around Mitrinovic and Mairet.

In late 1929, in a representative series of lectures given before Mitrinovic's group that were entitled "Individual Psychology and the Sexual Problems of Adolescence and Adult Life," Crookshank declared that healthy sexuality is vital to "the fullest individual functioning." But he presented a decidedly more Victorian approach than that favored by Adler and most of his Central European colleagues. Thus, Crookshank recommended that adolescents be deflected from engaging in masturbation by becoming involved in swimming. "A young man is usually responsive to suggestions of personal responsibility and chivalry," he added, "and he may be told that, although there are different codes of morality and conduct . . . certain things . . . *are not done.*" Crookshank conceded, though, that "the deliberate relief of physical tension [i.e., masturbation] is not always unavoidable."

He emulated Adler's viewpoint by praising marriage and monogamy as the highest form of human cooperativeness. In this same lecture series, Crookshank also condemned infidelity as a serious "breach of contract" and rejected unfettered sexual expression as a meaningful path toward human fulfillment. In these aspects, he and Adler shared a similar perspective.

"The doctrine of my reforming friends is, therefore, anarchical," Crookshank contended sarcastically. "My consolation is that they will find, as all other anarchists have found, that in establishing anarchy by general consent they have abolished anarchy, and substituted government. . . . When our friends have the right to walk about [London's] Hyde Park in a state of Nature, and to do whatever it is they want to do whenever they want to do it, they will come to find that their only chance of securing freedom is to behave sanely and wholesomely."

Such a conservative stance was not likely to endear Crookshank to the Bloomsbury Adlerians, and his own medical society had little interplay with them. More typical of his lectures was one presented in February 1930, before the York Medical Society. Published that year under the title "Types of Personality," Crookshank's talk emphasized the importance of making diagnosis more humanistic. "Medicine must be recognized to be, not the study of the false entities we call diseases, but a branch of anthropology—

the study of Man. . . . Our real task is to understand the individuality of our patients. In this way, Medicine becomes much more than an affair of the dead house, the laboratory, or even the farmyard, and a matter of human interest."

Crookshank's ability to articulate this cogent outlook well made him seem eminently qualified to head English activity for individual psychology. The Depression years of the early 1930s made Adler eager to prevent his popular approach from becoming subverted to wider political or social aims. Who, then, could better advance his psychological system in the British Isles than this well-regarded and sober-minded medical colleague? Unfortunately, within a few years, Adler's second choice for leadership would likewise come to haunt him.

CHAPTER EIGHTEEN

Thriving During the Depression

He is the children's New Dealer.
CLEVELAND PLAIN-DEALER

After completing his activities in London, Adler passed much of the rest of 1931 lecturing and consulting in a variety of European countries, including Denmark, Holland, Sweden, and Switzerland. But he spent the bulk of his professional time on work related to child guidance in Germany, writing to daughter Ali in Vienna that, "I am constantly busy. Sometimes [in the evening], I go to a movie. If I had time and could settle myself a little better, I could stay here." He was particularly happy to visit with his oldest daughter Valentine, who had moved to Berlin that fall for a new job with a Soviet publishing house. At the age of thirty-three, she was ready for major changes in her life, and would soon meet and marry a Hungarian journalist named Gyula Sas, who was working on foreign assignment there for the Soviet news agency *Imprecor*.

Less hurried than in previous years, Adler also spent considerable time in Vienna with friends and family members. Although he had spent few weekends at Salmannsdorf since buying the country property in 1926, its spacious garden had always been appealing. Its colorful gardener, Fritz, was a German who had known Hitler as an obnoxious childhood peer. Soon after taking over Salmannsdorf in 1926, Adler had found himself much too busy for regular gardening; nor was Raissa interested in doing the time-consuming physical work. They certainly had a problem, and then one day, a stranger appeared and requested to see Adler. Fritz explained that he been recently incarcerated for burglary. While serving his sentence, he had read one of Adler's stimulating books in the prison library and felt compelled to meet him.

The two chatted together for a while, and impressed with Fritz's earnestness, Adler offered him the gardening position. It was quickly accepted, and several days later, Fritz was sent to purchase a few items at a local greenhouse. Smiling, he returned with a huge number of plants, many more than Adler's money could possibly have procured. Realizing that Fritz was testing his own honesty, Adler firmly told him, "Go back to the greenhouse and return the plants you didn't pay for." Fritz did so immediately, and thereafter, proved a loyal employee.

Several years later, the Salmannsdorf estate became a full-time residence when Kurt and his childhood sweetheart Renée Grunberg decided to marry. Because he was still a university student in his mid-twenties and lacked an independent income, his parents generously vacated the country home for the newlyweds. Years later, Kurt recalled having felt grateful for such assistance, as well as for the fact that his famous father had not once intruded on his youthful, and ultimately short-lived, marriage by attempting to offer unsolicited advice.

By this time, red-headed Cornelia (Nelly) too had gotten married, to a Viennese law student named Heinz Sternberg. Having decided to become an actress, she was the only one of the four Adler children to reject a scholarly career. Perhaps for this reason, Nelly had experienced considerable tensions with Raissa. While away from Austria, Adler wrote Nelly frequently during this period, and sought to bolster her low self-esteem. Promising a new fur coat for her twenty-third birthday, Adler in a birthday letter dated mid-October assured Nelly that, "You haven't been at all too difficult up to now, and I am convinced that we will experience much joy together in the future. May your charm, your amiability and helpfulness, and your ability to work with others stay with you forever. Don't stop developing your great potential."

During the fall months of 1931, Adler continued to consult actively on psychiatric cases in Vienna. Among his most ardent young medical supporters was Rudolf Dreikurs, who later, as a prominent emigré Adlerian in the United States, often recalled his mentor's therapeutic mastery. On one occasion, Dreikurs requested Adler's help in diagnosing an elderly patient, hospitalized in a local sanatorium for an apparent depressive psychosis. As staff nurses and physicians gathered around to watch, Adler began his psychiatric examination.

He asked the old man a series of standard questions, and the patient started to reply very slowly, typical of clinical depression. "Then something astonishing happened," reminisced Dreikurs. "Adler, having asked the first question, did not wait until the patient in his slow way had answered it; he asked the second question. Again, Adler did not wait for the answer, but went on to the next question."

Dreikurs began to feel embarrassed by his teacher's seemingly incompetent behavior in conducting the interview. "But Adler continued calmly with his questions without waiting much for an answer until, lo and behold, the patient suddenly wanted to say something and began to speak quickly. From then," recollected Dreikurs, "Adler had quite a normal chat with the patient. Adler did not accept the verdict that depressed people had to be slow."

By the early 1930s, Ali had completed psychiatric training at the University of Vienna and, like Dreikurs, began to collaborate actively with her father. Father and daughter often discussed theory as well as specific cases together, and she gained the opportunity to learn directly his gentle, humorous manner with patients. One day, as Ali later recalled, an adolescent came to Adler and confided his problem, "I feel horribly guilty when I masturbate."

Adler looked at the worried youngster closely and warmly replied, "You mean to say you masturbate and feel guilty? That is too much. One would be enough: either masturbate *or* feel guilty. But both is too much."

On another occasion, Ali later reminisced, her father was called into a consultation involving a schizophrenic girl. In Adler's presence, the attending psychiatrist told her anxious parents that their daughter's case was "hopeless." Such a gloomy prognostication deeply upset Adler's sense of good patient care, and he immediately demanded of his colleague, "Now listen, how can we say such a thing? How can we actually know what is going to happen?"

Adler was also able to take time in seeing personally how his work had affected Austria's schools. Although Vienna was suffering during the global Depression, its Social Democratic administration remained sympathetic to educational reform. In mid-September 1931, educator Oskar Spiel and his colleagues Ferdinand Birnbaum and Franz Scharmer were delighted to receive permission to open their officially designated Individual Psychology Experimental School. Outwardly, it was hardly impressive, housed in a run-down building in the city's impoverished Twentieth District. The old high-school lacked adequate heat during the winter, and students often arrived hungry and shivering with cold. But from its inception, the unusual program gained international attention for its innovative classroom methods.

Based on Adler's notions that creativity and self-expression are vital to modern education, students were placed into a radically different learning milieu. Immediately, their desks were shifted from lockstep rows to a semi-circle for facilitating communication. Previously bare walls were adorned with colorful diagrams, photographs, and pictures to complement curricular topics. Most important, of course, was the new style of interrelationship. To help nurture students' maturity, especially their cooperative ability, the Adlerian administrators created five separate "communities." These involved day-to-day group learning projects, self-government, group discussions, peer tutoring, and shared life experiences through trips and related outside activities.

Central to the experimental school was an emphasis on fostering group learning. It was predicated on Adler's impassioned view that most parents fail to instill adequate social feeling in children, and that a host of juvenile and, later, adult problems therefore arise. If individuals could develop superb social skills, particularly empathy and cooperativeness, through schooling, then our entire society would benefit immeasurably. This conviction inspired those working at the experimental school.

Adler was much too busy to become personally involved in the school's ongoing functioning. But one spring day at the academic year's close, he decided to make a surprise visit. Unannounced, he quietly sat in the back of a classroom while the high-school students animatedly discussed one of his recent books. The topic was "the meaning of life," and guided occasionally by teacher Birnbaum, the youthful group arrived at the conclusion that life's meaning is found in creating a caring community. Although the students' parents were economically struggling and their own lives were hard, hope was in their eyes. By the conclusion of the discussion, Adler was visibly moved and, before the astonished adolescents, he wordlessly embraced their teacher.

———

Such promising developments in Austria gratified Adler, but he was glad about returning to New York in January 1932. His residence was the familiar Gramercy Park Hotel, just a few blocks from Davis's Manhattan townhouse and not far from the New School for Social Research. In the three years since Adler had last taught there, the innovative institution had grown considerably. During the previous year, the New School had opened its doors at West Twelfth Street on the edge of Greenwich Village. The neighborhood's bookshops, artists' lofts and studios, and inexpensive restaurants and bars provided a bohemian background for the New School's innovative curriculum. In coming years, the institution gained a reputation among sophisticated New Yorkers as the true intellectual center of the Village, far more so than New York University or Cooper Union, its academic neighbors.

Adler's course, entitled "The General System of Individual Psychology," comprised eighteen Friday evening lectures. Its focus lay on human nature, culture and education, and on such topics as the striving for superiority; the inferiority and superiority complexes; the psychological influence of occupation; love, marriage, and family life; the effect of inborn deficiencies; and problems originating in family discipline, such as those of the pampered or neglected child.

Joining Adler at the New School during this period was his Austrian colleague Olga Knopf. Born in 1888, she had attended medical school at Vienna and initially chose to specialize in gynecology. However, Knopf eventually became interested in psychiatry and particularly in Adler's approach. In the 1920s, Knopf was an active member of Adler's Viennese circle. She first lectured in America in 1931; the following year, Little, Brown published her new volume, *The Art of Being a Woman*. Decades later, Knopf would express gratitude for how her mentor had helped establish her in New York City. "Otherwise," she recalled, "I would surely have died in a Nazi concentration camp after they invaded Austria."

Coinciding with Adler's lecture series at the New School that winter was the appearance of his own new book, *What Life Should Mean to You*. With free-lance editing by Alan Porter, it was clearly aimed at a popular rather than professional audience. Better organized than several of his earlier works for the English-speaking world, the volume blended psychology and moralism. For Adler, social feeling was clearly the lynchpin for all worthwhile human life, ranging from marriage and parenting to academic success and even philosphical contentment. Thus opening with a chapter on "The Meaning of Life," he argued almost religiously that, "Every [person] strives for significance, but people always make mistakes if they do not see that their whole significance must consist in their contributions to the lives of others."

Adler's most readable book since *Understanding Human Nature* had appeared five years before, *What Life Should Mean to You* offered many insights on academic, vocational, and family issues commonly facing adults. His basic theme was that our approach toward life is rooted in early childhood, and inextricably affects the way we interact with parents and offspring, lovers and friends, and even neighbors and coworkers. Writing in a time when

American divorce was yet infrequent, Adler observed that, "In our present day civilization, people are often not well prepared for cooperation. Our training has been too much towards individual success. . . . [Before getting married] most are unaccustomed to consulting another human being's interests and aims, desires, hopes, and ambitions. They are not prepared for the problems of a common task."

Much of the book was descriptive rather than prescriptive. Adler offered his impressions of criminal behavior, learning problems, occupational difficulties, and other forms of what he likewise viewed as reflecting social maladjustment. As in earlier books, *What Life Should Mean to You* rejected possible hereditary influences on personality and recommended revitalizing public education to help raise a new generation with greater social feeling.

What Life Should Mean to You received mixed reviews. The *New York Times* favorably commented that, "Although [Adler] is one of the most eminent psychologists in the world, when he writes about psychology there is no other who can equal him in simplicity and non-technicality of language." But other sources, such as the *New Republic, Saturday Review of Literature,* and *Outlook and Independent,* criticized Adler's effort to simplify and popularize complex topics pertaining to the human psyche. "It is written plausibly and with great conviction," declared the *New Republic.* "Nevertheless, a terminology is not science; nor does emotional analysis suffice of itself to heal what nature and society have injured."

Some critics found Adler's moralistic judgments about marriage, divorce, and child rearing especially galling. To them, it seemed incongruous for a purported scientist in the 1930s to pass judgment on those who refused to embrace monogamy or parenthood as a life-style. In broader terms, they rejected as naive and self-serving his viewpoint that "In all the great movements of the world, men have been striving to increase social interest, and religion is one of the great strivings in this way. Individual psychology arrives at the same conclusion in a scientific way and proposes a scientific technique."

Nevertheless, *What Life Should Mean to You* generally met with positive reaction, and Little, Brown commissioned Adler later that year to write a new book tentatively entitled *The Child from Birth Up to Six Years of Age.* To be written in popular style, it would be aimed primarily at parents and offer practical advice from the perspective of individual psychology. The publisher saw the project as having a tremendous potential audience, and the book might even have preempted Benjamin Spock's famous best-seller, *Be-*

tween Parent and Child, issued a decade later. Unfortunately, Adler found it hard to begin writing his new book, possibly because of an overcommitted lecture schedule. As a result, the intriguing project never came to fruition.

In mid-May, Davis and his daughter Annalee, acting as trustees, opened a special bank account in Adler's name to help manage his professional income. With close to ten books in print and royalties coming from several different American and European publishers, he must have been grateful for such assistance. But the sixty-seven-year-old Davis was prepared to be far more helpful than Adler could possibly have imagined.

That spring, he contacted the board of trustees of the Long Island College of Medicine (today known as the Downstate Medical School of New York State) and expressed his interest in endowing a faculty chair for Adler there. Founded in 1858, the freestanding Brooklyn institution had long been affiliated with Long Island College Hospital. In 1929, the two institutions were legally disjoined and reorganized with two separate governing boards. In March 1931, the school received its new state charter, and its first president, James C. Egbert, was appointed the following year.

Undoubtedly, Davis knew of Adler's desire for a secure academic affiliation, although it is not clear whether other, more prestigious medical schools were similarly approached. Perhaps Davis had not even bothered. As a chief administrator of the Columbia University extension program before coming to the Long Island College of Medicine, Egbert had been extremely impressed with Adler's teaching for the division. In any event, by June 2, the recorded minutes of the trustees' meeting of the Long Island College of Medicine recount:

> Upon reference from the Education Committee, consideration was given to a proposal that Dr. Alfred Adler be made Professor of Medical Psychology, the offer being made by a Mr. Davis who would guarantee payment of annual salary of $8,500.00 for five years upon condition that Dr. Adler be given the appointment, and so long as he remained in the chair during the five year period. The matter was referred to the Education Committee for further study and report.

During the next few weeks, intense negotiations between Davis and the school's trustees proceeded amicably. By early July, most of the major details had already been resolved, and soon, with Adler's participation, all matters were agreed upon satisfactorily. He was to be appointed visiting professor of medical psychology for a five-year term, with all funds provided by Davis. The renumeration from Davis was good but hardly exorbitant; at the same institution, starting salaries for instructors with medical degrees were approximately three thousand dollars per year.

In addition, Adler would be allowed to direct a teaching clinic at the college, with Davis likewise guaranteeing all administrative, clinical, and clerical costs. Obviously impressed with his cordial generosity, the Education Committee reported to the trustees in late September their "full discussion of Mr. Davis and his possible permanent interest in the college."

No documentation is available concerning Adler's initial reaction to the appointment, clearly the most important academic position of his career. By summer, he was back with his associates in Vienna (among his foreign visitors was young Rollo May) and also traveling throughout Europe for lectures and consultations. Undoubtedly, Adler was delighted with Davis's generous and important assistance. Yet, rather strangely, neither Bottome nor any other biographer has ever substantiated the Quaker philanthropist's key role in bringing Adler to his College of Long Island faculty position. Possibly, they felt embarrassed that the appointment had been engineered by a single wealthy American rather than solicited by the school itself.

In any event, Adler now initiated the long process in gaining American citizenship. Raissa, it seems, still had no interest in relocating from Vienna with her husband, and probably remained suspicious of this multimillionaire so eager to promote individual psychology. Raissa may also have regarded her own Marxist-Leninist activity in Austria as a more important cause. Novelist Bottome later recalled that in mid-1934, she was introduced to Raissa at one of Adler's Viennese lectures.

"[She] was a small, compact figure of about sixty, with snow-white hair and uncompromising blue eyes, innocent of all guile, but full of determination. Raissa did not smile at me as we shook hands. It was a great occasion for me, and I may have said so, while expressing my deep debt to Adler's teachings."

But Raissa's swift reply was disconcerting. "I do not agree with all that Adler teaches," she said firmly. "Not that I am against his main principles of individual psychology, but I think these matters have an economic basis and should be dealt with politically, and my husband does not."

Regardless of Raissa's social perspective, Adler's medical appointment made news throughout the United States. Perhaps the most colorful account was *Time* magazine's, entitled "I on Long Island," and published in its October 10 issue:

Pugnacious little Alfred Adler, discoverer of the Inferiority Complex, used to spend a few months in the U.S. each year lecturing clubs, advising child psychologists, and displaying himself to learned institutions which wanted to entice him from Vienna. None won until this summer. Next week, Dr. Adler begins teaching students of Long Island College of Medicine medical psychology. The appointment runs for five years, and puts a big I on Long Island. For Dr. Adler is the scientist of the Ego.

At 62, Dr. Adler is grey but dynamic. When he lectures, he strides to & fro on the platform, wrinkles his nose so vigorously his eyeglasses quiver. He speaks English with an Austrian accent. There is something infantile about his features, something fugitively masked by his glittering eyes and sardonic smile.

From the outset, Adler greatly enjoyed lecturing to American medical students. His required course on medical psychology was not personally strenuous, involving a single weekly lecture to third-year medical students. Generally, the topics presented an introduction to individual psychology, with a special emphasis on common emotional disorders like insomnia, enuresis, and stuttering. From the content of the transcribed lectures, they offered little new material; Adler clearly was taking little for granted among his youthful audience. As reported by the college's Education Committee later in the academic year, Adler's teaching clinic had earned an excellent reputation. But professional jealousy seems to have triumphed, for he disappointedly learned that his colleagues had denied his requests to introduce a nonteaching format at the clinic and to conduct patient treatment.

While Adler was busy at both the Long Island College of Medicine and the New School in April 1933, ominous events were transpiring in Germany. On January 30, Adolf Hitler had become chancellor, and the Nazis lost no time in quickly seeking to consolidate power and destroy all potential opponents. On April 7, the Hitler regime issued the Law for the Re-Establishment of the Professional Civil Service throughout Germany. It specifically removed all "non-Aryans" from civil service positions including the universities. Four days later, the term *non-Aryan* was legally defined to include anyone with at least one non-Aryan grandparent. Almost immediately, many leading German physicians and scholars began planning to emigrate.

The New School's director Alvin Johnson saw an unprecedented opportunity for his institution. Within six months of energetic effort, he succeeded in raising sufficient funds to bring a dozen, and later a score, of Europe's most distinguished refugee scholars to the New School. To accommodate them, Johnson created a self-governing research institute within the New School called the University in Exile. Thus, he fulfilled his pledge of more than a decade before, to build the New School into a major institution of social science thought.

The original twelve refugees who arrived in 1933 and 1934 were chiefly responsible for giving the University in Exile its unique character. Like Adler, nearly all were German-speaking men (there was one woman among them) of secular Jewish backgrounds. Likewise, they were empirically oriented rather than "pure" philosophers, and politically antifascist and left of center to varying degrees. The only psychologist among them was Max Wertheimer, who had taught at the University of Frankfurt. Soon, his former colleague Erich Fromm would arrive in New York as a political refugee, along with such psychological luminaries as Kurt Goldstein, Kurt Koffka, and Wolfgang Kohler.

Adler seems to have had little contact with such European expatriates in the mid-1930s. Unlike many of them who struggled for years, often unsuccessfully, to reestablish themselves in the United States, Adler had come voluntarily, even eagerly, and not out of political persecution. Moreover, thanks to his wealthy benefactor, Adler enjoyed a full-time and relatively permanent faculty position in New York City. He also had countless opportunities for well-paying speaking engagements. Perhaps for this reason, these refugees never became close with Adler, who continued to maintain his own circle of American professionals and businesspeople.

━━━━

During Germany's fateful year of Nazi ascension to power, Adler saw the publication of two new books in his native tongue. *Der Sinn des Lebens* (*The Meaning of Life*) offered fifteen loosely related chapters on such familiar topics as early childhood memories, dreams, neurosis, and the inferiority and superiority complexes. Providing little fresh material to English-speaking readers, its American edition, entitled *Social Interest,* would not appear for five more years.

More innovative for Adler was *Religion and Individual Psychology,* a volume jointly written with Lutheran minister Ernest Jahn. Although interested in psychology, Jahn had been dismayed by Freud's atheistic *The Future of an Illusion,* and in 1927 offered his rebuttal in a work entitled *The Ways and Limits of Psychoanalysis.* "What I considered particularly destructive was Freud's assertion of religion being a neurosis, an illusion, at best an 'oceanic feeling,'" Jahn later recalled. "I saw ever definitely that in many people self-centeredness and striving for importance confused the setting of their goals. And this brought me to the work of Alfred Adler."

Finding quite relevant Adler's emphasis on social feeling (rather than sexual repression) as the key factor in pastoral counseling with couples and families, in 1931 Jahn published another book, *The Will to Power and the Feeling of Inferiority*. Shortly thereafter, the two men met in lively discussion.

"Adler's appearance has always remained unforgettable," Jahn reminisced. "He was a man wholly taken up by his idea, and without a trace of pathos, and yet filled with an enormous thirst for knowledge. At his suggestion, we undertook to present the theological and medical-individual-psychological aspects of therapy, respectively, in a book together."

Religion and Individual Psychology comprised two long chapters, one by Jahn and a response by Adler, who clearly expressed no interest in mysticism or revelatory experience. He shared Freud's distrust for all phenomena that could not be readily explained by mainstream science; indeed, several years earlier, Adler had broken with his German protégé Fritz Kunkel for espousing Jungian-like ideas about a "higher" unconscious. Like Freud, Adler was also suspicious of organized religion for its "power apparatus" and "not infrequent abuses." Realistically, he likewise rejected Jahn's theological view of love as the key to all healing, and commented that, "The healing process is much more difficult. Else it would be enough to surround every problem child, the neurotic, the alcholic . . . with love in order to cure him."

Yet, Adler readily valued certain aspects of religion. He referred to belief in God as "a gift of faith" and praised religious idealism for its emphasis on social feeling. For him, religion was at its most useful and meaningful when it encouraged people to care about one another selflessly. Perhaps with a measure of self-congratulation, Adler concluded that, "I regard it as no mean commendation when Jahn emphasizes that Individual Psychology has rediscovered many a lost position of Christian guidance. I have always endeavored to show that Individual Psychology is the heir to all great movements whose aim is the welfare of mankind."

═══

By early 1933, Davis was undoubtedly buoyed by his successs in creating a university chair for Adler, and next initiated a vigorous effort to bring his recent writing into American publication. Among Davis's agenting efforts were his friend's new German-language collaboration on religion and also his unpublished lectures at the Long Island College of Medicine. The proverbial well suddenly ran dry, however, as in mid-May 1933, Little, Brown's editor Stuart Rose sent a cordial rejection letter. After receiving what must have been an assertive letter from Davis the next day, Rose immediately returned the volume and copies of the Long Island College of Medicine lectures. His terse accompanying letter indicated that, "These do not seem to us to be in shape for book publication, and, while they undoubtedly possess many merits, we can scarcely consider them in that light until they have been put into more permanent form."

But Davis was accustomed to achieving his goals. Undaunted, he submitted in mid-July Adler's new German-language book, *Religion and Individual Psychology*. Again, he was turned down. "The book is a slight one," responded Rose on July 31, "and the publishers are asking an advance of $750.00 which we consider far too high." Because Adler and Jahn had not secured American rights, they had no legal recourse, and indeed, the book never received American publication.

Adler probably felt little disappointment. Returning from an active lecture tour of the Continent, in the early fall he submitted his official application for permanent United States citizenship. With an accompanying photograph of himself, he provided various biographical details and identified his wife, Raissa, and their four children as all living in Vienna. Finally, listing his race as "German," he indicated his current address as the Gramercy Park Hotel.

Besides teaching and demonstrating clinical work at the Long Island College that fall, Adler kept busy by offering two separate courses for public audiences in New York City. Although he was sudddenly experiencing difficulty in bringing new English-language books to publication, generally matters seemed to be going well for individual psychology in the United States.

The same was not true for his movement in England. In mid-November, Adler's well-respected London branch of the International Society for Individual Psychology came to disaster when Francis Crookshank committed suicide. In preceding years, the prolific middle-aged psychiatrist had rejected Adler's and Seif's repeated suggestions that he undergo psychotherapy with either of them.

The precise cause of Crookshank's suicide remains unclear to this day, although a scandal—possibly of a sexual nature—seems to have been its precipitant. A few years after the event, Bottome wrote rather elliptically that, "The tragedy of Dr. Crookshank . . . was that, while accepting the discoveries of Individual Psychology from an intellectual point of view, he had not accepted its moral discipline. . . . With him died the most convinced and the clearest exponent of Adler's psychology in England."

Bottome was not engaging in mere hyperbole, for Crookshank's death left a vacuum in Adler's British efforts that would never be filled. Although many practicing psychiatrists there would remain favorably disposed to individual psychology, no others would feel inspired to devote significant portions of their own careers to advance the Adlerian approach.

═══

But while individual psychology might have experienced a premature decline in England, it continued to grow in Adler's new homeland. In the 1930s, he gained the close friendship of yet another New England philanthropist of entrepreneurial wealth, Edward Albert Filene. Like Davis, Filene was strongly involved in public affairs and had a liberal outlook. He had become well known for establishing the United States Chamber of Commerce, the International Chamber of Commerce, and the Twentieth Century Fund. His famous friends included United States Supreme Court Justice Louis Brandeis and the journalist Lincoln Steffens. Through his frequent world travels, Filene had come to know such international figures as Georges Clemenceau, Neville Chamberlin, and Mohandas Gandhi, and United States presidents Woodrow Wilson, Herbert Hoover, and Franklin D. Roosevelt.

Edward Filene was also a rich man. Indeed, by the time he sought out Adler for therapeutic guidance, Filene's clothing-and-accessory store in downtown Boston was the largest of its kind in the world, and employed three thousand people. Yet, he had long regarded financial success as only a means toward a higher end, and throughout his life he sought appropriate outlets for his largesse. Thus, Filene became a prominent prewar figure among Boston's progressives, vigorously seeking to root out civic corruption through the help of muckraker Steffens and crusading attorney Brandeis. At the age of fifty-nine and still a bachelor, Filene donated his common stock in William Filene Son's Company to the Twentieth Century Fund by means of an irrevocable trust to be dissolved at his death. Later the stock was sold and the proceeds, amounting to some ten million dollars, became the bulk of the fund's endowment.

By the late 1920s during America's boom years, Filene commanded an international audience. Although hardly a revolutionary, he was nevertheless altruistic and civic-minded. In 1927, Filene was one of the few American businessmen invited by the Soviet government for a guided tour. Meeting with bureaucrats involved in distributing consumer goods, he returned with the conviction that communism would long endure but eventually embrace capitalistic aspects. For mildly praising the Soviet Union as an interesting "experiment," he was denounced as a communist sympathizer.

Undeterred by such criticism, Filene wrote books promoting his philosophy that enlightened capitalism—based on modern marketing and distributing—could help transform the world. In 1928, in an illustrative speech before the Sixty-Ninth Convocation of the University of the State of New York, he declared that, "In the final analysis, beauty is the greatest objective of the world. But we cannot teach spiritual truths effectively to starving people. One great way to make more beauty in this world is to make the obtaining of a living . . . so mechanical and so little time-consuming that we shall have time for avocations. . . . This can be accomplished by saving of waste, by more economic justice, by invention and better organization of production and distribution, [and] by better training of workers and leaders."

In 1931, Filene published his most philosophical work, *Successful Living in this Machine Age.* With a buoyant optimism in technology's ability to solve humanity's problems, the book shared Adler's faith in rationality and science as the keys to world betterment. Although internationally millions of unemployed workers were already suffering amidst the worst economic crisis in memory, Filene was confident about scientific management and planning. Under the new process of mass production (he extolled Henry Ford as a hero), "there will be such a volume of leisure as the world has never known. This approaching leisure is already manifesting itself in the eight-hour-day for workers and in the five-day week. . . . We are living in a new world. . . . Mass production is surely liberating man."

During the next few years, Filene gained important access to the Roosevelt White House. Few individuals of his wealth and social class were supporting the New Deal, so those who did were highly valued. As he became increasingly friendly with Adler, Filene began to view education and psychology more than mass marketing as key instruments for social betterment. He admired Adler's sense of idealism and his belief that emotionally healthy people have strong social feeling. Like the wealthy Charles Davis, Filene found in Adler a therapeutic reassurance that money and status were no sin, even during the worst Depression years, and could be valued as means to help others.

━━━

On February 6, 1934, Adler enjoyed one of his most festive experiences to date in the United States. Some two hundred well wishers, including pediatrician Ira Wile and City College president Frederick Robinson, celebrated his sixty-fourth birthday in a lavish banquet held at the Roerich Museum where he often lectured to the public. To Adler, it was a memorable occasion that must have evoked fond memories of similar large gatherings with friends and colleagues in Vienna.

But the Austria of his earlier days would soon be gone forever. Six days after Adler's public celebration, his homeland erupted into civil war. Culminating in a brutal, clerical-fascist takeover by Chancellor Engelbert Dollfuss, the swift events had not been entirely unforeseen by local political observers. Dollfuss, known as "Millimetternich" by friends and foes for his diminuitive size and lofty ambition, had become Austria's chancellor in 1932 after its parliamentary government had undergone yet another crisis. As agricultural minister at the age of thirty-one, he had been the only Christian Democratic cabinet member interested in becoming chancellor with an extremely shaky, one-vote parliamentary majority.

From the outset, the Dollfuss regime was forcefully opposed by the Social Democrats on the political left and by the Austrian National Socialists (Nazis), who were rapidly gaining strength on the right. When Hitler became Germany's chancellor in January 1933, he encouraged an ominous increase in arms and money to his Austrian Nazi allies. Less than five weeks later, Dollfuss seized the opportunity to engineer a coup of his own with the help of the paramilitary Heimwehr, supported by Mussolini.

The catalyst was a national railroad strike that Dollfuss was handling ineptly. When all three parliamentary leaders (Christian Social, Social Democratic, and German National) resigned for trivial reasons of formality, Dollfuss announced on March 7 that parliament had "suspended itself" and invoked an emergency decree to preserve law and order. Urged on by Mussolini and the Heimwehr commander Prince Ernst Starhemberg, Dollfuss banned the Social Democratic militia. Its leaders protested, but to the consternation of the rank and file, they did little more than that.

In June, Dollfuss outlawed the growing Austrian Nazi party as well. In retaliation, Hitler introduced an exorbitant tax on any German citizen traveling to or through Austria. The potent measure was aimed at ruining Austria's tourist industry, which, especially in the Alpine region, depended on German travelers. Then, as the Nazis escalated terrorist and anti-Semitic activity in Austria, Dollfuss and Starhemberg created an umbrella organization called the United Front. It was designed to unite all Austrians seeking to maintain their country's independence from Nazi Germany, and it included many Jews.

Initially, Dollfuss evidenced little overt anti-Semitism. But his Patriotic Front included Christian Socials and clerics who were decidely hostile to Austria's Jewry. Thus in 1934, Edmund Czermak, head of the Christian Socials and the nation's education minister, published a book on contemporary Jews. "We Germans gladly accord full respect to the Jewish people and their national religion," Czermak magnanimously remarked, while adding that, "In our national culture they cannot be allowed to have any say except as guests." He contended that Jews "have their real homeland in Palestine and give to their guest land only a limited part of their love," and in expressing special hatred for assimilationist Jews, Czermak declared that, "the religious German must decisively reject baptism as a [Jewish] entrance ticket."

After several months of unremitting pressure from Mussolini, who was providing major financial aid to the Heimwehr, Dollfuss finally decided to eliminate the entire Social Democratic movement, concentrated, of course, in Vienna. For its own part, the Social Democrats had long been seeking an alliance with the moderate Christian Socials to oust Dollfuss, and in February 1934, all matters came to a head.

On the evening of February 11, the Social Democratic leader Bauer secretly met contacts at a movie theater to plot possible action. But without his knowledge, militant workers at Linz had already been carrying out their own plan. On the morning of February 12, Vienna's electrical workers struck, an act that constituted an agreed-upon signal for a general strike of all industrial and civil workers to bring down the Dollfuss regime. Unfortunately, the zealous electrical workers took their illegal action before Bauer's organization had time to print mass posters announcing the general strike. Because the ensuing loss of electrical power halted the printing presses, many sympathetic Austrian workers never learned of the general strike, while others were already involved in pitched battles against armed government troops.

For the next four days, workers throughout Austria offered armed resistance to the Dollfuss forces. But lacking adept leadership and long demoralized by the Depression, the antifascists failed to mobilize sufficiently to triumph over the government. Resistance was undoubtedly strongest in Vienna's huge housing blocks built in the 1920s under the Social Democrats. During the particularly fierce siege of the apartment complex known as Karl-Marx-Hof, dedicated resisters were shelled into submission by troops of the Austrian army and the Heimwehr militia. A massacre ensued because the few Social Democrats with access to caches of arms had either refused to join the rank-and-file, or had been captured before the actual fighting began. According to Kurt Adler's later recollection, his mother was indirectly involved in the insurrection by assisting the Communists' first-aid division.

Dollfuss's triumph over the Social Democrats was suprisingly quick and complete. On the first day of civil war, several Austrian Social Democratic deputies were arrested, including the beloved Otto Glöckel (president of the Vienna's educational board) and several chairpersons of the city's district councils. Dollfuss immediately hanged eleven Social Democrats and was planning to execute still more when the British ambassador persuaded him to stop.

With Bauer and several other Social Democratic leaders having fled the country, Dollfuss lost no time in destroying their vaunted fourteen-year reign over Red Vienna. Indeed, among his chief aims in crushing the Social Democrats was to reverse decisively their far-reaching program in education and social welfare. Virtually all the educational reformers whom Adler had aided, including his close friend Furtmüller, were removed from power. Possibly because of her Russian origins and more activist political work (she served on Vienna's city council), Furtmüller's wife, Aline, was arrested and imprisoned for several months.

All the Adlerian child-guidance clinics, parenting and teacher-training programs, and curriculum innovations were abolished. As one Dollfuss appointee sarcastically declared, "We've had enough innovation for a while." The internationally admired experimental high school established by Adler's protégés Birnbaum, Scharmer, and Spiel was likewise shut down.

In late March, the Dollfuss government nullified the National Education Law of 1927, which Furtmüller had helped enact. Not only were the Social Democrats' educational reforms completely undone, the new fascist-clerical government went even further: It returned Austria's schools to their status before the basic reforms of 1908, when the *Realgymnasien* and *Reform-realgymnasien* had been established for working-class youngsters. Soon after, Glöckel and his fellow Social Democratic inmates were removed from Austria's central police prison and transferred to the decidedly more brutal detention camp in Wollendorf previously reserved for Nazi criminals.

On May 1, Austria's new Constitution went into effect. Article I abolished the former constitutional stipulation that any change in the document required approval by popular vote. Article II ratified the authoritarian Constitution already adopted. The Social Democratic party was banned and its allies, the Free Trade Unions, were dissolved. Immediately, Social Democratic members were expelled from all legislative bodies, all administrative positions, and all municipal, town, and village councils. Vienna's progressive school board, long sympathetic to the Adlerians, was abolished.

In late July, the country's Nazis attempted to seize control of the government by force. It is not clear how much advance complicity Hitler had in the well-organized effort, but teams of trained gunmen succeeded in the commando-style killing of Dollfuss and more than one hundred police officers before the attempted coup was stopped. Kurt von Schuschnigg, justice minister, became Austria's new chancellor. Only six weeks later in early September, the Ministry of Education issued with considerable publicity an edict designed to establish a "racially" segregrated school system: All Jewish students would henceforth be taught either by baptized Jews or by pensioned Christian teachers. No Austrian government had taken such a radical step toward reestablishing the Viennese ghetto since it had been officially dissolved in 1848. Indeed, Nazi Germany had not yet dared to make such a move concerning its own Jewish citizenry.

Nevertheless, little Austria was still far from true totalitarianism. Although barred from involvement with the newly reorganized public schools under fascist-clerical control, many of Adler's friends and colleagues, including his daughter Ali, were still permitted to maintain private practices in psychiatry and related fields. With scant possibility to emigrate successfully as their mentor had, they remained in Vienna and hoped for the best.

CHAPTER NINETEEN

American and European Vicissitudes

*Courage, an optimistic attitude,
common sense, and the feeling of
being at home upon the crust of the
earth, will enable [us] to face
advantages and disadvantages
with equal firmness."*

ALFRED ADLER

When Austrian democracy ended violently in early 1934, Adler was distressed but not surprised. Under Mussolini, fascism had triumphed in Italy for more than a decade. Neighboring Hungary was controlled by a particularly brutal fascist regime, and the Nazis had already begun transforming Germany into a totalitarian state. For little Austria to fall next in line had not been unexpected for Adler, and like many, he regarded the real question to be whether his homeland would long succeed in resisting Hitler.

Adler was also concerned about his family. Raissa was known for her left-wing activity and was endangered under the new regime. Indeed, as Kurt, who was attending graduate school at the university, later recalled, she was subsequently arrested for her involvement with the Communist party's first-aid unit, and spent several nights in jail. Although released unharmed, Raissa may have begun considering more seriously Alfred's request that she emigrate to the United States. As a practicing Viennese psychiatrist active in her father's child-guidance movement, Ali was certainly constrained by the authoritarian developments, but she did not feel personally threatened.

Vali and husband Gyula had left Germany after Hitler's takeover, initially resettling in Stockholm and then moving to Moscow. Nelly, the youngest of the four Adler children at the age of twenty-four, was still pursuing her career in Vienna as an actress. Neither she nor her attorney husband, Heinz, was politically involved and endangered. Nevertheless, Heinz's father would soon be imprisoned as a socialist enemy of the Dollfuss government.

Only two weeks after the fascists brutally triumphed in Austria, Adler hastily wrote Nelly and Heinz that, "It would be very nice if you both could come to New York and live with me. In addition to your own income, I would take care for your substinence and provide everything necessary for your needs. I hope you both could receive an immigration visa, with my guarantee to support you if necessary."

But no member of Adler's family was interested in emigrating to the United States, and during the spring, he continued his vigorous pace of teaching and cross-country lecturing. As always, he gained media attention for his remarks on parenting as well as education. Sponsored by Cleveland's Health and Parent Education Association in mid-April, Adler offered two lectures followed by queries from the audience. The *Cleveland Plain-Dealer* reported that, "Adler is not a big man physically, but he gives the impression of bigness." Dubbing him the "children's New Dealer" for his zealous child advocacy, the newspaper recounted that he answered "some questions briefly, others at greater length, but all with a kindly courtesy."

Regarding the use of corporal punishment in discipline, Adler emphatically stated: "I would never [physically] punish a child. It's a general rule— and there are no general rules. . . . It is an act of frustration. The child knows you are helpless and realizes that you don't know what to do."

Asked to identify the symptoms of "spoiled children," Adler tersely explained that they are "untidy, finicky in eating, mostly timid, mostly afraid to meet others, and [have] difficulty making friends."

Still other questions pertained to whether youngsters should have allowances (Adler favored the practice), attend Sunday school (Adler expressed support "if it makes children more socially adjusted), or learn to be thrifty (Adler advised teaching thriftiness but not miserliness). Undoubtedly, he had been asked such questions thousands of times before, but displayed no boredom or impatience. As his son Kurt later recalled, "Especially after fascism took over in Austria, he saw the United States as the most important place to spread the teachings of individual psychology. Lecturing to parents all over the country was a useful way to do this."

Still, Adler could occasionally flare up in anger during such encounters. On one occasion, after public lecturing in New York City, he was besieged at the podium by several individuals repeatedly hurling at him the same questions he had already just answered before the entire audience. Pushing his way free from the lectern, he muttered to a friend, "Let them waste their own time, not mine."

On another evening, one woman doggedly kept questioning Adler repeatedly, as he struggled out the crowded lecture hall and into the street toward a waiting taxicab. Without pause, she continued beside him all the way, hurling further questions. As Adler stepped into the taxicab, she began to follow, still pressing him for answers. Before a startled sidewalk crowd, he took hold of the woman and furiously pushed her out of the taxi, which then lurched off into Manhattan traffic.

Such episodes, however, were rare for Adler. He greatly enjoyed lecturing and usually adopted a genial, tolerant attitude toward even inane questioners. Indeed, by the mid-1930s in the United States, he had shifted most of his energy toward public speaking and was pleased to let Charles Davis handle affairs with publishers. But despite his wealth and influence, the Quaker philanthropist was having little luck in advancing his friend's literary career.

In a letter dated May 10, a frustrated Davis wrote, "The very frequent presentation to Little, Brown . . . of various books by Dr. Alfred Adler and which he would like to have published and which have been turned down by Little, Brown . . . leads us to believe that there is no longer any moral obligation or legal obligation to submit further books. . . . There have been so many presented for publication and turned down that it seems quite useless to submit more." Planning to embark for Europe later in the week, Davis requested prompt written confirmation that Adler's legal obligation for submitting new proposals was now discharged.

In a revealing letter dated May 14, 1934, Little, Brown's editor Rose somewhat huffily replied:

> I have your letter regarding the future books of Dr. Adler. It is our feeling that no book has been offered us since *What Life Should Mean to You* that deserved publication by us. As I recall the several books in German offered us for consideration, none of them was new and all either wholly or in part duplicated material of Adler's that has already been published in English. Also, it is to be remembered that when we commissioned Adler to write a book that we thought would be decidely worthwhile, he found himself unable to carry through with the plan.
>
> While we have no legal rights in the matter, we shall, of course, be glad to see anything that Dr. Adler may now write for the American market. Obviously, Dr. Adler's publishing affairs are in such a muddled state, due to the numerous books prepared for German or Austrian consumption and then offered here

by the foreign publishers, that it would be unwise to attempt the reissuing of these books in English.

The following week, Adler and Davis left for Europe together with Davis's oldest daughter, Helen, and her girlfriend Margaret Denham. Adler was scheduled for an important consultation in Switzerland and planning several new articles, but took time to relax. As Denham later recalled, the ship had a public game room with a game resembling miniature golf but played with a billiard ball and cue ball and stick. The first few holes were easy, but the last was extremely difficult. It required a very accurate spin of the white ball so as to set up another spin on the billiard ball and propel it through a narrow entrance into the final hole.

After a few tries, everybody jovially gave up and went out for a stroll on deck, except for Adler, who was seemingly intent on mastering the game by experimenting with every possible angle. After about an hour, Helen and Margaret returned to the gaming room to inspect his progress. Barely gazing at the pair and with a cigarette dangling from his lip, Adler softly said, "*Now*, I think I am going to do it." Holding their breath in anticipation, they watched as he carefully aimed and nudged the cue ball. It rolled slowly into the billiard ball, which then spinning, went right into the hole. Adler stood up, and smiling, put the cue away and walked off. For the rest of the voyage, he never went near the game again.

Later in May, Adler arrived in Switzerland, where he visited the celebrated ballet dancer Vaslav Nijinsky, hospitalized at the Sanatorium Bellevue in Kreuzlingen. Born to professional dancers in Kiev in 1890, Nijinsky had gained almost legendary fame for his spectacular leaps and sensitive interpretations.

In 1909, Nijinksy joined Sergey Diaghilev's touring ballet company (the Ballets Russes) and immediately became its principal dancer. Opening in Paris that spring, the Ballets Russes was critically acclaimed but Nijinsky's performance was considered phenomenal. He showed extraordinary bodily control, gracefulness, and acting virtuosity, with a incredible talent for seemingly rising into the air and suspending himself weightlessly. From 1907 through 1912, Nijinsky worked with the company's choreographer, Michel Fokine, in creating renowned ballet roles for himself. Subsequently, Nijinsky did independent choreography, and until 1917, performed ballet all over Europe, in the United States, and in South America. Praised internationally as the god of dance, he was once asked by an admirer, "How can you stay in the air so long?" Nijinsky's memorable reply was, "The real question is: Why should I ever come down?"

In 1913, he married Countess Romola de Pulszky Lubocy-Cselfalva, and when war broke out soon after, was interred in Hungary as a Russian subject. Shortly thereafter, Nijinsky was forced to retire at the age of twenty-nine with what was initially called a nervous breakdown. Fifteen years later in middle age, he was still hospitalized and completely unable to function in a normal manner. Romola had requested that Adler interview her husband and determine the likelihood of a cure. Probably alluding to Davis, Adler replied that a wealthy American and other benefactors were prepared to finance Nijinsky's treatment. His plan was to transfer the famous dancer to Vienna, where a private residence would be secured for him and there would be an attending psychiatrist trained in individual psychology. Adler also believed Nijinksy might benefit from music therapy, specifically, through piano lessons.

When Adler entered the sanatorium, the attending physician informed him that Nijinsky was always subdued and could not be induced to converse; even Romola was unable to persuade him. During the consultation, Adler found his famous patient to be well nourished and silently interested in his guests. Explaining his optimistic treatment strategy, Adler requested Nijinsky's cooperation in "going voluntarily" to Vienna. But as the attending physician recalled, the master dancer "smiled once in a while, but otherwise maintained his usual stiff attitude." Finally, he indicated that "he would not go," and Romola departed with Adler.

Nevertheless, Adler's single session with Nijinsky may have had a positive effect. For the first time in a very long while, a few weeks later he began responding with enjoyment to classical music. When asked about the possibility for a complete cure, Adler refused to offer false optimism; indeed, no other therapist succeeded in motivating Nijinsky. Although he would live another sixteen years, his condition never significantly improved. Eventually, Adler wrote that "In cases of this illness—schizophrenia—everything hinges on the establishment of a creative contact between doctor and patient. The possibilities of establishing such a contact must first be ascertained, since treatment is a task for two individuals; the abilities of both should be taken into consideration as this is a cooperative activity which is not only of a scientific but also of an artistic nature."

In emphasizing psychotherapy as an artistic endeavor, Adler had an inspiring effect on his friend Phyllis Bottome, and utimately spurred her success and fame. As a novelist, she had long been fascinated by the variety of hu-

man personalities existing in the world and, in the the early 1930s, underwent analysis with Adler's chief German associate, Leonhard Seif. A bearlike
man with a forceful manner, he had initially been a Freudian analyst. After
the war ended, Seif soon became involved with individual psychology and,
with Adler's enthusiastic support, gained an international reputation for
therapeutic mastery. Based in Munich, he lectured widely throughout the
Continent and abroad. With Germanic seriousness, Seif was rarely given to
Adler's unique brand of levity and banter with patients. But nevertheless,
he proved a fascinating figure to Bottome.

In 1934, her novel *Private Worlds* was published in England, and then
quickly promoted in the United States. Dedicated "to Leonhard Seif and
the Munich group of Individual Psychologists, my counsellors and friends,"
Private Worlds was probably the first fictionalized account of psychiatry to
attain best-seller status. Although today the plotline about a love affair between a mental hospital's physician-administrator and his female staff psychiatrist seems rather stilted, the book aroused tremendous interest, and
the following year, was even made into a Hollywood movie starring Charles
Boyer and Claudette Colbert.

Book reviews in the popular and professional press were laudatory. For
instance, the *New York Times* noted that, "It is axiomatic that Phyllis Bottome
is a very skillful story-teller [and] *Private Worlds* is pre-eminently a readable
novel [about life] in a perplexing new world." Adler's pediatrician-friend
Ira Wile wrote in the *Survey Graphic,* "With a frank recognition of her in-
debtedness to Adlerian individual psychology, she skillfully portrays her
characters as struggling for power in terms of their basic drives, in which
inferiority and inadequacy play a dominant role. . . . All those who have
served [in the field] whether as psychiatrist, psychologist, or social worker,
will find this excellent and most readable narration of the struggle for security and happiness intensely interesting and often delightfully reminiscent."

During the fall of 1934, Bottome came to the United States for an extensive author tour arranged by a New York lecture bureau. Feeling over-
whelmed by her newfound success and fame, she seized the opportunity to
undergo therapy with Adler: The key issue, in her opinion, was whether to
devote energy to public lecturing or to continue with writing. Adler suggested that she do both, and when Bottome looked "frightened and unconvinced," he advised "There is only one danger I find in life, and that indeed
is a real one. You may take too many precautions."

Adler usually practiced what he preached to patients. Now in his mid-
sixties, he was undeterred by the growing might of fascism in Germany and

Austria. Although these countries' authoritarian regimes had decimated organized individual psychology, he had presciently been shifting its base for several years to the United States. As Kurt Adler later recalled, "My father was certainly upset about events in Europe, but had no intention of abandoning his life work." Thus, in late 1934, he participated in discussions with several Chicago supporters to launch a new international journal to be published in English.

At the time, the Chicago group was generously backed by advertising executive Sydney Roth. Several years earlier, he had traveled to see Adler, who at the time was on a lecture tour in New York, for treatment of a chronic stutter that seemed to have originated during an unrelated childhood hospitalization. Today, such dysfluency is generally viewed not as chiefly a psychiatric problem, but as an inborn neurological condition exacerbated by stress. Adler spent several weeks working therapeutically to improve Roth's general self-esteem, which seemed to help his speech considerably. Decades later, Roth recollected Adler's inspiring advice: "Sydney, if you have to stutter, then go ahead and stutter. Just don't let it prevent you from doing anything you had intended."

In mid-February of 1935, Adler signed a legal agreement with Roth and his two colleagues, Edyth Menser and Ben Schenker, to serve as unpaid editor in chief for their new Chicago-based publication entitled the *International Journal of Individual Psychology*. The contract explicitly modeled the journal after the German periodical that Adler had been directing for many years; unfortunately, though, Roth's short-lived effort never achieved comparable influence.

For one thing, he and his partners lacked familiarity with academic publishing, and the articles typically lacked footnotes and references. A larger problem was that Adler's Austrian colleagues had little new material to provide, since their child-guidance clinics and other educational programs had been shut down by the fascist government in February 1934. In Nazi Germany, of course, the situation was much worse, and most Adlerian practitioners of Jewish background like Alice Rühle-Gerstel and Manes Sperber had long since fled the country and been living uneasily as refugees.

As for enticing American or English contributors, the new *International Journal of Individual Psychology* was never able to attract much professional interest. Therefore, it almost immediately began relying heavily on translations of previously published German-language articles by Adler or his Viennese collaborators like Dreikurs, Spiel, and Wexberg. Also prominent were reissues of earlier pieces by English-language clinicians like the recently deceased Crookshank, or even by nonacademic figures like Benjamin Franklin and H. G. Wells. Lacking prestigious academic affiliation and published in an oversized edition, the whole affair had an amateurish quality that did little to enhance individual psychology.

Perhaps Adler's advancing age provides another explanation for the journal's difficulties. Two weeks after affixing his signature to the legal agreement with Roth, he was forced to undergo emergency hospitalization and surgery for an infected carbuncle on his neck. Adler had been hoping that the cyst would heal by itself, but such proved not to be the case. On March 2, he wrote to Raissa that, "I am about to recover from a very serious illness. . . . This was a colossal shock for me, who never faced the possibility of being sick." Two days later, Adler informed Alexandra that, "The operation was performed today magnificently. I am free of pain and fever. You can be totally reassured that in three or four days I will be home again and will do my usual activities."

Adler's habitual optimism was quite unrealistic, for his postoperative recovery did not go as planned. A new infection suddenly set in, and in an era before antibiotics, the situation quickly became dangerous for him at age sixty-five. On March 16, a chastened Adler notified Raissa that his illness had been "very serious, but should be over in eight days." But even that estimate proved unrealistic, and it was not until mid-April that his health would improve sufficiently for a medical discharge.

During his seven weeks of hospitalization, Adler actively corresponded with Ali and Raissa. His tone was anxious and demanding, undoubtedly reflecting his impatience with lying in bed day after day in slow recovery. To be passive was something wholly alien. Adler was also worried over a host of major impending plans. The family home in Salmannsdorf had just been sold and was to be vacated in August, with his brothers Richard and Sigmund handling the sale. Ali was scheduled to begin a faculty position at Harvard Medical School in September, and Kurt was expected to join his parents in New York City around the same time. Recently divorced, he had just gained his doctorate in physics, and was thinking of switching to medical study in the United States. As for Adler's two other children, economist Valentine was living in Stockholm with her husband Gyula, while actress Nelly still intended to remain in Vienna with Heinz.

The Adlers' longtime apartment at Domininkanerbastei 10 would be vacated soon, and a host of packing and overseas shipping details had to be finalized. Partly for financial reasons, Adler had assumed a heavy European lecture tour for the upcoming months. His ambitious plan was for Raissa to emigrate immediately to New York, help find and set up a new apartment for them, and generally get acclimated to her new country in time for his fall teaching at the Long Island College of Medicine.

But as always, Raissa was fiercely independent. Reluctant enough about emigrating to the United States, she desired to remain in Vienna until early September. Thus, Raissa ignored Alfred's cordial letter dated March 2, inviting her to meet with his good friends Davis in New York City and Filene in Boston. On March 15, a more testy Adler relayed Davis's invitation to visit his family estate at Cape Cod, "where you will have a wonderful summer vacation and all the possibilities to improve your [English] language. If you don't accept this," Adler warned, "you will destroy all the advantages mentioned above . . . and the possibility to see me, after recovering from this horrible illness not in six months from now . . . which I would regret very much, but earlier."

Apparently, Raissa had neither telegrammed nor written him at all since his hospitalization, for the next day, Adler felt impelled to add, "All this hesitating is useless. . . . You have to come to New York as soon as possible because of all the reasons I pointed out to you in earlier letters. . . . All the difficulties are the result of the fact that you have always planned contrary to my arrangements. . . . Since sixteen days I am in the hospital with a bad cyst. You must have had the letter in which I was informing you of that since a long time. Today, I will telegraph in order to help your hesitating attitude."

Finally, the Adlers worked out a compromise. Raissa agreed to leave with Ali immediately for several weeks, but would return with Alfred to Vienna for the summer. She clearly was uninterested in socializing with her husband's friends or in maximizing her time to learn English before the final move from Austria. Indeed, her only grandchild, Margot, later recalled that Raissa "never learned to speak English well, and usually spoke solely in German to family members."

In a letter from Boston dated April 15, Ali recounted to Nelly and Heinz that, "Papa is doing very well, and thinks that the ship's doctor can change his bandage. . . . The latest news, you will probably already know: Mama is going with him to Europe: she has gotten what she wanted. I think this is good, especially because of Papa's [condition]. . . . I am constantly with foreigners now, and am always very reserved, even when something angers me a lot. I don't have a home yet, and am staying at the Statler Hotel until I find an apartment. For now, please write to me at the Boston City Hospital."

Arriving together in Vienna that summer, Alfred and Raissa took a residential suite at the fashionable Hotel Regina. Situated on the corner of Währinger Strasse and opposite the Votivkirche, the location coincidentally marked the site of Adler's pastoral boyhood in Währing. But busy with teaching and finalizing arrangements for permanently leaving Austria, he had little desire for nostalgic reminiscing about the distant past.

Clearly, the country's mood had darkened considerably. After the Nazis's abortive coup and murder of Dollfuss the previous summer, whatever sparks of cultural optimism that had still existed were now decisively gone. In that year of 1935, many of Austria's leading artistic and intellectual figures emigrated, including Arnold Schöenberg, Ludwig Wittgenstein, and Stefan Zweig. Although clerical-fascist Austria was not the brutal totalitarian place of Nazi Germany across the alps, democracy and liberal tolerance had disappeared.

The signs were everywhere. In the immediate aftermath of the February 1934 civil war, Dollfuss's regime took over Vienna's municipal government and removed fifty-eight Social Democratic physicians from its payroll; all but two happened to be Jewish. Soon medical school graduates applying for internships were required to present both birth and baptismal certificates. This practice effectively barred Jews from finishing their training at any hospital except the Rothschild Hospital, which could only accept a few interns each year. Consequently, the number of Jewish doctors in Vienna dropped below the 50 percent mark for the first time in over a half century. Increasingly thousands of Jews were finding themselves dismissed from municipal and public service positions in education, health, and medicine. Most Jewish journalists were allowed to cover only cultural and sporting events rather than major news. Leaders of the government-backed Fatherland Front openly promoted boycotts of Jewish merchants and the quasiofficial *Reichpost* carried a special page for "Advertisements by Christian Business Firms."

In the domain of public education with which Adler was intimately familiar, matters had rapidly gone downhill. At the university level, numerous books by professors and their doctoral students now dealt with the Jews and their supposedly dangerous traits. Some of these works cited the notorious *Protocols of the Elders of Zion* as a scholarly reference. The situation was no better in the country's elementary and secondary schools. Virtually all of Adler's dedicated colleagues in educational reform—Birnbaum, Furtmüller, Scharmer, Spiel—had seen their efforts swept away. Even worse, the powerful teachers association had become stridently profascist and anti-

Semitic; its journal spoke of "the totally demoralizing and corrupting Jewish influence which of necessity springs from the moral and intellectual characteristics of the race."

Nevertheless, Chancellor Schuschnigg was no megalomaniac like Hitler, and actually cultivated several famous Austrian Jews for political expediency. He reasoned that they attracted foreign visitors and their useful currency, and also enhanced his small country's international prestige. More importantly, since such prominent Jews were presumably free to settle almost anywhere on the globe, their willingness to remain in Austria signaled confidence in its ability to remain independent of Nazi Germany. Thus, it was probably not just Schuschnigg's appreciation for classical music that induced him to offer Bruno Walter the directorship of the Vienna Opera; nor was it purely out of scientific admiration that he sent birthday greetings to Freud. But fearful of handing the Nazis a propaganda boost, Schuschnigg's education minister warned the press that he would confiscate any newspaper that published or even mentioned the event.

"Vienna in 1935 was not the same city that had been our home for three years from 1920," bitterly recalled Bottome a few years later. Then we had found great misery and semi-starvation, but always a stirring towards life and hope. . . . In 1935 this lovely, brilliant city seemed nothing but an empty shell. Dollfuss had been murdered. The ruins of the model workmen's homes that he had destroyed were his monument. Yet it was the Nazis who murdered Dollfuss, not the Socialists; and it was the Nazis who would destroy Schuschnigg. . . . The sense of defeat was in the air and Adler, who loved Vienna . . . saw that it was going to be defeated. 'I shall never return to Vienna again,' he told us quietly. 'It is already a dead city; and we must let the dead bury their dead. Our business is with the living.' "

Adler was not merely speaking metaphorically. On July 23, Otto Glöckel died of heart failure at the age of sixty-one. The date marked less than a year since his release from Dollfuss's detention camp, where, in fragile health, Glöckel had been incarcerated along with Nazi terrorists and without any formal charges. Glöckel's release after eight months had been realized only through the sustained international outcry by such renowned friends as H. G. Wells. Respected for decades as a leading educational reformer and innovator, Glöckel was a beloved figure to many Viennese.

Despite police warning, more than five thousand mourners, mostly associated with the outlawed Social Democratic party, attended his burial following cremation a few days later. For the "crime" of dropping red carnations onto the coffin, several persons were quickly arrested by police. On leaving the churchyard, many more attendees were manhandled and a fourteen-year-old youth was beaten unconscious by officers wielding truncheons. As the furious assemblage began shouting, "Away with fascist brutality!" scores of additional police charged into the crowd and, wielding truncheons, indiscriminately arrested mourners and carted them off to jail.

Vienna's internationally acclaimed Salzburg music festival commenced the following week. "For the first time since 1933," the *London Times* ironically related, "the Salzburg festival was opened to the strains of pure melody unpunctuated by the bursting of bombs, the unrolling of forbidden swastiska banners, or the descent of Nazi manna from the clouds in the form of paper swastikas and leaflets from invading German airplanes." Acknowledging that "Chancellor Schuschnigg has proved himself in the past twelve months a more efficient trustee of the Dollfuss political legacy than his friends or foes ever expected," the *London Times* nevertheless opined that, "he has not yet shown the slightest indication that he is able or desires to repair Dr. Dollfuss' fatal error—antagonism of the great Socialist movement, which is pre-destined to be an all-powerful ally of any regime seeking to triumph over the forces of Nazism."

Although he had been long identified with the Social Democrats' educational efforts, it seems unlikely that Adler was among those at Glöckel's burial, which was probably too public and too potentially dangerous for his attendance. But now banned from involvement with public-school programs, Adler almost certainly was chagrined by dismaying events at the cemetery and throughout his homeland. Sadly confiding to friends that he expected never to revisit Austria, he devoted his professional time toward teaching two courses at his old meeting room at the Café Siller: one for medical students and the other for a more general audience.

For the latter course, Adler highlighted the importance of our early childhood memories and our contemporary dreams for revealing one's personality. The audience would place beside Adler anonymous slips of paper describing their dreams or early recollections, and he would proceed to discourse extemporaneously on their significance. Neither Adler nor his students knew to whom each paper belonged, but several persons afterward expressed their amazement and even awe at his clinical insights.

He also offered lectures on individual psychology for various touring groups of American and English university students. Describing the notion of "the four human personality types," Adler explained that each of us comprises a personal variation of either the aggressive or dictator, the masochistic or parasitic, the melancholic or retreating, and the socially minded or courageous individual. As recalled by Bottome, who rented an apartment in Grinzing with her husband to be near Adler, one evening an acquaintance who taught college in England brought her class to meet Adler informally over glasses of wine. Sitting around a huge table under an inn's trellised vines, the group was quickly joined by Austrian and German students. Each of the three nationalities took turns in singing their traditional folk songs, but the Viennese students had forgotten the words of their *Lieder*. Turning to Bottome, Adler murmured, "It's a bad sign when a country forgets its songs." To such intimates, he seemed uncharacteristically preoccupied and even depressed that summer. "Adler never *shared* his sadness with his friends," Bottome recollected, "still I think he liked to have them with him when he *was* unhappy. "

Undoubtedly, Adler's depressed mood was exacerbated in mid-August upon learning of Walter Beran Wolfe's sudden death in an automobile accident. During the transporting of a patient to a Swiss sanatorium, Wolfe had lost control of his car while swerving to avoid a mountaineering cyclist, and crashed into a tree. Only thirty-five years old, Wolfe had been Adler's most well-known psychiatric exponent in the United States. A prolific writer for both professional and lay audiences, he had authored several books including *A Woman's Best Years,* a 1935 nonfiction best-seller dealing with mid-life issues. With a flourishing private practice on Manhattan's fashionable Upper East Side, Wolfe had also gained respect for directing the Community Church's mental hygiene clinic for poor families. Not only was his premature death on a lonely Swiss mountain road a tragic personal loss for Adler, but it marked a significant blow to his hopes for gaining greater recogniton for individual psychology in his new country's psychiatric profession. Indeed, following Wolfe's death, no American-born psychiatrist to promote individual psychology would ever take his place effectively. Rather, the best-known psychiatric advocates in the United States would eventually become Adler's own children, Alexandra and Kurt, and his former Viennese associate, Rudolf Dreikurs.

By late August, it was time for the Adlers to leave Austria. He requested that Bottome and husband Forbes-Dennis join him for a last day at Salmannsdorf. Apparently, Raissa had made other plans and did not accompany them. Bottome recollected that they spent most of their time in the garden. A little boy was visiting the property with his parents, but Adler seemingly took little notice of him. Late in the afternoon, his dog walked stiffly beside him to the gate, as if sensing this was the end. Bottome recalled that it was the only time she had ever heard Adler sigh.

Patting the dog's head, he commented apologetically that the pet was "staying on with kind people that he likes very well, but I am afraid that they may forget to brush him—and he likes so much to be brushed." Adler gave his most treasured book of songs to Forbes-Dennis and, to Bottome, the last of the garden roses. As they headed to the driveway, the little boy ran down the road and cried out to Adler, "Come back. And stay forever!"

═══

But Adler never returned to Austria. He and Raissa, joined by Kurt, arrived in New York City on a warm day in early September. Disembarking from the *Aquitania,* the founder of individual psychology was immediately surrounded by a throng of reporters, who pressed him for details of his latest views and personal plans. In a story headlined "Idea of Women's Inferiority Immortal Myth, Dr. Adler says," the *New York Times* recounted how the "spectacled lecturer" insisted that American women continued to suffer from a sense of inferiority due to intense social conditioning. "From the very beginning, they are made to feel that they are not on a level with men. . . . There is no biological basis for this feeling; it is merely a fictitious invention of the male sex."

The *New York World-Telegram* reported how, at the same dockside interview, Adler had rejected the popular notions that artists are more neurotic than others, or that people generally are more unbalanced than in the past. "I think that modern Americans are no more neurotic than colonial Americans. And, further, I do not think that either the old or new American is more neurotic than his brother in Europe." In the same interview, Adler told the *World-Telegram* that the world might be a more harmonious place if children were taught right in the home to be helpful rather than burdensome. "I would not care, he announced, "if a law were passed that no child could leave school until he was socially adjusted."

Later in September, Adler was the feature of a *New York Herald Tribune* article occasioned by his visit to a local children's court. Invited by Judge Jacob Panken to spend the morning as an observer, Adler told the press that he had found little difference between American and Viennese cases of juvenile delinquency. "The old idea of punitive correction is crumbling fast, but we have not yet, even in the United States, any adequate apparatus to give the kind of treatment which these cases require. One trouble is that there can't be any rules," he commented. "I've been working in schools, courts, and clinics for more than twenty years with cases just like those I've heard this morning, and every case is still a new one for me."

Even in Adler's long career, it is unlikely that he had experienced much familiarity with a different aspect of child development: the celebrated Dionne quintuplets living in Callander (Ontario), Canada. In October, Adler traveled there by train to share his impressions in an article for *Cosmopolitan* readers. It was part of a larger lecture tour he had scheduled for eastern Canada that month.

Born in 1933, the Dionne "quins," as they were known, had attracted tremendous publicity. After meeting the family at home, Adler offered his viewpoint in a lucid article entitled "Separate the Quins," published the following spring. Although the toddlers seemed fairly well adjusted at the time, Adler was concerned about their future.

> Life in a glass house is not conducive to normal human development. Five little guppies living in a fish bowl may not be distracted by constant exposure. But babies are not fishes. Children accustomed to being exhibited are never happy unless they elicit attention. . . . There is danger ahead.
>
> The quintuplets are not symbols in an equation or guinea pigs in an experiment, but human beings. Science takes a justifiable interest in their development. . . . But if we consider the happiness of the children, it would seem advisable to destroy the uniqueness of their position, and to make them forget that they are quintuplets.

In controversial but prescient advice that evoked widespread outrage, especially in Canada, Adler recommended that the Dionne quins be separated from one another and placed in five different families. Noting that the appropriate goal was not to "create a little troupe of trained monkeys, but five separate individuals," he urged that each one later receive vocational training in accordance with her particular interests and skills. "If they remain together, the lure of the stage or the circus may prove irresistible. Instead of fulfilling their separate destinies, they would, in that case, continue to exploit the biological accident that made them quintuplets."

After traveling from rural Callander east to Montreal, Adler suffered a painful automobile accident on October 26. As reported by United Press, he had been crossing a city street when suddenly struck by a car, and was rushed to a local hospital where he recovered from minor injuries.

Later that week, Davis received a condolence letter from the director of Toronto's Pleiades Club, where Adler had been scheduled to speak:

> Again, may we offer you the deepest sympathy in your anxiety over your beloved friend. . . . When you are able to speak to him about his Canadian visit,

you might tell him that the very anticipation of his coming has helped psychiatry throughout the country as it has not been aided in years. It has brought many together who had differences and an impetus given to cooperation that I think would cheer him even in a sickroom.

━━━━━

During the fall of 1935, Adler began serving as mentor to a tall, outgoing young psychologist who would later exert great impact on the discipline: Abraham Maslow. Born and raised in Brooklyn to Russian-Jewish immigrants, he had recently completed doctoral work at the University of Wisconsin. After an unhappy year struggling financially through the Depression, he and his Russian-born wife, Bertha, had just arrived back in New York City. There Maslow was serving as a postdoctoral research assistant to the venerable Edward L. Thorndike, an educational psychologist at Columbia's Teachers College.

It may have been through his acquaintance, Heinz Ansbacher, now pursuing graduate psychology at Columbia, that Maslow first heard about Adler's Friday evening meetings at the Gramercy Park Hotel. Quite familiar with individual psychology through his doctoral training at Wisconsin, the twenty-seven-year-old Maslow soon became a regular visitor to Adler's informal classes and, eventually, spent increasing time with him socially as well. "Abe talked about Adler all the time," later reminisced Bertha, "and was tremendously excited by his theories."

Indeed, Maslow had conducted his doctoral dissertation at Wisconsin to compare experimentally Adler's versus Freud's theory of the basic driving force to adult personality. Since Maslow's behaviorally oriented department permitted only animal research, Maslow contrived an elaborate study that succeeded in showing that the dominance position of monkeys in their social hierarchy determined their sexual behavior—and not the other way around, as Freud might have argued. That is, the more dominant the monkey (whether male or female), the more active it was sexually. Also, the incessant heterosexual and homosexual mounting that monkeys displayed often seemed to be a form of dominance-submissive behavior. Maslow found that among monkeys, "Sexual behavior is used as an agressive weapon often, instead of bullying or fighting, and is to a large extent interchangeable with these latter power weapons."

From such observations, Maslow advanced an original theory of primate sexuality. He contended that within the monkey social order there exist two distinct but related forces that culminate in sexual relations among individuals: the hormonal urge to copulate, and the need to establish one's dominance with respect to overlords and subordinates. Based on these intriguing findings, Maslow excitedly planned to obtain data through primate research that might enable him to look at human sexuality, such as marital relations, in a new way. He ended one published paper by recommending that Adler's notion about sex and power be reassessed in view of this primate research.

Adler found such research fascinating as an empirical validation of his own theories, and proudly published one of Maslow's research articles in the German edition of the *International Journal for Individual Psychology*. He was intrigued by Maslow's determination to shift his study of dominance and sexuality to human relations; after all, sexology was a taboo subject in American universities of the time. Maslow's plan was to interview college women about their sexual feelings and experiences, and relate these to personality aspects, specifically, to what he called *dominance-feeling* (self-esteem).

By January 1937, Maslow had completed work with about one hundred women and fifteen men. That month, based in part upon discussions with Adler, he submitted for publication the first of several papers on his emerging findings: essentially, that the higher a woman's self-esteem, the more active and varied her sexual behavior. Conversely, women with low self-esteem tended to be sexually shy and inhibited. Although American sexual mores have obviously changed since the late 1930s, Maslow's observations seem fundamentally valid today. In fact, during the 1960s, author Betty Friedan cited his sexological studies to help promote a new approach, distinct from the Freudian, to female psychology.

During this period, Adler exerted a strong influence on his younger colleague. He played the role of mentor well, offering encouragement and advice as requested. Adler also turned Maslow's attention to the idea of social feeling as a basic human trait.

But perhaps inevitably, the two assertive men suffered snags between them. On one memorable occasion, Maslow was dining with Adler at the Gramercy Park Hotel's restaurant and casually asked a question that implied Adler's former discipleship under Freud. Adler suddenly became very angry, his face flushed, and he began to talk so loudly that heads turned in their direction. He insisted that he had *never* been a student, follower, or disciple of Freud but had always been an independent physician and researcher. The very notion that he had been Freud's disciple, he nearly shouted, was a "lie and a swindle" concocted long ago after their break by Freud himself. Maslow, who had never heard Adler speak of Freud at all, was stunned by the outburst.

Although twenty-five years had elapsed since Adler had quit the Vienna Psychoanalytic Society, his early association with Freud remained a tremendous sore point. In virtually all other respects, Adler in late middle age felt secure about his international status. Yet, it seems that no amount of popular and professional acclaim could erase his bitterness in being still depicted as Freud's onetime follower. As one who had always prided himself as a free thinker and self-made man, such a characterization was the worst insult. In order to spread further the truth of individual psychology, Adler would need to maintain and even expand his worldwide activities.

CHAPTER TWENTY

A Father's Anguish

I will mention one last test—the fear of
growing old and the fear of death.
These will not terrify the person who
is certain of his own immortality
in the form of his children and
in the consciousness of his
having contributed to the
growth of civilization.

ALFRED ADLER

Living with Raissa and Kurt at the Gramercy Park Hotel was undoubtedly an adjustment for Adler, but he seems to have handled
it well. Little changed outwardly in his habitual schedule of activities, for he continued to teach and lead demonstration clinics at the Long
Island College of Medicine. Adler also maintained weekly classes at his hotel suite. Psychologists, physicians, educators, and others attended regularly, but no organization ever successfully emerged as had been in the case
in Vienna.

Never drawn to administrative or organizational work, Adler probably
lacked the supportive help necessary to create a viable association in New
York. He generally relied upon a succession of former patients like Helen
Davis for clerical assistance, and rarely held a consistent secretary. Even at
the time, many of Adler's admirers were chagrined by the haphazard way
that he managed his professional affairs during these final years.

More businesslike was the way Adler conducted his extensive lecturing
throughout the United States. By now, he was well represented by a private
Manhattan agency exclusively handling his lucrative bookings. Typically
earning up to two hundred and fifty dollars per lecture (with sometimes
several talks a day) before civic groups and women's clubs in cities like Boston, Chicago, Columbus, Detroit, Grand Rapids, Milwaukee, Oklahoma
City, Saint Paul, and Waco, Texas, he was likely one of America's top-earning
public speakers by the mid-1930s.

Obliged to leave fascist Austria as a political refugee, Raissa tried to adapt to her new situation. She had no friends in New York, and must have felt especially lonely when Alfred was away on lecture tours. Writing to actress Nelly in Vienna soon after her twenty-sixth birthday, Raissa recounted that, "In general, we are doing quite well, but unfortunately I must contradict everything that Papa wrote about me. I am neither enamored with New York nor do I have companions. . . . However, my language is getting better, which makes me happy. Talking on the telephone is getting easier. Kurt speaks very well. His pronunciation is really good. I don't think it will be hard for him to become a real American. Papa isn't becoming one; his travels to Europe have probably contributed to that."

Indeed, Kurt was quickly acclimating himself. Busy with auditing premedical courses and a seminar taught by the renowned Austrian physicist Isidor Rabi at New York University downtown, he was seldom home. Having nearly been denied his doctorate in physics and mathematics by vindictive fascists at the University of Vienna, he was grateful to be resettled in the United States with a new life ahead. Kurt's definite plan was to become a psychiatrist like his famous father and his sister Ali, who had begun a teaching fellowship at Harvard.

On a visit to her in the Boston area that fall, Alfred Adler stopped in New Haven for lecturing. His schedule included talks before the staff at the Yale Institute of Human Relations and also at the Children's Community Center nearby on Quincy Avenue. The next morning, the institution's director met Adler for breakfast and initiated the conversation with a bit of teasing: "[Well], I trust you had pleasant dreams last night." With surprising asperity, Adler replied, "I *never* dream!"

Later, the director would chuckle with colleagues over the episode, but it was not an isolated statement. Although recent laboratory research suggests otherwise, Adler taught at the time that once we have mastered unresolved inner conflicts, our dreams largely disappear. Such a viewpoint directly contradicted Freud, who saw the human unconscious as wielding far greater power.

━━━

As the 1936 presidential election began during the cold winter months, Adler's friend Filene became an important fund-raiser for Roosevelt's re-election campaign against Kansas governor Alfred Landon. Filene, as has been noted, was one of America's few truly wealthy to support the New Deal so enthusiastically, and later that year would address millions in a pre-election radio appeal for Democratic votes. As for Adler himself, he maintained a low profile on political matters. Perhaps he still felt extremely uneasy about how individual psychology in Europe had become enmeshed in interparty politics: first declared an appendage to Marxism-Leninism by German supporters like Sperber and Rühle-Gerstel, and then struck down in Austria by the fascist Dollfuss regime. Meanwhile, Adler's longtime colleague, Leonhard Seif, had decided to keep his Munich clinic operating under Nazi auspices. Inviting his Jewish-born mentor for a friendly visit, Seif offered his personal promise that Hitler's police would not harm him. Adler laughed in response.

He must certainly have felt glad to be established safely in the United States, for the mid-1930s witnessed the arrival of a succession of renowned European refugee scholars and psychoanalysts who were struggling to rebuild their lives in this unfamiliar continent across the Atlantic. Virtually none was as fortunate as Adler in securing a long-term teaching position with philanthropic backing like Davis.

Besides Adler's ceaseless public lecturing, he continued to write for the popular press; editors were usually eager for his well-known byline on psychological topics. His *Cosmopolitan* piece on the "Dionne quins" had generated particular excitement. As the *Boston Globe* reported at the time, "In city after city, people jump at him from doorways, wait for him in hotel lobbies and buttonhole him at dinners by asking: 'Do you really think the quintuplets ought to be separated?' Not surprisingly therefore, unscrupulous magazine publishers sometimes printed excerpts from Adler's books without permission and touted these as "new articles" written by the famous physician. In January 1936, Adler produced a short piece for *Forum* entitled "Are Americans Neurotic?" In European aristocratic fashion, Freud and Jung had declared shallow and repressed much of the bustling, daily life in the United States. But Adler now suggested that it probably contained less neurosis than in other countries because of "better opportunities for useful activity."

Praising American efficiency, Adler perhaps somewhat autobiographically commented how the New World had always attracted "the cream of active, adventurous individuals—settlers, pioneers, people for whom the homeland had grown too narrow [and] limited. . . ." While conceding that "the lack of social interest in different countries cannot be measured exactly," his impression, he wrote, "is that there is not less social interest in the United States than in other countries, [but] perhaps a little more."

Later in the year, Adler had a popular article published in *Esquire* on the rather different theme of, "Love is a Recent Invention." Stylistically re-worked by journalist George Vierick, the piece argued breezily that roman-tic love "did not come into existence until woman was emancipated from her social and economic shackles. . . . Only the enslavement of the machine gave the average man and woman sufficient leisure to develop the more exalted emotions." Insisting as he had for years that love "is a task for two" and requires "an equal partnership," Adler ended the piece by offering eight practical guidelines for achieving "the dyad of perfect love" in roman-tic relations. He stressed that true intimacy involves emotional and spiritual, and not just sensual, compatibility.

Undoubtedly buoyed by the appearance of these pieces in America's mass magazines, Adler continued to seek a publisher for his recent German-language works. In the spring, he corresponded with Harper & Row regard-ing *Religion and Individual Psychology*. Although its editor was cordial and met with Adler to discuss possible projects, nothing ever materialized. Ei-ther from advancing age, disinterest, or lack of time due to extensive public speaking, Adler had long ceased working on any new books. The few excep-tions involved his transcribed lectures, and American publishers were no longer interested in those.

═══

On April 24, Adler stepped aboard the S.S. *Manhattan* bound for London. Raissa and family friend Evelyn Roth (Sydney's wife) accompanied him for the voyage and subsequent lecture tour arranged by Bottome and husband Forbes-Dennis. By now, the middle-aged British couple had become devoted supporters and efficiently organized Adler's upcoming schedule of talks throughout England and Wales. Besides offering presentations before vari-ous professional and civic groups, Adler also gave a series of general lec-tures at London's Conway Hall on "The Science of Individual Personality."

With Raissa along, Adler allotted more time for socializing and cultural activities than was his usual impulse. On May 19, they attended three one-act plays by Noel Coward, with the playwright acting in the leading parts. The second play was *The Astonished Heart*, about a psychiatrist who solves his own desperate love entanglement by committing suicide. Adler found the play quite intriguing, and was pleased to meet backstage afterward with Coward. Although Bottome later alluded to a friendship between the two men after the playwright-actor excitedly read one of Adler's books, histori-cal research suggests this was unlikely.

While in London that week, Adler also met with Romola Nijinsky, wife of the renowned dancer whom he had visited two years before in a Swiss sanatorium. Contracted with Simon & Schuster to publish her husband's diary that year, Romola had requested the London meeting to persuade Adler to write the preface. He readily agreed, later recalling that:

> There were two reasons [I did so]. . . . One was [that] the *Diary* gives a very clear insight into how a great artist, despairing and hopeless, no longer relates himself toward outside social problems. . . . The other reason was to direct the attention of educators, psychiatrists, and psychologists to how much can be understood in matters of mind and psyche, and how often we could prevent and cure. I cannot forget what one of my patients once answered when I asked him, 'What do you believe was the reason that I could succeed to cure you after all these years of misery?' He answered, 'I became sick because I had lost all hope. And you gave me hope.'

Published later in 1936, Nijinsky's diary became a psychiatric classic for its vivid self-portrait of schizophrenia in an immensely creative figure. But for reasons never made precisely clear, Romola refused to print Adler's preface, and instead wrote her own. Possibly, his candid remarks about Nijinsky's vast egotism and selfishness were too upsetting for his wife to accept.

Soon after returning to the United States, Adler left for his second visit to the San Francisco area. Enjoying the opportunity to be with their father, Ali and Kurt accompanied him for the time-consuming train ride, but Raissa chose to remain behind in New York City. Arriving in California in late July, Adler's chief responsibility involved teaching a course for teachers sponsored by the Williams Institute in Berkeley.

Situated on a hill overlooking the San Francisco Bay, the stately building held a beautifully decorated interior of statues, tapestries, and velvet carpets. Outside its marble-pillared frontage were expansive lawns, cool fountains, and trees. Recently shifted from junior college to four-year academic status, the Williams Institute was named after its founder and director, Cora L. Williams. Of the many American educators and health professionals interested in Adler's work, she was certainly among the most iconoclastic.

A native midwesterner, Williams had spent her early childhood in rural Minnesota and received her bachelor's degree in mathematics from the University of California at Berkeley in 1891. She had taught high-school mathematics in Oakland and Santa Ana, and later in graduate study at her alma mater, enrolled in its first course on non-Euclidian geometry. "The greatest freedom of mind and soul came through [my] study of the fourth dimension and the higher spaces," she later recalled. "Of course, people laughed at me, saying 'There is no such thing!' Then the Einstein theory came and everybody was talking about it."

Williams became the first woman to teach mathematics at the Berkeley university and authored several texts, including *Introduction to Absolute Geometry* and *Four Dimensional Reaches*. Eventually, her interests transcended mathematics to reach general education, which she regarded as woefully obsolete. Impelled to actualize her creative ideas, she cofounded the private A to Zed School in Berkeley. Initially, it was designed as a demonstration center for teachers interested in contributing to methods of fostering student achievement through structured group activities. Later, in 1917, she established the innovative and progressive Cora L. Williams Institute.

The Williams Institute had received international acclaim since its inception, and been visited by educators from as far away as Sweden to observe and study its techniques for blending individual and group study. In a 1925 magazine interview, Williams commented that, "The all-important thing for us human beings to learn is how to come together so as to be lifted and not lowered by the integrative process. . . . We are living our lives more and more in the group, or rather, in many groups. It stands to reason that these larger contacts require larger powers, deeper insights, than were needed for individual contacts. And yet we go on educating our youth to think only as individuals."

Articulating her unique educational philosophy in books like *Creative Involution*, Williams eventually instituted a "school for authorship" on her campus, and brought visiting writers, scientists, and philosophers to serve as guest faculty. She had a strong commitment to teaching fine arts, and in sentiments eminently consistent with Adler's, Williams once remarked that, "Education is more than a science, it is an art, the greatest of all arts—the art of creating souls. As there is in every block of marble, a beautiful statue awaiting the hand of the sculptor, so there exists in every child a beautiful soul if we know how to evoke it."

Arranged by social worker Sibyl Mandell, the Williams Institute course on individual psychology involved a daily lecture; college or teacher credit was provided for students. As Mandell later recalled, each day after Adler presented, he would join the class for a leisurely lunch. One afternoon, a woman became indignant at the repetitive fare of sandwiches and hot beverage. Having expected fancier meals in honor of their world-renowned Viennese instructor, she exclaimed, "Dr. Adler, I've told them that it's outrageous to make you eat sandwiches every day: a great man like you."

"Madam," he replied, "if there is anything of greatness in me, it's *not* because of anything I've *eaten*."

Adler immensely enjoyed his second trip to San Francisco Bay area. A photograph taken at the Williams Institute shows a smiling and paternal Adler with his arms happily draped around Ali and Kurt. While his sister sometimes attended the sessions, Kurt spent most of his time engaged in horseback riding and exploring Berkeley's scenic hills overlooking the dazzling bay.

One of Mandell's prize memories that summer was driving her old Ford one day with Adler sitting beside her. Mandell's sister and Ali relaxed on the back seat. Suddenly, Adler began happily singing the "Wiener Lieder" as all listened and smiled. Before summer's end, he definitely decided to return the following year for another teaching stint at the Williams Institute and even made plans to establish his "West Coast headquarters" in Berkeley.

During these weeks, Adler traveled down to Los Angeles for several days. His itinerary is not known, but according to Bottome, several prominent Hollywood starlets became his patients during the 1930s. A magazine photograph from the period shows Adler and film mogul Carl Laemmle genially chatting together aboard the S.S. *Bremen*. Had Adler lived longer, it seems quite possible that he may have become more involved with Hollywood's tight-knit film community, especially after his Viennese friends Gina and Otto Kaus became part of it.

———

Back in New York City with Raissa and Kurt for the fall of 1936, Adler was very excited to receive a friendly letter from Albert Einstein, who had heard him lecture about individual psychology. As recounted by Davis's daughter Priscilla, Adler had been invited to their home as usual for dinner. He rang the doorbell, and after entering, oddly offered no greeting but stood silently in the foyer. Then with a beaming smile, Adler finally said slowly and dramatically, "I have a new follower. Guess who?"

Davis and Priscilla shrugged in bafflement. Then very slowly and beaming all the while, Adler replied: "Albert Einstein."

Soon after, Adler wrote to the renowned mathematician to elicit his detailed opinion about individual psychology's place in modern science. In a German letter dated February 4, 1937, Einstein modestly replied:

> Your letter causes me embarrassment. Although I have had some lucky ideas in one field of knowledge, I must confess that my opinions in others are worth no more than those of others who are also completely ignorant. This is true

especially in the field of psychology because nature has not endowed me with special sensitivities to grasp intuitively the state of the soul. In addition, my knowledge in your field is not founded on systematic studies.

With this reservation in mind, let me tell you how I see you. Freud was the first who has brought the power of the sub-conscious into the light and you have followed him in this undertaking. While Freud has almost exclusively used the sexual desires and the sphere of anxiety as his motive, you have systematically used the complex of *social* sentiments: one could almost call it . . . anxiety about the social position.

I am really convinced that this complex of feelings and of the dreams connected with them plays a role that is not less important than the sexual complex. It is without doubt a merit that you have investigated this essential aspect in greater detail.

Adler's subsequent correspondence with friends suggests that he found Einstein's letter disappointing. Having devoted more than twenty-five years to refuting Freud's emphasis on sexuality, he could hardly have felt pleased by Einstein's assurance that individual psychology offered an equally valuable contribution. But the famous mathematician knew little of theoretical psychology, and most intelligent lay persons in Europe and the United States probably held a similar viewpoint.

During the winter of 1937, Adler kept busy with his usual schedule of activities. One evening at his informal seminar, therapist Marguerite Beecher and her husband offered a presentation entitled "Building Social Awareness in Schools." The topic intrigued Adler greatly and he invited the couple to discuss it more fully in his *International Journal for Individual Psychology*. To the Beechers' surprise, Adler revealed that the short, dapper man sitting on the couch was Edward Filene, increasingly interested in promoting individual psychology. Adler requested that the Beechers send the influential merchandiser a copy of their paper, and perhaps he might fund a relevant project. To the Beechers' delight, Adler soon informed them that Filene was indeed interested in supporting a proposed teacher-training program consistent with their goals. Before any such plan was finalized, however, both Adler and Filene left for their respective European summer activities.

Another talented individual destined to have unfinished business with Adler was Abraham Maslow. The two had become quite friendly during the eighteen months of their acquaintanceship, and one evening that winter, Maslow was attending Adler's informal class as usual. After the lecture, whose topic remains unknown, a heated group discussion ensued, and Maslow offered his vocal opinion. Soon, he was shocked to find himself thrust into the room's corner by Adler, who stared at his young colleague and challenged, "Well, are you for me or against me?" Shocked and hurt by the implications of Adler's remark, Maslow decided not to return soon for another soiree. It would be their final interaction, and one that Maslow would regret for decades later.

Writing to Forbes-Dennis in late February, Adler recounted with customary cordiality his upcoming itinerary for the spring and summer. Reviewing some of his lecture plans, he indicated arrival in France on April 21, and expressed gratitude for all that Forbes-Dennis had done in arranging the extensive British lecture tour, Adler's most ambitious to date.

It would involve several days of presentations in Aberdeen, Scotland, in late May, before journeying southward in June to various English cities and then a week's presentations in London. Immediately after that Adler was scheduled to teach a two-week course at the University of Edinburgh with his daughter Alexandra collaborating; both were very pleased about the mutual project. In July, they would offer two additional two-week courses, one at the University of Liverpool and the other at the University of Exeter. Adler would conclude this rigorous pace with a final lecture in London on August 2, and then sail back with Ali to the United States on the *Queen Mary*. He planned to spend the latter half of August teaching again at Berkeley's Williams Institute.

During May, Adler's latest professional article appeared in print. Solicited by the *American Journal of Sociology*, it would be his final English-language piece. Along with Freud, Pierre Janet, Jung, and Adolf Meyer, Adler had been asked to offer his perspective on the "social confusion and disorganization" afflicting contemporary Western civilization. Essentially, he argued for a new societal institution to foster greater social feeling during early childhood, as "all efforts made until now appear to be insufficient. Medical care, law enforcement, education, and even religious teachings have not brought about the desired results. . . . As I have tried to prove in a scientific way, all failures of individuals and of masses . . . are always failures because of a lack of social interest."

Adler specifically called for greatly expanding public education:

> In nursery schools and in all other schools we could make the children fitted for a greater social interest if they are found to be lacking in it. This work would be conducted by specially trained teachers and well-selected experts. All the schools would then become the center of the social progress of the next generation, who would not only be fitted to carry on a more socially adjusted life but would be enabled to cope with confronting problems better than we are.

315

As for how to achieve this vast societal task, Adler urged that "a tremendous army of teachers [be trained], who would be qualified for the education of social interest, their unavoidable influence toward the parents and families of the children, the spreading of a new spirit in all other welfare institutions and agencies, and in all the religious and political movements."

Clearly for Adler, individual psychology offered the best hope for creating a world based on cooperation rather than competition. But not all his family felt this way. Raissa still believed that Marxist-Leninist concepts of class struggle and the elimination of capitalism were more relevant than notions of childhood inferiority. At thirty-eight, their oldest daughter, Vali, still living as an expatriate in the Soviet Union, shared this outlook. There she was employed as an economist, while her husband Gyula continued to work for *Imprecor*, the Soviet foreign news agency; the two were still childless.

———

All had seemingly been going well for the couple until mid-January of 1937. Beginning then, Adler's correspondence had gone completely unanswered, and he and Raissa had gradually become concerned and then worried. In a March 16 letter to Nelly in Vienna, Raissa anxiously recounted that:

> Our letters and telegrams came back. Vali is not in Moscow. We do not know what is going on with her at all. But I believe that my feeling that she did not leave Moscow of her free will is correct. I am hoping that she is not in some inhospitable area. Gyula is also not at home. . . . Hopefully, he is with her.

By late March, the Adlers began to grasp at straws. Writing again to Nelly, Raissa confided that perhaps they had been only overreacting. Ever the optimist, Alfred had temporarily convinced Raissa that possibly the whole matter was simply due to Moscow's erratic postal service, and that nothing was actually amiss with Vali and Gyula.

Two weeks later, such wishful thinking had apparently evaporated. Fearing for his daughter's safety, Adler on April 3 wrote with anguish to his friend Forbes-Dennis:

> We are now in great distress. As you know, my daughter Vali is since 4 years in Moscow, married with a newspaperman of the name Sas. He is Russian, Vali has been till two years ago Austrian. If she has changed later to be Russian we do not know, but it seems to be a law that it has to be done after 3 years in Russia. Her name is now: Valentina Adler-Sas, Doctor of Sociology.

Since the middle of January of this year, we have not heard of her. One of the many letters came back with the remark: DOES NOT LIVE ON THIS PLACE. . . . [But my sister-in-law verified the address as accurate] We [then] sent some food, which [was] delivered not to Vali, but to [my] sister-in-law.

I inquired at the Russian Consul in New York 14 days ago. He wired my request but I had no answer.

She has been since birth my most intimate child. I have seen her two years ago in Stockholm in the best of health.

She always agreed with me regarding Trotsky as a nuisance, or as I am convinced, a paranoic.

You understand that we are so much in the dark that we are thinking of all possible and impossible things.

If at least, we would like to know where she is, and how she is [and] what I and my friends can do . . . to bring her out of Russia. It would be much better for us than this terrible uncertainty. She is the loveliest and most considerate person you can imagine.

In this terrible need, I thought of you. Perhaps you could do something in influencing some person whose word in Russia would be of importance. It would relieve my anxiety. I do not know how far you could go. . . . She was always very friendly to the present regime. If you mention me, not Mrs. Adler (because she is Russian born), do not omit all my titles. You know it is far from vanity.

Politically, Adler was astute in suspecting that Vali might be endangered for his family's formerly close association with Trotsky. But he probably did not know that her linkage with another Bolshevik leader might be even more directly related to her sudden disappearance. For both Vali and her husband had been friendly with Karl Radek, recently arrested by Stalin's police as a major enemy of the Soviet regime.

The Polish-born Radek was the son of affluent and assimilated Jews. As a young man, he had been close with the revolutionary Rosa Luxemburg in Zurich. Jailed by czarist police in 1906 at the age of twenty, he later emigrated to Berlin. Equally conversant in Polish and German, Radek became well-known there as an iconoclastic journalist of communist outlook. He liked to dress in a sloppy, bohemian style and to tell off-color jokes. It was at the 1910 World Congress of the Second International in Copenhagen that Radek first met Lenin. But it was not until Radek fled to Switzerland during the war to avoid conscription as an Austrian citizen that he first encountered a large group of Russian socialists and became close with Lenin.

Despite Radek's rise to power after the October revolution, he was never elected to the select five-person Politburo. Lenin seemed to regard him as emotionally immature, and Trotsky too seemed uncertain of the journalist's reliability. In 1927, Radek unsuccessfully joined forces with the Trotsky faction to stop Stalin's growing consolidation of power. As punishment, Radek was exiled to the Siberian towns of Tobolsk and Tomsk, where he spent much of his time corresponding with fellow exiles, including Trotsky, and started writing a biography of Lenin.

But in 1928, Radek began to break emotionally from the harsh Siberian life, and decided to shift his allegiance to Stalin. In a public memorandum widely circulated that summer, Radek condemned Trotsky's political views. The following year, he published a laudatory article about Stalin's economic program, to the shock and dismay of Trotsky who had already been deported to Turkey for his continued opposition.

During the early 1930s, Stalin allowed Radek a small amount of intellectual freedom, even independence. He began writing regularly for various Bolshevik journals in a style that never directly criticized Stalin's leadership, but nevertheless showed wit and originality in a bureaucratically controlled press where such qualities had become almost extinct. In 1932, Radek was granted permission to accompany the Soviet delegation to the Geneva disarmament conference, albeit in a minor role and under heavy surveillance.

By the next year, Radek had ingratiated himself sufficiently with Stalin to be appointed an editor of *Izvetsia*, the government's official press organ. The editorship did not place Radek in a policy-making position, but it restored him to the public eye, a spot he had always enjoyed, and it gave him an opportunity to renew his contacts with Western correspodents and even to travel abroad again. It was probably at this time that Vali and her journalist husband Gyula became friendly with Radek. Later, like many Westerners living in Moscow, the couple admired him as one of the few "Old Bolsheviks" still in circulation. His political wit was also renowned.

To ingratiate himself increasingly with Stalin, Radek stepped up his written attacks against Trotsky as a power-mad murderer, and then authored a major piece for the influential American journal *Foreign Affairs* in which he depicted Stalin as a champion of global peace. The following year, Radek extolled Stalin in *Pravda* and other periodicals as the most glorious leader the party, the Soviet Union, and the entire world had ever known. As a reward, Stalin gave Radek further important assignments; these included disseminating "socialist realism" at the First Soviet Writer's Congress in 1934, and in 1935, helping to draft the new Soviet Constitution.

Outwardly, Radek's career was blossoming. But in 1934, Stalin decided for reasons that remain historically unclear to purge the Bolshevik party and eliminate all who showed a willingness—or even the slightest potential—to challenge him. Initially, Radek heartily joined in the sweeping campaign engineered by Stalin, but probably saw that his own chance of survival was dim. At the top party levels where Radek moved, the criteria for liquidation were clearcut: long-standing (that is, pre-Stalin) revolutionary commitment and past involvement in the international socialist movement. Both factors clearly applied to Radek.

On December 1, 1934, popular Politburo member Sergei Kirov was assassinated in a plot that historians now credit to Stalin himself. To uncover and destroy whom he described as counterrevolutionary enemies of the Soviet Union, Stalin immediately unleashed what came to be known as the Great Terror. Within days, dozens of people imprisoned on unrelated political charges were shot in Kiev, Leningrad, Minsk, and Moscow. The following month, the first political-criminal trial of key Bolshevik leaders, including Lev Kamenev and Grigory Zinoviev, was initiated. In August 1936, these and fourteen other prominent party figures were retried for additional crimes, including directly plotting Kirov's murder, in a far more grotesque show trial held in Moscow. Tortured to extract confessions and deprived of the right to independent counsel, most defendants were immediately shot after the proceedings.

Radek must have been alarmed that the accused had named him as having joined in plans to overthrow the government. By now, rumor also had it that Radek was the originator of every anti-Stalin joke circulating in Russia. In September, his popular articles suddenly ceased appearing in the Soviet press, and on October 7, *Pravda* announced what many now suspected: Radek had been arrested and would stand trial for treason.

Brought to trial on January 24, 1937, Radek confessed to even the most ludicrous charges. He proclaimed prior knowledge of virtually every anti-Stalinist group said to exist in the Soviet Union, and recounted in vivid detail an incredible alleged plot by Trotsky's supporters to seize control of the country by maneuvering it into a disastrous international war and then installing him as supreme leader. By testifying to such farfetched intrigue, Radek may have been seeking to save himself from a death sentence or simply indicating to foreign observers that the whole trial was a farce.

Although his ten-year prison sentence seemed surprisingly light to foreigners, Radek's confession hardly caused a halt in the Great Terror permeating even the highest levels of the Soviet system. Of the thirty-three men who served in the Politburo between 1935 and 1938, fifteen were executed or died while imprisoned, two committed suicide, and two were assassinated. Radek himself disappeared immediately after the trial, and was never heard from again. The Soviet government rendered him a nonperson, that is, obliterated all references to his name as though he had never existed. For decades after, rumors circulated about Radek's fate. Most historians now believe that he died in prison after only two years.

About such matters in the Soviet Union, Adler knew only what he read in newspapers like the *New York Times*. But having long despised the Bolsheviks' predilection for terror as an instrument of social policy, he must have suspected the worst about Vali's disappearance. Before long, the sixty-six-year-old Adler began to have trouble sleeping at night, and his health began to deteriorate. As Kurt, then living with him, later emphasized, "My father had always been very vigorous and strong. All this endless worrying about Vali affected him greatly."

Just before leaving for his European lecture tour in late April, Adler suddenly developed a severe cold with flulike symptoms. According to his psychiatric colleague Frederic Feichtinger at Long Island College of Medicine, "[Adler] stayed away from the clinic and hospital for several days, which was very unusual for him. When he came back to work, he looked very tired, and I asked him how he felt. He then told me that, in addition to having a cold, he was coughing up blood." Alarmed, Feichtinger urged his colleague to see a doctor immediately for a complete checkup before embarking for Europe. But with a kindly smile, Adler replied, "Look, I'll tell you one thing: don't ever worry about me. Everything will be all right."

He then confided his new plan to open a private medical office in New York for the first time, instead of seeing patients in his sitting room at the Gramercy Park Hotel. Now that he was living with Kurt and Raissa, they all probably felt the need for more space. Inviting Feichtinger and another faculty colleague to join him, Adler advised, "Look for an office, and when I come back, we'll start our private practice."

———

Sailing for France together in mid-April, the Adlers continued to hope desperately for word about Vali. With Raissa remaining in familiar Paris where she spoke the language and had friends, Alfred began what was probably the most demanding lecture tour of his life: nearly ten continuous weeks of engagements through France, Belgium, Holland, and then over to Great Britain. As usual, he enjoyed speaking about individual psychology to professional and civic audiences, but his daughter's disappearance continued to induce anxiety. In a representative letter mailed from Holland to Nelly, he wrote on April 29, "Vali causes me sleepless nights. I am surprised how I can endure it." Some ten days later, in a letter to Forbes-Dennis, Adler recounted that he had already given thirty lectures, and that he hoped to gain news about his oldest daughter's whereabouts. On May 18, in another postcard to his Scottish friend, Adler boasted, "Tomorrow I finish my 42nd lecture. It has been very easy for me."

But after presenting a talk at the Child Study Association in the Hague, Adler felt chest pains and phoned his medical colleague Joost Meerlo. Accompanied by a cardiologist, Meerlo promptly arrived at the hotel. Although Adler's pain had subsided, the specialist advised an immediate cardiological evaluation and complete rest. But Adler was determined to maintain his relentless lecturing pace and departed for England the next day.

During his three days of public lectures in the London area, Adler hosted interviews in his hotel room with local journalists seeking something enticing for readers. One reporter knew particularly little about psychology and asked presumptuously, "Dr. Adler, do you mind if I ask a peculiar question? Are you especially fond of sex?" Staring at the man curiously for a moment, Adler evenly replied: "In my psychology, we do not pick our parts. We look at a human being as a whole. Since sex is a function belonging to the life of man and natural to it, we accept it as such—but perhaps I should not call it my *favorite* function!"

Another journalist anxiously asked, "Do you think my son's beating me at chess means he's *really* got a better brain than I have?" Soothingly, Adler answered that, "It might not be so. I myself have frequently been beaten by men who I do not suppose were any more intelligent than myself. I have even known quite stupid people who played chess well."

After the reporters left, Adler smilingly turned to Bottome, who had observed the entire scene, and laughed, "What do you suppose those fellows made of all we tried to tell them?" But his mood that week was not all levity. After speaking before hundreds at the University of London, he found himself surrounded on the lecture platform by friends and well-wishers. Among them was Ernest Papanek, an Austrian educator whom Adler knew fairly well. "Did you now leave Vienna for good?" he asked Papanek.

"No," was Papanek's swift reply. "My family is still living there, and I hope to return soon and join them."

Adler stared with astonishment and then said, "Are you crazy? Take your family out immediately and go to the United States. Number one: the Nazis will soon be in Vienna. Number two: war will come. And number three: the United States is the best place not only to live, but also to work."

Bottome and Forbes-Dennis accompanied Adler for his overland trip to

Aberdeen, Scotland. There, he was scheduled to offer four days of lectures before medical students and faculty, student teachers and their professors, and others associated with the University of Aberdeen. His host was psychology professor Rex Knight, who came to greet Adler at the Caledonia Hotel. After exchanging mutual greetings in the lobby, the two men sat down briefly to chat on a sofa. Suddenly, a handsome young man swaggered over. "I hear that you two gentlemen are psychologists. I bet there's nothing that either of you can tell me about myself."

Knight looked quizzically to Adler for an answer, who raised his eyes and gazed deliberately at the young man. "Yes, I think there's something that I can tell you about yourself." As the stranger smiled expectantly, Adler continued. "You're very vain."

"Vain!" was the startled reply. "Why should you think that I'm vain?"

"Isn't it vain," Adler said simply, "to come up to two unknown gentlemen sitting on a sofa and ask them what they think about you?"

As the young man left baffled, Adler turned back to Knight and commented, "I've always tried to make my psychology simple. I would perhaps say that all neurosis is vanity, but that might be too simple to be understood."

Following his lectures of May 27, Adler penned a quick letter to Raissa in Paris, revealing his new plan to find Vali's whereabouts. With Davis providing the funds, he would travel personally to Moscow and finally put an end to all their anxious speculation. Later that evening, Adler suggested to Forbes-Dennis that they relax a bit by going to a movie. Initially, his friend was reluctant, wanting to do further planning for the upcoming lecture of England, but Adler was gently adamant. As Bottome later recalled, the two men went off cordially together and saw a film entitled *The Great Barrier*. It dramatized how a modern tunnel had been excavated through the American Rocky Mountains, and how, overcoming numerous accidents and setbacks, the dedicated engineers were finally able to achieve their goal. Adler found *The Great Barrier* very appealing. Having risen from lower-middle-class obscurity to international acclaim in championing his psychological system, Adler may have viewed the movie as an apt metaphor for his own, full life.

The fourth and final day of Adler's lecture series at the University of Aberdeen was Friday, May 28. He was scheduled to travel southward from Scotland immediately afterward for speaking engagements in the cities of York, Hull, and Manchester, before returning to London, where Ali was planning to meet him in about ten days for their joint college teaching.

After dining alone for breakfast, Adler decided to leave the hotel for a walk. A moment later, he collapsed. A police ambulance was called, and found him still breathing but lying unconscious on the Union Street pavement. He was lifted onto the stretcher, and the ambulance sped off. A few minutes later, Adler while en route to the local hospital died of a heart attack. He was sixty-seven years old.

News of Adler's demise reverberated throughout the world. In his native Vienna, the *Neue Freie Presse*'s detailed obituary was probably the first to bring the shocking news to admiring compatriots as well as longtime opponents. The obituary praised him as a "unique thinker, whose theories have for decades been at the center of public discussion and [which] have found as many spirited supporters as embittered opponents. . . . Alfred Adler's name and his theories have penetrated far beyond the borders, not only of today's Austria, but also those of the old monarchy. In England and especially America, he is counted as one of the famous learned Austrians."

In England, the *London Times* traced Adler's influential career through his latest lecture tour. Writing in his *New English Weekly*, editor Mairet extolled Adler's emphasis on education as a force for social improvement, and added that, "He has done more: his psychology is in itself an outline of ethics . . . of almost a Confucian simplicity and realism."

Across the Atlantic, United Press likewise covered the story of Adler's sudden death in Scotland. The news bulletin noted that "[he] ranked with Sigmund Freud as one of the world's great psychologists" and mainly highlighted the stormy relationship between the two thinkers.

The *New York Times* was similar to its London counterpart in offering a detailed and balanced account of Adler's influential career. Several days later, the *New York Times* took the occasion of his death to write a broader feature about psychoanalysis and its apparent decline in popularity compared to communism among America's intelligentsia. The *Times* sarcastically observed that, "In the high tide of psychoanalysis, its disciples were certain that it was a new science; now they are beginning to doubt whether it was really a science or just a way of insulting your friends with impunity."

Perhaps the most intriguing of the American obituaries was published by the *New York Herald Tribune*. Like most accounts, it labeled Adler as the "father of the inferiority complex" and as a member, with Freud and Jung, of the influential "trinity of what was to become almost as much a new religion as a new science." These three figures and their many adherents, the *Tribune* remarked, "were to remake the mental surfaces of their times and leave an impression on civilization fairly comparable . . . to that with which Charles Darwin had devastated a preceding generation."

"Adler, who rejected the specific apparatus of psychoanalysis, whose views were less dogmatic and more fluid than Freud's, may have helped to correct some of the worser effects of the school, while he helped to spread its general gospel," suggested the *Tribune*. "Standing somewhere between Freud, the scientist, and Jung, the prophet, he performed an invaluable service in the pioneer labor of this formidable trinity. He leaves his monument, as will the others, in the world around him."

With Raissa and Ali, Kurt and Nelly, and many friends throughout Europe and the United States converging on tiny Aberdeen, the funeral service was held at King's College Chapel on June 1.

The Trap of Personality

Not all were saddened by the news of Adler's death. Back in Vienna, an ailing Freud was pleased that he had outlived his younger and longtime foe. No doubt, Freud felt irritated by the *Neue Freie Presse*'s laudatory obituary, for more than a quarter century after their bitter break, he still hated Adler for having dared attempt a rival psychological movement. When Arnold Zweig expressed regret about Adler's demise, Freud caustically wrote that, "For a Jewish boy from a Viennese suburb, a death in Aberdeen, Scotland is an unprecedented career and a proof of how far he had come. Truly, his contemporaries have richly rewarded him for his service in having contradicted psychoanalysis."

Such professional jealousy and enmity soon became eclipsed by much larger world events. On March 11th, 1938, the Nazis invaded Austria and quickly took over the country. Several of Adler's medical colleagues, like Rudolf Dreikurs and Olga Knopf, had already heeded their mentor's advice to settle in the United States. Others active in his Viennese association, like Seidler and Sicher, left their homeland for freedom immediately after Hitler's takeover.

Still others were less fortunate. Aline and Carl Furtmüller first fled to France and then Spain, where they were imprisoned for several months; they finally reached the United States before its involvement in World War II. Many perished in Nazi concentration camps throughout Europe, among them Adler's longtime associates Margaret Hilferding and David Oppenheim, and his own sister Irma.

When the war ended, a few of Adler's non-Jewish associates resumed their professional work in Austria. Birnbaum and Novotony helped in the restarting of the original German-language edition of the *International Journal for Individual Psychology* and began to hold regular meetings. With Furtmüller returning to assume directorship of the Pedagogical Institute, the array of school-related programs that Adler had pioneered in establishing slowly revived and expanded. But most of his initial circle of ardent educational reformers, including Furtmüller and Birnbaum, died soon after the war.

In Great Britain, no really significant individual psychology movement lasted beyond Crookshank's death in 1933. While Adler's two lecture tours in 1936 and 1937 had generated considerable excitement, it was in retrospect mainly centered around his own personality and international reputation. After his death, only a modest effort was sustainable for Adlerian psychology in the British Isles.

In the United States where Adler had spent most of his final decade, the situation was essentially comparable. The Chicago-based *Journal of Individual Psychology* ceased publication within months of Adler's demise, and many of his books soon went out of print. In this sense, his extensive publishing output, media coverage, and worldwide speaking engagements were illusory. After his death, it became obvious how much of individual psychology as an intellectual movement outside Austria had been dependent upon its energetic creator to attract and hold true interest.

In this regard, the idealistic Adler fell into the "trap of personality," a trap largely of his own making. He was so immediately successful in attracting favorable American audiences and media attention that he failed to see that the excitement largely centered around his own genial, charismatic personality, and not his theoretical system. The same was true for Adler's therapeutic approach. Wherever he practiced or consulted, even sophisticated patients like Davis and Filene were greatly impressed with his clinical touch. But it was not Adler's treatment methodology they prized, but his own qualities as a master therapist: his warmth, optimism, and ability to inspire them to accomplish their best amidst life's challenges.

Ironically, therefore, a system that called itself *individual psychology* ultimately hinged on the force of a single individual, its founder. Perhaps Adler was too modest to see this accurately; perhaps its implications were too troubling as he aged in a foreign land. Possibly, no one among his ardent following had the courage to tell him.

This situation occurred for several reasons that lay beyond Adler's control. He had long been dogged by followers who sought to subordinate his system to international power politics. The triumph of Nazism and Austrian fascism quickly destroyed the genuine movements he had laboriously established in those countries. By then relocated to the United States, Adler was already over sixty and lacked the loyal professional allies of his Viennese years. Also, America in the 1930s was mired in the Depression; the zeitgeist had shifted decisively away from psychology and toward economic-political concerns like the New Deal for solving society's pressing problems.

Nevertheless, Adler's emphasis on democratizing psychological insights has remained a powerful influence through the present day. Far more than either Freud or Jung, with whom he will probably always be linked historically, Adler was energetically involved in bringing his ideas into the everyday home and classroom; there, the greatest numbers of people could benefit. The triad of methods that he helped to popularize—self-help, parent training, and teacher training—have all been gaining increased acceptance in recent years. While probably decrying the commercialization of such efforts today, Adler would be pleased by the unprecedented availability of psychological knowledge through books, magazines, newspapers, and electronic media to help individuals, couples, and families.

Of course, many of Adler's specific ideas have become absorbed into the scientific and even cultural mainstream. These have particularly included such concepts as compensation and over-compensation, the effect of birth order upon personality, and the role of early feelings of inferiority vs. self-esteem in determining our later success in school, social relations, and career achievement. His key notion that marriage and parenting always involve power issues has gained wide credence, especially with the emergence of family therapy as a special field. Almost without exception, though, such insights have been rarely credited to Adler and his actual writings seldom read.

Yet, Adlerian psychology did not altogether disappear in the years immediately following its founder's demise. Several biographical accounts, including a semiauthorized work by novelist Bottome, helped keep his name in the public eye. A posthumous translation of *Der Sinn des Lebens* (The Meaning of Life) was translated and successfully published as *Social Interest* in 1938. Two years later, Dreikurs, based in Chicago, established an active local group and also an international newsletter for individual psychology. Over time, the publication, the *Journal of Individual Psychology*, grew in the 1950s to become a well-respected professional journal, broadly advancing the new humanistic approach developing in the United States. Its leading theorists included Rollo May, Carl Rogers, and Abraham Maslow, all three of whom later acknowledged their intellectual debt to Adler. They highlighted his philosophical stance that human beings are always goal-directed and must therefore be understood as more than bundles of biological impulses.

As Maslow declared shortly before his own death in 1970, "For me, Alfred Adler becomes more and more correct year by year. As the facts come in, they give stronger and stronger support to his image of man . . . especially . . . to his holistic emphasis."

Returning to live in Vienna after surviving a Nazi concentration camp, Viktor Frankl achieved great influence in developing existential psychiatry, or what he calls *logotherapy*. Frankl admiringly described his former mentor as "the man who was the first creatively to oppose Sigmund Freud. What he, in so doing, achieved and accomplished was no less than a Copernican switch. No longer could man be considered as the product, pawn and victim of drives and instincts . . . Beyond this, Alfred Adler may well be regarded as an existential thinker and as a fore-runner of the existential-psychiatric movement." In a similar vein, the influential literary critic Harold Bloom has described Adler as "the first to argue that the neurotic is not suffering from his past, he is creating it."

Unfortunately, Adler's personal American friends generally did little to promote his system. Edward Filene died in 1937 before he could support the types of teacher-training programs the New York Adlerians were seeking to establish. Charles Davis never ceased quoting his beloved Viennese friend, but turned to other causes in the postwar era, particularly world government and nuclear disarmament. At the age of eighty-three, Davis sought to generate publicity for these issues by seeking the Republican nomination for president in 1948. After a period of declining health, he died in 1951.

As emigrés, Alexandra and Kurt Adler developed successful psychiatric careers, and in the 1950s, helped sustain a small but viable international organization for individual psychology. Still in existence, it continues to attract professionals, especially in the United States and Central Europe where their father was most active. Heinz and Rowena Ansbacher, based at the University of Vermont, were probably the most important American academicians to place Adler's work in historical and theoretical perspective. They coedited three major anthologies of Adler's diverse writings. Although now in his early nineties, Heinz Ansbacher continues his prolific career explicating Adlerian concepts for contemporary psychology.

Daughter Nelly, divorced from Heinz, emigrated to the United States after the war. She remarried and led a happier life in her new homeland, but did not gain much success with her acting career. Raissa outlived her famous husband by nearly twenty-five years. She settled in New York City and enjoyed correspondence with prominent political and cultural figures. She led a quiet existence, near Kurt, who remarried, and his daughter Margot, the only direct descendant of Alfred Adler.

Valentine's situation in the Soviet Union remained unknown for many years. In disheartening news too late for her father, Senator Henry Cabot Lodge Jr. of Massachussetts (serving on the United States Senate's Committee on Military Affairs) relayed information in late 1937 that Vali had been arrested by Stalin's security police on January 20 of that year. Charged with espionage, she was languishing in a Moscow prison whose officials were firmly rebuffing all outside attempts to provide food or communicate with her. In the same letter to the Adlers' attorney in Boston, Lodge chillingly reported that, "Practically every member of the former local Austrian colony, which numbered over two hundred, is now imprisoned in the Soviet Union, and that sixty-nine . . . have been arrested since September. The Austrian Legation has been unable to determine whether these persons are being detained in prison, have been sent to Siberia, or shot."

Approximately ten years after Valentine's disappearance, the Adler family finally succeeded in discovering her fate. With Albert Einstein serving as an intermediary between the Adlers and Stalin's government, the abhorrent truth was revealed: In approximately 1942, Vali had died in a Siberian prison camp at the age of forty-four. It is difficult to say how Adler would have taken the news intellectually. In his optimistic system of individual psychology, there was little effort devoted to understanding the inner subtleties of a Hitler or Stalin.

In recent years, Adler's specific work has begun making a definite comeback. In the United States and Germany, two international journals offer interdisciplinary articles rooted in individual psychology. Several of Adler's books have been reprinted in new editions, and efforts are now underway to translate into English and publish many of his earlier German-language articles. A number of his theoretical notions are being rediscovered and empirically validated, such as the adult significance of our earliest childhood memories. His emphasis on the father-child bond as an important aspect of healthy family life is gaining widening social relevancy as men and women seek new patterns of relationship. In this regard, Adler stood virtually alone among his European colleagues in calling for a radical change in the debilitating gender roles within the family and workplace. His longtime advocacy of incorporating character building (specifically, fostering greater social feeling) in education is likewise proving prescient, as violent juvenile delinquency has begun affecting the very climate of many public schools.

Today, Adlerian institutes and therapeutic training centers are growing modestly throughout the United States, Central Europe, and elsewhere. Although he surely would be dissatisfied with Freud's unquestionably greater impact upon Western civilization, it seems likely that Adler would be content to see how much of his impassioned life's work has proven beneficial to the world.

References

BOOKS BY ALFRED ADLER

A Study of Organ Inferiority and its Psychical Compensation: A Contribution to Clinical Medicine (original German, 1907). Translated by S. E. Jellife. New York: Nervous Mental Diseases Publishing Company, 1917.

The Neurotic Constitution: Outline of a Comparative Individualistic Psychology and Psychotherapy (original German, 1912). Translated by B. Glueck and J. E. Lind. New York: Moffat, Yard, 1917.

Heilen und Bilden: Arzlich-Padagogische Arbeiten des Vereins für Individualpsychologie (Healing and Education: Medical-Educational Papers of the Society for Individual Psychology). Munich: Reinhardt, 1914. With Carl Furtmüller. Published in German.

The Practice and Theory of Individual Psychology (original German, 1922). Translated by P. Radin. London: Routledge Kegan Paul, 1925.

Understanding Human Nature (original German, 1927). Translated by Walter B. Wolfe. New York: Greenberg, 1927.

The Case of Miss R: The Interpretation of a Life Story (original German, 1928). New York: Greenberg, 1929.

Individualpsychologie in der Schule: Vorlesungen für Lehrer und Erzieher (Individual Psychology in the School: Lectures for Teachers and Educators). Leipzig: Hirzel, 1929. Published in German.

Guiding the Child: On the Principles of Individual Psychology (original German, 1929). Edited by Alfred Adler, translated by Benjamin Ginzburg. New York: Greenberg, 1930.

Problems of Neurosis: A Book of Case Histories. Edited by Philip Mairet. London: Routledge Kegan Paul, 1929.

The Science of Living. Edited by Benjamin Ginzburg. New York: Greenberg, 1929.

The Education of Children. Translated by Eleanor and Friedrich Jensen. New York: Greenberg, 1930.

The Pattern of Life. Edited by Walter B. Wolfe. New York: Greenberg, 1930.

The Problem Child: The Life Style of the Difficult Child as Analyzed in Specific Cases (original German, 1930). Translated by G. Daniels. New York: Capricorn Books, 1963.

What Life Should Mean to You. Edited by Alan Porter. Boston: Little, Brown, 1931.

Religion und Individualpsychologie (Religion and Individual Psychology). Vienna,

Leipzig: Passer, 1933. With Ernst Jahn. For partial English translation, see: *Superiority and Social Interest,* 1964.

Social Interest: A Challenge to Mankind (original German, 1933). Translated by J. Linton and R. Vaughan. London: Faber & Faber, 1938.

The Individual Psychology of Alfred Adler: A Systematic Presentation in Selections from his Writings. Edited by Heinz L. and Rowena R. Ansbacher. New York: Basic Books, 1956.

Superiority and Social Interest: A Collection of Later Writings. Edited by Heinz L. and Rowena R. Ansbacher. Evanston, Ill.: Northwestern University, 1964.

Cooperation Between the Sexes. Edited and translated by Heinz L. and Rowena R. Ansbacher. Garden City, N.Y.: Doubleday, 1978.

BOOKS ABOUT ALFRED ADLER

Adler, Kurt A., and Deutsch, Danica, eds. *Essays in Individual Psychology.* New York: Grove Press, 1959.

Ansbacher, Heinz L. and Ansbacher, Rowena R., eds. *The Individual Psychology of Alfred Adler: A Systematic Presentation in Selections from his Writings.* New York: Basic Books, 1956.

Bottome, Phyllis. *Alfred Adler: A Portrait from Life.* New York: Vanguard, 1957.

Dinkmeyer, Don C., Pew, W. L., and Dinkmeyer, Don C., Jr. *Adlerian Counseling and Psychotherapy.* Monterey, California: Wadsworth, 1979.

Ellenberger, Henri F. *The Discovery of the Unconscious.* New York: Basic Books, 1970.

Ganz, Madeline. *The Psychology of Alfred Adler and the Development of the Child.* Translated by Philip Mairet. New York: Humanities Press, 1953.

Internationalen Vereinigung für Individualpsychologie. *Alfred Adler, Zum Gedenken.* Vienna: Vereins für Individualpsychologie, 1957.

Mairet, Philip. *ABCs of Adlerian Psychology.* London: Routledge and Kegan Paul, 1926.

Manaster, Guy, ed. *Alfred Adler as We Remember Him.* Chicago: North American Society of Adlerian Psychology, 1977.

Mosak, Harold H., ed. *Alfred Adler: His Influence on Psychology Today.* Park Ridge, New Jersey: Noyes Press, 1973.

Orgler, Hertha. *Alfred Adler, The Man and His Work.* New York: New American Library, 1963.

Rattner, Josef. *Alfred Adler.* Translated by Harry Zohn. New York: Ungar, 1983.

Rom, Paul. *Alfred Adler und die Wissenschaftliche Menschenkenntnis.* Frankfurt: Waldemar Kramer, 1966. New York: Ungar, 1984.

Rühle-Gerstel, Alice. *Freud und Adler.* Dresden: Verlag Am andern Ufer, 1928.

Rühle-Gerstel, Alice. *Der Weg zum Wir.* Munich: Ernst Reinhardt, 1980.

Sperber, Manes. *Alfred Adler: der Mensch und seine Lehre: ein Essay.* Munich: Bergmann, 1926.

Sperber, Manes. *Masks of Loneliness: Alfred Adler in Perspective.* Translated by Krishna Winston. New York: Macmillan, 1974.

Stepansky, Paul E. *In Freud's Shadow, Adler in Context.* Hillsdale, New Jersey: Analytic Press, 1983.

Way, Lewis. *Adler's Place in Psychology.* New York: Collier, 1962.

SELECTED ARTICLES ABOUT ALFRED ADLER

"Adler and the Vienna College of Professors." *Journal of Individual Psychology,* 1966, 22, 235–36.

Adler, Alexandra. "Recollections of My Father." *American Journal of Psychiatry,* 1970, *127* (6), 771–72.

Adler, Kurt. "A Personal Autobiography." *Journal of Individual Psychology,* 1981, *37* (2), 196–204.

Adler, Raissa. Minutes of the Society for Free Psychoanalytic Research, September 1912 to January 1913. *Journal of Individual Psychology,* March 1982, *38* (1), 22–27.

Ansbacher, Heinz L. "The Significance of the Socio-economic Status of the Patients of Freud and of Adler." *American Journal of Psychotherapy,* 1959, *13*, 376–82.

———. "On the Origin of 'Holism.'" *Journal of Individual Psychology,* 1961, *17*, 142–48.

———. Review of R. B. Winn, ed. "Soviet Psychology: A Symposium." *Journal of Individual Psychology,* 1961, *17*, 229–30.

———. "Rudolf Hildebrand: A Forerunner of Alfred Adler." *Journal of Individual Psychology,* 1962, *18*, 12–17.

———. "Was Adler a Disciple of Freud? A Reply." *Journal of Individual Psychology,* 1962, *18*, 126–35.

———. "The Structure of Individual Psychology." In B. B. Wolman and E. Nagel, eds. *Scientific Psychology: Principles and Approaches.* New York: Basic Books, 1965.

———. "Adler and the Vienna College of Professors." *Journal of Individual Psychology,* 1966, *22*, 235–36.

———. "History of an Anecdote Used by Adler." *Journal of Individual Psychology,* 1966, *22*, 237–38.

———. "Life Style: A Historical and Systematic Review." *Journal of Individual Psychology,* 1967, *23*, 191–203.

———. "Adler and the 1910 Vienna Symposium on Suicide." *Journal of Individual Psychology,* 1968, *24*, 181–91.

———. "Alfred Adler in the Great Soviet Encyclopedia." *Journal of Individual Psychology,* 1969, *25* (2), 183–85.

———. "Suicide as Communication: Adler's Concept and Current Applications." *Journal of Individual Psychology,* 1969, *25*, 174–80.

———. "Alfred Adler: A Historical Perspective." *American Journal of Psychiatry,* 1970, *127*, 777–82.

———. "Alfred Adler and G. Stanley Hall: Correspondence and General Relationship." *Journal of the History of the Behavioral Sciences,* 1971, *7*, 337–52.

———. "Religion and Individual Psychology: Introduction." *Journal of Individual Psychology,* 1971, *27*, 3–9.

———. "Alfred Adler and Humanistic Psychology." *Journal of Humanistic Psychology,* 1971, *11*, 53–63.

———. "Adler's 'Striving for Power' in Relation to Nietzsche." *Journal of Individual Psychology,* 1972, *28*, 12–24.

———. "Psychology: A Way of Living." In T. S. Krawiec, ed. *The Psychologists.* New York: Oxford University Press, 1974.

References

———. "Adler and Virchow: New Light on the Name 'Individual Psychology.'" *Journal of Individual Psychology,* 1974, *30,* 43–52.

———. "The Development of Adler's Concept of Social Interest: A Critical Study." *Journal of Individual Psychology,* 1978, *34,* 118–52.

———. "On the Origin of 'Social Interest' in Adler's Writings." *Journal of Individual Psychology,* 1980, *36,* 117–18.

———. "Discussion of Alfred Adler's Preface to The Diary of Vaslav Nijinsky." *Archives of General Psychiatry,* 1981, *38,* 836–41.

———. "The Significance of Alfred Adler for the Concept of Narcissism." *American Journal of Psychiatry,* February 1985, *142* (2), 203–07.

———. "Alfred Adler's Influence on the Three Leading Cofounders of Humanistic Psychology." *Journal of Humanistic Psychology,* Fall 1990, *30* (4), 45–53.

———. "Alfred Adler, Pioneer in Prevention of Mental Disorders." *Individual Psychology,* 1992, *48* (1), 4–34.

———. "Alfred Adler's Concepts of Community Feeling and Social Interest." *Individual Psychology,* in press.

———. "Alfred Adler's Description of the Case of Vaslav Nijinsky in the Light of Current Diagnostic Standards." *Individual Psychology,* in press.

———. "Adler and the Development of Freud's Thought." Burlington, VT: Unpublished paper, 1990.

Ansbacher, Rowena R. "Sullivan's Interpersonal Psychiatry and Adler's Individual Psychology." *Journal of Individual Psychology,* 1971, *27,* 85–98.

Brodsky, Paul. "Lydia Sicher (1890–1962)." *Journal of Individual Psychology,* 1962, *18* (3), 184–86.

Carlson, Jon, and Dinkmeyer, Don. "Adlerian Marriage Therapy." *American Journal of Family Therapy,* 1987, *15* (4), 326–32.

Dreikurs, Rudolf. "Ferdinand Birnbaum: A Biographical Sketch." *Journal of Individual Psychology,* 1947, *6,* 157–61.

Federn, Ernst. "Was Adler a Disciple of Freud? A Freudian View." *Journal of Individual Psychology,* May 1963, *19,* 80–82.

Furtmüller, Carl. "Alfred Adler: A Biographical Essay." In Alfred Adler, *Superiority and Social Interest.* Evanston, Ill.: Northwestern University Press, 1964.

Gowing, Lawrence. *Paintings in the Louvre.* New York: Stewart, Tabori, and Chang, 1987.

Leibin, V. M. "Comments on 'Minutes of the Society for Free Psychoanalytic Research.'" *Journal of Individual Psychology,* March 1982, *38* (1), 28–31.

"Like Father, Like Daughter: Dr. Adler Carries On." *Miami Herald,* April 18, 1971, sec. G.

Mandell, Sibyl. "Adler's Contribution to the Varying Functions of a Psychologist." *Journal of Individual Psychology,* 1947, *6,* 65–67.

Maslow, Abraham H. "Was Adler a Disciple of Freud? A Note." *Journal of Individual Psychology,* 1962, *18,* 125.

Papanek, Helene. "Adler's Psychology and Group Psychotherapy." *American Journal of Psychiatry,* 1970, *127* (6), 83–86.

Schick, Alfred. "The Cultural Background of Adler's and Freud's Work." *American Journal of Psychotherapy,* 1964, 7–24.

————. "Psychotherapy in Old Vienna and New York: Cultural Comparisons." *Psychoanalytic Review*, 1973, *60* (1), 111–26.

Seidler, Regine. "Ferdinand Birnbaum's Contribution to Individual Psychology." *Journal of Individual Psychology*, 1947, *6*, 162–63.

————. "Alfred Adler and the Teachers." *Journal of Individual Psychology*, 1947, *6*, 51–53.

Spiel, Oskar. "The Individual Psychological Experimental School in Vienna." *Journal of Individual Psychology*. 1956, *12* (1), 1–11.

Stein, Henry T. "Twelve Stages of Creative Adlerian Psychotherapy." *Individual Psychology*, 1988, *44* (2), 138–43.

Stein, Henry T. "Adler and Socrates: Similarities and Differences." *Individual Psychology*, 1991, *47* (2), 242–46.

"Tributes to Alfred Adler on His 100th Birthday." *Journal of Individual Psychology*, 1970, 26 (1), 10–14.

Wasserman, Isidor. Letter to the editor. *American Journal of Psychotherapy*, 1958, *12*, 623–27.

Wittels, Fritz. "The Neo-Adlerians." *American Journal of Sociology*, 1939, *45*, 433–45.

GENERAL REFERENCES

Allen, Frederick Lewis. *Only Yesterday and Since Yesterday, A Popular History of the 20's and 30's*. New York: Harper and Row, 1986.

Alexander, Franz, Samuel Eisenstein, and Martin Grotjahn, eds. *Psychoanalytic Pioneers*. New York: Basic, 1966.

American Journal of Psychiatry. "Ira S. Wile: In Memoriam." 1944, *100*, 583–84.

Barea, Ilse. *Vienna*. New York: Knopf, 1966.

Barker, Elisabeth. *Austria 1918–1972*. Coral Gables, Fla.: University of Miami Press, 1973.

Bettelheim, Bruno. *Freud and Man's Soul*. New York: Knopf, 1983.

Beller, Steven. *Vienna and the Jews, 1867–1938: A Cultural History*. Cambridge: Cambridge University Press, 1989.

Berkley, George E. *Vienna and its Jews: The Tragedy of Success*. Cambridge, Mass.: Abt Books, 1988.

Berton, Pierre. *The Dionne Years*. New York: Norton, 1977.

Bird, Caroline. *The Invisible Scar*. New York: Longman, 1966.

Blanton, Smiley. *Diary of My Analysis*. New York: Hawthorne Books, 1971.

Bloom, Harold. *Sigmund Freud*. New York: Chelsea House, 1985.

Bluhm, William T. *Building an Austrian Nation*. New Haven: Yale University Press, 1973.

Blum, Mark E. *The Austro-Marxists, 1890–1918: A Psychobiological Study*. Lexington: University of Kentucky Press, 1985.

Boardman, Barrington. *From Harding to Hiroshima*. New York: Dembner, 1988.

Bottome, Phyllis. *The Challenge*. New York: Harcourt, Brace, 1953.

————. *The Goal*. New York: Vanguard, 1962.

————. *Private Worlds*. New York: Grosset & Dunlap, 1934.

References

Bottomore, Tom, and Patrick Goode, eds. *Austro-Marxism.* Oxford: Clarendon, 1978.

Brome, Vincent. *Ernest Jones: Freud's Alter Ego.* New York: Norton, 1983.

Brook-Shepherd, Gordon. *Royal Sunset, The European Dynasties and the Great War.* Garden City, N.Y.: Doubleday, 1987.

Brunner, Jose. "Psychiatry, Psychoanalysis, and Politics During the First World War." *Journal of the History of the Behavioral Sciences,* 1991, *27,* 352–65.

Buckley, Kerry W. *Mechanical Man: John Broadus Watson and the Beginnings of Behaviorism.* New York: Guilford, 1989.

Burnham, John C. *Jelliffe: American Psychoanalyst and Physician.* Chicago: University of Chicago Press, 1983.

Clark, Ronald W. *Freud: The Man and the Cause.* New York: Random House, 1980.

Clendening, Logan. "Sex Madness." *Forum,* October 1930, 208–12.

Cohen, David. *J. B. Watson: The Founder of Behaviourism.* London: Routledge Kegan Paul, 1979.

Coles, Robert. *Anna Freud.* Reading, Mass.: Addison-Wesley, 1992.

Collier, James Lincoln. *The Rise of Selfishness in America.* New York: Oxford University Press, 1991.

Collins, Joseph. "The Doctor Looks at Companionate Marriage." *Outlook and Independent,* December 21, 1927, 492–95.

Coser, Lewis. *Refugee Scholars in America.* New Haven: Yale University Press, 1984.

Covert, Catherine Lucille. *Freud on the Front Page: Transmission of Freudian Ideas in the American Newspaper of the 1920s.* Ann Arbor, Mich.: University Microfilms, 1975.

Crunden, Robert M. *From Self to Society, 1919–1941.* Englewood Cliffs, N. J.: Prentice-Hall, 1972.

Crankshaw, Edward. *Vienna, The Image of a Culture in Decline.* ?: 1976.

Decker, Hannah S. *Freud, Dora, and Vienna 1900.* New York: Macmillan, 1991.

Davidson, Adele K. *The Collected Works of Lydia Sicher: An Adlerian Perspective.* Fort Bragg, Ca.: QED Press, 1991.

DeJonge, Alex. *Stalin and the Shaping of the Soviet Union.* New York: Morrow, 1986.

Deutscher, Isaac. *The Prophet Armed, Trotsky: 1879–1921.* New York: Oxford University Press, 1954.

Diamant, Alfred. *Austrian Catholics and the First Republic.* Princeton: Princeton University Press, 1960.

Douglas, Emily Taft. *Margaret Sanger: Pioneer of the Future.* New York: Holt, Rinehart & Winston, 1970.

Dreikurs, Rudolf. "Guiding, Teaching, and Demonstrating." *Journal of Individual Psychology,* 1967, *23,* 145–57.

Dublin, Louis I. "Birth Control: What It is Doing to America's Population." *Forum,* November 1931, 270–75.

Ecksteins, Modris. *Rites of Spring: The Great War and the Birth of the Modern Age.* Boston: Houghton Mifflin, 1989.

Eissler, K. R. *Freud as an Expert Witness: The Discussion of War Neuroses between Freud and Wagner-Jauregg.* Translated by Christine Trollope. Madison, Conn.: International Universities Press, 1986.

Encyclopedia of World Art. New York: McGraw-Hill, 1960.

Evans, Richard. *Conversations with Carl Jung and Reactions from Ernest Jones.* Princeton: Van Nostrand, 1964.

References

Evans, Richard I. *Dialogue with C. G. Jung.* New York: Praeger, 1981.

Filene, Edward A. *Successful Living in this Machine Age.* New York: Simon and Schuster, 1931.

Frankl, Viktor. *Man's Search for Meaning.* Translated by Ilse Lasch. Boston: Beacon, 1963.

Freidenreich, Harriet Pass. *Jewish Politics in Vienna, 1918–1938.* Bloomington: Indiana University Press, 1991.

Freud, Sigmund. *Civilization and its Discontents.* Translated by James Strachey. New York: Norton, 1962.

———. *The Future of an Illusion.* Translated and edited by James Strachey. New York: Norton, 1961.

———. "A History of Psychoanalysis," in *The Basic Writings of Sigmund Freud.* Translated and edited by A. A. Brill. New York: The Modern Library, 1914.

———. *The Interpretation of Dreams, Standard Edition,* Vols. 4 and 5. London: Hogarth, 1958.

———. *Three Essays on the Theory of Sexuality, Standard Edition,* Vol. 7. London: Hogarth, 1953.

Fuller, Robert C. *Americans and the Unconscious.* New York: Oxford University Press, 1986.

Furtmüller, Carl. *Denken und Handeln.* Munich: Ernst Reinhardt, 1983.

Gabbard, Krin, and Glen O. Gabbard. *Psychiatry and the Cinema.* Chicago: University of Chicago Press, 1987.

Gay, Peter. *Freud: A Life for Our Time.* New York: Norton, 1988.

———. *Freud, Jews and other Germans: Masters and Victims in Modernist Culture.* New York: Oxford University Press, 1978.

Grosskurth, Phyllis. *The Secret Ring.* Reading, Mass.: Addison-Wesley, 1991.

Gruber, Helmut. *Red Vienna, Experiment in Working-Class Culture.* New York: Oxford University Press, 1991.

Grunberger, Richard. *The 12-Year Reich, A Social History of Nazi Germany, 1933–1945.* New York: Holt, Reinhart and Winston, 1971.

Grunfeld, Frederic V. *Prophets without Honor: A Background to Freud, Kafka, Einstein and their World.* New York: Holt, Rinehart and Winston, 1979.

Grunwald, Max. *Vienna.* Philadelphia: Jewish Publication Society of America, 1936.

Gulick, Charles A. *Austria from Habsburg to Hitler,* Vols. 1 and 2. Berkeley: University of California Press, 1948.

Hale, Nathan G. *Freud and the Americans.* New York: Oxford University Press, 1971.

Hardyment, Christina. *Dream Babies: Three Centuries of Good Advice on Child Care.* New York: Harper and Row, 1983.

Harms, Ernest. *Handbook of Child Guidance.* New York: Child Care Publications, 1947.

Higgins, Mary, and Chester M. Raphael, eds. *Reich Speaks of Freud.* Translated by Therese Pol. New York: Farrar, Straus, & Giroux, 1967.

Hoffman, Edward. *The Right to be Human: A Biography of Abraham Maslow.* Los Angeles: Tarcher, 1988.

Hoffman, Paul. *The Viennese: Splendor, Twilight, and Exile.* New York: Doubleday, 1988.

Hornstein, Gail A. "The Return of the Repressed: Psychology's Problematic Relations with Psychoanalysis, 1909–1960." *American Psychologist,* 1992, *47,* 254–63.

"Intellectual Provocateur." *Time,* June 26, 1939, 59–63.

Jackson, Robert. *International Trotskyism.* New Brunswick, N.J.: Rutgers University Press, 1991.

Janik, Allen, and Stephen E. Toulmin. *Wittgenstein's Vienna.* New York: Simon and Schuster, 1973.

Jenks, William A. *Vienna and the Young Hitler.* New York: Columbia University Press, 1960.

Johnson, Gerald W. *Liberal's Progress.* New York: Coward-McCann, 1948.

Johnston, William M. *The Austrian Mind: An Intellectual and Social History 1848–1938.* Berkeley: University of California Press, 1972.

Jones, Ernest. *The Life and Work of Sigmund Freud,* Vols. 1–3. New York: Basic Books, 1953–1957.

Jones, J. Sydney. *Hitler in Vienna.* New York: Stein and Day, 1983.

Journal of the American Medical Association. "Ira Solomon Wile." October 30, 1943, 582.

Jung, Carl. "Your Negroid and Indian Behavior." *Forum,* 1930, *83* (4), 193–199.

Jungk, Peter Stephan. *Franz Werfel, A Life in Prague, Vienna, and Hollywood.* Translated by Anselm Hollo. New York: Grove Weidenfeld, 1990.

Kirchwey, Freda, ed. *Our Changing Morality, A Symposium.* London: Kegan, Paul, Trench and Trubner, 1925.

Klein, Carole. *Gramercy Park, An American Bloomsbury.* Boston: Houghton Mifflin, 1987.

Klein, Dennis B. *Jewish Origins of the Psychoanalytic Movement.* New York: Praeger, 1981.

Gustav Klimt Landscapes. Translated by Ewald Osers with an essay by Jonannes Dobai and a biography of Gustav Klimt. Boston: Little, Brown, 1981.

Knopf, Olga. *The Art of Being a Woman.* Boston: Little, Brown, 1932.

Lerner, Warren. *Karl Radek: The Last Internationalist.* Stanford: Stanford University Press, 1970.

Lesky, Erna. *The Vienna Medical School of the 19th Century.* Baltimore: Johns Hopkins University Press, 1976.

Lieberman, E. James. *Acts of Will: The Life and Work of Otto Rank.* New York: Free Press, 1985.

Luft, David S. *Robert Musil and the Crisis of European Culture, 1880–1942.* Berkeley: University of California Press, 1980.

MacDonald, Mary. *The Republic of Austria 1918–1934.* London, Oxford University Press, 1946.

Mann, Arthur, ed. *The Progressive Era.* New York: Holt, Rinehart and Winston, 1963.

Marquis, Alice Goldfarb. *Hopes and Ashes, The Birth of Modern Times.* New York: Macmillan, 1986.

Maslow, Abraham H. *Motivation and Personality.* New York: Harper & Brothers, 1950.

———. *Toward a Psychology of Being,* 2nd edition. Princeton: Van Nostrand, 1968.

Masson, Jeffrey M. *The Complete Letters of Sigmund Freud to William Fliess, 1887–1904.* Cambridge, Mass.: Harvard University Press, 1985.

May, H. F. *The Discontent of the Intellectuals: A Problem of the Twenties.* Chicago: Rand McNally, 1963.

May, Rollo. *The Cry for Myth.* New York: Norton, 1990.

Mayer, Herbert Carleton. "Whose Children Are They?" *Forum,* November 1930, 294–99.

McCartney, Carlile A. *The Habsburg Empire, 1790–1918.* New York: Macmillan, 1969.

McElvaine, Robert S. *The Great Depression, America 1929–1941.* New York: Times Books, 1984.

McGrath, William J. *Freud's Discovery of Psychoanalysis: The Politics of Hysteria.* Ithaca, N.Y.: Cornell University Press, 1986.

McGuire, William, ed. *The Freud/Jung Letters.* Princeton: Princeton University Press, 1974.

McKinney, Fanny Lee. "The Movies and the People." *Outlook and Independent,* May 16, 1923, 882–83.

Medvedev, Roy. *Let History Judge, The Origins and Consequences of Stalinism.* New York: Columbia University Press, 1989.

Menaker, Esther. *Otto Rank: A Rediscovered Legacy.* New York: Columbia University Press, 1982.

Miller, Daniel R., and Guy E. Swanson. *The Changing American Parent.* New York: Wiley, 1958.

Mitrinovic, Dimitrije. *Certainly, Future.* Translated and edited by H. C. Rutherford. Boulder, Co.: East European Monographs, 1987. Distributed by Columbia University Press.

Morton, Frederic. *A Nervous Splendour, Vienna 1888/1889.* London: Weidenfeld and Nicolson, 1979.

———. *Thunder at Twilight, Vienna 1913/1914.* New York: Scribner's, 1989.

Myers, Garry Cleveland. "Spank it Out!" *Forum,* Feburary 1931, 88–91.

Musil, Robert. *The Man Without Qualities.* Translated by Eithne Wilkins and Ernst Kaiser. New York: Capricorn, 1965.

Nervous Child. Ira S. Wile, Obituary. October 1943, *3* (1)

Nietzsche, Friedrich. *On the Genealogy of Morals and Ecce Homo.* Translated by Walter Kaufmann and R. J. Hollingdale. New York: Random House, 1967.

Noakes, Jeremy, and Geoffrey Pridham, eds. *Documents on Nazism, 1919–1945.* New York: Viking, 1975.

Nunberg, Herman, and Ernst Federn, eds. *Minutes of the Vienna Psychoanalytic Society, vols. 1–4.* New York: International Universities Press, 1962–75.

Ogden, Annegret S. *The Great American Housewife.* Westport, Conn.: Greenwood, 1986.

O'Higgins, Harvey. "Your Other Self." *Outlook and Independent,* November 28, 1928, 1227–29, 1259–60.

Ostwald, Peter. *Vaslav Nijinsky: A Leap into Madness.* New York: Lyle Stuart, 1991.

Pawel, Ernst. *The Labyrinth of Exile.* New York: Farrar, Straus and Giroux, 1989.

Perrett, Geoffrey. *America in the Twenties.* New York: Simon and Schuster, 1982.

Rabinbach, Anson. *The Crisis of Austrian Socialism.* Chicago: University of Chicago Press, 1983.

———, ed. *The Austrian Socialist Experiment.* Boulder, Co.: Westview Press, 1985.

Rasey, Marie J. *It Takes Time: An Autobiography of the Teaching Profession.* New York: Harper & Brothers, 1953.

References

Recouly, Raymond. "A Visit to Freud." *Outlook and Independent,* September 5, 1923, 27–29.

Regier, C. C. *The Era of the Muckrakers.* Gloucester, Mass.: Peter Smith, 1957.

Reich, Wilhelm. *Passion of Youth.* Translated by Philip Schmitz and Jerri Tompkins. New York: Farrar, Straus & Giroux, 1988.

———. *Sex-Pol: Essays 1929–1934.* Translated by Anna Bostock, Tom DuBose, and Lee Baxandall. Edited by Lee Baxandall. New York: Vintage, 1972.

———. *People in Trouble.* Translated by Philip Schmitz. New York: Farrar, Straus & Giroux, 1976.

Rice, Emanuel. *Freud and Moses, The Long Journey Home.* Albany: State University of New York Press, 1990.

Roazen, Paul. *Encountering Freud.* New Brunswick, N.J.: Transaction, 1990.

———. *Freud and His Followers.* New York: New American Library, 1976.

———. "Psychoanalytic Ethics: Edoardo Weiss, Freud, and Mussolini." *Journal of the History of the Behavioral Sciences,* 1991, *27,* 366–74.

Ross, Dorothy. *G. Stanley Hall, The Psychologist as Prophet.* Chicago: University of Chicago Press, 1972.

Rozenblit, Marsha L. *The Jews of Vienna, 1867–1914: Assimilation and Identity.* Albany: State University of New York Press, 1983.

Rutkoff, Peter M., and William B. Scott. *New School: A History of the New School for Social Research.* New York: Free Press, 1986.

Sanford, John A., ed. *Fritz Kunkel: Selected Writings.* New York: Paulist Press, 1984.

Sann, Paul. *The Lawless Decade.* Greenwich, Conn.: Fawcett, 1971.

Schnitzler, Arthur. *My Youth in Vienna.* Translated by Catherine Hutter. New York: Holt, Rinehart & Winston, 1970.

———. *Plays and Stories.* Edited by Egon Schwarz. New York: Continuum, 1982.

Schorske, Carl E. *Fin-de-Siecle Vienna: Politics and Culture.* New York: Knopf, 1980.

Segal, Ronald. *Leon Trotsky.* New York: Pantheon, 1979.

Sperber, Manes. *God's Water Carriers.* Translated by Joachim Neugroschel. New York: Holmes & Meier, 1987.

———. *The Unheeded Warning, 1918–1933.* Translated by Harry Zohn. New York: Holmes & Meier, 1991.

Spiel, Hilda. *Vienna's Golden Autumn.* New York: Weidenfeld and Nicholson, 1987.

Spiel, Oskar. *Discipline without Punishment: An Account of a School in Action.* London: Faber & Faber, 1962.

Spock, Benjamin, and Mary Morgan. *Spock on Spock.* New York: Pantheon, 1989.

Steffens, Lincoln. *The Autobiography of Lincoln Steffens.* New York: Literary Guild, 1931.

Stekel, Wilhelm. *The Autobiography of Wilhelm Stekel.* New York: Liveright, 1950.

Steiner, Kurt. *Politics in Austria.* Boston: Little, Brown, 1972.

Sulman, A. Michael. *The Freudianization of the American Child: The Impact of Psychoanalysis in Popular Periodical Literature in the United States, 1919–1939.* Ann Arbor, Mich.: University Microfilms, 1972.

Taft, Jesse. *Otto Rank.* New York: Julian Press, 1958.

Tebbel, John, and Mary Ellen Zuckerman. *The Magazine in America, 1741–1990.* New York: Oxford University Press, 1991.

Terner, Janet, and W. L. Pew. *The Courage to Be Human.* New York: Hawthorne, 1978.

Timms, Edward, and Naomi Segal, eds. *Freud in Exile*. New Haven: Yale University Press, 1988.

Torrey, E. Fuller. *Freudian Fraud*. New York: HarperCollins, 1992.

Trotsky, Leon. *My Life*. New York: Grosset & Dunlap, 1960.

Tucker, Robert C. *Stalin in Power*. New York: Norton, 1990.

Urbach, Reinhard. *Arthur Schnitzler*. Translated by Donald Davian. New York: Unger, 1973.

Vaihinger, Hans. *The Philosophy of "As If": A System of the Theoretical, Practical, and Religious Fictions of Mankind*. Translated by C. K. Ogden. New York: Harcourt, Brace, 1925.

Wardle, Christopher J. "Twentieth-Century Influences on the Development in Britain of Services for Child and Adolescent Psychiatry." *British Journal of Psychiatry*, 1991, *159*, 53–68.

Warner, Silas L. "Freud's Antipathy to America." *Journal of the American Academy of Psychoanalysis*, 1991, *19* (1), 141–55.

Watson, John B. *Psychological Care of Infant and Child*. New York: Norton, 1928.

Wexberg, Erwin. *Individual Psychology and Sex*. Translated by W. Beran Wolfe. London: Jonathan Cape, 1931.

Wile, Ira S. "Are Modern Parents Failures?" *Hygeia*, March 1931, 223–27.

———. *National Encyclopedia of American Biography*, vol. 35, 459. New York: James T. White, 1949.

———. "The 1933 Symposium: Certain Aspects of Treatment in Psychiatric Work with Children." *American Journal of Ortho Psychiatry*, July 1933, *3*, 310–36.

———. *Sex Education*. New York: Duffield and Company, 1912.

———, ed. *The Sex Life of the Unmarried Adult*. London: George Allen and Unwin, 1934.

———. "What is Happening to the Family?" *Hospital Social Service*, 1929, *19*, 525–35.

Wile, Ira S., and Mary Day Winn. *Marriage in the Modern Manner*. New York: Century, 1929.

———. "Emotional America." *Outlook and Independent*, May 8, 1929, *152*, 48–49, 77.

Wistrich, Robert S. *The Jews of Vienna in the Age of Franz Joseph*. Oxford: Oxford University Press, 1989.

Wittels, Fritz. *Sigmund Freud: His Personality, His Teachings, and His School*. New York: Dodd, Mead, 1924.

Wolfe, Walter B. "Romance vs. Marriage." *Forum*, September 1931, 166–72.

———. "Psycho-Analyzing the Depression." *Forum*, April 1932, 209–14.

———. *A Woman's Best Years*. New York: Long & Smith, 1934.

———. *Nervous Breakdowns*. New York: Farrar & Rinehart, 1933.

Young-Bruehl, Elisabeth. *Anna Freud*. New York: Summit, 1988.

Zweig, Stefan. *The World of Yesterday*. New York: Viking, 1943.

Notes

The following notes refer to books and articles in the Bibliography and to additional references indicated. Newspaper clippings on Adler in various archives did not always indicate page numbers.

Abbreviations for Primary Sources:

AAC   Alfred Adler Collection, Division of Manuscripts, U.S. Library of Congress, Washington, D.C.

AFA   Adler Family Archives (private documents possessed by Dr. Kurt Adler and Margot Adler)

AI   Author's Interview

GC   Sanford J. Greenberger Collection, Special Collections; University of Oregon Library, Eugene, OR.

GM   Guy Manaster (Editor), *Alfred Adler: As We Remember Him.*

HE   Henri F. Ellenberger, *The Discovery of the Unconscious.*

PB   Phyllis Bottome, *Alfred Adler: A Portrait from Life.*

v Alfred Adler, "Character and Talent," *Harper's Monthly Magazine,* Vol. 155, 1927, 66.

PART I

1 Alfred Adler, *Superiority and Social Interest,* ed. Heinz L. Ansbacher and Rowena Ansbacher. New York: Norton, 1979, 42.

CHAPTER ONE
A Viennese Boyhood

3 Adler, *Social Interest,* 74.
3 "civil and political rights . . .": George E. Berkley, *Vienna and its Jews.* Cambridge: Abt Books, 1988, 34.

5 "As far as I can look back . . .": Alfred Adler, "Something About Myself," *Childhood and Character,* Vol. 7, 1930, 7.
6 "The situation was so . . .": *Ibid.,* 6.
6 "One of my earliest recollections . . .": PB, 30.
7 "If the sorrows of a chicken . . .": Adler, "Something About Myself," 6.
7 "clothed all in black . . .": *Ibid.*
8 "How could a mother . . .": *Ibid.*
8 "Give yourself no more . . .": *Ibid.*
8 "My decision was confirmed . . .": *Ibid.,* 8.
9 "I was not altogether surprised . . .": PB, 34.
9 "Rich and poor . . .": Berkley, *Vienna,* 43.
11 "a good industrious . . .": PB, 27.
11 "The only sure prevention . . .": AI, Kurt Adler, April 5, 1992.
12 "Every well-to-do family . . .": Stefan Zweig, *The World of Yesterday,* New York: Viking, 1943, 28.
15 "The success changed . . .": Adler, "Something About Myself," 7.
16 "It was more than . . .": Zweig, *The World of Yesterday,* 28.
17 "For eight years . . .": *Ibid.,* 30.
17 "For a teacher . . .": *Ibid.,* 32.
17 "For us school was compulsion . . .": *Ibid.,* 29.

CHAPTER TWO
The Making of a Radical Physician

19 Alfred Adler, *The Pattern of Life,* 136.
20 "Treatment, treatment . . .": William M. Johnston, *The Austrian Mind.* Berkeley: University of California Press, 1972, 228.
20 "the most important diseases . . .": HE, 581.
21 "It is true . . .": Erna Lesky, *The Vienna Medical School,* trans. J. Williams and I. S. Levij. Baltimore: Johns Hopkins University Press, 1976, 287.
21 "Only a good man . . .": *Ibid.,* 280.
22 "There was an intense . . .": Carl Furtmüller, "Alfred Adler: A Biographical Essay," in Alfred Adler, *Superiority and Social Interest,* ed. Heinz L. Ansbacher and Rowena Ansbacher. New York: Norton, 1979, 333.
23 "Grouped into so-called . . .": Zweig, *The World of Yesterday,* 64–65.
24 "[The] main avenue . . .": *Ibid.,* 61.
24 "Food is being hoarded . . .": Ilse Barea, *Vienna.* New York: Knopf, 1966, 310–311.
25 "[typical] were brief liasons . . .": Zweig, *The World of Yesterday,* 79.
26 "In order to protect . . .": *Ibid.,* 77.
27 "respectful Miss . . .": AAC, Container 1, General Correspondence, 1891–1898. Letter dated July 11, 1897.
27 "with heartfelt greetings . . .": *Ibid.*

27 "respectful Miss . . .": ACC, Container 1, General Correspondence, 1891–1898. Letter dated August 13, 1897.

27 "I have burned my bridges . . .": *Ibid.*

27 "Raissa! My soul . . .": AAC, Container 1, General Correspondence, Undated. Undated letter.

28 "When there is news . . .": AAC, Container 1, General Correspondence, 1891–1898. Letter dated September 17, 1897.

28 " 'Just think' . . .": *Ibid.*

28 "Your father has not . . .": AAC, Container 1, General Correspondence, 1891–1898. Letter dated October 4, 1897.

29 "I am already starting . . .": *Ibid.*

CHAPTER THREE

On His Own

30 Adler, *Social Interest*, 19.

31 "If I had made . . .": PB, 48.

32 "But no one . . .": PB, 52.

33 "for the time being . . .": Paul Hofmann, *The Viennese: Splendor, Twilight, and Exile*. New York: Doubleday, 1988, 143.

34 "the most formidable German mayor . . .": *Ibid.*

34 "not hating Jews . . .": AI, Kurt Adler, April 5, 1992.

35 "To know a danger . . .": Heinz L. Ansbacher, "Alfred Adler: Pioneer in Prevention of Mental Disorders," *Journal of Individual Psychology*, Vol. 48 (1), March 1992, 4.

35 "to describe the connection . . .": *Ibid.*

36 "it is the unbridled competition . . .": Paul Stepansky, *In Freud's Shadow: Adler in Context*. Hillsdale, NJ: Analytic Press, 1983, 17.

37 "contemporary academic medicine . . .": Ansbacher, "Pioneer in Prevention," 5.

38 "Since the second child . . .": AAC, Container 1, General Correspondence, 1902–1909. Letter dated September 30, 1902.

38 "When I first came . . .": PB, 48.

39 "Look at how they . . .": AI, Kurt Adler, April 5, 1992.

39 "the most valuable . . .": Stepansky, *In Freud's Shadow*, 18.

39 "in the little worries . . .": *Ibid.*, 19.

40 "Only then will humanity . . .": Ansbacher, "Pioneer in Prevention," 5.

40 "There was a time . . .": *Ibid.*, 8.

40 "It is high time that . . .": *Ibid.*

40 "Life cannot be simply reduced . . .": *Ibid.*

40 "finally provide the undergirding . . .": Stepansky, *In Freud's Shadow*, 19.

41 "curtail and eliminate . . .": Alfred Adler, "Demoralized Children," *The Practice and Theory of Individual Psychology*, trans. P. Radin. London: Routledge and Kegan Paul, 1925, 350.

41 "the splendor of Hungary . . .": AAC, Container 1, General Correspondence, 1902–1909. Letter dated September 30, 1902.

42 "Very honored . . .": "Father of the Inferiority Complex," *New York Herald,* March 17, 1929. By permission of Sigmund Freud Copyrights, Wivenhoe, UK.

CHAPTER FOUR

Early Years with Psychoanalysis

44 Alfred Adler, "Individual Psychology and Psychoanalysis," Alfred Adler Correspondence, unpublished lecture, December 14, 1930, 2.

45 "a scientific fairy-tale . . .": Peter Gay, *Freud: A Life for Our Time.* New York: Norton, 1988, 93.

46 "complete harmony among . . .": *The Autobiography of Wilhelm Stekel,* ed. Emil A. Guntheil, New York: Liveright, 1950, 116.

48 "she was the complete . . .": Gay, *Life for Our Time,* 59–60.

48 "The [society] gatherings followed . . .": *Ibid.,* 174.

48 "the atmosphere of the foundation . . .": *Ibid.*

49 "no government can affect . . .": Stepansky, *In Freud's Shadow,* 19.

49 "[as] the manager . . .": *Ibid.*

49 "the hesitating social precautions . . .": *Ibid.,* 20.

49 "a gain for our ruling classes . . .": *Ibid.*

50 "We owe to Freud . . .": Ansbacher, "Pioneer in Prevention," 6.

50 "Possibly, the powerful accent . . .": *Ibid.*

50 "Not to treat and cure . . .": *Ibid.*

50 "The most important . . .": *Ibid.*

50 "confidence in . . .": *Ibid.*

50 "The child's self-confidence . . .": *Ibid.*

50 "weak and sickly children . . .": *Ibid.*

50 "pampered and overprotected . . .": *Ibid.*

50 "under no circumstances . . .": *Ibid.*

50 "leave the child freedom . . .": *Ibid.*

51 "The Theory of Epic . . .": Carl Furtmüller, *Denken und Handeln,* ed. Lux Furtmüller. Munich: Ernst Reinhardt, 1983, 15.

53 "He confided that . . .": AI, Kurt Adler, May 19, 1992.

53 "ticket of admission . . .": Marsha L. Rozenblit, *The Jews of Vienna, 1867–1914: Assimilation and Identity,* Albany, N.Y.: State University of New York Press, 1983, 134.

53 "I considered myself . . .": *Ibid.,* 6.

53 "We were raised . . .": *Ibid.*

53 "the generation which followed . . .": *Ibid.,* 7.

55 "The fact that things . . .": Dennis B. Klein, *Jewish Origins of the Psychoanalytic Movement,* New York: Praeger, 1981, 148.

55 "Develop in him . . .": *Ibid.*

56 "He attributed great importance . . .": Herman Nunberg and Ernst Federn, eds., *Minutes of the Vienna Psychoanalytic Society,* Vol. 1, 1906–1908. New York: International Universities Press, 1962, 42.

56 "[Freud stated that] . . .": *Ibid.*

56 "good cooks are always . . .": *Ibid.*, 46–47.

56 "his own cook . . .": *Ibid.*, 47.

57 "the interesting psychic . . .": Alfred Adler, *A Study of Organ Inferiority and Its Psychical Compensation,* trans. S. E. Jellife. New York: Nervous Mental Diseases Publishing Company, 1917, 65.

57 "This seems to me . . .": *Ibid.*, 53.

58 "In our children . . .": Stepansky, *In Freud's Shadow,* 25.

58 "Whereas today the old . . .": *Ibid.*

CHAPTER FIVE
Breaking with Freud

59 Alfred Adler to Alexander Neuer, Alfred Adler Correspondence, unpublished, January 18, 1928.

60 "deeper psychological understanding . . .": E. James Lieberman, *Acts of Will: The Life and Work of Otto Rank.* New York: Free Press, 1985, 96.

60 "sir who should be [called] . . .": Furtmüller, *Denken und Handeln,* 16.

61 "From early childhood . . .": Heinz L. Ansbacher and Rowena Ansbacher, eds. *The Individual Psychology of Alfred Adler.* New York: Basic Books, 1956, 34.

61 "to see, to hear, and to touch . . .": *Ibid.*, 35.

61 "revolutionary heroes . . .": *Ibid.*, 36.

61 "charity, sympathy, altruism . . .": *Ibid.*

62 "Alfred Adler, in a suggestive paper . . .": *Ibid.*, 37.

62 "are sufficiently striking . . .": *Ibid.*, 40.

62 "to touch, to look . . .": *Ibid.*, 39.

62 "A large part of the child's . . .": *Ibid.*, 41.

64 "On a sunny day . . .": AI, Kurt Adler, April 5, 1992.

64 "class consciousness . . .": Herman Nunberg and Ernst Federn, eds., *Minutes of the Vienna Psychoanalytic Society,* Vol. II, 1908–1910. New York: International Universities Press, 1962, 173.

65 "class consciousness liberates . . .": *Ibid.*, 178.

65 "Marx's entire work . . .": *Ibid.*

65 "the enlargement of consciousness . . .": *Ibid.*, 174.

65 "substitute for religion . . .": *Ibid.*, 176.

65 "has offered remarkable . . .": Herman Nunberg and Ernst Federn, eds., *Minutes of the Vienna Psychoanalytic Society,* Vol. III, 1910–1911. New York: International Universities Press, 1974, 356.

65 "Pupils' suicides can no longer . . .": *Ibid.*, 496–497.

65 "School is not only like life . . .": *Ibid.*, 497.

66 "the older generation . . .": Vincent Brome, *Ernst Jones: Freud's Alter Ego.* New York: Norton, 1983, 26.

66 "a heavy cross to bear . . .": *Ibid.*

66 "a theoretician, astute and original . . .": Gay, *Life for Our Time,* 220.

66 "decent . . .": *Ibid.*, 221.

66 "We must hold on to him . . .": *Ibid.*

66 "Most of you are Jews . . .": Fritz Wittels, *Sigmund Freud: His Personality, His Teachings, and His School.* New York: Dodd, Mead, 1924, 140.

67 "a chillier and more formal . . .": Brome, *Freud's Alter Ego,* 86.

67 "I am satisfied with . . .": Lieberman, *Acts of Will,* 121.

68 "In 1908, I hit upon . . .": Ansbacher and Ansbacher, eds., *Individual Psychology,* 38.

68 "These objective phenomena . . .": Alfred Adler, *The Individual Psychology of Alfred Adler: A Systematic Presentation of Selections from His Writings,* ed. Heinz L. Ansbacher and Rowena R. Ansbacher. New York: Basic Books, 1956, 46.

68 "it is the goal . . .": *Ibid.,* 50.

69 "For about seven years . . .": Alfred Adler, "On Suicide, With Particular Reference to Suicide Among Young Students," Preface to *Discussions of the Vienna Psychoanalytic Society—1910.* ed. Paul Friedman, New York: International Universities Press, 1967, 30.

70 "Adler's theories be for once . . .": Nunberg and Federn, eds., *Minutes,* Vol. III, 59.

70 "sexuality is aroused . . .": *Ibid.,* 104.

70 "In general, it is . . .": *Ibid.,* 105.

70 "if sexuality is not the center . . .": *Ibid.,* 106.

70 "never wanted to dispute . . .": *Ibid.,* 111.

70 "there is no principle . . .": *Ibid.*

70 "a wanting to be more . . .": *Ibid.,* 142.

70 "The budding of a feeling . . .": *Ibid.*

71 "That woman is devalued by man . . .": *Ibid.,* 141.

71 "Whether and how much libido . . .": *Ibid.,* 144.

71 "All these teachings . . .": *Ibid.,* 147.

71 "Instead of psychology . . .": *Ibid.*

72 "behind what one sees . . .": *Ibid.,* 149.

72 "acknowledged the worth . . .": *Ibid.,* 151.

72 "found fault with them . . .": *Ibid.*

72 "personal relations with . . .": *Ibid.,* 155.

72 "valuable study on organ . . .": *Ibid.,* 175.

72 "the most important disclosures . . .": *Ibid.,* 172.

72 "Adler's views are not . . .": *Ibid.,* 173.

73 "incompatability of his . . .": *Ibid.,* 177.

73 "I must avenge . . .": Lieberman, *Acts of Will,* 126.

73 "as for the internal . . .": Gay, *Life of Our Time,* 223.

74 "fencer's postures . . .": *Ibid.*

74 "I have always stayed . . .": *Ibid.*

74 "nonsensical castration . . .": *Ibid.*

74 "Upon learning of the impending . . .": Furtmüller, *Denken und Handeln,* 300–301.

75 "Herewith, I would like to notify . . .": Adler, *Social Interest,* 344.

76 "he confronts those members . . .": Nunberg and Federn, Vol. III, 281.

76 "a few rather useless . . .": Lieberman, *Acts of Will,* 126.

CHAPTER SIX
The Birth of Individual Psychology

78 Alfred Adler, "Fundamentals of Individual Psychology," trans. Heinz L. Ansbacher, *Journal of Individual Psychology*. Vol. 26(1), 1970, 39.

79 "driven mad by ambition . . .": Gay, *Life for Our Time*, 223.

79 "paranoid . . .": "Ex-Disciple Accuses Freud of Intolerance," *New York Times*, May 23, 1926, 16.

79 "Adler isn't a normal man . . .": *The Autobiography of Wilhelm Stekel*, ed. Emil A. Gutheil, New York: Liveright, 1950, 142.

79 "My first impulse was to join . . .": *New York Times*, May 23, 1926, 16.

79 "courtyards and sheltered alleys . . .": PB, 79.

80 Surviving minutes from sessions: Raissa Adler, "Minutes of the Society for Free Psychoanalytic Research, September 1912–January 1913." *Journal of Individual Psychology*, Vol. 38(1), March 1982, 22–27.

80 "having listened to empty debates . . .": *Ibid.*, 26.

80 "an unbearable human being . . .": Gay, *Life for Our Time*, 232.

80 "in the pay of Adlerism . . .": *Ibid.*

81 "When we were growing up . . .": AI, Alexandra Adler, October 6, 1990.

81 "We children, who always joined . . .": Alexandra Adler, "Recollections of My Father," *American Journal of Psychiatry*, Vol. 127(6), December 1970, 71.

81 "He would never, never hit us . . .": AI, Alexandra Adler, October 6, 1990.

81 "I found at once . . .": GM, 19.

81 "My father was not at all . . .": AI, Kurt Adler, April 5, 1992.

81 "Your teacher is an idiot . . .": *Ibid.*

82 "The Society in whose name . . .": Alfred Adler, Publisher's Foreword, *The Papers of the Society for Free Psychoanalytic Research*, Munich: Reinhardt, 1912, vi–vii.

86 "It is here, in the special ambience . . .": Helmut Gruber, *Red Vienna*, New York: Oxford University Press, 1991, 33.

86 "They were well-educated people . . .": *Ibid.*

86 "And who, if you please . . .": Hofmann, *The Viennese*, 43.

86 "I always knew that Herr Doktor Bronstein . . .": *Ibid.*

86 "It is during this period . . .": Alfred Adler, The Study of Child Psychology and Neurosis. *The Practice and Theory of Individual Psychology*, trans. P. Radin. London: Routledge and Kegan Paul, 1925. 61.

87 "the most important element . . .": Alfred Adler, "Individual-Psychological Treatment of Neuroses," *The Practice and Theory of Individual Psychology*, 41–42.

87 "the uncovering of the life-plan . . .": *Ibid.*, 44.

87 "The name of Individual Psychology . . .": Carl Furtmüller, Preface to *Journal for Individual Psychology*, Vol. 1(1), 1914, iii.

88 "We do not aim at . . .": *Ibid.*, iv.

88 "for both abnormal and normal psychology . . .": Heinz L. Ansbacher, Alfred Adler and G. Stanley Hall, "Correspondence and General Relationship," *Journal of the History of the Behavioral Sciences*, Vol. 7, 1971, 337.

88 "Sex anxieties are themselves . . .": *Ibid.*

88 "To my mind, there is very much . . .": *Ibid.*, 338.
89 "Your sustained interest . . .": *Ibid.*, 341.
89 "Presumably, the object . . .": Ernest Jones, *The Life and Work of Sigmund Freud,* Vol. II. New York: Basic Books, 46.
89 "his bomb . . .": Gay, *Life for Our Time,* 241.
89 "gathered around me with the expressed intention . . .": Sigmund Freud, "The History of the Psychoanalytic Movement," *The Basic Writings of Sigmund Freud.* Trans. and ed. A. A. Brill. New York: The Modern Library, 1938, 946.
89 "a colleague who had himself experienced . . .": *Ibid.*
90 "I had the opportunity . . .": *Ibid.*, 965.
90 "Do you believe that it is . . .": *Ibid.*
90 "radically false . . .": *Ibid.*, 972.
90 "a single new observation . . .": *Ibid.*, 970.
90 "The view of life . . .": *Ibid.*
90 "these [scientific criticisms] have not . . .": *Ibid.*, 971.

CHAPTER SEVEN
The Great War

92 "Noted Scientist Tells of Serious Austrian Problems," *San Francisco Chronicle,* Feburary 10, 1929.
92 "for the first time in thirty years . . .": Jose Brunner, "Psychiatry, Psychoanalysis, and Politics During the First World War," *Journal of the History of the Behavioral Sciences,* Vol. 27, October 1991, 356.
93 "on the wrong side . . .": *Ibid.*
93 "All my libido is given . . .": *Ibid.*
93 "Dear Mrs. Adler . . .": AAC, Container 1, General Correspondence, 1911–1918. Letter dated June 30, 1914.
93 A photo-postcard she sent Alfred: Raissa Adler to Adler, AAC, Container 1, General Correspondence. Undated.
93 "Shall wait.": PB, 117.
93 "It was initially . . .": AI, Kurt Adler, April 5, 1992.
94 "What's the matter? . . .": GM, 22.
94 "These were exciting . . .": Kurt Adler, "A Personal Autobiography," *Journal of Individual Psychology,* Vol. 37(2), 1981, 200.
95 "According to him . . .": HE, 585.
95 "explanations of only a purely speculative . . .": *Ibid.*, 586.
96 "interesting and reasonable . . .": *Ibid.*
96 "ingenious . . .": *Ibid.*
96 "as grotesque . . .": *Ibid.*
96 "Is it desirable . . .": *Ibid.*
97 "Had Freud brought us . . .": PB, 109.
97 "People sometimes say . . .": V. M. Leibin, Comments on "Minutes of the Society for Free Psychoanalytic Research." *Journal of Individual Psychology,* Vol. 38(1), March 1982, 30.

98 "Success can only be achieved . . .": Brunner, "Psychiatry, Psychoanalysis, and Politics During the First World War," 354.
98 "As the psychoanalyst Max Nonne . . .": *Ibid.*, 355.
99 "that his long-time colleague . . .": *Ibid.*
99 "who, as slave-drivers . . .": *Ibid.*
99 "By comparing the sleeping postures . . .": Alfred Adler, *The Problems of Neurosis*, ed. Philip Mairet. New York: Harper and Row, 1964, 152–153.
99 "The treatment of neuroses . . .": Alfred Adler, "New View-Points of War Neuroses," *The Practice and Theory of Individual Psychology*. New York: Harper and Row, 1964, 291.
100 "Your telegram reached me . . .": PB, 93.
102 "This sudden missionary idea . . .": *Ibid.*, 123.
102 "medical ideas and purely medical considerations . . .": Adler, "New View-Points of War Neuroses," 291.
102 "The enormous amount of data . . .": *Ibid.*, 301.
103 "behind every neurosis . . .": *Ibid.*, 305.
103 "Attempts should be made . . .": Alfred Adler, "Compulsion Neurosis," *The Practice and Theory of Individual Psychology*, 200.
103 "If we were to put . . .": *Ibid.*, 201.
103 "great synthesis of uniting . . .": Alfred Adler, "Dostoyevski," *The Practice and Theory of Individual Psychology*, 283.
103 "the richest fulfillment of human worth . . .": *Ibid.*
103 "Man must look . . .": *Ibid.*, 288.
104 "[Dostoyevski's] achievements as a psychologist . . .": *Ibid.*, 290.
104 "Physicians will eventually become . . .": Alfred Adler, "Individual-Psychology Education," *The Practice and Theory of Individual Psychology*, 317.
104 "so that they may become . . .": *Ibid.*
104 "a man whose childhood . . .": *Ibid.*, 321.
105 "It is, of course . . .": *Ibid.*, 326.

CHAPTER EIGHT
A Psychological Revolutionary

106 Alfred Adler, *Social Interest*, 126.
106 "When the republic of Austria was proclaimed . . .": Manes Sperber, *The Unheeded Warning*, trans. Harry Zohn. New York: Holmes and Meier, 1991, 3.
107 "Hardly was the train . . .": Zweig, *The World of Yesterday*, 285.
107 "The famine was unrelieved . . .": Sperber, *Unheeded Warning*, 3.
107 "We never had much money . . .": AI, Kurt Adler, April 5, 1992.
108 "Austria is what's left . . .": Modris Eksteins, *Rites of Spring*. Boston: Houghton Mifflin, 1989, 47.
108 "mutilated trunk bleeding . . .": Berkley, *Vienna*, 143.
108 "rump state . . .": *Ibid.*
108 "pathetic relic . . .": *Ibid.*
109 "death warrant . . .": *Ibid.*, 142.

109 "I don't mind dying . . .": Hofmann, *The Viennese*, 162.

109 "Eighty percent of the intellectuals . . .": Harriet Pass Friedenreich, *Jewish Politics in Vienna, 1918–1938*. Bloomington, IN: Indiana University Press, 1991, 92.

110 "the bodyguards of Jewish capitalism . . .": Hofmann, *The Viennese*, 160.

110 "As Leopold Plasehkes . . .": Friedenreich, *Jewish Politics in Vienna*, 88.

111 "Adler's ambition never faced . . .": Furtmüller, "Alfred Adler: A Biographical Essay," 372.

112 "The rule of Bolshevism . . .": Ansbacher and Ansbacher, eds., *Individual Psychology*, 457.

113 "the enforcement of socialism . . .": *Ibid.*, 456.

113 "a Hercules who strangles . . .": *Ibid.*

113 "Human nature generally answers . . .": Ansbacher and Ansbacher, eds. *Individual Psychology*, 457.

113 "Now [some people] want . . .": *Ibid.*, 458.

113 "It is not the people . . .": *Ibid.*

113 "Herded together, with blinkers on . . .": *Ibid.*

113 "they were no longer whipped dogs . . .": *Ibid.*

114 "The present generation . . .": Zweig, *The World of Yesterday*, 83.

114 "the well-fed, self-satisfied . . .": Alfred Adler, "The Individual Psychology of Prostitution," *The Practice and Theory of Individual Psychology*, 329.

114 "a deficient social feeling . . .": *Ibid.*, 334.

115 "a stigma and a reproach . . .": *Ibid.*, 338.

115 "This explanation may not . . .": *Ibid.*

115 "Of the 'blessings' that came . . .": Alfred Adler, "Demoralized Children," *The Practice and Theory of Individual Psychology*, 339.

115 "We know the demerits . . .": *Ibid.*, 346.

115 "curative pedagogy . . .": *Ibid.*, 350.

116 "Even in times of complete peace . . .": *Ibid.*, 349.

116 "the determination and prosecution . . .": K. R. Eissler, *Freud as an Expert Witness*, trans. Christine Trollope. Madison, CT: International Universities Press, 1986, 11.

117 "the immediate cause of all war neuroses . . .": *Ibid.*, 76.

117 "The physicians had to play . . .": *Ibid.*

117 "This kind of generosity . . .": *Ibid.*, 118.

119 "for nothing about him . . .": Sperber, *Unheeded Warning*, 43.

119 "You spoke like an individual psychologist . . .": *Ibid.*, 46.

120 " 'was simple,' reminisced Dreikurs . . .": Janet Terner and W. L. Pew, *The Courage to be Imperfect: The Life and Work of Rudolf Dreikurs*. New York: Hawthorne, 1978, 53.

120 "How can you treat . . .": *Ibid.*

121 "In contradistinction to your view . . .": Wilhelm Reich, *Reich Speaks of Freud*, eds. Mary Higgins and Chester M. Raphael. New York: Farrar, Straus, and Giroux, 1967, 143.

121 "It is far more logical . . .": *Ibid.*

122 "The World War hindered . . .": Erwin Wexberg, Preface to *Heilen und Bilden* (To Heal and to Educate). Munich: Bergmann, 1922, v.

122 "It is no coincidence . . .": *Ibid.*

122   "Just as we do not want . . .": *Ibid.*, vi.
122   "The ideas of individual psychology . . .": *Ibid.*
122   "By this decision . . .": Heinz L. Ansbacher, "Adler and the Vienna College of Professors," *Journal of Individual Psychology*, Vol. 22, 1966, 235–236.

CHAPTER NINE
Red Vienna

124   Alfred Adler, "Bolshevism and Psychology," trans. Heinz L. Ansbacher, *Int. Runsch. Zurich*, 4.
125   "On a given day, a worker . . .": Anson Rabinach, *The Austrian Socialist Experiment*. Boulder, CO: Westview, 1985, 5.
128   "there were no trained . . .": Regine Seidler, "Alfred Adler and the Teachers," *Journal of Individual Psychology*. Vol. 6, 1947, 51.
128   "[these] served as much . . .": *Ibid.*, 52.
128   "The findings were generalized . . .": *Ibid.*
129   "It is well known . . .": Olga Knopf, "Orophylactic Educational Guidance in Parents' Associations," *Guiding the Child*, ed. Alfred Adler, trans. Benjamin Ginzburg. New York: Greenberg, 1930, 89.
130   "Children who are impudent . . .": David M. Levy, "Individual Psychology in a Vienna School," *Social Service Review*. Vol. 8, June 1929, 210.
132   "Their records are at once . . .": Madeline Ganz, *The Psychology of the Child*, New York: Humanities Press, 1953, 123.
133   "The rapid economic development . . .": HE, 618–619.
135   "[Adler enabled the teachers to] . . .": Furtmüller, "Alfred Adler: A Biographical Essay," 379.
135   "have for many years . . .": *Ibid.*
137   "great social and cultural achievements . . .": Hofmann, *The Viennese*, 196.
138   "that today Austria stands . . .": Gruber, *Red Vienna*, 77.

CHAPTER TEN
Beyond Austria: International Prominence

139   Alfred Adler, "Inferiority Sense Held to be Our Chief Enemy," *New York Times*, September 20, 1925, 13.
141   "The socialist reformers showed little . . .": Gruber, *Red Vienna*, 156–157.
141   "one researcher at the time . . .": *Ibid.*, 159.
142   "When we examine . . .": Alfred Adler, *Cooperation between the Sexes*, ed. and trans. Heinz L. Ansbacher and Rowena R. Ansbacher. Garden City, NY: Doubleday, 1978, 27.
142   "Should one force . . .": *Ibid.*, 29.
142   "Alone in the interests . . .": *Ibid.*, 30.
144   "But perhaps the boy is right!": PB, 171.
144   "He gave us up . . .": *Ibid.*
144   "I never quite trusted . . .": AI, Kurt Adler, April 5, 1992.

145 "We hold to the stodgy . . .": Alfred Adler, *Diskussionsbemergkungen zum Vortrage des Prof. Max Adler* [Discussion comments on the lecture by Prof. Max Adler]. *Journal for Individual Psychology.* Vol. 3, 1925, 222.

145 "The raising of spiritual . . .": *Ibid.*

146 "I find the studies of Marx . . .": *Ibid., 223.*

146 "Of course, we should not . . .": *Ibid.*

146 "That Max Adler . . .": *Ibid.*

147 "One of the most important . . .": *New York Times,* September 20, 1925, 12.

147 "shown how the imperialistic . . .": *Ibid.*

147 "Motives of hatred . . .": *Ibid.*

147 "Most of the methods . . .": *Ibid.*

148 "I divined that the hurt . . .": Sperber, *Unheeded Warning,* 50.

148 "To me, he was an exemplary teacher . . .": *Ibid., 49.*

148 "I was stupid enough . . .": *Ibid., 85.*

151 "soon was installed as director . . .": PB, 231.

151 Editor Philip Mairet and several: Philip Mairet, *Autobiographical and Other Papers,* ed. C. H. Sisson. Manchester: Carcanet, 1981, 131–132.

151 "I have passed my two lectures . . .": AAC, Container 1, General Correspondence, 1926. Letter dated November 9, 1926.

151 "vivid and anxious dream . . .": PB, 204.

PART II

153 "Inferiority Complex Cause of All Ills," *San Francisco Chronicle,* February 4, 1929.

CHAPTER ELEVEN
A New World in Social Upheaval

155 Freda Kirchwey, *Our Changing Morality.* London: Routledge and Kegan Paul, 1925, viii–xix.

157 "there had been a very . . .": Frederic Lewis Allen, *Only Yesterday and Today.* New York: Harper and Row, 1986, 94.

158 "a portable living room . . .": James Lincoln Collier, *The Rise of Selfishness in America.* New York: Oxford University Press, 1991, 151.

158 "a house of prostitution on wheels . . .": *Ibid., 100.*

158 "brilliant men, beautiful jazz babies . . .": *Ibid., 101.*

158 "neckers, petters, white kisses . . .": *Ibid., 101–102.*

158 "The potentialities of motion pictures . . .": Paul Sann, *The Lawless Decade.* Greenwich, CT: Fawcett, 1971, 86–87.

159 "Men and women are ignoring . . .": Kirchwey, *Our Changing Morality,* v–vi, ix.

161 "The man, through a long-outworn . . .": Alfred Adler, "Marriage as a Task," *The Book of Marriage,* ed. H. Keyserling. New York: Harcourt, Brace, 1926, 363.

162   "You will find no demagogic oratory . . .": *Outlook and Independent.* Vol. 147, November 9, 1927, 314.

162   "for the extraordinary value . . .": *Saturday Review of Literature.* Vol. 4, December 24, 1927, 468.

162   "there are problems of human . . .": *Survey Graphic.* Vol. 59, December 1, 1927, 321.

162   "temporary marriage [which] can be . . .": *New York Times,* November 27, 1927, 4.

163   "the greatest experience of my life . . .": Catherine Lucille Covert, "Freud on the Front Page," *Dissertation Abstracts International.* Ann Arbor: University Microfilms, 1975, 143.

163   "I was full of enthusiasm . . .": *Ibid.,* 139.

165   "Mabel Dodge writes about Mother Love . . .": E. Fuller Torrey, *Freudian Fraud.* New York: HarperCollins, 1992, 27.

165   "Every case of nervous invalidism . . .": *Ibid.,* 28.

166   "That there will be found . . .": R. S. Woodsworth, *The Nation.* Vol. 103, 1916, 396.

166   "What united experimental . . .": Gail A. Hornstein, "The Return of the Repressed: Psychology's Problematic Relations with Psychoanalysis, 1909–1960," *American Psychologist.* Vol. 47(2), Feburary 1992, 256.

166   "psychoanalysis . . . removes . . .": Covert, "Freud on the Front Page," 245.

167   "satisfaction of thwarted curiosity . . .": *Ibid.,* 141.

167   "latest intellectual fad . . .": Covert, "Freud on the Front Page," 54.

167   "The extraordinary symbolism . . .": *Ibid.,* 248.

168   "If there is anything . . .": Torrey, *Freudian Fraud,* 31.

168   "Don't Tell Me What . . .": Covert, "Freud on the Front Page," 213.

168   "a really great love story . . .": Gay, *Life for Our Time,* 454.

168   "like an unpleasant . . .": *Ibid.,* 563.

169   "Freud had an antipathy . . .": Silas L. Warner, "Freud's Antipathy to America," *Journal of the American Academy of Psychoanalysis.* Vol. 19(1), 1991, 142.

169   "he knew a lot about America . . .": *Ibid.,* 142.

169   "Thirty-three years ago . . .": Gay, *Life for Our Time,* 562.

169   "if fate had not smiled . . .": *Ibid.,* 563.

169   "governed by authority . . .": *Ibid.,* 562.

169   "by the dollar . . .": *Ibid.*

169   "too American . . .": *Ibid.,* 563.

169   "America should bring in . . .": *Ibid.*

170   "American dyspepsia . . .": Warner, "Freud's Antipathy to America," 146.

170   "these people cannot even . . .": *Ibid.,* 147.

170   "free and easy manner . . .": *Ibid.*

170   "America is a mistake . . .": *Ibid.*

170   *Echt Americanish* ("It's American-like"): Ronald Clark, *Freud, The Man and the Cause.* New York: Random House, 1980, 278.

171   "All its popularity . . .": Gay, *Life for Our Time,* 564.

171   "Psychiatrists and neurologists . . .": Warner, "Freud's Antipathy to America," 148.

171   "These same men . . .": *Ibid.,* 149.
171   "Many of these evils . . .": *Ibid.*
172   "sojourn among such savages . . .": *Ibid.,* 151.
172   "nice that you . . .": *Ibid.*
172   "What is the use . . .": Gay, *Life for Our Time,* 563.
172   "America is useful . . .": *Ibid.*
172   "Is it not sad . . .": *Ibid.,* by permission of Sigmund Freud Copyrights, Wivenhoe, UK.

CHAPTER TWELVE
Planting the Flag

173   Alfred Adler, "The Drive for Success in America," *International Journal for Individual Psychology,* Vol. 5, 1927, 226.
174   "The Freudian psychologists . . .": Ira S. Wile, *The Challenge of Childhood.* New York: T. Seltzer, 1925, 160–161.
176   "I quite agree with H. G. Wells . . .": *New York World,* December 26, 1926.
176   "Men and nations cannot bear . . .": *Ibid.*
176   "In Russia, no usual reformers . . .": *Ibid.*
176   "The behavior pattern of persons . . .": *Ibid.*
176   "Mussolini's behavior patterns . . .": *Ibid.*
177   "In life, you can find . . .": Alfred Adler, "The Feeling of Inferiority and its Compensation," *Bulletin of the New York Academy of Medicine.* Vol. 3, April 1927, 255.
177   "before a difficult problem . . .": *Ibid.*
177   "fears a defeat even more . . .": *Ibid.*
178   "There, in a cosmopolitan, democratic group . . .": *Providence Journal,* December 13, 1926.
178   "famous Viennese psychologist and neurologist . . .": *Providence Journal,* January 15, 1927.
178   "popularly known as . . .": *Ibid.*
178   "Every individual from birth . . .": *Ibid.*
178   "The three great questions . . .": *Ibid.*
178   "helping the child . . .": *Ibid.*
179   "Dr. Adler, our ancestors . . .": GM, 50.
179   "Yes, yes. . . .": *Ibid.*
179   "He had selected his term . . .": *Ibid.,* 72.
180   "If your child sleeps . . .": *Detroit News,* February 11, 1927.
180   "very exciting . . .": AAC, Container 1, General Correspondence, 1920–1927. Letter dated February 11, 1927.
180   "I am terribly spoiled . . .": *Ibid.*
180   "I can't remember when . . .": *Ibid.*
181   "That is the will of God . . .": Lieberman, *Acts of Will,* 268.
181   "before as many Chicago teachers . . .": *Chicago Daily Tribune,* February 23, 1927.
181   "Children need optimism . . .": *Ibid.*

182 "Tomorrow, I will give my last . . .": AAC, Container 1, General Correspondence, 1920–1927. Letter dated March 3, 1927.

182 "Here, again, great acclaim . . .": *Ibid.*

182 "Every child is . . .": *Detroit News,* April 21, 1927.

183 "What is an inferiority complex? . . .": *Boston Globe,* April 10, 1927.

183 "American interest in psychology . . .": *New York Times,* April 10, 1927, 5.

CHAPTER THIRTEEN

Coming Home

184 Alfred Adler to Alexander Neuer: Alfred Adler, "The Drive for Success in America," ed. L. Zilahi. *International Journal for Individual Psychology,* Vol. 5, 1927, 226.

184 "Due to the incomparably higher . . .": *Ibid.*

184 "leadership and most important institutions . . .": *Ibid.*

185 "a substantial number of American . . .": *Ibid.,* 227.

185 "It is very rare . . .": *Ibid.*

185 "working population has won . . .": *Ibid.*

185 "The social tendencies of . . .": *Ibid.*

185 "much greater role in cultural . . .": *Ibid.*

185 "Although [they] are active . . .": *Ibid.*

186 "In most cases, the wrong . . .": *Ibid.,* 228.

186 "more spoiled than in Europe . . .": *Ibid.*

186 "a constant race . . .": *Ibid.,* 227.

187 "profoundly disappointed . . .": Phyllis Bottome, *The Goal.* New York: Vanguard, 1962, 138.

187 "I had expected a Socratic genius . . .": *Ibid.*

187 "He spoke with horror . . .": *Ibid.,* 139.

187 "We are all fellow men . . .": *Ibid.*

187 "In those hours . . .": *Ibid.,* 140.

188 "An armed police contingent . . .": Wilhelm Reich, *People in Trouble,* trans. Philip Schmitz. New York: Farrar, Straus, and Giroux, 1976, 24–25.

189 "The everyday appearance . . .": *Ibid.,* 33.

189 "Shooting is popular nowadays . . .": *Ibid.,* 39.

189 "We are so convinced . . .": *Ibid.,* 77.

190 "It seemed to me that he lacked . . .": *Ibid.,* 81.

193 "socio-economic order . . .": Alice Rühle-Gerstel, *Der Weg Zum Wir* (The Road to We). Munich: Ernst Reinhardt, 1980, 13.

193 "a new unity . . .": *Ibid.,* 221.

193 "class conflict and courage . . .": *Ibid.*

193 "activity of real class consciousness . . .": *Ibid.*

193 "[It] particularly appealed to me . . .": Sperber, *Unheeded Warning,* 86.

194 "remain just as independent . . .": *Ibid.,* 87.

CHAPTER FOURTEEN
Return to America

196 *Publishers Weekly,* Vol. 115, January 28, 1928, 347.
196 "melancholia, pampered youth, and suicide . . .": *New York Times,* February 5, 1928, 19.
196 "denied that, contrary to popular belief . . .": *Ibid.*
196 "All psychological illness is based . . .": *Ibid.*
197 "rubbish [for] many circumstances . . .": *Ibid.*
197 "every suicide is a cowardly escape . . .": *Ibid.*
197 "We cannot develop without struggling . . .": *Ibid.*
198 Temperament and Endocrine Secretion: Alfred Adler, *Understanding Human Nature,* trans. Walter B. Wolfe. New York: Greenberg, 1927, 180.
198 "Untamed Instincts . . .": *Ibid.,* 248.
198 "The purpose of this book . . .": *Ibid.,* author's preface, unpaginated.
199 "It is not our *objective* experiences . . . . . .": *Ibid.,* 245.
199 "class injustice . . .": *Ibid.,* 120.
199 "class differences . . . have created privilege . . .": *Ibid.,* 121.
199 "the economic basis, the technical form . . .": *Ibid.,* 27.
199 "All our institutions . . .": *Ibid.,* 123.
199 "masculine dominance is not a natural thing . . .": *Ibid.,* 125.
199 "[t]here is no justification . . .": *Ibid.,* 127.
199 "poisons . . .": *Ibid.,* 145.
199 "It is our duty . . .": *Ibid.,* 147.
199 "If parents were good educators . . .": *Ibid.,* 279.
200 "is not adapted to this task . . .": *Ibid.,* 283.
200 "Up to the present time . . .": *Ibid.,* 284.
201 "If you want an interesting life . . .": *Publishers Weekly,* Vol. 156, October 1, 1949, 1569.
201 "Do you have an inferiority complex . . .": *Publishers Weekly,* Vol. 115, January 28, 1928, 347.
201 "Adler demands that . . .": *Survey Graphic,* Vol. 123, April 15, 1928, 60.
202 "To understand human nature . . .": S. D. House, *Bookman,* Vol. 67, March 28, 1928, 98.
202 "The Adlerian approach . . .": S. D. House, *Saturday Review of Literature,* Vol. 4, March 31, 1928, 716.
202 "[Adler's] philosophy is colored . . .": *Ibid.*
202 "It is a pleasure . . .": *Ibid.*
203 "Of all psychiatrists, Dr. Adler . . .": *American Journal of Sociology,* Vol. 34(2), September 1928, 391.
204 "When you see such an interest . . .": AAC, Container 1, Lectures 1928–1929. Case Conference, February 10, 1928, Morning Session, 10.
204 "Perhaps we will find . . .": *Ibid.,* 12.
204 "It is not necessary . . .": AAC, Container 1, Lectures 1928–1929. Case Conference, February 10, 1928. Afternoon Session, 7–9.

204 "I had the privilege . . .": Heinz L. Ansbacher, "Alfred Adler's Influence on the Three Leading Co-Founders of Humanistic Psychology," *Journal of Humanistic Psychology.* Vol. 30(4), Fall 1990, 47.

205 "Individual psychology and its significance . . .": New School for Social Research, spring 1928 catalogue, 34.

206 "does not lie in the fact . . .": AAC, Container 2, Article, "A Brief Comparison of Individual Psychology and Psychoanalysis," trans. Sibyl Mandell. Undated, 2.

206 "social feeling is what enables . . .": Alfred Adler, "Feelings and Emotions from the Standpoint of Individual Psychology," *Feelings and Emotions: The Wittenberg Symposium,* ed. M. L. Reymert. Worcester, MA: Clark University Press, 1928, 318.

207 "Criminals are made, not born . . .": *Ibid.,* 320.

207 "inferiority complex . . . . This feeling . . .": *Ibid.,* 318.

207 "friend and old pupil of Dr. Sigmund Freud . . .": *Time,* October 29, 1927.

207 "Dr. Adler indicated that . . .": *Wittenberg Torchlight,* May 8, 1928.

207 "You will never find . . .": AAC, Container 1, Lectures 1928–1929. Reports of Medical Meetings, "Psychiatrists Meeting with Dr. Alfred Adler," May 4, 1929, 1.

208 "Tell the mother that . . .": *Ibid.,* 2.

208 "To a certain degree . . .": *Ibid.,* 7.

208 "I propose always . . .": *Ibid.,* 3.

208 "The mother notices . . .": *Ibid.,* 2.

208 "Do not fight . . .": *Ibid.,* 14.

208 "I cannot deny that . . .": *Ibid.,* 6.

209 "I never promise . . .": *Ibid.,* 17.

CHAPTER FIFTEEN

The Great Popularizer

210 William Leon Smyser, "Father of the Inferiority Complex," *New York Herald,* March 17, 1929.

211 "Some of [the papers] were Adler's . . .": Heinz L. Ansbacher. Introduction to *Problems of Neurosis,* by Alfred Adler. New York: Harper and Row, Torchbook Edition, 1964, xxiii.

211 "rewriting the whole . . .": *Ibid.*

211 "saw what I had done . . .": *Ibid.*

211 "Adler made any corrections . . .": Mairet, *Autobiographical and other Papers,* xiv.

211 "He was never a very . . .": *Ibid.*

211 "professor of the University of Vienna . . .": AAC, Container 1, General Correspondence, 1928–1929. Letter dated November 1928.

212 "reactionary . . .": Heinz L. Ansbacher, "Alfred Adler in the Great Soviet Encyclopedia," *Journal of Individual Psychology.* Vol. 25(2), November 1969, 185.

212 "psychological basis of the ideology . . .": *Ibid.*

212 "a polyglot mixture of paupers . . .": Smyser, "Father of the Inferiority Complex."

212 "[the spectacle of] Adler's debating . . .": *Ibid.*

213 "Love is the basis . . .": *Ibid.*

213 "Mr. Freud has bad luck . . .": Alfred Adler, *Uber den nevosen Charakter* [The Neurotic Character] 4th ed. Munich: Bergmann, 1928, 24.

214 "The art of individual psychology . . .": Alfred Adler, *The Case of Miss R.*, New York: Greenberg, 1929, 4.

215 "divine how . . .": *Ibid.*, 306.

215 "of her compulsion neurosis . . .": *Ibid.*

215 "because of its unique subject . . .": *Publishers Weekly.* Vol. 116, February 4, 1929, 486.

215 "A young girl tells . . .": *Ibid.*

216 "The United States is like an ocean . . .": "Inferiority Complex Cause of All Ills," *San Francisco Chronicle,* Feburary 4, 1929.

216 "In the mid-afternoon . . .": GM, 50.

216 "keep him away . . .": *Ibid.*

216 "was not prepared . . .": *Ibid.*, 51.

216 "a loop around . . .": *Ibid.*

217 "is far from prepossessing . . .": "Famous Psychologist is Guest on Campus," *Mills College Weekly,* February 13, 1929, 2.

217 "The most revealing glimpse . . .": *Ibid.*

217 "on the bearing of the system . . .": New School for Social Research, spring 1929 catalogue, 17.

217 "psychological influence of occupation . . .": *Ibid.*

217 "love, marriage, and family life . . .": *Ibid.*

218 "problems in behavior . . .": *Ibid.*

218 "misadjusted childhood, neuroses . . .": *Ibid.*

218 "the nature of nationalism . . .": *Ibid.*

218 "Readers of this book . . .": W. Beran Wolfe, "Adler and our Neurotic World," Introduction to *The Pattern of Life* by Alfred Adler. New York: Greenberg, 1930, 9.

219 "so that Carl will feel honored . . .": *Ibid.*, 107.

219 "It is a common situation . . .": *Ibid.*, 73.

219 "not to whip him . . .": *Ibid.*, 126.

220 "The less you have him . . .": *Ibid.*, 267.

220 "It is never desirable . . .": *Ibid.*, 111.

220 "Individuals who have no social interest . . .": *Ibid.*, 187.

220 "Moreover. . . . Stories of good people . . .": *Ibid.*

221 "Let's go. It's no use . . .": GM, 72–73.

221 "has an eloquence . . .": Smyser, "Father of the Inferiority Complex."

221 "Even today, [Adler and Freud] . . .": *Ibid.*

221 "Scientific education has again . . .": *Ibid.*

223 "I wish I could picture . . .": John B. Watson, *Behaviorism.* New York: Harper Collins, 1925, 248.

224 "once a child's character . . .": John B. Watson, *Psychological Care of Infant and Child.* New York: Norton, 1928, 3.

224 "I believe that the . . .": *Ibid.*, 186.

225   "Any religion that helps . . .": *New York Times,* January 19, 1929, 18.

225   "Since children are made . . .": Watson, *Psychological Care,* 7.

225   "to the first mother . . .": *Ibid.,* dedication page.

225   "The oldest profession of the race . . .": *Ibid.,* 11.

225   "There is a sensible way . . .": *Ibid.,* 81.

225   "the child should learn . . .": *Ibid.,* 84.

226   "Mother love is a dangerous . . .": *Ibid.,* 87.

226   "It is a serious question . . .": *Ibid.,* 5.

226   "The old theory was . . .": *Ibid.,* 173.

226   "Every college and university . . .": *Ibid.,* 182.

226   "theorist" should be "backed up . . .": David Cohen, *J. B. Watson, The Founder of Behaviorism.* London: Routledge and Kegan, Paul, 1979, 212.

226   "on every intelligent mother's shelf.": *Ibid.,* 218.

227   "a godsend to parents . . .": *Ibid.*

227   "democracy safe for himself . . .": Kerry W. Buckley, *Mechanical Man.* New York: Guilford, 1989, 166.

227   "I have always been amused . . .": *Ibid.,* 167.

229   "We recognize the vital importance . . .": Arthur Schlesinger, Jr., *A History of American Presidential Elections.* New York: Chelsea House, 1971, Vol. 3, 2591.

230   "In his manic times . . .": E. Mott Davis to James Gould, private collection of James Gould, August 18, 1985.

230   "He was constantly anxious . . .": *Ibid.*

231   Davis would not only bankroll . . . : Ted Frothingham, "Charles Davis: Amazing Millionaire," *Cape Cod Times,* June–August, 1972; AI, Jean Nandi, November 22, 1992.

232   "It's a little thing . . .": Frothingham, "Charles Davis."

232   "Carl, you're like a little boy . . .": *Ibid.*

CHAPTER SIXTEEN

Relocating to New York

233   Alfred Adler, "Religion and Individual Psychology," in *Alfred Adler: Superiority and Social Interest,* ed. Heinz L. Ansbacher and Rowena Ansbacher. New York: Norton, 1964, 279.

234   "My husband thanks you cordially . . .": Raissa Adler to Leon Trotsky, Trotsky Archives, Shelf A46, Item 111, The Houghton Library of Harvard University, July 6, 1930.

234   "There is an acute revolutionary situation . . .": Raissa Adler to the Politburo of the Central Committee of the Austrian Communist Party, Trotsky Archives, Shelf A46, Item 13741, The Houghton Library of Harvard University, January 27, 1930.

236   "The greatest contribution of independent . . .": *New York Times,* November 6, 1929, 14.

236   "The Religious Significance of the . . .": *Bulletin of The Community Church of New York,* December 1929, 5.

237   "Because an individual has . . .": Alfred Adler, *The Science of Living.* New York: Greenberg, 1929, 385.

238 "These complexes are not . . .": *Ibid.,* 104.
238 "whether carried on in . . .": *Ibid.,* 80.
238 "in which children must sit . . .": *Ibid.,* 82.
238 "the children are their teacher's friends . . .": *Ibid.*
238 "so set in tradition . . .": *Ibid.,* 83.
238 "normal children, if there be such . . .": *Ibid.,* 84.
238 "The best point of attack . . .": *Ibid.,* 83.
238 "Dr. Adler, famous Viennese physician . . .": *New York Times,* October 27, 1929, 18.
238 "What would you do? . . .": Adler, *Problems of Neurosis,* 72.
239 "are indications of . . .": *Ibid.,* 90.
239 "In a certain popular music-hall . . .": *Ibid.,* 91.
239 "We do not, of course . . .": *Ibid.,* 121.
239 "Dr. Adler is well known . . .": *New York Times,* August 24, 1930, 12.
240 "from yesterday, I have begun . . .": Alan Porter to Charles Davis, Miscellaneous Correspondence, April 2, 1930.
241 "Other articles which I have . . .": *Ibid.*
241 "It is not hard to understand . . .": Alfred Adler, "Individual Psychology and Crime," *Journal of Individual Psychology,* Vol. 32, November 1976, 135.
242 "a cheap superiority complex . . .": *Ibid.,* 141.
242 "change every single criminal . . .": *Ibid.*
242 "we find that in hard times . . .": *Ibid.,* 142.
242 "can act as a challenge . . .": *Ibid.*
242 "not mention the names of criminals . . .": *Ibid.*
242 "We should not imagine that criminals . . .": *Ibid.,* 143.
242 "its ten million dollar fund . . .": *Detroit Educational Bulletin,* Vol. 13(4), December 1929, 4.
242 "Ever since it first found . . .": *Detroit News,* January 4, 1930.
243 "I would urge . . .": *Ibid.*
243 "Only living humans . . .": *Ibid.*
243 "always understand how . . .": AAC, Container 1, Lectures 1930. "Dr. Adler's Lecture to Teachers," January 13, 1930, 6.
243 "You should use sympathy . . .": *Ibid.*
243 "We do not know . . .": *Ibid.*
243 "Life will correct it . . .": Marie I. Rasey, *Toward Maturity.* New York: Hinds, Hayden, and Eldridge, 1947, 195.
244 "Now you will stay here . . .": Marie I. Rasey, *It Takes Time.* New York: Harper and Brothers, 1953, 161.
244 "The summer ended . . .": *Ibid.,* 162.
245 "Persons who spend . . .": *Detroit News,* February 26, 1930.
245 "in my despair, I went . . .": Heinz L. Ansbacher, "Psychology: A Way of Living," *Journal of Individual Psychology.* Vol. 37(2), 1981, 154.
246 "Dr. Adler is a strong believer . . .": Editor's introduction to "Alfred Adler, Something About Myself," *Childhood and Character,* April 1930, 6.
247 "had been taken over . . .": *New York Times,* March 24, 1930, 13.

CHAPTER SEVENTEEN
"Books Like Firecrackers" and Mass Politics

248 "Inferiority Sense Held to be Our Chief Enemy," *The New York Times,* September 20, 1925, 12.

249 "Usually on the basis . . .": *New York Times,* October 5, 1930, 10.

249 "Dr. Wolfe's preface reveals . . .": *Outlook and Independent,* April 30, 1930, 710.

249 "Perhaps that is why . . .": *Ibid.*

250 "shows how children are readjusted . . .": *New York Times,* October 5, 1910, 10.

251 "These weapons may be compared . . .": Alfred Adler, *The Education of Children,* trans. Eleanor and Friedrich Jensen. New York: Greenberg, 1930, 78–79.

251 "What is essential . . .": *Ibid.,* 96.

252 "There are many persons . . .": *Ibid.,* 221.

252 "An educator's most important task . . .": *Ibid.,* 84.

252 "We are entering a period . . .": *Ibid.,* 249.

252 "One finds much good sense . . .": *New York Times,* October 5, 1910, 10.

253 "Alfred Adler's new books . . .": *Outlook and Independent,* July 30, 1930, 508.

253 "While it has slowly . . .": *Books,* May 11, 1930, 10.

254 "in acknowledgment of the . . .": HE, 590.

254 "a deserving pupil of Freud's . . .": PB, 214.

256 "not merely is this . . .": Sigmund Freud, *Civilization and its Discontents,* ed. and trans. James Strachey. New York: Norton, 1961, 57.

256 "the sense of guilt . . .": *Ibid.,* 81.

256 "It forms the basis . . .": *Ibid.,* 60.

256 "indestructible . . .": *Ibid.,* 61.

257 "After spending a week . . .": Mairet, *Autobiographical and Other Papers,* 132.

258 "Willi Reich was a stocky . . .": Sperber, *Unheeded Warning,* 137.

258 "The whole . . . system . . .": Raissa Adler, "Children's Education in the Soviet Union," *Journal for Individual Psychology.* Vol. 9, 1931, 297.

259 "Today, it is no longer feasible . . .": Alice Rühle-Gerstel, "The Role of Psychology in the Social Upheaval," *Krise der Psychologie, Psychologie der Krise* [The Crisis of Psychology, The Psychology of Crisis]. Berlin: Fachgruppe für dialetisch materialistsche Psychologie, 1932, 52.

259 "Here is something to think about . . .": Sperber, "The Present State of Psychology," *Krise der Psychologie, Psychologie der Krise* [The Crisis of Psychology, The Psychology of Crisis]. Berlin: Fachgruppe für dialetisch materialistsche Psychologie, 1932, 15.

260 "I could not find anything . . .": PB, 150.

260 "the moment I heard . . .": *Ibid.*

261 "No two individuals are . . .": Alfred Adler, "The Structure of Neurosis," *Lancet,* Vol. 1, January 17, 1931, 136.

261 "not very deep and must be taught . . .": *Ibid.*

261 "be started at school . . .": *Ibid.,* 137.

261 "At what stage does the semi-sanity . . .": *Ibid.*

261 "No general rules . . .": *Ibid.*

262 "The problem I want to discuss . . .": Alfred Adler, "The Meaning of Life," *Lancet*, Vol. 1, January 31, 1931, 225.
262 "It is often said . . .": *Ibid.*, 226.
262 "not rightly prepared for life . . .": *Ibid.*, 226–227.
262 "We say that the ability . . .": *Ibid.*, 228.
263 "masterpiece" of creativity . . . : Alfred Adler, "The Practice of Individual Psychology," *Lancet*, Vol. 1, January 24, 1931, 139.
263 "By her neurosis . . .": *Ibid.*
264 "the Religion of the Aryan Will . . .": H. C. Rutherford, *Certainly, Future: Selected Writings by Dimitrije Mitrinovic.* Boulder, CO: East European Monographs, distributed by Columbia University Press, 1987, 12.
265 "an organized European Senate . . .": *Ibid.*, 95.
265 "The Black, the Red, and the Yellow races . . .": *Ibid.*, 98.
265 "The world has no direct use . . .": *Ibid.*, 104.
265 "We wish to be fair . . .": *Ibid.*, 102.
265 "Everywhere the Jewish mentality . . .": *Ibid.*, 97.
265 "a monster, not a man . . .": *Ibid.*, 329.
265 "Now, at the same time . . .": *Ibid.*
265 "Until mankind understands . . .": *Ibid.*, 335.
265 "Nothing could have penetrated . . .": *Ibid.*, 336–337.
266 "The Individual Psychology of Adler . . .": *Ibid.*, 334.
266 "The contribution which Adler has made . . .": *Ibid.*, 349.
266 "Comparatively suddenly, the whole world . . .": Mairet, *Autobiographical and Other Papers*, 205.
266 "financial parasitism . . .": *Ibid.*, 201.
266 "That idea must be found . . .": *Ibid.*, 205.
267 "Dimitrije would have taken . . .": *Ibid.*, 132–133.
268 "psycho-physical parallelism . . .": *British Medical Journal*, Vol. 2, November 4, 1933, 848.
268 "To him a patient . . .": *Ibid.*
268 "remarkable . . .": *Lancet*, Vol. 2, November 4, 1933, 1066.
268 "In argument, Crookshank . . .": *Ibid.*
269 "to the fullest individual functioning . . .": Francis G. Crookshank, "Two Lectures on Individual Psychology and the Sexual Problems of Adolescence and Adult Life," *Psyche.* Vol. 10, April 1930, 7.
269 "A young man is usually responsive . . .": Crookshank, "Two Lectures on Individual Psychology and the Sexual Problems of Adolescence and Adult Life," *Psyche.* Vol. 11, July 1930, 24.
269 "breach of contract . . .": *Ibid.*, 40.
269 "The doctrine of my reforming friends . . .": Crookshank, *Psyche.* Vol. 10, April 1930, 7.
269 "Medicine must be recognized . . .": Crookshank, "Types of Personality, with Special Reference to Individual Psychology," *Lancet*, Vol. 1, March 8, 1930, 547.

CHAPTER EIGHTEEN
Thriving During the Depression

271 "Finds Tantrums Test of Parents," *The Cleveland Plain-Dealer,* April 4, 1934.
271 "I am constantly busy . . .": AAC, Container 1, General Correspondence, 1930–1934. Letter dated March 18, 1931.
272 "Go back to the greenhouse . . .": GM, 36–37.
272 "You haven't been at all . . .": AAC, Container 1, General Correspondence, 1930–1934. Letter dated October 16, 1931.
273 "Then something astonishing happened . . .": GM, 62.
273 "But Adler continued calmly . . .": *Ibid.*
273 "I feel horribly guilty . . .": *Ibid.,* 56.
273 "Now listen, how can we say . . .": *Ibid.,* 57.
275 "Otherwise," she recalled, "I would . . .": *Ibid.,* 33.
275 "Every [person] strives . . .": Alfred Adler, *What Life Should Mean to You.* Boston: Little, Brown, 1950, 8.
276 "In our present day civilization . . .": *Ibid.,* 268.
276 "Although [Adler] is one of the . . .": *New York Times,* September 13, 1931, 12.
276 "It is written plausibly . . .": *New Republic,* Vol. 68, November 4, 1931, 333.
276 "In all the great movements . . .": Adler, *What Life Should Mean to You,* 11–12.
276 "Little, Brown commissioned Adler . . .": GC, *Child from Birth Up to Six,* contracts and correspondence.
277 "In mid-May, Davis and his daughter . . .": GC, Misc. Correspondence, Statements. Exchange sheet dated March 7, 1933 indicates that the savings account was opened by Annalee and Charles Davis for Alfred Adler on May 20, 1932.
277 "Upon reference from the Education Committee . . .": Long Island College of Medicine Archives, Medical Research Library of Brooklyn, SUNY Health Services Center at Brooklyn, Board of Trustees' Bound Minutes, June 20, 1930 through June 3, 1940, 71–72.
278 "full discussion of Mr. Davis . . .": Long Island College of Medicine Archives, Medical Research Library of Brooklyn, SUNY Health Services Center at Brooklyn, Minutes of the Committee on Education of the Board of Trustees, September 29, 1932, 1.
278 "[She] was a small, compact figure . . .": Phyllis Bottome, "Frau Dr. Adler (Mrs. Raissa Adler)," *Journal of Individual Psychology,* Vol. 18, November 1962, 28.
278 "I do not agree with all . . .": *Ibid.*
278 "Pugnacious little Alfred Adler . . .": "I on Long Island," *Time,* Vol. 20, October 10, 1932, 26.
279 "As reported by the college's . . .": Long Island College of Medicine Archives, Medical Research Library of Brooklyn, SUNY Health Services Center at Brooklyn, Minutes of the Committee on Education of the Board of Trustees, January 16, 1933, 1.
279 "had denied his requests . . .": *Ibid.*
280 "What I considered particularly destructive . . .": Ernest Jahn, new Preface to "Religion and Individual Psychology," in *Superiority and Social Interest* by Alfred Adler, ed. Heinz L. and Rowena Ansbacher. New York: Norton, 1979, 272.

281 "Adler's appearance has always remained . . .": *Ibid.*, 273.
281 "power apparatus" and "not infrequent abuses . . .": Alfred Adler, "Fundamental Expositions of Individual Psychology," *Superiority and Social Interest,* 279.
281 "The healing process is much more difficult . . .": *Ibid.*, 306.
281 "a gift of faith . . .": *Ibid.*, 277.
281 "I regard it as no mean commendation . . .": *Ibid.*, 307–308.
281 sent a cordial rejection letter . . .: Stuart Rose to Charles Davis, GC, Little, Brown & Company Correspondence, May 16, 1933.
282 "These do not seem to us . . .": Stuart Rose to Charles Davis, GC, Little, Brown & Company Correspondence, May 18, 1933.
282 "The book is a slight one . . .": Stuart Rose to Charles Davis, GC, Little, Brown & Company Correspondence, July 31, 1933.
282 he submitted his official application: AAC, Container 3, Miscellany. U.S. Naturalization Service Declaration of Intention, signed October 17, 1933.
282 "The tragedy of Dr. Crookshank . . .": PB, 233.
283 "experiment . . .": Gerald Johnson, *Liberal's Progress.* New York: Coward-McCann, 1948, 195.
284 "In the final analysis, beauty . . .": *Ibid.*, 206.
284 "there will be such a volume of leisure . . .": Edward A. Filene, *Successful Living in the Machine Age.* New York: Simon and Schuster, 1931, 12.
284 "Some two hundred well-wishers . . .": *New York Times,* February 8, 1934, 21.
286 "We Germans gladly accord . . .": Berkley, *Vienna,* 215.
286 "In our national culture . . .": *Ibid.*
286 "have their real homeland in Palestine . . .": *Ibid.*
286 "the religious German must . . .": *Ibid.*
286 According to Kurt Adler's later recollection: AI, Kurt Adler, November 16, 1992.
287 "We've had enough innovation . . .": Ernest Papanek, *Austrian School Reform.* New York: Fell, 1962, 110.

CHAPTER NINETEEN
American and European Vicissitudes

289 Alfred Adler, *The Problems of Neurosis,* 48.
289 she was subsequently arrested: AI, Kurt Adler, November 16, 1992.
290 "It would be very nice . . .": AAC, Container 1, General Correspondence, 1930–1934. February 24, 1934.
290 "Adler is not a big man physically . . .": *Cleveland Plain-Dealer,* April 14, 1934.
290 "the children's New Dealer . . .": *Ibid.*
290 "some questions briefly . . .": *Ibid.*
290 "I would never [physically] punish . . .": *Ibid.*
290 "untidy, finicky in eating . . .": *Ibid.*
290 "if it makes children . . .": *Ibid.*
290 "Especially after fascism . . .": AI, Kurt Adler, November 16, 1992.
291 "Let them waste . . .": AI, Kurt Adler, April 5, 1992.

291 "The very frequent presentation . . .": Charles Davis to Little, Brown, GC, Little, Brown & Company Correspondence, May 10, 1934.

291 "I have your letter . . .": Stuart Rose to Charles Davis, GC, Little, Brown & Company Correspondence, May 14, 1934.

292 "*Now,* I think . . .": GM, 40.

293 "smiled once in a while . . .": Peter Ostwald, *Vaslav Nijinsky, A Leap into Madness.* New York: Lyle Stuart, 1991, 288.

293 "he would not go . . .": *Ibid.*

293 "In cases of this illness . . .": Alfred Adler, Preface to "The Diary of Vaslav Nijinsky," *Archives of General Psychiatry,* Vol. 38, July 1981, 834.

294 "to Leonhard Seif and the Munich group . . .": Phyllis Bottome, *Private Worlds,* dedication page.

294 "It is axiomatic . . .": *New York Times,* April 1, 1934, 8.

294 "With a frank recognition . . .": Ira Wile, *Survey Graphic,* Vol. 70, August 1934, 268.

294 "frightened and unconvinced . . .": Bottome, *The Goal,* 230.

295 "My father was certainly upset . . .": AI, Kurt Adler, November 16, 1992.

295 "Sydney, if you have to stutter . . .": GM, 34–35.

295 In mid-February of 1935: GC, *Journal of Individual Psychology* Correspondence, contract dated February 12, 1935.

296 "I am about to recover . . .": AAC, Container 1, General Correspondence, 1935–1936. March 2, 1935.

296 "The operation was performed today . . .": AAC, Container 1, General Correspondence, 1935–1936. March 4, 1935.

296 "very serious, but should be over . . .": AAC, Container 1, General Correspondence, 1935–1936. March 16, 1935.

297 "where you will have . . .": AAC, Container 1, General Correspondence, 1935–1936. March 15, 1935.

297 "All this hesitating is useless . . .": AAC, Container 1, General Correspondence, 1935–1936. March 16, 1935.

297 "never learned to speak English well . . .": AI, Margot Adler, August 21, 1993.

297 "Papa is doing very well . . .": Alexandra Adler to Cornelia Adler, AAC, Correspondence 1935. April 15–16, 1935.

298 "Advertisements by Christian Business Firms . . .": Berkley, *Vienna,* 228.

299 "the totally demoralizing and corrupting . . .": *Ibid.,* 230.

299 "Vienna in 1935 was not . . .": Phyllis Bottome, *The Goal,* 249–250.

300 "For the first time since . . .": *London Times,* August 4, 1935, E5.

300 "Chancellor Schuschnigg has proved himself . . .": *Ibid.*

301 "It's a bad sign . . .": Bottome, *The Goal,* 252.

301 "Adler never *shared* his sadness . . .": PB, 186.

302 "staying on with kind people . . .": *Ibid.,* 187.

302 "Come back. And stay forever! . . .": *Ibid.*

302 "From the very beginning . . .": *New York Times,* September 7, 1935, 17.

302 "I think that modern Americans . . .": *New York World-Telegram,* September 6, 1935.

302 "I would not care . . .": *Ibid.*

302 "The old idea of punitive corrections . . .": *New York Herald Tribune,* September 24, 1935.

303 "Life in a glass house . . .": Alfred Adler, "Separate the Quins!," *Cosmopolitan,* March 1936, 90.

303 "create a little troupe . . .": *Ibid.*

303 "If they remain together . . .": *Ibid.*

303 "Again, may we offer . . .": Lucy S. Doyle to Charles Davis, AAC, Container 1, General Correspondence, 1935–1936. October 25, 1935.

304 "Abe talked about Adler . . .": AI, Bertha Maslow, May 14, 1987.

304 "Sexual behavior is used . . .": Edward Hoffman, *The Right to Be Human.* Los Angeles: Tarcher, 1988, 61.

304 author Betty Friedan cited: Betty Friedan, *The Feminine Mystique.* New York: Norton, 1974, 326.

305 "a lie and a swindle . . .": Abraham Maslow, "Was Adler a Disciple of Freud? A Note," *Journal of Individual Psychology.* Vol. 18, 1962, 125.

CHAPTER TWENTY

A Father's Anguish

307 Alfred Adler, *Social Interest,* 66.

308 "In general, we are doing quite well . . .": Raissa Adler to daughter Cornelia, AFA, Raissa Adler Correspondence, undated.

308 "[well], I trust you had . . .": GM, 40–41.

309 "In city after city . . .": Pierre Burton, *The Dionne Years.* New York: Norton, 1978, 126.

309 "better opportunities for useful activity . . .": Alfred Adler, "Are Americans Neurotic?" *Forum.* Vol. 26, January 1936, 45.

309 "the cream of active . . .": *Ibid.*

309 "the lack of social interest . . .": *Ibid.*

310 "did not come into existence . . .": Alfred Adler, "Love is a Recent Invention," *Esquire,* May 1936, 56 and 128; reprinted in *Journal of Individual Psychology,* Vol. 27, 1971, 147.

310 "is a task for two . . .": *Ibid.,* 148.

310 "an equal partnership . . .": *Ibid.*

310 "the dyad of perfect love . . .": *Ibid.,* 149.

310 corresponded with Harper and Row: GC, Miscellaneous Correspondence and Statements. Letters dated January–March 1936 between Alfred Adler and Eugene Exman of Harper and Row.

311 "There were two reasons . . .": Alfred Adler, Preface to *The Diary of Vaslav Nijinsky,* 835.

311 "The greatest freedom of mind . . .": "Miss Cora Williams, Eminent Berkeley Educator," *Berkeley Gazette,* April 27, 1924.

312 "The all-important thing . . .": "Cora L. Williams, Preparing Youth for the 'Big Game' of Life," *California Monthly,* September 1925, 22.

312 "Education is more than a science . . .": "Miss Cora Williams," *Berkeley Gazette,* April 27, 1924.

312 "Dr. Adler, I've told them . . .": GM, 39.

313 A magazine photograph: AAC, Container 3, Miscellany. Unidentified photograph with credit, S. S. Bremen.

313 "I have a new follower . . .": GM, 48.

313 "Your letter causes me . . .": Albert Einstein to Adler, AAC, Container 1, General Correspondence, 1937. Translated, Feburary 4, 1937. Permission granted by the Albert Einstein Archives, the Hebrew University of Jerusalem, Isreal.

314 "To the Beecher's delight . . .": GM, 88–89.

315 "Well, are you for me . . .": Hoffman, *Right to Be Human,* 105.

315 Writing to Forbes-Dennis: Adler to Forbes-Dennis, AAC, Container 1, General Correspondence, 1937. February 25, 1937.

315 "social confusion and disorganization . . .": Editor of *American Journal of Sociology* to Adler, Alfred Adler Correspondence, regarding "Psychiatric Aspects Regarding Individual and Social Disorganization," June 16,1936.

315 "all efforts made until now . . .": Alfred Adler, "Psychiatric Aspects Regarding Individual and Social Disorganization," *American Journal of Sociology.* Vol. 42(6), May 1937, 779.

315 "In nursery schools . . .": *Ibid.,* 780.

316 "a tremendous army of teachers . . .": *Ibid.*

316 "Our letters and telegrams . . .": Raissa Adler to daughter Cornelia, AFA, Raissa Adler Correspondence, March 16, 1937.

316 "We are now in great distress . . .": Adler to Forbes-Dennis, AAC, Container 1, General Correspondence, 1937. April 3, 1937.

320 "My father had always . . .": AI, Kurt Adler, June 20, 1992.

320 "[Adler] stayed away from . . .": GM, 97.

320 "Look, I'll tell you one thing . . .": *Ibid.*

320 "Look for an office . . .": *Ibid.*

320 "Vali causes me sleepless nights . . .": GM, 23.

321 "Tomorrow I finish . . .": Alfred Adler to Forbes-Dennis, AAC, Container 1, General Correspondence, 1937. May 13, 1937.

321 "Dr. Adler, do you mind . . .": PB, 254.

321 "Do you think my son's . . .": *Ibid.*

321 "What do you suppose . . .": *Ibid.*

321 "Are you crazy . . .": GM, 84–85.

322 "I hear that you . . .": GM, 54.

322 "Yes, I think . . .": *Ibid.*

323 "unique thinker, whose theories . . .": *Neue Freie Presse,* May 29, 1937.

323 "He has done more . . .": *New English Weekly,* June 1937, 153.

323 "[he] ranked with Sigmund Freud . . .": *Boston Globe,* May 19, 1937.

323 "In the high tide of psychoanalysis . . .": *New York Times,* May 31, 1937, 14.

323 "father of the inferiority complex . . .": *New York Herald Tribune,* May 29, 1937.

323 "trinity of what was to become . . .": *Ibid.*

323 "were to remake the mental surfaces . . .": *Ibid.*

EPILOGUE
The Trap of Personality

325 "For a Jewish boy . . .": Gay, *Life for Our Time,* 615.
327 "For me, Alfred Adler . . .": Tributes to Alfred Adler on his 100th birthday, *Journal of Individual Psychology.* Vol. 26(1), 1970, 13.
328 "the man who was the first . . .": *Ibid.,* 12.
328 "the first to argue . . .": Harold Bloom, *Sigmund Freud.* New York: Chelsea House, 1985, 57.
329 "Practically every member . . .": Senator Henry Cabot Lodge, Jr. to Samuel B. Horovitz, GC, Miscellaneous Correspondence, December 10, 1937.

Index

371